Most Scandalous Woman

A book in the Latin American and Caribbean
Arts and Culture publication initiative.
Latin American and Caribbean Arts and Culture
is supported by the Andrew W. Mellon Foundation.

MOST SCANDALOUS WOMAN

Magda Portal and the Dream of Revolution in Peru

Myrna Ivonne Wallace Fuentes

UNIVERSITY OF OKLAHOMA PRESS : NORMAN

Library of Congress Cataloging-in-Publication Data

Names: Wallace Fuentes, Myrna Ivonne, author.
Title: Most scandalous woman : Magda Portal and the dream of
    revolution in Peru / Myrna Ivonne Wallace Fuentes.
Description: Norman : University of Oklahoma Press, 2017. | Includes
    bibliographical references and index.
Identifiers: LCCN 2017003569 | ISBN 978-0-8061-5747-4 (hardback)
Subjects: LCSH: Portal, Magda, 1901–1989. | Poets, Peruvian—20th
    century—Biography. | Women poets, Peruvian—Biography. | Women
    politicians—Peru—Biography. | Revolutionaries—Peru—Biography. |
    Political poetry, Peruvian—History and criticism. | Peru—Politics
    and government—1919–1968. | BISAC: HISTORY / Latin America /
    South America. | BIOGRAPHY & AUTOBIOGRAPHY / Political.
Classification: LCC PQ8497.P75 Z93 2017 | DDC 861/.62 [B]—dc23
LC record available at https://lccn.loc.gov/2017003569

LATIN AMERICAN
AND CARIBBEAN
ARTS AND CULTURE

Copyright © 2017 by the University of Oklahoma Press, Norman,
Publishing Division of the University. Manufactured in the U.S.A.

1 2 3 4 5 6 7 8 9 10

*In memory of María del Milagro Peralta, another woman
of steel who made today possible.*

*For the future: Adeline, Galeb, Molly Rose, Elisha, and Violet.
May you all fly on "miraculous winds" of your own creation.*

Contents

Contents

Illustrations

Acknowledgments

OVER THE MANY YEARS and miles that I have traveled with this book, I have accrued many, many debts—financial, intellectual, and personal. I would like to recognize and thank the following people and institutions for their support of what at times must have seemed like a never-ending quest.

The archival research for the dissertation that was the heart of part one of this book was made possible by major grants from the Ford Foundation's Peruvian Exchange Dissertation Fellowship and the Fulbright-Hays Fellowship. At Duke University, I received additional generous support from the Duke-UNC Latin American Studies Consortium, the Ford Foundation Summer Exchange Fellowships to Peru, a Ford FLACSO Summer Research Fellowship to Chile, a Duke Graduate School Summer Award for International Research, and a summer research grant from the Program for Critical U.S. Studies.

Roanoke College generously supported additional research and writing time to complete the book with Faculty Starter Grants, a Faculty Scholar Fellowship, and a Summer Research Award.

I have been exceedingly fortunate to call two extraordinary departments my intellectual homes: the Duke University History Department, where I trained for graduate school, and the Roanoke College History Department, where I have been teaching for the last ten years amid a group of gifted historians whose intellectual curiosity and insight challenge and impress me over every lunch bunch. I thank them for their friendship and support. Thanks also go to Katie Kurtessis, who adopted this project for four years as my URAP undergraduate research assistant.

I would like to thank the teachers and mentors at Duke who exposed me to new ways of thinking, opened new theoretical playgrounds, and made me a historian, especially Pete Sigal, Daniel James, Malachi Hacohen, Irene Silverblatt, and Jocelyn Olcott. The Duke-UNC Consortium in Latin American Studies was my second academic home, and I thank Natalie Hartman for her friendship and support throughout my graduate career. The Duke Latin American history graduate program's annual workshop of works in progress offered invaluable feedback on this project when it was just two dissertation chapters and then again when the book manuscript was complete; it is entirely fitting that their feedback and support bookend this project.

My friends and colleagues from those graduate school years have become my fellow travelers and constant companions, even when we are far away. I thank, for their friendship, Erin Conroy and her crazy midnight beach runs; Katy Fenn and her legendary pad thai; Daniel Levenson-Wilk, to whom I will one day return his missing Dire Straits CD; James Palmer and his impromptu visits; and Shauna Sanders, who remains with us. My Latin American *compañeros* from the Duke UNC program remain one of my secret weapons, with their continued support, wit, and insight—*especially* when March rolls around. Thanks to Adriana Brodsky, Daniel Golonka, Mark Alan Healey, Jane Mangan, Jody Pavilack, Bryan Pitts, Bianca Premo, David Sartorius, Elizabeth Shesko, Alejandro Velasco, Kristin Wintersteen, and Caroline Yezer. Gonzalo Lamana and Tom Rogers, with whom I shared so many seminars, projects, and conversations, have become two of my touchstone examples of academic collegiality. I thank them for that and for their friendship, as well as for that of Gabriella Lukacs and Hannah Knott Rogers.

In Peru, André Samplonius helped me navigate Lima's National Library and used-book stands as much as APRA's early history; I thank him for his invaluable research assistance. Sara Beatriz Guardia introduced me to Portal's niece, Rocío Revolledo Pareja, who graciously allowed me to access Portal's papers and has given me permission to use Portal's poetry and photographs. I am also grateful for the intellectual home provided by the Instituto de Estudios Peruanos and for the help of their library staff.

In Venezuela, I thank the Rómulo Betancourt Foundation and the friendship of Reuben Zahler, with whom I maneuvered the crazy months of 2002. In Argentina, I thank the Fulbright office in Buenos Aires and

Kristi Petty, Rebekah Pite, and Natasha Zaretsky for their friendship. May we all meet again to dance the *porteño* night away.

I would also like to thank Kathleen Weaver and the staff at Penn State University Press for their generous help with securing the illustrations for this book. Finally, I thank the editorial staff at the University of Oklahoma Press, especially my sharp-eyed copyeditor, for guiding the book through its last stages.

My family has patiently and lovingly supported me throughout this project, a much longer journey than they expected. I thank my parents, Myrna and Walter Wallace; my partner, Kevin Rains; and my brothers, Roy and Daniel, for their love and support and for the gift of quiet hours to finish yet another draft over family holidays and countless evenings and weekends. During the course of writing this book, I lost both grandmothers, and their memories and the future promise I see in my beloved sons, Galeb and Elisha, and my nieces, Adeline, Molly Rose, and Violet, ground me in the "real life" that is, in the end, what really matters. May my grandmothers rejoice in the laughter of their great-grandchildren, and may those children find their own happiness in creating a future of love, light, and justice.

Finally, those of us who have had the great fortune to have John French as a mentor know the gift that is his historian's insight, prodigious knowledge, and indefatigable energy, attention, and love for his students. While any errors of fact or interpretation in the pages that follow are mine alone, there are precious few pages where John's influence has not made this work better, as we pored over countless drafts in workshops, on phone calls, and over kitchen tables. I thank him for that, and for training me as a historian and making me the scholar and teacher I am today. But more than that, I thank John and Jan Hoffman French for their friendship, their resilience, and their human example. They remain our Maestros de Juventud.

Most Scandalous Woman

Introduction

IN 1926, A YOUNG PERUVIAN woman made a fateful choice: she picked up a gun, wrested her infant daughter from her husband, and ran away to build a new life that would carry her to the commanding heights of Latin American revolutionary politics. By rebelling against patriarchal restrictions and forging a revolutionary vocation, Magda Portal (1900–1989) chose freedom—as self-realizing liberation—and emerged as one of Latin America's best-known and most successful female politicians and one of Peru's most scandalous women.

Portal's story begins at the turn of the twentieth century, when Lima, Peru's capital, lurched into modernity. Young bohemian men crowded into Lima's new, thriving cafés, intoxicated by the Russian and Mexican Revolutions, burning with the certainty of purpose inspired by an elder statesman's pithy slogan: "The old to the tomb, and the young to the task."[1] Reading, gossiping, and writing, they dreamed of demolishing the old viceregal capital's stuffy artistic, political, and spiritual order. Bohemian Lima produced two rival men who emerged as touchstones of Latin America's new radical politics: the Marxist *indigenista* José Carlos Mariátegui (1894–1930) and the anti-imperialist Víctor Raúl Haya de la Torre (1895–1979). Portal circulated freely in these circles as a journalist and prize-winning poet who introduced Peruvian readers to modernism (known as *vanguardia*). In 1928, Portal was the only woman Mariátegui praised as a poet in his masterpiece, *Seven Interpretive Essays on Peruvian Reality*. That same year, she was also the only woman among the young exiles who signed the founding document of the Alianza Popular Revolucionaria Americana, the American Popular Revolutionary Alliance, or APRA, a

3

political project Haya created that would dominate Peru's politics for fifty years. Yet if Mariátegui and Haya challenged the ideas of what was politically possible, Magda Portal became Peru's most scandalous woman by challenging what was possible in love and life as well as in politics.

Portal's story is a gripping tale of audacity and courage, suffering and betrayal; it is the moving, human story of one woman's romantic and political choices for freedom. It also charts a series of relationships, such as those with her mother and male peers—including the brothers with whom she would fall in love. None of these relationships was more important than that between Haya and Portal, two brilliant, unorthodox people married to Peru: one deified as the "dominant personality of twentieth-century Peruvian history"; the other largely neglected.[2] Yet, in important ways, each cleared the path for the other: at the peak of APRA's national leadership, Portal and her incongruous presence as a vehement, professionally violent woman provided the context to tacitly overlook Haya's own gender unorthodoxies as a closeted homosexual.

To understand why Portal, a young lower-middle-class woman, developed the exceptional will she needed to break away from the norms of decency constraining women like corsets, we can turn to her political writings, a corpus of end-of-life interviews, and her poetry. Portal secured her poetic reputation early: in 1926, Jorge Luis Borges selected Portal and César Vallejo as the two Peruvian representatives for an anthology of new Hispano-American poetry.[3] But Portal is no Vallejo, whose seminal *Trilce* is often compared to *Ulysses* and *The Waste Land* in both merit and influence. Critics have conceded that while Portal's poetry is important to her political biography in revealing "her intimate feelings, especially the pain and grief caused by solitude," many have dismissed her poetry as "prosaic": her work is socially "revolutionary, certainly; poetry, rarely."[4]

But it was Mariátegui who realized what Portal's poetic contributions meant, how her intimate, feminine voice was different and why it mattered. "Magda Portal," he proposed, "is something very rare and very precious in our literature: a *poetisa*." He christened Portal Peru's first "poetess" because she cleaved Peruvian literature and culture away from the colonial literary models and semifeudal traditions considered bankrupt by the new intellectual generation he headed.[5] Her male literary peers broke from colonial values by revalorizing the indigenous and creating *indigenismo*. Portal did it by introducing an explicitly female voice, an authentically feminine poetry that confronted head-on the challenge of female sexual experience, imagining and clearing a path to an active female sexual agency proscribed by her time and place. Her verses were scandalous and titillating; they were indecent. There were other women writing poetry, but they tended to write what Mariátegui described as "asexual" poetry about anything but female sexual desire and the predicaments it caused. Portal, he judged, had achieved a truly female poetry. Even before she launched into her meteoric political trajectory with APRA, Mariátegui caught a glimpse of something about Portal in her poetry and in her personality that everyone sensed but few tried to grapple with and understand: her audacity, her courage, her willingness to transgress, her messianic will, her radical honesty.

In poetry, in politics, and in her lived experience as a woman, Portal expanded the horizons of her life possibilities and forced her way into exclusive male worlds. Across decades, she made her writing, her life choices, and her revolutionary politics into vehicles of emancipation, both personal and collective. Having chosen creative freedom in print and personal freedom in her own sense of self and in her love life, Portal became a professional revolutionary—the woman with a gun—and played a central role in APRA and its dream of revolution.

Haya founded APRA as a youth movement with continental aspirations combining the demands and momentum of two insurgent social forces: the cultural capital and future political promise of reformist university youth and the social justice demands of an increasingly mobilized working-class labor movement. Haya was the energy and the vision creating and hurtling APRA forward. Of the second-line founding "apostles," Portal was the only woman and one of only two founding signatories of both APRA's 1928 Plan de México and the 1930 charter of APRA's Peruvian section, which became the Partido Aprista Peruano, the Peruvian APRA Party, or PAP. In the early 1930s, APRA's continental ambitions collapsed, leaving APRA as a national Peruvian political project. Though they would not reach the presidency until 1985, nearly sixty years later, APRA was unquestionably Peru's most important political party. They mobilized thousands and could expect to command around a third of the national vote, a tidal force in any multiparty parliamentary system. When that failed, they launched dozens of attempted coups, several of which threatened widespread insurrection. Loathed and feared by the military and the oligarchical elite, they would be hunted down and proscribed for years at a time, only to emerge strong enough to be wooed into coalitions, considered kingmakers. Generations would be "born under the star," the red Aprista star that was their emblem, each point representing one of the original five Aprista demands: anti-imperialism, Latin American political unity, nationalization of lands and industry, internationalization of the Panama Canal, and solidarity with the world's oppressed.

What can explain such intense identification of Aprista "red (star) diaper" babies and leaders who called and considered themselves "apostles?" Apristas became a community of fate, a group subjected to specific historical conditions who translated that collective identity into a "willed affiliation" we call solidarity, that "special claim . . . individuals have on each other's energies, compassion, and resources."[6] Their enemies dismissed it as a rabid "collective madness," but Apristas understood this partisan cohesion, this solidarity, the revolutionary delusion necessary to challenge an unforgiving system, as a shared "Aprista faith." For a quarter century, Portal stood at the heights of APRA as one of its most powerful and visible national leaders as it matured into Peru's most powerful—and most persecuted—mass movement and party. Pivotal in organizing APRA, she edited its most important doctrinal magazines and formulated Aprista positions on women, all while rallying thousands of cheering partisans and introducing thousands of women into political life. She expanded the meanings of female citizenship in a world where women had neither suffrage nor citizenship.

Agitating and organizing, Portal crisscrossed Peru, Bolivia, Mexico, the Caribbean, Argentina, Chile, and Venezuela for twenty years as a standard bearer for the revolutionary but non-Communist APRA. In this transnational, cosmopolitan pan-American landscape of cultural and political possibility, she befriended a generation of leftist politicians, including future presidents like the Venezuelan Rómulo Betancourt and the Chilean Salvador Allende. Even as APRA's original revolutionary, anti-imperialist ideas softened over the course of the tumultuous twentieth century, it was this Aprista faith that remained, binding them all—leaders and followers—together.

When government repression against APRA broke into near civil war, Portal was implicated in a conspiracy to assassinate the president in 1932 and saw her romantic partner, her compañero, jailed for a decade. She lived hand to mouth as an involuntary political exile, then as a hunted fugitive, before being captured and thrown in prison herself. Her direct association with revolutionary and personal violence, incongruous given her gender, class position, and feminine persona, simultaneously titillated and worried allies and opponents alike. While making her more effective, it also alienated her from other leaders: she was like them, maybe stronger, but never *one* of them. But Portal was not the only complication in the national leadership's gender politics: Haya was also maneuvering in dangerous waters as the open secret of his homosexuality rippled throughout society. Together at their party's summit, Portal and Haya made possible the ideological space for each other.

Their shared Aprista faith unified the leadership for twenty years, long past when most revolutionary projects splinter apart. In 1950, however, after a failed military mutiny, Portal stood before a court martial and became the first national leader to break the faith and leave APRA, viciously attacking her onetime comrades and baffling her closest allies. Portal demolished her dream of revolution and broke their shared solidarity, their Aprista faith.

Why do women in politics bear deeper emotional costs? Answering this question means taking emotion and sentiment seriously as analytical categories, and unpacking how and why defying these gendered norms was, and remains, so difficult. The tragic ends of a later generation of Latin American women revolutionary leaders underscore the emotional and psychological toll of such transgressions: the Chileans Beatriz and Laura Allende and the Cuban Haydeé Santamaría, for instance, all committed suicide. Thirty years earlier, Portal faced down similar suffering in her personal life and the cumulative aggressions of her political life by jettisoning from APRA, now a mature party that she argued had betrayed its original revolutionary ideas.

Ultimately, Portal's compelling life story allows us to explore both the power of revolutionary affiliation—what makes people revolutionaries and how successful revolutionary projects keep adherents and leaders—and the gendered limits of these revolutionary affiliations. Focusing on subjectivity, "the cognitive, active, feeling, experiencing self," means exploring how this generation of young bohemians understood their own choices as they grew older and how they battled to lead their nation.[7] Mapping this political cohort's interpersonal dynamics reveals the emotional layers and textures of the lived experience of the period's revolutionary politics. Along the way, their story, the story of South America's non-Communist revolutionary Left, also tells us the story of twentieth-century Peru.

Drafting memoirs that death would prevent her from completing, Magda Portal begins: "Everyone knows that I evolved from a poet into a struggler for social justice, without abandoning poetry."[8] We begin, therefore, by weaving together the two worlds of Peru's literary vanguardia and the political history of APRA, which both begin with perhaps fifteen self-styled bohemian students in the sleepy northern Peruvian city of Trujillo. In 1915, this informal literary group, the "Trujillo Bohemia," gathered to read poetry and rail at the injustice of their lives. Politics was never their purpose or aim, but criticizing Trujillo's literary culture led them to challenge its elite political culture. They needed to "burst out of our little world"; conforming "would have been the negation of our very beings." So they clashed "with everything and everybody," and "ferociously attacked" everything undergirding Trujillo, including its "institutions, public powers, social conventions, university, an insolent and exploiting plutocracy, its sacred falsehoods, class customs, lack of honesty and honor, a humiliating servileness, its exploitation of the worker, its bureaucracy, professional politics, and general presumptuous ignorance."[9] They were the very definition of young, aspiring iconoclasts.

Two of these young bohemians would rise the highest: Víctor Raúl Haya de la Torre and Peru's most critically acclaimed poet, César Vallejo. Even then, at the beginning of their lives, poetry and politics were woven together. Haya vividly remembered how, reading Vallejo's poems, a highly learned professor exclaimed, "*¡Esto es inaudito!*" "Inaudito," simultaneously meaning "not previously heard" and "monstrous, not to be heard," aptly captures, even a century later, the surprise, indignation, and rage of their elders, the august university professors. Facing down their elders' ferocious reception taught Haya and his young peers the values that would guide them for the rest of their political lives. "We learned, before we turned twenty, to defend good and just causes by defending Vallejo. And we knew how to love and respect, understand and admire, the superior and authentic values of a genius . . . certain in ourselves we were not wrong."[10] These values—recognizing and defending genius, a willingness to sacrifice material and social validation for their convictions, facing down society bolstered only by their own self-certainty—would define the Aprista faith and ethical code that Haya, another figure of charismatic political genius, spun around himself and his revolutionary dreams after he moved to Lima, Peru's capital and principal city.

Much like Paris and New York City's Greenwich Village, the world of early-twentieth-century Lima was an exciting, heady, "effervescent" blend of iconoclastic artistic creativity, radical political agitation, and rapid social transformation.[11] Young Peruvian artists and students proudly called themselves *bohemios* and cast themselves in a mold they adapted from international—especially French—books, newspapers, and magazines, coalescing into small groups to advance their creative literary ambitions.

Portal and other young poets began composing as Latin American poetry transitioned from *modernismo* to a variety of avant-garde, or vanguardia, tendencies. In the 1920s, this new vanguardia generation looked to North Atlantic aesthetic innovations, including modernism, futurism, dadaism, and surrealism, to fuel their own experimentation. Thematically, they turned away from the cosmopolitan to more intimate, national, and even familial themes. Technically, they eschewed formal perfection for innovations like free verse, innovative spelling, and striking typographical arrangements, and declared "themselves answerable to nothing, pushed the limits of acceptable subjects and forms, and proclaimed a heady freedom from traditions, social environment, and reality itself."[12]

Reflecting back more than fifty years later, Portal fondly recalled that the vanguardia appealed to her and her peers because "America, its youth, searched for action, not contemplation," aching "to intervene in the happenings of History not just as simple spectators, but instead as participants in the great tasks of the intelligentsia." For her generation of rebel youth, rebellion against suffocating traditions in their poetry and especially in their universities "illuminated the paths of America with its pronouncements of rebellion toward everything in the past, to its mental parameters, and its dependence on Europe's old cultures."[13]

It was, after all, an age of iconoclastic earthquakes, and none were more important than the revolutions remaking the world of the political possible. Headlines trumpeted the disastrous end to the Great War and Europe's destabilization in its aftermath, Russia's implausible Bolshevik victory and the creation of the Soviet Union, and the convulsions of a revolution that had already lasted a decade and decimated a Mexican generation. These cataclysmic events, demolishing ever faster a world their parents had taken for granted, cleared mental and creative maps for their children, who now faced their futures with an unprecedented sense of possibility.

These youths burned with the certainty, the inevitability, that the next step on the world stage was theirs. "Men of a free republic," one of their regional manifestos proclaimed, "we have just broken the last chain that even in the twentieth century tied us to the ancient monarchical and monastic domination. . . . We are stepping into a revolution; we are living an American hour."[14] In this new world, energy and agency had moved west. Europe had proven bankrupt. The tiny circles of Latin American intellectuals, or *letrados*, to use Ángel Rama's persuasive concept,[15] had since colonial times played outsized roles in politics and art because of their powerful cultural influence as literate specialists. This newest generation of Latin American letrados coaxed their sense of agency to ever higher, even heroic heights and saw themselves as a renovating counterelite, an intelligentsia of reforming and revolutionary letrados.

Portal and her peers in poetry and politics were certain they had been born into a Peruvian hour. Together, they would construct a vision of what Peru needed to become, of what it could, of what it *would*, become. If politics and poetry were married, then these young people were each married to a Peru of revolutionary possibility. Making that vision real meant dedicating, sacrificing, and throwing themselves into intense collective relationships that lasted the length of their twentieth-century lives.

Such a romantic political imagination was the sign of the times, and not just for utopian Soviets or Peruvian poets. Warily watching the rise of North Atlantic "sentimental humanist" politicians of all tendencies who nurtured similar dreams of renovating politics and new worlds, the U.S. conservative cultural critic Irving Babbitt argued that such a romantic political imagination was profoundly dangerous. Reading Babbitt, Justin Garrison describes this romantic political imagination, soaked in high emotion and exhilaration, as investing "life and politics with . . . marvelous possibilities." But, the danger lay in that its "extravagant dreams" refused to acknowledge "what is actually known about human beings in history," and its overly optimistic perspective on human nature elided our baser urges like selfishness and a will to power. Instead, Babbitt counseled, politicians should cultivate a moral political imagination, "rooted in a down-to-earth assessment of what life is really like." With a clear-eyed assessment of inherent human weaknesses, it accepts that a "better life requires much moral effort" and is necessarily much more modest in ambition. "Politics at its best can achieve some nobility—a measure of order, justice, and civilization—but it has to be a limited enterprise."[16]

But not all revolutions are political. Like other women in the teens and twenties, Portal became what we today call a New Woman, one pushing against the traditional definitions of womanhood, demanding new personal freedoms, all intent on being freer than their mothers' generation. New Women, like flappers in ever shorter hemlines, courted scandal everywhere; in Lima—highly traditional, uniformly Catholic, a city that looked back, still invested in its colonial glory as a viceregal capital—they were anathema. As much as Portal's story is about a political dream, it is also about her dreams of liberation from these gendered constraints Lima assumed were both natural and necessary. In the tug of war between a romantic and moral political imagination, Portal had to create and inhabit the romantic and heroic precisely because what was known about human beings in her time and place fundamentally constrained women, and everybody "knew" that women were unsuited for political life. Portal's two formative "extravagant dreams," transforming society along broadly Socialist lines and transforming women into political agents, were equally dangerous.

Historians of Latin American women have grappled with understanding the motivations driving women to politics in the face of its many social costs.[17] But understanding motivation, especially motivation for rebellion, demands an agent-centered approach that looks at the dynamic interface between human beings and culture, that fluid point of contact where human subjectivities confront, try to understand, challenge, and accept the structures of meaning organizing their lives. This is a fluid point of contact because neither human subjectivities nor that repertoire of shared understandings we call culture are ever static, much less stable. Motivations are never given and are often neither rational nor reasonable.

Social history can tell us about the conditions and pressures acting on groups. It can outline the contours, for instance, of women's restricted social lives or their economic vulnerability as a group in early-twentieth-century Peru. Cultural history shifted to focus on social discourses and their meanings, dissecting, for instance, the layers of meaning in concepts such as "honor" and "decency." But we don't experience the world as members of larger collectives, and our culture does not just inscribe its discourses on us. The analytical site where these come together is the individual human being, who while certainly molded and constrained by social and economic parameters it shares with others, nonetheless has leeway to accept, reject, or remix cultural discourses in idiosyncratic ways.[18] This interface between human subjective experience and culture, where, in William Sewell's term, "fateful" decisions to accept or rebel against hegemonic models are taken, cannot be studied at the macro level, as forces on a collective identity where identical inputs suggest identical outputs; our analytical scale instead narrows to the individual struggling against these collective abstractions that populate our worlds and our minds.

Since the 1990s, a "New Biography" in historical writing has emerged to address this gap between the collective abstractions of empirical social science and a cultural history that can assume individuals are already always inscribed by social discourses.[19] This "biographical turn" has moved from "simply charting the course of individual lives" to "examining those lives in dialectical relationship to the multiple social, political, and cultural worlds they inhabit and give meaning to." In Oscar Handlin's words, biography spotlights the interaction of a person and society, the place where "the situation and the individual illuminate each other."[20] Writing his biography of William Blake, E. P. Thompson called these "the nodal points of conflict"; the historian's objective became exploring the way Blake's "mind meets the world." Such an exploration tells us something about Blake, to be sure, but as Alice Kessler-Harris noted, it also allows us to "see through the life" and "ask how the individual life helps us to make sense of a piece of the historical process."[21] In its focus on how individuals perceive the world, such New Biography scholarship is part of what Gabrielle Spiegel identified as the field's "largely implicit" neo-phenomenological approach returning to "an actor-centered perspective" in the wake of the methodological discontents of both social and cultural history.[22]

This book also studies a person, her world, and the structures of consciousness she inherits and ultimately transforms to understand it. It is most interested in Portal's interactions with two particular structures of consciousness—one well explored, one not. The first was a patriarchy still surprisingly conserved in its colonial Spanish contours, a consciousness intent on restriction and conformity she shared with all Peruvian women, although with different inflections based on class and racial background. She shared the second with a small group of committed partisans: an Aprista romantic, if not heroic, political imagination and agency, a nebulous cloud of shifting ideas, aspirations, and feelings they called their Aprista faith. While APRA is not at the center of Latin American politics, analyzing the political agency, collective subjectivity, and solidarity of the Apristas can illuminate other Latin American projects of romantic political imagination—from the renovating politics of Arielism at the start of the century, the mid-century seductions of Communism, and the revolutionary dreams of the Cuban Revolution and those inspired by it in the century's second half. Unique among Aprista leaders, Portal had two transformative projects—the general one they all shared of Aprista renewal, revolution, and faith, and the specific one of gender transformation. And because she was a vanguardia poet, a type of poetry that self-consciously rejected the European themes of the past to focus on the "intimate," she had a canvas on which to leave traces of the emotional and psychological processes of these two transformations.

This, then, is a longitudinal study of one individual's interiority constantly struggling against patriarchy, only understandable as an individual ecology. Portal succeeded in her own rebellion; she did break free from the psychological hold patriarchy had over her will. But a total escape, a complete liberation, was impossible. As Lois Banner noted, individuals internalize and rebel against social roles, "both policing and individuating themselves according to cultural conventions," and we can add that this is a perpetually incomplete, dynamic process.[23] This is not, to borrow a chemical concept, a chemical transformation that fundamentally and irrevocably transforms one substance into another. Instead, like water that can freeze, melt, and refreeze with its environment, "buy-in" into these powerful social constructs can shift from one state into another as our own conditions and environments change. Instead of focusing on moments of victory when Portal breaks with patriarchal expectations, our longitudinal focus considers how Portal understood the experience of having to combat these norms structuring the foundations of experience and psychology for both men and women repeatedly throughout her life course. This book maps her continuing struggle, in which moments of elated triumph and despondent suffering punctuate much longer periods of frustration, exhaustion, and ambivalence, a struggle that was the full price Portal willingly paid for demanding to be free as a woman, to expand her own life possibilities, and to dream of revolutionary change.

The architecture of Portal's lived experience was a series of relationships. Biography, by its nature, takes the individual as the object of analysis.[24] Portal's story is best understood instead as a series of dyads: and none more important than her relationship with Haya. Studying such an intense longitudinal, affective world of relationships and how these relationships over time affect personality and motivation means looking for how gendered dynamics affect Portal's internal emotional landscape through time, along a series of relationships that last decades. How do these relationships, structured inevitably by historically contingent gender performances and personas, define and change interior worlds, dreams, and motivations?

The study of women and gender in Latin American history, which began in the 1970s as part of a social scientific agenda powered by second-wave feminist energies, tended to see Portal as, at best, an ambivalent figure, "not an original thinker," and historically noteworthy because of her "unflattering attitude towards her own sex." In this reading, Portal became a paradigmatic example of leftist women's troublesome ideological position and represented the feminist shortcomings of the entire Latin American Left, which, "like the political right, tended to view women as highly conservative, politically malleable, and subject to the influence of the church, despite eloquent evidence to the contrary." Portal's reluctance to extend full and immediate suffrage to all women indicted her as "antifeminist," as did her disdain for Peruvian feminists whom Portal considered class enemies. Scholars also criticized Portal's "tutelary attitude" toward working-class women.[25] Aprismo as a political ideology and intellectual movement, however, was founded on such "tutelary attitudes" toward the working class, and scholars have addressed the inherent paternalism in such tutelary discourses.[26] Instead of simple "anti-feminist alienation," Portal's position needs to be read within this larger APRA worldview.

In fact, Portal's insight that women needed special tutoring was the heart of her theoretical focus on women's psychology as the main barrier to their full political participation. Women did need additional tutoring because their structurally subaltern position inculcated self-doubt—self-subalternization. Nobody is inherently rebellious; in fact, as social animals, humans seek the safety of the group and its rules, no matter how onerous. Rebellion, especially for structurally subaltern actors, needs to be explained. Portal recognized that women's psychological liberation was a necessary prerequisite to formal politics; without the first, the second was impossible and meaningless, insights other systematically exploited theorists, such as Frantz Fanon, would also advance later.

Latin American political feminists have, on the whole, remained deeply invested in "preserving femininity and respectability," a regional generalization that rang true in Peru, where a woman was judged a success "not on her individual capabilities and accomplishments, but on how faithfully she reflects the prevailing image of womanliness."[27] Latin American feminist reformers carefully patrolled their behavior to maintain an unblemished reputation as decent women, constantly asserting their own individual identification with other well-adjusted women of their time and class, even if, or especially because, they challenged the excesses of male privilege in politics.

Portal radically departed from these other middle-class Latin American feminists who were such "gentle reformers." As opposed to elite women who battled for feminist causes in institutional venues, Portal chose instead to fight her battles extralegally, as a revolutionary conspirator and insurgent. Unlike feminists who worked so hard to maintain their personal reputations as decent ladies, or "*damas decentes*," Portal flagrantly disregarded normative notions of feminine decency in her own personal conduct. In a society prizing female sexual chastity, she professed an openly sexual sensibility in her poetry and practiced a scandalous sexual freedom in her own relationships with men. In a society valorizing women as mothers, Portal was openly ambivalent about maternity and continued her revolutionary activity long after the birth of her only child, exposing her daughter to a childhood rife with political danger. She adopted standards of behavior society granted only to men in her personal life and sexual relationships, including flirting, initiating illicit relationships, and perhaps most tellingly, leaving relationships. Portal demanded the quintessentially masculine prerogative of a sovereign love life.

Assuming such a masculinist orientation meant fighting against shame and humiliation, the potent emotional weapons social institutions pointed against transgressors as they patrolled the boundaries of the decent, the moral, and the normal. Shame was a ferociously effective tool of psychological and social control. Individuals did not leap over these potentially debilitating emotional weights once and for all after recognizing the conditions of their oppression. The emotional price to pay for social transgression lags behind and cannot be fully eradicated. It must be constantly faced and fought—but could it be transformed?

Because I try to discern these historical processes through the lens of one person, through Portal's private psychological negotiations, her public life, and her private sense of self, this is an individual and unrepresentative story that untangles the reasons why and the process through which one woman made herself exceptional. But this unrepresentative story has much to tell us about the horizons of possibility during the first three decades of the twentieth century. It uncovers the social mores and gendered standards of her time, not just because Portal allows us to see the limits imposed by normative notions of feminine decency, but because she responded by crafting a political and affective agency that her world could only understand as a masculine orientation.

We can best assess the challenge Portal posed in projecting such a militantly masculine self by studying her from multiple angles: as a politician, as a poet, and as a person within a network of affective relationships. Consequently, this analysis superimposes these three layers of her experience, layers other scholars have often dealt with separately. It begins by analyzing Portal's poetry and her political ideas and then contextualizing these two strands of her intellectual production within her lived experience, including a personal affective life that combatively refused the limits imposed by gendered notions of decency. Of course, we must be careful about reading Portal's poetry too literally, seeing "the works and the life as one, to read the first-person pronoun only in limited biographical terms."[28] Strict versions of such an "intentional fallacy" set the tone for much of the New Criticism school dominating mid-twentieth-century literary theory, which viewed the literary text as self-contained and therefore understandable on its own without recourse to either historical context or authorial intent. Such critics argued that "the design or intention of the author is neither available nor desirable as a standard for judging . . . literary art."[29] But as the critic William Empson countered, we search for intention "all the time" in human activity, and literature should be no different. Intention, he thought, was the "fallible but indispensable human source of any writing that matters."[30] We should also remember that the

Magda Portal, Juegos Florales, 1923, Universidad Nacional de San Marcos.
Courtesy estate of Magda Portal, Rocío Revolledo Pareja,
and Penn State University Press.

vanguardia and lyric traditions Portal composed in encouraged exploration of interiority and emotion. A final guard against an overly reduction-
ist logic conflating biography with a person's ideas or artistic production is
Gerald Izenberg's method of approaching the work first, and turning to the
author's biography only after encountering internal logical inconsistencies
that need to be explained.[31] Izenberg formulated his method to explicitly
deal with psychohistory, and while I am not offering a psychoanalytical
reading, I also draw conclusions about Portal's motivations based on my
analysis of her internal life, her emotions, and her psychology.

Instead of tracing every turn in her evolving ideas on politics, aesthetics,
and feminism, I excavate and reconstruct the rich context that nourished
her ideas and motivated her into taking action by tracing out the inter-
group dynamics of bohemian poetry groups and revolutionary cells. I
unpack how participants may have understood "key terms" such as "decente," "poetisa," "mother," "compañera," and "personality," charting how
these words evolved and illuminating the idiosyncratic subtleties of meanings available to contemporaries but lost to us in our everyday usage.

Instead of focusing primarily on Portal's pioneering legacy as a founder
of APRA or a vanguardia poet, I search for the barriers Portal encountered
as a woman who aspired to be a journalist, a poet, a revolutionary and as a
woman who operated in environments dominated by men who became
comrades, friends, and lovers. The following chapters ask what dilemmas
these barriers presented, the difficulties she had in overcoming them and
why she chose to do so, and how these traumatic experiences changed her.
Portal's story, like any human being's, could have had multiple endings:
she could have chosen to become and remain a poet, a revolutionary, a
politician, a wife, a mother. Taken as a whole, Portal's choices in love, life,
and politics were the foundation of an emancipatory vision that prized her
freedom as an individual over the "other-centered" demands of the hegemonic model of Latin American womanhood as self-abnegation.

Her choices in politics revolved around her lifelong relationship with a
dream of revolution that grew to encompass this Aprista band of brothers.
The principal relationship was with Haya, a relationship as committed and
fraught as any "secret marriage." After debuting on the national stage in
1923, both created a sacred union, a platonic ideal, toward their shared goal,
and less than seven years later, Haya was almost elected president. Once
she is transformed into Magda Portal, the self-actualized revolutionary

partisan in the commanding heights of Aprista leadership, I trace out her dreams of revolution, her two transformative projects in gender consciousness and revolutionary politics. And, in the end, I try to discern how—and why—she demolished that emancipatory revolutionary dream in 1950.

In part I, I follow Portal and Haya through their scandalous debuts and learn how María Magdalena Julia del Portal Moreno became Magda Portal, how she forged her revolutionary agency, her fearless, radical honesty, her will to action. In part II, I follow Portal and her Aprista brethren as their revolutionary dream becomes a national movement, a meteoric rise to power that catapulted them to the center of Peru's political stage. In part III, I explore the contours of a postwar world and the personal and political crises that shook Portal to her core and led her to become the first national leader to break the Aprista faith after twenty years of shared militancy. As this cohort of young poets who became national leaders journeyed through three tumultuous decades in their shared dream of revolution, Portal is the constant thread I follow as I uncover and try to explain the choices she made that changed her and, just as surely, her world.

Part I

Becoming Magda Portal

Víctor Raúl Haya de la Torre, 1923. Courtesy Walter P. Reuther Library, Archives of Labor and Urban Affairs, Wayne State University.

Magda Portal, 1920. Courtesy estate of Magda Portal, Rocío Revolledo Pareja, and Magda Portal Papers, Benson Latin American Collection, University of Texas at Austin.

CHAPTER ONE

Scandalous Debuts

O N WEDNESDAY, MAY 23, 1923, five thousand university students and workers charged out from San Marcos University into the streets of Lima, protesting against President Augusto B. Leguía. Even though Peru's constitution barred him from a second term, Leguía was courting conservative and clerical support for reelection by coordinating with the Catholic Church to consecrate Peru to the Sacred Heart of Jesus. As the crowd surged to the city center, mounted police drew their swords, charged, and fired guns into the crowd, killing a student and a worker. When the protesters finally reached the Plaza Mayor, a tall, charismatic university student with an aquiline nose and a ready smile that revealed a riot of teeth rose before them and voiced their rage, pointing at the presidential palace, thundering, "The real villain is the tyrant hiding there!"

The following day, the same student led protesters in "rescuing" their fallen comrades' cadavers from the morgue and carrying them back to the university. They hunkered down, waiting for the government attack to reclaim the bodies. But Leguía backed down, and no attack came. The next day, when six times as many people, perhaps thirty thousand, gathered for the funeral, the student leader's commanding oratorical powers moved the immense crowd all over again, circling back again and again to the Fifth Commandment, ritually and furiously repeating, "Murderers, the Fifth means thou shalt not kill!" That very same day, Lima's archbishop called off the consecration.[1]

Leguía, a veteran politician, had actually enjoyed tremendous student support when he ran for president four years earlier in 1919, in no small measure because he backed the students' demands for University Reform modeled on a reform movement that had exploded in the sleepy Argentine provincial city of Córdoba a year earlier in 1918. In Argentina, this Reforma Universitaria had started with a student strike demanding internal administrative reforms at the highly traditional University of Córdoba and only became a national issue when the president, Hipólito Yrigoyen, intervened. But once ignited, La Reforma soon burst into a continental student demand, what an entire generation took to be "their" Reformista revolution. In this iconoclastic, heroic, and patricidal narrative, a generation of young progressive male students confronted the abuses of a fiercely reactionary institution refusing to embrace modernity, finally vanquishing the remnants of Spanish colonialism. This Reforma Universitaria became a potent strain in a rich landscape of new, seductive, and exhilarating iconoclastic ideas in politics and culture, including anarchism, anarcho-syndicalism, the Russian Revolution, and the artistic upheavals of postwar Paris.

Much as Argentine students viewed Yrigoyen, Peruvian students believed they had found an ally in their president. However, after just a year in office, to the students' shock, dismay, and anger, Leguía turned on the university and shut it down in 1922.[2] These Sacred Heart protests were the most visible national manifestation of the growing student opposition against him, the most spectacular protests against Leguía's reelection efforts. They made the young student leader, already impossible to miss at the university and in the leadership circles of proletariat Lima, a national hero. His canny organizing and leadership of the protests, coupled with his spectacular success as a powerfully evocative, emotional, and mobilizing public speaker, made him into a household name. The front cover of *Mundial*, one of Lima's most popular magazines, lampooned Leguía's lumbering, clumsy attack in Peru's "football match of the moment," easily thwarted by a youthful San Marcos goalkeeper: Víctor Raúl Haya de la Torre.

Haya had come to prominence in labor circles four years earlier in January 1919, during a strike for an eight-hour day in Lima's small but important textile industry. Haya had advocated for a "popular university" where university students would educate laborers after hours. Sensing an ideological ally within the elite, labor leaders approached him, hoping he could organize support in the university to help sway the government. As the strike broadened to a general strike and the government agreed to negotiations, the workers sent Haya in as chief negotiator, hoping his shared class background with government negotiators would pay dividends. The government capitulated and the eight-hour day was won, catapulting Haya to the highest echelons of leadership and prestige in Lima's working class.

Since childhood, Haya had been interested in politics. The son of two downwardly mobile aristocratic families in the northern coastal province of Trujillo, he had been a voracious reader from an early age, a lover of sport, and a child possessed of what he later called a well-developed "political imagination" who spent hours creating elaborate republics, with presidents, cabinets, and ministers. Dragging his brothers into his play, they ignored their other toys and instead "directed political campaigns."[3] From the first, everyone could tell he was rushing, with bottomless ambition, toward the largest stages. Haya's school buddies in Trujillo called him the "Prince of the Grand Venture."[4]

Haya left Trujillo in 1917 to pursue law at San Marcos, where he met many of the men who would form the nucleus of the future Aprista leadership, principal among them Manuel Seoane. Seoane was from an aristocratic Limeñan family—his father was a jurist and a literature professor, and his mother descended from an independence hero. Seoane had entered San Marcos to study law, like his older brother, father, and grandfather before him.[5] The tall, good-humored, and good-looking ladies' man befriended Haya, with whom he shared a mutual love of books and sports. Their nicknames—Seoane was "El Cachorro," the puppy, to Haya's "El Viejo," the old man—names they would keep through the decades of their long friendship and political collaboration, were terms of endearment that already performed the power relations emerging between them.

In 1921, Haya brought his dream of the popular university to life. The González Prada Popular University (Universidad Popular González Prada; UPGP) brought together dozens of university students with hundreds from the capital's emerging proletariat for evening classes on everything from geography and hygiene to philosophy. The UPGPs quickly grew into "community organizations" addressing not just educational deficits but also workers' "personal, social, and cultural problems" with recreational opportunities like sports events, social opportunities like dances for workers and their families, and material benefits such as medical clinics.[6]

The Sacred Heart protests in May 1923, then, were the spectacular national debut of Haya as both an iconoclast and a political force to be reckoned with: a student leader commanding the respect of his class peers who was also a hero to Lima's proletariat, the organizer blessed with both a leader's natural charisma and powerful oratorical gifts. Derailing the consecration was both a personal victory for Haya and a collective victory for the growing resistance against Leguía and his reelection plans. In the long run, these Sacred Heart protests fused together the bonds between university students and workers that became the foundation of APRA as a political movement. For Haya, these two days were "Apra's baptism of fire," and José Carlos Mariátegui echoed his sentiment, calling them "the historical baptism of the new generation."[7] But in the months following the protests, the fruits of the victory were uncertain. Would the heady days of May prove a "hollow victory," as Leguía now turned his full attention to the growing student opposition and their unmistakable leader?

Even though the Church had backed off, Leguía could also claim victory, since repressing the protests had effectively silenced the most vocal university students.[8] In July, he further punished the rebellious students when police violently attacked the inauguration of a UPGP branch.[9] Increasingly exasperated with his young opponent, Leguía had tried enticing Haya with a lucrative offer to study in Europe; when Haya refused, the president moved to sterner measures and started hunting him down. By August of 1923, three months after the dramatic May protests, Leguía still sat comfortably in Peru's Presidential Palace and Haya was in hiding.

A dapper, charismatic figure, Leguía embodied Peru's ascendant middle class. A provincial bereft of any aristocratic last names, Leguía, like Haya, was born in the northern sugar-producing zones. After studying business and commerce, he worked as an *empleado*, a white-collar employee, for several foreign concerns, including the New York Life Insurance Company.[10] A fixture of Lima's social life—Leguía never missed the Sunday horse races—he also avidly courted publicity. The magazines and newspapers that featured the president daily were happy to oblige; their emerging urban readership "deified" the elegantly dressed president and reveled in his revival of "the courtesan traditions" of the ancient colonial capital; journalists were frustrated "if the President didn't appear in the photos of a party."[11] Flashing cameras followed him everywhere, including the endless receptions honoring him for the public works transforming Lima from a colonial capital to a bustling twentieth-century city, a visible manifestation of how, as the "Giant of the Pacific," he was transforming Peru, ever-rising proof of his rule as a force of progress and modernity.[12]

On August 25, 1923, a Saturday night, Leguía attended the elite Teatro Forero, the kind of place where lavish banquet tables were set with gold and silver menus, for yet another opportunity to elegantly present himself before his adoring press.[13] His daughter had been invited to award the prize at the Juegos Florales, a university poetry contest. It promised to be a night to remember, in the lavish praise of *Mundial*: a carefully orchestrated "exquisite evening party of everlasting memory" captured in its full-page photographs displaying the president's daughter as "queen" of the games in front of a "court" of ten young Limeñan beauties and four children.[14] After quelling student opposition in the May and July crackdowns, the president must not have had unruly students on his mind. The students, however, had other plans. They had orchestrated an ambush for that night, this time a symbolic tussle on a flower-strewn stage where the ammunition was humiliation and loss of face instead of the live fire on Lima's bloodied streets, where weeks before Haya had debuted as an iconoclastic political leader leading the Sacred Heart protests. Now, on this stage, the action and the spotlight would focus on another young iconoclast—a beautiful twenty-three-year-old woman.

Loreley

A young woman who has just won a prestigious prize conferring national attention waits nervously backstage. At the appointed time, she should step forward into the spotlight to triumphantly declaim her winning poems before the gathered students and the city's elite. The audience only knows she has won; they have not yet heard or read the poems she submitted under a new pseudonym she chose just for this occasion: Loreley. An imposing rock on the Rhine, in the minds of German poets, Loreley was a woman so beautiful she bewitched any man who looked in her eyes and who, vainly searching for her beloved, met her death falling from the precipice into the river; a bewitching siren who combed her long blond hair on the rocks that killed unfortunate mariners. Peruvians, more likely to read French than German, were most familiar with the Loreley story as immortalized by Guillaume Apollinaire in his 1904 poem "La Loreley." Choosing this pseudonym signaled the young woman's identification with poetry, certainly, and more generally with Europe. It also gives us a glimpse of who this young woman, also beautiful, thought she might be: a Limeñan siren, a tragic figure but also a powerful danger to men, with eyes, like in Apollinaire's poem, flashing, fiery, trembling, and shining like precious stones, the color of the Rhine.[15]

That night in that theater where Loreley waited backstage was like any of the other innumerable glittering nights of Limeñan high society: an opportunity for the wealthy to gather and document their shared glamour. But on the Juegos Florales stage that night, two worlds with sharply different artistic and political values collided. The upstart world of bohemian Lima erupted onto the scene of a traditional but dying Lima of elite sensibilities, a traditional world of academic knowledge and prestige revolving around the university and gentlemen poets (*poetas gran señores*), a world of cloistered domestic spaces and careful, watchful patriarchal authority. Besieged in the classroom by students using the Reforma Universitaria to challenge authority, traditional Limeñan elites and intellectuals faced an equally dangerous challenge from a new bohemian Lima, a world driven by an effervescent street life focused on cafés like the Parisian-inspired Palais Concert. In their new public sphere, young intellectuals created tightly intimate groups and collective identities, potent alternatives to the traditional patronage relationships that demanded they serve as ornaments in the public lives of their betters.[16] This second bohemian world, the "ephemeral *belle epoque* of the Leguía-allied middle sectors," nurtured networks of students and workers that would eventually form both APRA and the Peruvian Communist Party, and produced some of the most important intellectual works of twentieth-century Peru, including Mariátegui's *Seven Interpretive Essays on Peruvian Reality* (1928) and his pivotal literary magazine *Amauta* (1926–1930).[17]

When San Marcos students reinstated the Juegos Florales poetry competition after a five-year hiatus, it seemed another step in the return to normalcy after Leguía's traumatic closing of the university the year before.[18] Though the contest was organized by students, the judges and sponsors were established and respected men of letters led by José Gálvez, a noted poet and San Marcos literature professor, the host of the awards ceremony that Saturday night.[19] Gálvez was a "poeta gran señor," a traditional Limeñan intellectual, a larger-than-life personality who walked Lima's streets certain that others recognized, acknowledged, and admired him and his literary gifts and whose wealth and prestige allowed him—invariably him—to host salons in his impressively grand private library.[20] But if

Gálvez epitomized traditional elite and academic authority, he was also a leader in the political opposition who visibly challenged the president's re-election efforts, even resigning a diplomatic post in 1921.[21]

There was little suspense that Saturday night, as the winning poets had been announced a few days before. A young poet from Arequipa, Alberto Guillén, a close friend of Haya's, won the first prize in the lyrical poem category.[22] Haya had "discovered" Guillén en route to a student congress in Cuzco that Haya had convened in March of 1920. Guillén joined the Reformistas, and with the financial help of his new San Marcos friends, the young poet traveled back with them to Lima, carrying only a few poetry books and a toothbrush.[23] In the capital, he joined Haya's small circle of friends. Luis Alberto Sánchez, who would establish enduring and unassailable personal and political ties with Haya spanning the twentieth century, and would rise to be a high-ranking general in APRA, second only to Manuel Seoane, fondly remembered how his own friendship with the future APRA leader blossomed in that circle. Sánchez and Haya drew closer together because, he recalls, they shared a mutual appreciation for culture and sports and a "common enthusiasm for the recently discovered poet Alberto Guillén."[24]

That Saturday night, then, the anti-Leguía students attending this university literary and social function were coming to applaud one of their own, just three months after the Sacred Heart protests and a few weeks after Leguía's attack on their beloved UPGP. For the students struggling to form a viable opposition to a regime that seemed only to grow stronger with each passing day, this night presented an opportunity for a symbolic victory allowing them one glorious night to challenge the president and to matter politically.

Leguía's daughter was to award the prizes, and to ensure Leguía himself would attend, Guillén asked Gálvez to invite the president. Since Guillén was one of the president's young clients, this was a reasonable request. Three years earlier, Leguía had paid for Guillén to travel to Madrid, where he interviewed no fewer than thirty-eight men of letters. He published these interviews, stressing only the worst character traits of each, goading the authors to gossip, and highlighting the petty envies and egotisms among them. Back in Lima, Guillén had just republished these salacious and scandalous interviews along with a highly laudatory dedication to Leguía, establishing Guillén as Leguía's client and cementing the young poet's reputation for creating attention-getting scandals.[25] In the commonly understood logic of the patronage ties binding young intellectuals to older, more powerful men, it would not have surprised Leguía that Guillén, in an effort to further his career, wanted the most important poets and politicians to witness his literary triumph as the Juegos Florales first prize winner. Leguía's acceptance of such an invitation from a young and promising—albeit mischievous—client tied the younger man ever closer to him, while allowing Guillén to further acknowledge Leguía's status.

When Leguía arrived and took his box at the theater, the students and antigovernment partisans in the audience, with the deaths just three months earlier on May 23 still fresh in their memories, hissed loudly.[26] Contriving to use Guillén's clientelist ties to invite the president precisely to publicly humiliate Leguía by disrespecting him in a public venue, on a stage that was as much for establishing and reaffirming political and patronage bonds as it was for reciting poetry, seems to us today to be little more than prankish behavior with little power to shock. In that time and place, however, it cut against a deeply felt clientelist logic of how young men advance by behaving toward, and currying favor from, older men. As such, what reads to us as childish, churlish behavior is also a creative political response using humiliation as a "weapon of the weaker" to simultaneously register the students' disgust and scoff at a traditional patriarchal system of patronage demanding their total deference.

With the students' opportunity for such safer, semi-anonymous repudiation over, Guillén began the ceremony by presenting the honorary court, including the "queen," the president's daughter, María Isabel. The organizing committee read the jury's judgment, awarding in addition to Guillén's first prize, an "exceptional" prize to a young Limeñan woman, Magda Portal—Loreley—for a series of three short poems collectively entitled "Nocturnes." The queen formally presented Guillén the Golden Violet prize and Portal the Silver Violet.[27] Music began playing.

This musical intermission was buying time. Portal was to publicly recite her winning poems; when she did not step forward, she interrupted the natural flow of the ceremony, giving the gathered students, still a little giddy from their own fireworks at the start of the night, reason to believe something else was afoot. Refusing to follow the expected script, Portal added to the night's drama, and the students folded her into their own emerging story of their battle against Leguía the dictator. Not reading her prizewinning poems became the foundation of an Aprista myth.

Writing in 1935, fellow Aprista Óscar Herrera recounted seeing Portal backstage waiting to be called to receive her prize: "When they raised the curtain, I saw her grow pale; it seemed to me that it was because of the excitement, but later, when the unctuous José Gálvez invited her, very ceremoniously, to take the stage, I saw how her face, so delicate and youthful, lit up and turned severe, and how the expressive lines of a firm decision were drawn on it. 'No,' she told Gálvez. 'I do not want to greet Leguía, not even to be courteous. I renounce the prize.'" Her refusal to take the stage led Gálvez to hastily explain "that a sudden indisposition of the *señorita* Portal impeded her from reading her verses and from receiving the well-deserved applause from the audience." "Everyone understood" the political nature of her gesture, Herrera noted gleefully, and it garnered her an ovation.[28] Looking back on these heady months from 1935, Manuel Seoane remembered: "I know that many years ago—in the time of naïve Juegos Florales, of gems and stratagems—Magda Portal won a prize and this let her snub Leguía."[29] For her first biographer Daniel Reedy, her protest at the 1923 awards ceremony was a dramatic metamorphosis, the point when a "youthful melancholic girl transformed herself into a rebel who refused to accept poetic laurels from the hands of someone she considered an autocrat," the turning point when "she emerged from her cocoon and the future revolutionary, Magda Portal, took flight."[30]

Portal's actions—or, better said, her choice for inaction—forcefully punctuated that night the students had tried to appropriate, to matter politically if only for a few moments of bravado, transforming it into a more enduring and direct repudiation of Leguía. Later, the students moved quickly to capitalize on this amplified victory in this latest skirmish against the president. Guillén immediately turned around and published a poem the very next month in *Claridad*, the UPGP newspaper Haya edited. Now legitimized as a prizewinning poet, Guillén published a poem dedicated to Haya, "who brings Dawn in his arms," under the banner of "Page of the Laurelled Poet." One stanza scoffed: "Build monuments? Yes, very good. Some dumb ones deserve them. But before that, men should teach dogs to have a less irreverent leg."[31] Readers could not fail to connect Leguía with "raising monuments," given his economic plan built on large public works projects, and the unavoidable mental image Guillén painted of an "irreverent dog" urinating on his powerful patron unmistakably humiliated the president. Within the clientelist logic that demanded Guillén's respect for and loyalty to Leguía for, among other things, paying for his European tour, the poem was a slap in Leguía's face.

While Guillén lobbed his humiliating attacks against the president, Haya, who had been underground, hiding from the Leguía government for more than three months, faced a challenge from his own power base when Limeñan students selected Manuel Seoane to run against him for the presidency of the university student federation. Seoane barely won, only to learn that Leguía had captured Haya and thrown him in prison. Haya was now on a hunger strike. In solidarity with their beleaguered classmate, Seoane proposed that Haya take the presidency while he settled for the vice presidency instead. Haya was elected unanimously.[32]

Turning an electoral defeat into a unanimous victory was an early indication of Haya's political gifts. In these heated, negotiated alliances, as pressure from Leguía's police and university opponents mounted, a key dyad was born, forging a political bond between these two young men, a political brotherhood they would share for the rest of their lives. But alliance is an anemic term to describe their fervent brotherhood, their intimate trust. From this point forward, no matter the repression to come, the distance between them as they scattered in exile, no matter how hot the flame of their political conviction burned—and it could get very hot for a man willing to go on hunger strikes for politics—Haya and Seoane were brothers. Just a week after Haya regained his student leader position in October 1923, Leguía deported him, and he began a series of voyages that would take him from the Soviet Union, through Europe, to Mexico and Central America. As the dominoes fell in Leguía's increasing repression, Seoane himself soon followed, deported to Argentina a year later in mid-1924.

Back in Lima, when students again organized the poetry competition a year later in 1924, they had to go it alone, since no older and respected (albeit dissident) men of letters would serve as judges or sponsors, and since "no young girl from society wanted to accept being queen of a party of rebellious students." Lacking a queen, the students had to make do with one of their own standing as king.[33] "It hadn't happened that way the year before," Luis Alberto Sánchez remembered, "when the daughter of Leguía,

María Isabel, presided over the handing of a prize to Magda Portal." The student actions at the 1923 Juegos Florales still scared away respectable sponsors, patrons, and society girls from participating a year later, suggesting Lima's elite considered them more than simple high jinks. Sánchez's reminiscences also underscore how in his memory, Portal winning and receiving the prize from the hand of the president's daughter came to define that night for him.

Who was this young woman memorialized in this Aprista myth? Unlike Guillén, Portal was not part of the inner circle around Haya, and although she socialized with Reformista students, she was tied more closely to provincial students focused on literary, not political, pursuits. Portal had briefly met Haya days after his breakthrough performance leading the May 23 protests, but she would not see him again until years later in 1927. In a 1978 interview, she stressed that at this time she knew nothing about politics—she "was only a poet."[34]

María Magdalena Julia del Portal Moreno

On May 27, 1900, in Barranco, a seaside suburb of Lima, Doña Rosa Moreno de Portal gave birth to María Magdalena Julia Portal Moreno, the second of four children fathered by Pedro Portal. In the key traumatic moment of her infancy, when young Magda was only five years old, her father died suddenly, in just hours, from bronchial pneumonia. His unexpected death became a psychological wound she could only recall later in life as a "violent circumstance." Her mother was left with four children and no means of supporting them, and the rest of young Magdalena's childhood was marred by financial uncertainty and poverty, her earliest memories haunted by constant moves to cheaper rental housing, selling family goods to make ends meet, and evictions. The economic free fall was cushioned somewhat when her mother remarried in 1907, to Juan Crisóstomo Pareja Rodulfo, and had another four children, these last with the Pareja surname, while the first four kept the last name Portal.[35]

The Lima Portal was born into in 1900 was in many ways still the highly stratified, traditional, colonial viceregal capital, a city where men dared not enter the central Plaza de Armas unless they wore a jacket and tie, where "decent" people did not carry their packages in public, where those of too dark a hue knew where they could and could not go. Decency here had a particular meaning comprehensible to Peruvians at the time and, to a startling degree, to Peruvians today. Instead of using material criteria like income and capital to rank people along a socioeconomic scale, Peruvians distinguished between *gente decente* and *gente de pueblo* by reworking colonial definitions that transformed the abyss between manual and nonmanual work into moral categories. Decency was not about "transitory circumstances" like getting or losing a job; it was an intrinsic, unchanging quality that described who you really were and always would be.

Labor was key. Gente decente did not work with their hands, and they had domestic servants, but "dress, speech, bearing, and manner all played a role, as did the place where one resided, the company one kept, the way one lived." Decent Peruvians had light skin and a respected family name or ancestry, or they cultivated the proper bonds of clientelism with another elite family. In this Catholic society, they observed and marked key life transitions with the appropriate religious rituals and celebrations, including baptism, First Communion, *quince años*, church marriage, and a proper funeral.[36] Every day, Peruvians instinctively classified people based on subjective snap impressions of their decency. Decency mapped Peruvians' life possibilities, and it mattered most for those people on its margins who met only some of the requirements, those slipping off its precarious slopes—people like young Magda Portal.

From a very early age, Portal had started writing; her mother had taught her to read when she was just three years old. Doña Rosa had always prized reading and writing. "My mother was a woman who loved reading," Portal recalled. "She very much liked to read the works of her time, romantic novels that made her tear up, but which I never laid eyes on." Like mother, like daughter. Portal was also entranced with the written word, fondly recalling that even as a little girl of four or five, "the kind of toy I liked best was something in print, any sort of thing—a book or a magazine." The young girl would walk around and around the interior patio of the family home with these books and magazines under her arm, making up and telling herself stories.[37]

She attended various schools, including one she described as "something for decent young ladies," sponsored by women of high Limeñan society, meant to instruct the daughters of the middle class and prepare them for the new jobs opening in Lima's offices as secretaries and office employees.[38] She "read anything that fell into her hands," and by the time she was about twelve, she remembers the director of her school learning that she had filled her notebooks with verses and taking them away. But her mother paid special "attention to my attempts to write," Portal remembered, and would "scold her severely" whenever she "discovered" young Magda destroying original drafts of unsatisfactory writings. By sixteen, she finished her studies "with much difficulty," although her drive to learn was fierce enough that she made herself sick trying to complete two grades in one single year.[39]

But Lima was changing, and changing fast. Just as Portal entered the radical physical changes and everyday euphorias and tragedies of her adolescent years, Lima was also transitioning from an aristocratic and almost cloistered community of elites into a teeming modern capital. Modern technologies like the electric lights colonizing the late night and the speeding automobiles running over everything were overrunning the "beautiful placidity of the Lima of old," a placidity organized and reigned over by a small elite aspiring to a "closed caste." This small group of families "surrounded with respect, reverence, and adulation" wore beautiful outfits tailored in Europe, married only among themselves, watched their children grow up and attend school together, and planned their lives around meeting each other at Mass; at the bullfights; at the horse races; or in the halls of commercial, academic, and political power.[40]

Traditional Lima's "beautiful placidity" weighed most heavily on "decent" women who experienced their world as sharply divided between an interior domestic world and an outside world to be avoided. An extremely cloistered life was especially expected of elite women. In 1905, Teresa González de Fanning lamented that being a decent woman and a good mother meant "becoming moldy in the enclosure of her house," and she warned, in what one hopes was hyperbole, of "girls who, from the time that they were taken to be baptized in the parish church, do not breathe fresh air again until they enter the street feet first," dead and on the way to their own funeral.[41]

But now, economic changes and new public venues were fundamentally altering how Lima socialized. These golden twenties exploded with new wealth, the likes of which Peruvians had not seen since the heady days of the guano boom, and brought in their wake other rapid economic changes and social possibilities. Peruvians at the time attributed this new wealth to the economic stimulus of World War I, although much of the stimulus was due to Leguía's economic policies, which stressed welcoming foreign capital at all costs and pumping it into large public works, which in turn generated massive public debt. Lima grew into a "bustling commercial center," and the banks, insurance companies, and commercial houses that before had operated out of humble storefronts now blossomed into "massive, sumptuous offices." In 1917, a German shopkeeper opened Peru's first department store, an elegant four-story building, complete with "elevators, all the modern conveniences, and the last word in European styles," on the Plaza de Armas facing off with the National Cathedral, the symbolic heart of Lima.[42]

Drawn to these sumptuous new department stores, veritable palaces of material consumption, Limeñans created new rituals of sociability focused around shopping and public display. The old guard, suspicious of such new incentives for women to leave their domestic refuge for the pleasures of the street, anxiously worried about the new consumerism's pernicious influence. Starting at their very doors, they fretted, department stores were "a series of surprises that narcotized women; fooled them like innocent creatures, making them lose all sense; obligated them to leave the home's budget, resigning themselves with true heroism to the fasting of the stomach."[43]

Everything, not just commerce, now seemed to be undermining decency. Shopping promenades like the Jirón de la Unión, cafés like the Jardín Estrasburgo and the Palais Concert, restaurants, theaters—public venues that had played little part in earlier forms of elite sociability and political life—effectively replaced parties and dinners in private homes.[44] José Gálvez, our poeta gran señor, had in fact enjoyed a respectable success in the 1920s with nostalgic evocations of the traditional forms of elite sociability of a Lima disappearing around him. A generation before, he mourned, elite families still hosted most social interactions at home, genteel affairs, *tertulias*, with clearly understood rules, limits, purposes, and chaperones. Gálvez angrily accused the "cinema, the theaters, the *paseos públicos*" of "vilely assassinating the tertulia." Families no longer dictated the social calendar by scheduling calling days and instead "young men find girls in the *cinema*, at the *tennis* [clubs], at the Palais, wherever."[45]

Lastenia Larriva de Llona, an elite Limeñan matriarch, also worried about this troubling demise in the importance of the family home in the elite's social life. "It was a custom in my time to eat early, and immediately after, the owners of the house were already prepared to receive their guests, and the tertulia, very cordial and pleasant, lasted until eleven or twelve at night," she fondly remembered. In contrast, she warned, "today, and I worry at confessing it—there is no longer a home. Marriages are arranged in the streets, far from the parents' view, who often do not even know their daughters' admirers, until the daughters themselves introduce them."[46] Traditional tertulias could not compete with these new venues and their relaxed forms where modern young people met and socialized.

Consternation at the idea of daughters arranging their own emotional life or parading in the public streets highlighted in sharp relief how, at heart, the concern was about gendered notions of piety, chastity, and young women's sexual purity. Lima's elite youth, Larriva de Llona maintained, were "not yankees," and should not venture alone in public like young women in the United States, since young Limeñan men could not be trusted to respect them. Those who ignored her advice were "reckless girls" who naively believed they knew who their boyfriends really were after just "strolling in his company, or going with him to the cinema." These new public spaces were "schools very different from that of the family, temples where pagan gods are worshiped, very different from the sanctity of the home, in which the God who is revered teaches Honesty and Chastity!"[47]

These changes in social life affected everyone in Lima, not just the elite at the top of the social pyramid. But the elites' feverish anxieties arose because this small closed caste was losing exclusive control of their social spaces, as elite youth were seduced outside the home to bohemian Lima's streets, shops, and cafés, where they met, interacted, and now courted people who would never have made it inside Larriva de Llona's tertulia. These new undesirables included the provincial migrants pouring into the capital, drawn by Lima's opportunities and traveling on the new roads and railroads Leguía was building. These more modest sectors were as much pushed out into the street by their increasingly cramped and uncomfortable living conditions; striving to keep housing affordable as the population exploded, the Interior Ministry essentially froze rents for modest-income housing, which reduced incentives for further construction, only exacerbating the housing crunch. The only silver lining was that Lima's severe housing shortage fed its bustling cafés and "bohemian air," creating its vibrant street life.[48]

Magda Portal, then, lived in a time and place surrounded by changing and evolving buildings, mores, and possibilities. After she finished her formal education at sixteen, she immediately went to work to help make ends meet at home, landing her first job at a photography studio. But in 1918, Portal's stepfather died, plunging the family into financial troubles yet again. His death left her mother three months pregnant, and the family had trouble paying their bills even after combining the incomes of Portal and her older sister. Once again, the family had to move from house to house.[49]

Portal's family was not alone in falling into one of the most obvious contradictions about decency and wealth in Peru. On the one hand, "decency," and the middle-class status it conferred, did not depend on wealth. Since the very language of decency that Peruvians all spoke and understood based social status on innate moral categories, money could only be an "acquisition, not an intrinsic quality" able to mark one's place in the social hierarchy. For instance, some older women, who could convincingly claim to be decent based on their family names, their education, their Catholic piety, and their racial background, chose to live in "abject poverty" in the center of Lima because living in those decaying *casonas*, traditional colonial-era mansions, added to their social prestige. Choosing to live at a "decent" address was worth endangering their health. But Peruvians also marked and read decency by a vast repertoire of expensive social and cultural performances requiring wealth.[50] Those caught in this seeming contradiction of the "decent poor," especially women, elicited considerable sympathy from Lima's elite as "the true victims" of Lima's misery: "the señoritas who belong to good families and who have fallen into misfortune," who "hide their poverty, as if it were opprobrious, the martyrs who succumb because they work until the late hours of the night to support themselves, but are so poorly remunerated that their delicate organisms cannot bear such rude labor and they die ignored by society."[51]

"Middle-class families maintained a type of shyness and did not exhibit their penury," instead suffering "in the hopes that some miraculous wind would blow to compensate the moments of extreme poverty," Portal wrote later, echoing the judgment passed by her contemporary, the historian Jorge Basadre, who explained that the "tragic" condition of the Peruvian middle class derived "from their heroic efforts" to differentiate themselves from the working masses. "In their dress and presentation, they were condemned to a lifestyle and to social rituals that were constantly superior to their effective capabilities. Their lives were intimate tragedies, carefully concealed."[52] But outside of sympathy and sporadic charity, there were no structural answers for these decent poor—Magda Portal included. People waited or suffered, carefully concealing their "intimate tragedies," accepting discreet charity, or fantasizing of their "miraculous wind."

Portal lived with her mother and siblings near San Marcos University, and on her way back home from work, she would pass by the imposing doors of the university, "amusing" herself by gazing inside into the sheltered and cultivated patios and interior gardens that "fascinated" her. One day, her curiosity won out, and she stepped in. Walking inside, she discovered a classroom where a professor lectured on philosophy. Portal found a seat in the back of the classroom and sat down. Nobody paid any attention to her as she sat there quietly and listened. Emboldened, she stealthily attended classes on subjects that interested her; she listened, read, and studied.[53]

In a city with a population of nearly a quarter million in 1920, only about two thousand attended San Marcos University, and literally only a handful were women. Five had battled the hostile resistance and harassment of other students and professors and entered the Faculty of Medicine.[54] Remembering these few female students, Luis Alberto Sánchez tellingly focused on their feminine beauty and attributes, noting how one "did not stand out in her beauty, although she was always an excellent colleague." Another, "in contrast, very young and of a delicate air, with fine features and her hair down like a schoolgirl, awakened sympathy and, yet, respect."[55]

While Portal would have liked to formally enroll and study law, medicine, history, or even philosophy, she was different from these other women students: her family's poverty made that an impossible dream. Portal remembers her greatest wish was to "learn everything," fundamentally a yearning for escape from a life circumscribed by her natal family's poverty.[56] It took more than curiosity for Portal to walk in, sit down, remain, and return to these university classes. In these classrooms, as surely as she satisfied intellectual curiosities, Portal was looking for an escape from her precarious status as a decent but poor young woman. What kind of "miraculous wind" did she dream about?

For most women, especially beautiful young women, escape would be a new family. In these classrooms, where she was the only woman, Portal met young men, decent men, men from wealthy families whose prospects must have seemed limitless. Other young women, constrained by Lima's notions of female decency, could only hope to meet potential suitors in one or two carefully guarded spaces. "All the young girls in search of boyfriends" had to resort to attending the eleven o'clock Mass at Lima's central cathedrals of Santo Domingo or San Pedro precisely so that the young men at the ever-popular Palais cafe could watch them walk—slowly, one presumes—to and from Mass.[57] Portal did not wait to display herself strolling to Mass, the usual marriage market; she was meeting young men in a new, unsanctioned, and unchaperoned space, a new venue without established courtship rules or normative behavioral expectations.

This was the other way she was different from the more demure, decent female university students like the one Luis Alberto Sánchez remembered as "very studious, always smiling and distant," and who talked to the young men "but not excessively." A letter she published in 1923, answering a somewhat risqué *Mundial* survey, captures the very different personality Portal projected. "With whom would you flirt?," the magazine asked coyly. Portal shot back: "For flirting [*coquetear*] nothing beats liars. . . . Word of honor! Never flirt [*flirteo*] with a man who only speaks the truth. . . . They infuriate me." She assured *Mundial*'s readers that "the man who does not know how to lie will never completely win over a woman, because by nature, even when we doubt what they tell us, their telling of it pleases us."[58] While Portal's reply strikes us today as playful, in 1923, publishing her take on a modern form of sociability so new and foreign it was still referred to interchangeably with its English name, flirteo, was, to use her term, audacious. This was, after all, the same Lima where young decent women were expected to eschew all public displays, especially those having to do with courtship and romance.

It was also from 1918, Portal remembered, after her stepfather's death and the wolf returned to her door, that she started escaping from her family's recurring financial troubles with young loves, "responding to the frenzies that presented themselves."[59] Male students saw in Portal a beautiful young woman willing to play and flirt with sexual transgression. This was her first—and perhaps foundational—iconoclasm: refusing to bow before female sexual propriety. Curiosity may have drawn her into the university, but staying and coming back was an audacious step, the step that started it all, the step she no doubt hoped would fundamentally alter the course of her life.

Likely leveraging connections she made with other young writers at the university, Portal elbowed her way into Lima's burgeoning publishing world. On May 28, 1920, *Mundial* published her story "Violetas." The life-changing decision to step into the university did not end in escape through marriage, but instead in escape through a public writing life. Women, even women of middling status like her mother, were reading and writing. But what made Portal different from her mother and her mother's "intimate tragedies," her mother's lack of agency in a life that buffeted her around to no end, was finding a way to publish that writing and create a public persona, a public reputation—another life.

Of course, this public writing life was still somewhat socially suspect and carried more than a whiff of scandal. In the public imagination, women who entered the public arena, leaving behind the respectable cloistered domesticity of the family home or nuptial bed, courted shame and disrespect, and were culturally intelligible to contemporaries mostly as prostitutes.[60] Looking back, the words Portal used to describe her younger self, "curious" and "audacious," give us a sense of a woman leaving something— the "intimate tragedies" of her downwardly mobile natal family—for something else, something she was audacious enough to take a risk for, to reach out and grasp.

Another life, another name. For a little over a year, starting in May 1920, Portal published under a pseudonym in *Mundial*: Tula Soavani. Her next two pieces carried both her pseudonym and her name, and by December of 1922 she had discarded the Soavani pseudonym entirely and published openly under her given name.[61] Using a pseudonym was a way to protect her feminine honor, although they were commonly used by men as well: Mariátegui wrote under the name Jean Croniquer. Portal, however, was quite self-consciously playing with names and identities. The poet César Vallejo once told her, "'Magda Portal, what a beautiful ring your name has, while I am a simple Vallejo, not even a Valle.' A curious thing to say, which impressed me and made me think," Portal remembered. "In fact," she confessed, "my name is not exactly Magda Portal. I have three or four names—María Magdalena Julia Portal Moreno. And, since I didn't like any of them, one day I simply shortened my name to Magda Portal. . . . I had to go to court to change it legally. By law you have to use your complete name. It was audacious in those days to change your name." She didn't like her name, her courtly name of Virgins and pretensions toward decency that life had chosen for her. The new, shorter name she chose for herself performed the escape she had dreamed of: a door to another life.[62]

Magda Portal

Back at the Juegos Florales that Saturday night, as the strains of the musical intermission faded, a poet did step forward to read "Nocturnes"—the host, José Gálvez. There were three poems in the series, all written from a female perspective.[63] In the first poem, "Weariness," the female narrative voice tosses and turns, unable to sleep, imagining shadows "that ruin her hair and drown their long fingers in her idea," as her heart counts "the beats of my swollen womb." In "Possession," the second poem, the shadow feels her eyes and face with silken hands while she is immobile, and has "the audacity to take it all." The poem ends exclaiming "Look how / the shadow possesses / my body!" The last poem, "Fear," begins with the narrator expecting the shadow: "I will have this fever that beats today in my brow / and I will be seated, / taciturn / with my gaze tenaciously nailed to the door" from where the shadow will emerge. The "dark / bitter / yearned-for shadow! / will take the flames of deep concern from my eyes / and poking in my depths, will take the red / lived rubies of my youth" and will then leave quietly, leaving her "seated, taciturn / and the fever that today beats in my brow will have fled."[64]

Sex, delight, shame, fear—even in the voice of a respectable older man like José Gálvez, this was potent and scandalous stuff. The students gathered that night in the elite theater, a privileged space for the respectable, decent Lima of their parents, who nonetheless considered themselves daring iconoclasts, must have loved it—loved hearing the poems recited and loved savoring their multiple and layered voyeuristic pleasures.

It was about sex; that was clear enough. But what kind of sex? The female narrator describes herself repeatedly as immobile and taciturn, and an ominous silence drapes all three poems, including the last one, explicitly titled "Fear." Is this a coercive encounter, a rape? But the narrator "yearns" for the "dark / bitter" shadow, which will sate the "fever" consuming her, suggesting it is about her sexual satiation. The shadow has the "audacity to take it all" from the narrator; or is it that she has the audacity to give it all? Sex, of course, has consequences—the "swollen womb" mentioned in the first poem. But the series is not about the past, or about remorse, the all-too-common tale of a fallen woman. The last poem, "Fear," is written in a future tense; it's pitched not as a remorseful memory so much as fantasy, expectation, and promise, however dark. And ultimately, it was that ambivalence, that yearning, that desire for more, that made this scandalous—this was a series that dared to consider and explore the complicated, ambiguous emotional landscape of female sexual agency. "Magda Portal," Mariátegui would write, "is something very rare and very precious in our literature: a poetisa." As Peru's first "poetess," Portal introduced an explicitly female voice, an authentically feminine poetry that was neither "asexual" nor "sterile," abruptly breaking free from Peruvian literature's colonial legacy.[65] Mariátegui saw clearly that Portal's poetry exploring female sexual agency—the fear haunting Lima decente—was an explosive challenge to traditional literature.

Portal's actions that night at the Juegos Florales first spoke to the students because she interrupted the normative script of these events, but they must have resonated with the students even more when they actually heard the poems, that frontal attack on everything Lima cherished about female sexual purity and chastity, all of these feeding their iconoclastic impulses. Playing with taboo topics such as coercive sex and female sexual agency, destroying cherished ideas about morality and virtue, these poems were the very definition of iconoclasm.

These poems—these scandalous poems—made Portal's reputation; they were her own scandalous debut. Portal knew, of course, just how scandalous they were. Why else would she have entered the contest not as Tula Soavani, her professional pseudonym, but as "Loreley," a new pseudonym never used before, essentially a "burner" pseudonym? No one forced her to enter the contest or to submit these three specific poems. This was another audacious risk she was willing to take to grasp at another life just out of reach. The new pseudonym was a prudent mitigation should she not win, assuring there were no real consequences for her or her professional name.

But she did win. And this prize singled her out as one of Lima's most talented poets, recognition and validation on a national stage. The approbation, prestige, and reputation she garnered with this prize could make concrete her escape from the middling life of "intimate tragedies." These poems were in a real sense her own "miraculous wind," a Prince Charming of her own making. This achievement was so foundational that more than fifty years later, recounting her life history, she always made sure to mention that she won the Juegos Florales—this was always the start of her public autobiography.[66]

The national exposure offered by the Juegos Florales established her as one of the very few public women in Peru, but this brought new risks along with new opportunities. As a reporter, Portal's name was already in print. Exposure nourished her escape to another kind of life, her public writing life. But Lima's codes of feminine modesty considered any exposure scandalous. As a young iconoclast, she relished some of that scandal, of course. Portal's profession as a journalist and a poet and her enthusiastic adoption of new forms of sociability like flirting already marked her as modern and willing to challenge traditional notions of decency. But when did that exposure tip from daring iconoclasm into humiliation?

Winning a prize at the Juegos Florales meant two types of exposure lay before her: at the awards ceremony, she would receive the prize on stage and read her winning verses. A few days later, *Mundial* would also publish its trademark multipage photographic spread documenting the evening, the first time Portal's photograph, and not just her name, would be published. Photographs, still a new technology in Lima, had different rules, even in the most modern of North Atlantic cities. When a reporter wanted to take a picture of the all-female staff of the Parisian paper *La Fronde*, a female journalist demurred: "I don't know if I could. . . . I need to ask my husband and he is not here. A wife owes obedience to her husband."[67]

Lima's code of public feminine modesty also looked askance at publishing the photographs of decent women. A few months earlier, in February during Lima's summer Carnival when the city elected and crowned a Carnival queen from Lima's young debutantes, *Mundial* ordered reporters to tramp through the city streets knocking on the doors of the daughters of the elite, "begging" them for a portrait for their lavish montage "Who Will Be the Carnival Queen?" The magazine "knew perfectly well" that their four-page feature was missing many of the young women who could "aspire to Carnival's scepter," and explained that many of the young beauties refused their request for a photograph because of their "inherent modesty." Not so easily defeated, *Mundial* convinced a photographer "who avariciously guards the nicest archive of pretty faces" to hand over thirty of the thirty-eight portraits they published, resorting, or at least claiming to resort, to subterfuge to print almost all their portraits.[68] Even if the women wanted to see themselves in *Mundial*, the code of public feminine modesty made Lima's decent young ladies all demur, or at least pretend to demur, such scandalous exposure.

In a choice between exposure as a prizewinning poet and Lima's codes of gendered propriety, Portal chose exposure—her public writing life, her escape. In *Mundial*'s full-page photo spread a few days later, Portal appears in a full body shot, dressed in a flowing and loose dark dress. She stands next to the dapper Guillén, their images superimposed over the flower-strewn stage of the queen's court, right next to the title of the page: "Los Juegos Florales." A final decorative embellishment, a large bouquet of flowers, graces the immediate left of the title, fully obscuring the middle section of Portal's body. The photographers and editors at *Mundial*, where

Detail from "Los Juegos Florales," *Mundial*,
August 31, 1923. Courtesy University of
California, Berkeley Libraries.

Portal had been publishing for years, did what they could to hide the fact that by August of 1923, Magda Portal was six months pregnant.

Maneuvering around Lima's codes of feminine modesty, her friends and allies tried to protect Portal as she walked this fine line between iconoclasm, scandal, and humiliation. But while they could somewhat protect her on the pages they edited, who was looking out for her on that stage, when the normal course of events would have her stand before elite Lima reciting her poems about female sexual agency, visibly pregnant and unwed?

Later, Portal revealed that José Gálvez had visited her at home a few days after the judges reached their decision, begging her to concede first place to the second-place winner, the young Guillén, offering her a "special prize" equal in condition to, but instead of, first place. He explained that when the jury realized their first-place winner had a female pseudonym, they had concluded that they nonetheless had to award the prize to a male, because it would be "impossible" for the president's daughter to "offer homage" to her since they were both "ladies."[69] Gálvez might have used the rather courtly excuse that a queen could not render homage to a lady as a euphemistic way of protecting a young Portal from needless exposure as unmarried and pregnant. Or perhaps the jury wanted to guard the honor of María Isabel Leguía and keep her from having to share the stage with a scandalous Magda Portal.

Male critics read Portal's "Nocturnes" with evident pleasure for its voyeuristic view of a woman's tormented interiority, in *Mundial's* review, of a woman whose "sentimental life has been trampled by Pain," whose life has been "robbed" of joy by her unsanctioned pregnancy.[70] The jury's decision did not focus on the elements of positive female sexual agency in Loreley's poems, instead commending them for the "tortured and feminine soul throb[bing] profoundly [with] the mysteries and anguish of everyday tragedy," what traditional Lima could understand and perhaps accept as a risqué morality tale, a voyeuristic lens into a fallen woman's misfortune.[71] But when Loreley was revealed to be Magda Portal, a risqué choice on their part threatened to explode into a more serious scandal. Now it wasn't just about the poems. The scandal mushroomed and shifted to focus on a young woman who thumbed her nose at every cherished notion of female chastity and honor. At issue was Portal's willingness to publicly admit to sexual behaviors that everyone knew happened, but which everyone still wholeheartedly condemned. A close reading of "Nocturnes" revealed a tumultuous stew of high emotion, including shame. But not just shame. If she were truly ashamed, and appropriately contrite, why reveal anything about it in print? In traditional Lima, any decent woman would know better; Portal was so indecent she felt none of the appropriate shame and even trumpeted her sin on a national stage. The scandal was now both her obvious sexual transgression and her refusal to assume its associated shame.

But Portal could never completely escape shame; even this rebellious iconoclast was fundamentally conflicted. She refused Gálvez's face-saving opportunity to step back from this exposure into a more acceptable private domesticity, instead accepting her prize and posing in the awards ceremony photograph, risking irreparably destroying her reputation as a decent woman. This was not an easy choice to make, and it was the essence of Portal's lifelong and inescapable struggle between normative definitions of gendered decency and the demands of her public life as an intellectual. But when the moment came to take the stage, she chose not to step in front of the audience and read her scandalous verses. With her *Mundial* allies' skillful attention to photographic montage, perhaps most who glanced over the photograph later noticed nothing. Perhaps she had managed to thread the needle between daring iconoclasm and public ridicule and humiliation.

That night was not a metamorphosis from melancholic poet to revolutionary militant. Portal was not conspiring with the San Marcos students to heighten the students' insult to the president. Instead, she was engaged in her own interior battle, balancing her needs to be both a public poet and a decent woman. But in every way that mattered, for Portal this psychological struggle was political because it was the foundational motivation for a life oriented around challenging limits to her freedom. She did not—could not—"win" this conflict between feminine decency and individual agency. A total victory was impossible. But she was now a prizewinning poet featured on the pages of a national magazine. Like Haya, Portal's scandalous debut established her as one of Lima's most representative iconoclastic youth.

CHAPTER TWO

Crazy, Boundless Heart

IN 1919, LISTING QUALITIES young Limeñan men should search for in a "model wife and perfect mother," the Limeñan matriarch Lastenia Larriva de Llona counseled them to look for "sincere piety, absolute purity, innate chastity, and modesty without affectation . . . a young woman who is a loving and submissive daughter."[1] By 1923, Magda Portal, a published journalist, a prizewinning poet, and a pregnant unmarried woman, was the living repudiation of the gendered propriety Lima held dear. Her pregnancy advertised her lack of purity and chastity. Appearing on stage and in print in her scandalous condition, she was certainly not modest. Above all, her scandalous conditions—her pregnancy, her immodesty, her refusal to let shame keep her from pursuing the escape her public writing life provided—all proved she was not a submissive daughter.

How could Doña Rosa Moreno de Portal, Portal's mother, understand what had befallen her daughter, what her daughter had become? Widowed, Doña Rosa led a family of women, a household without a patriarch in a society where men provided honor and protected decency.[2] Portal's transgressive behavior thus reflected poorly on Portal's mother, proving she had failed to teach Magda how to behave properly. But "fallen" daughters also suggested "fallen" mothers. Adapting emerging scientific—and pseudoscientific— ideas about evolution and biological inheritance, Peruvians now also held mothers, and not just the family patriarch, responsible for a daughter's chastity. A child's physical or moral shortcomings increasingly indicated a similar failing in the parent who had passed the unfortunate trait down, as in Clorinda Matto de Turner's novel *Herencia*, where a mother's irresponsible frivolity proved a "fatal heritage of the blood" for a daughter who could not

Magda Portal with her mother, Rosa Amelia Moreno del Risco; her grand-
mother, Juana del Risco; and daughter, Gloria. Courtesy Estate of Magda Portal,
Rocío Revolledo Pareja, and Penn State University Press.

control her sexual impulses when faced with a seducer. For Doña Rosa, Portal's scandalous exposure on the Juegos Florales stage and in the pages of *Mundial* was nothing less than a knife through her heart. Any mother would have agonized about a shameless, fallen daughter's compromised future, but Portal's behavior hurt even more because people would accuse her of being a bad mother who could not control her daughter and even worse, might wonder if, like daughter like mother, Doña Rosa herself was sexually indecent.

"My mother was very blond with very blue eyes," Portal remembered. "The neighborhood called her 'Madame' when they spoke of her, as a sign of respect, but she did not like that, she preferred that they call her '*señora*.'"[3] Her mother descended from a Spanish family, which, along with her fair-skinned phenotype, was a strong claim to decency. Portal's father, however, descended from a French family, so why the insistence on "Señora" over "Madame?" While "Madame" literally translates in Spanish to "Señora," colloquially "*madama*," like in English, meant prostitute or madame, and Limeñans strongly associated prostitutes with French women. Instead of a sign of respect, her neighbors' insistence on calling her mother "Madame" may have ridiculed her mother's social aspirations, mocking the family's claims to decency. A fallen daughter now "proved" what people had suspected—that this entire household, and especially this mother, was unfit, indecent, and sexually suspect. That Portal even mentioned it suggests to us that implications of sexual impropriety, no matter how slight, deeply disturbed her mother.

And the daughter? How did Portal feel about these transgressions? In September 1921, two years before her scandalous debut at the Juegos Florales, Portal published a short poem titled "Prayer." "Lord, Lord! I desire to be good / desire to / forget my biting sorrow / desire to submerge myself in a beatitude / that will rob me of the enormous power of my restlessness / . . . / I want to be straight as an arrow and / advance in life / without wavering in the path, curious and rash / like channeled water, / like forceless wind, / like a caged bird, like a soundless voice . . . / I want to abandon my / fierce arrogant attitudes, / my rebellious instincts, my primitive strengths. / I want to trap the crazy, boundless heart, / I want to make it not cry, I want to make it not / (sing . . . / Oh Lord, you can do it, by your wounded side / grant me, grant me freedom from sin / from completely unraveling against my tumultuous sorrow . . . / I want you to make me simply good."[4]

Compared to "Nocturnes," this prayer, this plea to change, suggests the remarkable distance Portal will travel in two years as she becomes a vanguard New Woman, a scandalous iconoclast. A prayer was a safer way to explore the personal qualities tormenting a young Portal—the "enormous power of my restlessness," her "fierce arrogant attitudes," her "rebellious instincts," her "primitive strengths"—an inventory completely contrary to Larriva de Llona's checklist. With the striking language of "fierce" and "primitive" animalistic strengths to be "caged" and "trapped," this 1921 poem suggested that Portal's personality, her "crazy, boundless heart," needed to be overcome and tamed. In this poetic prayer, Portal chronicles all the ways she cannot conform to the strictures of decent Lima, even though she desperately wishes she could.

Portal offered this prayer to the reading public, but just as certainly to her mother and to herself. Still struggling with Catholic decency, she labeled as "sin" the excesses of her "crazy, boundless heart." Cast as a religious exercise recognizing temptations, it was still culturally acceptable, especially since it pleaded for strength to resist these temptations, the physical ones she would later chronicle in "Nocturnes," but also more generally the temptation to escape her life and its restrictive conditions, escape from her own intimate tragedies created by looming poverty and gendered notions of decency, the structural conditions limiting her freedom.

But the poem was also startlingly introspective and self-aware; Portal recognized what and who she was, the essence of her character. Her "crazy, boundless heart" cries because it transgresses her society's dictates, but she recognizes how that same transgression makes it "(sing . . . ," the opening parenthesis and spacing performing how singing happens privately, alone, in hiding, the ellipses suggesting the singing was only the beginning of something. Portal, even at twenty-one, recognized and celebrated in herself these ferocious, arrogant, fierce strengths. Casting these unspeakable desires as sinful temptations that needed and deserved to be expunged allowed her to write and publish about her conflictive emotions while also allowing her to recognize who she was.

This poem, which might at first seem to be her recognition of sin and acceptance of shame, is therefore instead a head-on confrontation with her own ambivalence, ambivalence about the many binaries animating this prayer: temptation and celebration of self, demureness and decency, modesty and haughty pride. In another, more implicit binary, the poem marked the difference between the audacity of a daughter who had found a public platform for her writing and the self-abnegation of a mother who wrote and read only in private. Ultimately, in this poem Portal begs to be made "simply good" instead of being who she actually is: a complicated, conflicted, ambivalent woman trying to become something else.

At the Juegos Florales, Portal confronted a personal, psychological struggle between expectations of decency limiting women's freedom and the demands of a public writing life she considered her escape from her downwardly mobile life, a choice perfectly distilled when Gálvez came to her home suggesting she step back from the social risks of public exposure that were part and parcel of a public writing life. Choosing any exposure carried risks for her and inevitably promised to hurt her mother and further erode her mother's precarious claim to decency. To claim her freedom, Portal had to hurt and endanger her mother, the first emotional price to pay for her public life in what would prove to be a long list.

For the tumultuous three years between 1920 and 1923, as Portal fashioned her adult personality and pushed the boundaries of acceptable behavior, she negotiated the emotional distance from her mother, particularly difficult because her mother was her only living parent. Portal also struggled, however, to create a sense of self true to all the inner qualities she wanted to set free, qualities like curiosity, daring, and courage, those temptations driving her to affiliate with the intensely attractive homosocial world of bohemian Lima. To be true to herself meant courting unavoidable conflict with her mother's expectations for Portal's behavior.

That perpetual struggle, and the choices she would need to make again and again between decency and public life, became the foundation of her political identity because it made the structural conditions limiting her freedom explicit to her and forced her to confront them. It's an intuition that at this point she is not yet analyzing; that will come later. As she explored the world of men around her at the university and as a journalist, Portal began to feel out the edges of the psychological and structural dilemmas of being a woman.

In narrating her own dramas and predicaments, Portal will come to realize that her psychological conflicts arose from structural conditions and to recognize that shame was a powerful tool keeping people—particularly women—convinced that these psychological conflicts were inevitable individual torments, not structural conditions that could be changed. In any viable society, everybody believes to some degree in the hegemonic social fictions ordering their world; everyone is oppressed. But what leads some to start fighting that oppression, to even recognize it as oppression instead of a righteous plan or the inevitable way things are? Portal's central intellectual conundrum was finding a way to dampen the shame demanding that she trap her "crazy, boundless heart" and instead unleash those primitive, fierce, arrogant, rebellious energies toward a larger political project. As an individual of her time and place, she could not jettison the shame entirely; she would always be ambivalent. But she could make that internal conflict less overwhelming, enough to allow her to move forward, dry her tears, and sing out loud.

A Family of Women in a World of Men

In every way that mattered, Doña Rosa could not even imagine the new world of bohemian Lima, with all its delights and dangers. Her generation had lived life "with slowness, conventionality, and moderation . . . not far from the atmosphere and the psychology of their mothers and their grandmothers."[5] Through her work as a reporter for *Mundial*, Portal gained access to a world closed to her mother or other *señoritas decentes*, and she desperately wanted to affiliate with this exciting new world of men, to be one of the boys. *Mundial*, a glossy, folio-sized magazine bursting with photographs, was also new. Founded only in 1920, it quickly became "an obligatory stop for any intellectual passing through Lima," gathering "all those of liberal ideas."[6]

Mundial's young owner ran the magazine in a casual and clubby manner, a "boy's club." After losing his wife in 1923, he promptly dedicated himself not just to "amorous adventures" but also to cultivating his own rich life of masculine friendships. Every day at noon he invited *Mundial* contributors to swim with him, followed by a cold shower, which Luis Alberto Sánchez fondly remembered were "vigorously administered" by Germán, the old *manguerista*, "hose handler." No doubt refreshed, they had lunch and drinks together. After lunch, the action moved for the rest of the day to *Mundial*'s offices, where they entertained visitors to Lima and read each others' works.

At night, their companionship shifted to other, more private locales: Lima's many popular brothels. While decent women feared, even in jest, the slightest implication of any transgressive sexual behavior, respectable men had an entirely different relationship to prostitution, an unquestioned part of the Limeñan night. Men of all ages and political persuasions met each other in Lima's brothels, where savvy *madames* imported the latest French literary texts for their bohemian clientele to discuss over cognac or absinthe. "There were no other places for them to comfort themselves," Luis Alberto Sánchez explained, concluding poetically, if somewhat melo-dramatically, that "the fact is that is how we killed the night, the endless night of a village fighting to transform itself into a city."

This bohemian world was also, then, a world of men, a world of intense male bonding with homoerotic overtones. Being a young woman effectively barred Portal from such companionship; inviting female colleagues to join them swimming and bathing would have been inconceivable. Fascinated by this homosocial world, Portal longed to join its intense camaraderie. This world, however, explicitly defined itself by excluding women, and even Sán-chez recognized that the few bohemian intellectuals who happened to be women had no place in it, a condition he described as "the orphanhood of lettered women." An orphan in this public world of men, Portal found back doors into bohemian Lima with, in her words, audacity, curiosity, and courage—all traits highlighting that she was, above all, not timid.

The bohemian Lima calling to Portal was a world of artists, poets, and journalists, most of whom had some tie with the University of San Mar-cos, and many had just recently arrived from the provinces, young men who relished Portal's audacity and daring behavior. She moved easily through these male circles, befriending men who became famous artists, such as the poet César Vallejo or the painter José Sabogal.[7] Sabogal painted her portrait, and Portal had her picture taken in a photography studio she fondly remembered as a "cordial refuge" where these young bohemians gathered, drinking together from whatever vessel they could find at hand. These young New Men, especially those from traditional provincial cities they found stultifying, were also somewhat drunk on Lima. Trujillo, one explained, "was like a monastery," where no one gathered except for Christmas and the Peruvian independence holidays, after which "I used to feel sad, thinking that I should have to spend another year without being able to meet my fellow men. Everybody shut themselves up inside their houses. The whole of life went on behind closed doors and behind the barred windows of the silent city."[8]

Compared with those barred windows and cities silent as monasteries, opportunity charged through the teeming streets of Lima like the new electric currents. They had found it very difficult to socialize with young women in the provinces. "Falling in love was, of course, a problem," one complained. "To meet a woman, we had to stand on guard at street corners, day after day, and when the beauty showed herself from behind a blind or at a half-opened door, we had to take advantage of this to throw her a note written on paper that had yellowed with the waiting." Audacious and daring, Portal was a live wire who flirted, who flouted her sexual freedom by speaking freely about sex, who shared their adventures, who drank, who wrote. By meeting and socializing with modern young women like Portal, provincial men gained access to bohemian Lima's excitement, a world where they did not have to wait for days to catch a glimpse of a girl.

"We were all friends and equals" in this group, Portal remembered later, claiming she "never argued" with them. Portal "was especially close" to provincial students at San Marcos, she explained, because Lima's intellectuals, who had "always been a bit arrogant and patronizing," were "a little egotistical" toward provincials. Her friends were "all in rebellion against Lima. They taught me to dislike Lima." Portal bonded with her provincial friends in part because they did not consider her a typical Limeña. Vallejo "felt close to me 'because I didn't act like I was from Lima.'" Her provincial friends would tell her, "'It's hard to believe you're from Lima, since you don't talk that much.' The women of Lima talked and talked, without saying very much at all."[9]

Portal became so identified with provincial students that she often pretended to be from the provinces herself, explaining somewhat enigmatically that she wanted to give them "space, to give them context." But the "space and context" she created also served her ends. Excluded because of her gender, Portal took advantage of her structural privilege as a Limeña among provincials to become "one of the boys" even as these particular subaltern boys chafed against Limeñan slights, both subtle and egregious. She found herself increasingly implicated in their drama of regional identity as they began to construct and assert a militant anti-Limeñan identity. Portal's ties to these regional groups also allowed—or perhaps encouraged— her to further contrast herself from normative Limeñan feminine sociability, as suggested by how sharply she still remembered their "compliment" that she didn't prattle on like other vain, frivolous limeñas.

Working as a journalist also created opportunities for a curious Portal to explore and document a wider world. On June 10, 1921, she published "China-Town: The Things Not Everyone Sees."[10] In this piece, the reader follows the young journalist to Lima's bustling Chinatown, a world marked by the nasal sounds of spoken Chinese and the smell of lard and garbage she describes with obvious distaste. Alongside photographs of typical storefronts, Chinese food, and a smiling Chinese clerk, Portal commands her readers to see "those things that not everyone sees," including a poor beggar, miserable and hungry, who tries desperately to buy food with his last three cents, only to be denied over and over.

How did Portal herself come to "see" this wrenching sight? This adventure begins in Lima's lively recreational life, where, Portal remembered, "drinking and taking drugs was what went on in the bohemian world we were a part of." Her friends experimented with ether, cocaine, and opium. "I used to get together with this group, even when they were taking drugs. . . . The most I ever dared was sniffing ether, which was relatively harmless. They moistened a handkerchief with ether and gave it to me to smell. We all tried it. It was a stupid thing really. I felt nothing." Portal underlined that "my friends cared about me and protected me, though I was terribly curious about the drugs. I wasn't a baby by any means."[11] Being a baby meant both being innocent and being under tutelage, even as her friends, being decent Limeñans after all, protected her. Protected her from what? From the dangers bohemian Lima loved flirting with, or from her own "terrible curiosity?" Stupid or not, Portal's "terrible curiosity" often impelled her to accompany her friends as they set out to purchase their drugs around Lima. One time, one of her friends invited her to smoke opium with the "addicts" in Lima's Chinatown. Curious, Portal agreed and ventured out alone into Chinatown; when she did not see her friends at the agreed-upon apartment, however, she fled.[12]

This memory is about young people indulging in forbidden pleasures, but also about Portal's attempts at "constructive acts of affiliation" with the world of bohemian Lima. The setting is important: Luis Alberto Sánchez casually remembers how "the people of *Mundial*" were the first ones to champion and patronize the first "decent" Chinese restaurant in Chinatown, the Kuong Tong.[13] Chinatown was exotic, yes; but in 1920s Lima, it was also considered dangerous, distasteful, degenerate—certainly inde-cent.[14] For these New Men, visiting Chinatown was not a cosmopolitan adventure so much as slumming. By publishing this piece, Portal poi-gnantly asserted to these "people of *Mundial*" that she was one of them.

For New Women in North Atlantic cities, drinking and at least trying drugs was about more than physical intoxication. For these women, drinks were also "elixirs of modernity" and "potions of transcendence into a gen-derless life . . . a domain of profound community."[15] For Portal, however, this was not so much a metaphysical escape from her gender as a back door into an exclusive realm of masculine sociability. Portal recalled drinking with her friends, "the majority [of whom] were men and I did not note it, because it was always like that," again stressing her uniqueness as the only woman in this male world. This representation of self ignored the other women—admittedly few—in bohemian Lima's literary and jour-nalist worlds.[16] Portal could never swim with her male colleagues at *Mun-dial* or join them in their "vigorous" drenching at the hands of the skillful Germán; neither could she share and discuss her poetry with them over an after-dinner absinthe at their favorite brothel. But by ignoring these other exceptional women, and sharing what bohemian pleasures she could with her male friends, like exploring Chinatown or experimenting with drugs, she reaffirmed that she, at least, was one of the boys. And if the rules of this world excluded women, Portal would exclude them, too.

Portal was certainly audacious and curious, as well as more than a little rash and daring. Yet her curiosity about taking drugs and participating in all such extra-domestic adventures was also drenched in ambivalence, as her attempts at being "one of the boys" vied with deeply entrenched notions of decency. Portal qualified her attendance at these bohemian parties, subtly implying she felt, at least in part, that her presence was transgressive: "I used to get together with this group *even* when they were taking drugs," or "the most I *ever dared* was sniffing ether," which she be-lieved "was the most innocent." Right after confessing her "terrible curi-osity," Portal adamantly stressed that "I didn't care for drugs, but I used to watch the others, who would say, 'No, don't look at us. It's better if you don't look.' "[17]

Better for whom if Portal didn't look? This entire adventure highlights the important role attributed to the act of seeing: Portal's friends plead with her not to look at them taking drugs, and her Chinatown report emphasizes the importance of seeing by demanding that her readers witness the miserable beggar: "Did you see him, reader?"

Who gets to see? Portal's Chinatown adventures and the emphasis on the act of "seeing" was a challenge to restricted access, revealing the high social stakes at play when women worked as journalists. By seeing for herself and directing the gaze of her oblivious *Mundial* readers, Portal directly challenged naturalized gendered assumptions about who can wield the power to look and who has to be content with being watched. But if female reporters could now physically travel farther than before—leaving the private space of a family home and entering the public space of a city street, trading works of novelistic fantasy and imagination for works of fact-based journalism—psychologically, they could not completely jettison their internalized assumptions of how others perceived, evaluated, and judged them. As John Berger noted in his 1972 classic, *Ways of Seeing,* "Men look at women. Women watch themselves being looked at. This determines not only most relations between men and women but also the relation of women to themselves. The surveyor of woman in herself is male: the surveyed female."[18]

Several nights after the incident when she fled the opium den after not connecting with her friends, she confessed her "cowardice" to them, but "none of them reproached me."[19] Her obvious surprise that her male friends did not find it shameful that she ran away highlights her fierce desire to remember this particular adventure as courageous, and demonstrates how she viewed herself and her actions through what she assumed were her friends' eyes. She held herself to the standard that she imagined her friends would apply to other men—her internal surveyor watched and judged her from a male point of view. Actually, she held herself to a much more militant standard of masculine courage than her male friends applied to their own behavior, especially considering the courage it took to push back against twenty years of socialization.

Portal's ambivalence shines through in how she judged herself against two separate standards of gendered behavior—not just against an exaggerated vision of her colleagues' masculinity, but also always against what her society expected of the very same decent young women whom she scoffed at for their "timidity." And that voice in her head was fully embodied. She was reluctant to try harder drugs, she confessed, because "the truth is I was concerned about my mother. She would have been hurt if she had ever seen me under the influence of a drug."[20]

The proximate danger Doña Rosa worried most about, however, was likely Portal's ever closer relationship with young bohemian men. Perhaps at the university, or in *Mundial's* offices, Portal met the three Bolaños brothers, all poets recently arrived from Huancayo: Federico, Reynaldo, and Óscar. Dark, handsome, so tall he slouched, Federico cultivated a brooding, melancholic, poetic personality. Esteban Pavletich, another student who in 1922 lived in the same pension with the Bolaños brothers, remembers meeting Portal as part of a larger group of San Marcos students. He fell in love with her, but Portal did not reciprocate his hopeless infatuation, already in love herself with Federico Bolaños, the father of her child.[21]

Woman-Mother

Magda Portal had a new life, a happy ending: a dark, handsome poet at her side, a man who shared her literary orientation and somewhat melancholic take on life, two bohemians who found happiness in each other. The new life stretching out before her was full of promises: a child and a public writing life as a poet immeasurably bolstered by her Juegos Florales prize. Federico took Portal back home with him to Huancayo for the last trimester of her pregnancy. Portal only mentioned these months, her first separation from her mother, in passing, disclosing that she wrote a few poems "when I was in the mountains in Peru, attempting to recover my health."[22] Something was gnawing at her. After two months among the Andes in Huancayo, she returned to Lima to give birth.

Portal gave birth to a daughter, Gloria Alicia, on November 11, 1923. "Nature gave me the gift of Maternity," she recalled later. "At the end of November, my daughter was born, who was to occupy a place of exception in my life. I want to exclude or point as little as possible to anything relating to this fruit of my youth, which in a certain way accuses me of not having been totally a mother because of my instinctive refusal to not fully realize myself as a woman."[23] Another startling example of her clear-eyed ambivalence is this astoundingly rich and frank comment that motherhood was Nature's complicated gift, but one she can't talk about. Portal was not fully a woman, she feared, and therefore not fully a mother.

Peru's Catholic, patriarchal society celebrated motherhood as a woman's ultimate—and only—legitimate role and highest joy. Portal certainly loved Gloria, and as such, her daughter was that promised uncomplicated, undiluted joy. But motherhood, with its boundless demands on her freedom and individuality, also clarified how unbearable these limits were to her. Both joyful and terrifyingly constricting, motherhood, she was beginning to understand, was the ultimate structural constraint on human freedom. Once a mother, a woman was now forever marked as two: herself and her child. Her society celebrated that union of mother and child, Virgin and Christ, elevating its associated sacrifices to an almost divine plane; Larriva de Llona taught her daughters that "when you say woman, you say self-abnegation. . . . The entire life of a woman . . . is nothing more than a tapestry of large and small sacrifices, especially from the divine instant she feels herself a mother." As Jocelyn Olcott has argued for Mexico, self-abnegation in Peru was a fundamental lens through which all Peruvians understood women, motherhood, and femininity. "Selflessness, martyrdom, self-sacrifice, an erasure of self and the negation of one's outward existence," self-abnegation, according to Olcott, "simultaneously elevated and subjugated" women.[24]

Portal could not stand, much less celebrate, such self-abnegation, the negation of her hard-fought self and its crazy, boundless heart. She could not help but focus instead on what was lost: a woman's ultimate sovereignty as an individual. In her writing, she began using compound constructions such as "*mujer-madre*," "woman-mother," explicitly separating these two identities, an analytically important step in a patriarchal world so invested in subsuming women into mothers that it could not imagine one without the other. But Portal still agonized about rejecting the self-abnegation her society demanded of mothers and therefore women. It was her cursed spirit, which, though cursed, was still ultimately what she was.

Eight months after giving birth, Portal married Bolaños in a Catholic ceremony on July 30, 1924.[25] Why did they not marry before the birth, which would have spared both Portal and Gloria from the social stigma of an illegitimate birth? "Legal matrimony has value because of the child," Portal recognized later, but did it hold little value to her? Bolaños seems to have been willing, if not anxious, to formalize their union; why else would he have taken her home to his mother, when other men might have abandoned such a compromised affair? Why had she left the privacy and anonymity of a quiet birth in the provinces and returned to Lima and its prying eyes?

Portal's decisive concern was neither the illegitimacy of her child, nor capturing Bolaños in marriage, but instead recapturing her mother. When she did take her wedding vows, she was not cementing her relationship to Bolaños so much as rehabilitating her more important relationship with her mother. The restlessness gnawing at Portal was about Bolaños, about her mother, about her own child. Portal's happy ending was not enough. Having found ways to affiliate with bohemian Lima's world of men, what did motherhood mean for her hopes to be free?

As she had for the past three years, Portal worked out her joys, terrors, and ambivalences in verse. Portal's emerging sense of self hinged largely around a complicated tapestry of identification with and repudiation of her mother. Portal knew enough about her mother's youth to see key similarities in their biographies, another reason to psychologically distance herself from her mother. Doña Rosa married at a "very young age," before she had even turned sixteen, to a man "almost twice her age." Portal believed her mother had married to leave an unhappy home. "Very possibly she never experienced the emotion of first love," Portal lamented. "That's probably true, for those were difficult times. When my mother finished school, a Catholic school run by nuns, she chose to marry rather than go on living in the same house as her stepfather. Her own father had died."[26]

Maternal disaffiliation and resistance to motherhood as the standard definition of being a woman also played a critical role in the psychological self-definition of other modernist women artists. In bohemian New York, such a "psychology of disaffiliation" was common enough that "the disavowal of the mother came to be almost a trademark of female modernism."[27] Doña Rosa, however, was who Portal had left. After the death of her father and stepfather, Portal could only turn to her mother for support, and her poems lovingly recall a treasured intimacy she shared with her. Portal's unsanctioned pregnancy, betraying her mother and all the norms of decent middle-class behavior her mother held dear, fundamentally threatened this primary relationship.

Portal's pregnancy and their shared experience of motherhood, however, also offered her powerful psychological avenues to identify, even commune, with her mother. In her private papers, we find a beautiful handwritten "Touching Prayer" Portal wrote in 1924 to give to Doña Rosa on Mother's Day. Now herself a mother of a six-month-old infant, Portal acknowledged the day she knew her mother's "full measure" was the one when "my young tree bore its fruit," and "feeling my own heart, I could know how soft yours was. How your heart was what I felt in my hands."[28]

Motherhood—her relationship to her mother, contemplating her own impending motherhood, and the lived reality of being a new mother—consumed Portal between 1923 and 1924, driving her to develop a scorchingly honest register in her lyrical, confessional poetry. She didn't immediately publish these, the most searching and emotional poems she had written to date. Five years later in 1929, some appeared as a series titled "Vidrios de amor" / "Shards of Love," in *Repertorio Americano*, a highly regarded Costa Rican literary and political review with a Latin American readership.

The power of "Shards of Love" rests on the cumulative weight of eighteen poems dissecting the emotional landscape of motherhood, one after the other. The series begins with desperation, regret, and a wrenching plea for forgiveness for destroying a mother's hope: "woman-mother / center of my attractions / forgive me."[29] From there, eighteen poems explore a complicated emotional terrain centered on guilt and shame for separating from her mother, as well as growing vulnerability and fears of abandonment as the impossible desire to recapture a lost maternal intimacy recedes and disappears. Something terrible has happened. In the fourth poem, in an emotional confrontation that devastates them both, "the tragedy" of the mother's "false laugh" echoes through the page and the years, as does the mother's ultimatum: ". . . 'then go' / the trembling of her body / like a branch / tossed by the wind." There is so much regret, so much to want to forget. In the seventh poem, she wakes up in the Andes after a rain, and "like the morning / I was sweet—with no memory—and pale."

But these poems are not just about the conflicts over gendered propriety driving Portal out of her mother's home. In the sixteenth poem, contemplating her own infant daughter she wants to protect from her own fierceness, Portal yearns to be, for her daughter's sake, "happy, ingenuous, a girl / as if all of the bells of happiness pealed an eternal Easter in my heart." What keeps her from being happy, ingenuous, the girl she should be? What gnaws at Portal is the realization, clearer each day, that her happy ending, this new life, is not enough for her crazy, boundless heart. Those qualities that have driven her for years have not quieted. Her trip to the Andes only proved, in the eleventh poem, that travel is a "necessity of my conscience" but also her "eternal sorrow / trembling restlessness." In the twelfth, faced with her mother's suffering, she "raised my column of strength / like an indifferent granite," a strength that proved the daughter's "circular selfishness," a selfishness both self-contained and eternal in the face of her mother's love. In the sixteenth, a strangled question, a piercing demand: "Where did I come from with my ferocity / to not conform?"

But while the series begins with pleas for forgiveness, it ends by accepting an insurmountable distance from her mother and proclaiming her allegiance instead to solitude: "and your eyes turned into seas / of distance / I know now that I will always be / like a distant light / and that your innards will no longer tremble / when they feel my steps—/ that is why I take refuge in you / solitude—mother of the strong / and for the last time / I say this song." The solitude resulting from Portal's rejection of her mother and Lima's normative expectations of behavior births her strength. Rejecting self-abnegation was so very painful, but it was also generative: it made her strong.

In this challenging and wrenching poetic series, Portal's primary emotional struggles centered on her turbulent relationship with her mother and her dawning awareness of her own maternity and its claims on her freedom and individuality. Portal's published work, short journalistic pieces and poetry about her relationship with her lover, presented her public face to Lima as a young bohemian poet with a playful, modern attitude toward sex and affective relationships. These writings show a private face she kept carefully turned away from Lima's public scrutiny; a private self struggling with the stigma of her unsanctioned pregnancy and sexual transgression that her mother felt as deeply, if not more so, as Portal herself; a private self built around these ambivalent reflections on motherhood.

Another striking aspect of "Shards of Love" as a series was Portal's new reliance on fluid language and metaphors. A few examples of this imagery draw from nature, like rain, or hydraulic processes, like boiling. But natural processes do not attract Portal as much as the waters of the body—tears and blood. Drowning, with its accompanying connotations of helplessness and being overwhelmed, makes several appearances. The sixteenth poem ends: "I do not remember a cry like that of this night / like I have drunk the whole sea / and it was fighting to come out through my breast." There are powerful images of rivers, with their connotation of rushing power, or the inverse, the aching lack of a dry riverbed. In the fifteenth poem, the poet imagines a conversation in which the memory of her mother asks "Until when?" and a "deep, deep voice / like an interior river / 'See you soon.'" The sea or the ocean makes several evocative appearances, usually to punctuate the insurmountable nature of distances, such as the "oceans of distance" between her and her mother in the fifth poem. Three times she compares her mother's eyes to oceans: "the green seawater / of your pupils," in the fifteenth poem and, in the seventeenth, "your green eyes— wide, wet seas / distilled their pain drop by drop unrestrained." Finally, in poem eighteen, these two potent images come together as the poet describes how her mother's "eyes turned themselves into seas of distances."

What is going on here? All in all, such fluid imagery appears thirty-nine times. This marked emphasis on fluids, water, seas, or oceans had not appeared previously in her work before 1923 and 1924. Instead, her previously published writings in *Mundial* were anguished love poems, portraits of Lima (Chinatown, a convent), and sad stories where young girls, blond and light-eyed, invariably poor yet decent and sexually innocent, encounter the world of bohemian Lima but never fully enter it, alter egos through which she rehearses taking the curious, audacious, and courageous leaps to affiliate with bohemian Lima. Portal's later poems will return to fluid imagery—especially the sea and ocean—which will, in fact, become one of her most important themes, one she revisits again and again over the course of her poetic career. "Shards of Love" is the first extended treatment in her body of work of one of her central thematic concerns.

This fluid imagery is organic, dynamic, and forceful. In its most immediately accessible meanings, it expresses the experience of forceful emotional change; both the poet-daughter and the mother swing frantically between emotional extremes. In "Prayer," she had used the imagery of a "powerful wind"; her male vanguardia peers tended toward more mechanical metaphors, like an unstoppable machine. But water can be deadly in a way that wind can't; it is both essential and potentially deadly, like mothers.

Digging further, we find that the association between women and water is deeply entrenched in Western thought. Klaus Theweleit, building on Freud, has argued that it reflects a deeply rooted form of female oppression.[30] In this reading, a central anxiety of a man's life is differentiating himself from women by seeing himself as "a body with fixed boundaries," in eternal opposition to boundless, fluid women. Real women dissolve into vague, fluid bodies of water: oceans, seas, vaginas, depersonalizing individual women and transforming them into an endless watery oasis where men achieve transcendence in sexual pleasure not with women, just *through* them. Associating women with expansive bodies of water and fluid processes depersonalizes individual women as objects of desire into an abstract, boundary-less ocean-woman, who then loses power over him because any one woman is essentially all women, interchangeable, and no single woman has the power to breach his psychological boundaries. Actual, individual women are rendered powerless when transformed into this archetype of woman-water. This mental association allows men to make individual women "safe" because men don't need to fear the power of an individual woman over them and their sense of self; it makes both the psychological process of "falling" into romantic love and the physical act of orgasmic sexual release safer, taming their moments of abandon when the self threatens to dissolve into the outside world.

A similar, essentially defensive instinct may be at play in "Shards of Love." "I would like to see you flooded / flooded—flooded—" Portal wrote in the second poem, a violent fantasy in which her mother is destroyed, overwhelmed, and washed away. With these associations, Portal struggles to diminish the emotional hold her mother and the world of decent Lima she represents have over her, bolstering her emerging sense of self. Theweleit's woman-water archetype "oppresses through exaltation, through a lifting of boundaries, an irrealization and reduction to principle."[31] Portal dissolves her mother's individual personality into a similar abstracted ideal, a reduction to mother as principle, an archetype of woman-mother, diffusing her power. In the first lines of the first poem, Portal distinguishes between the formal and informal forms of address, highlighting the two mothers here—Doña Rosa and all Mothers: "because over your [*tu*] voice / your [*su*] voice is raised."[32] Portal is reconciling the individual woman and the role of mother, separating the individual human being from the superimposed social identity. Portal would still be using this same phrasing more than fifty years later.[33]

As an archetype, woman-mother may have begun as a way to safeguard Portal from both her mother's emotional power and from the gendered notions of appropriate behavior her mother had come to represent for her. Once pregnant, however, Portal herself began to "dissolve," first with the physical experience of a fetus developing within her, the most literal violation of ego boundaries, and then, once Gloria was born, "dissolving" into motherhood and its unceasing demands. Now, the woman-mother archetype also allowed Portal to escape from the power of motherhood as an ideal, as the sole definition of being a woman, and as a prison. Now abstracted, Portal could also begin thinking about motherhood and its associated limitations as a larger structural problem for all women, and not just about her own cursed spirit.

Cleaving woman and mother apart in this way, Portal stepped into a female masculine orientation. Is this a male fantasy or fantasies of maleness? This was not about inhabiting a different physical body. Portal was, in fact, deeply invested in expressing a femme identity, and her white, small, beautiful body was important not just because it gave her decency and sexual capital she could leverage when affiliating with bohemian Lima's young men, but also because it gave her, to use her phrase, "space and context" to think and act like a man in her society. Just by looking at her, everyone could tell she still met the physical definitions of being a decent young lady. Her normative, in fact beautiful, appearance allowed Portal to feel and implicitly claim she had never fully rejected hegemonic definitions of Peruvian womanhood.

Instead, Portal was discovering ways to think, act, and be in her world with the unconscious privileged agency of men. She was finding ways to turn down that internal voice—Freud's superego, Berger's surveyor, Lima's socialization, that internal policing that spoke in her head in her mother's voice. Turn down, because as a human socialized in her society, she could not turn it off. Ambivalence about her masculine way of being would never go away, but Portal was finding ways to break through the ambivalence enough to act in ways only men in this time and place were supposed to act. These fantasies and archetypes, these masculine ways of feeling, may seem common, even trite. And they are. But when women take up such stereotypically masculine tropes, meanings shift. Men can fantasize about armed women, but that is very different from an actual woman picking up a gun. Portal's ambivalence arose from feeling both sides of such loaded associations: being both drowned, overwhelmed by the ocean, while being capable of drowning men. Portal was grappling with the interiorization of female-male distinctions and feeling out ways to resist it.

Ultimately, to release her own personal qualities: curiosity, audacity, and courage, but now also ferocity and ambition, those qualities she had pleaded with God to take from her in "Prayer," Portal had to diffuse her mother's, and motherhood's, emotional power over her. These qualities threatened Portal by encouraging her to transgress against traditional notions of gendered propriety, thus driving a wedge between her and her mother. But if the problem was not her "indecent" behavior but instead her mother's and motherhood's emotional hold over her, then Portal needed to defend her self against her mother and not against her "ferocity to not conform." In fact, these inner qualities, once so feared, become protective. The wedge they drive between her and her mother now help her differentiate and realize herself. They have transformed from destructive into productive and defensive. Turning to the poetic imagery she had introduced in "Shards of Love," they can now turn into the rivers, the boiling pressure, the steam that can power a new sense of self.

And this was another alchemy; Portal could now take the repertoire of imagery developed in this breakthrough and use it to imagine herself as a female poet in a new way, reimagining female interior subjectivity. When romanticism transformed Western art and thought, a foundational contribution was "discovering" the creative imagination. At heart, this meant understanding art and thought not as the most faithful imitation or representation of something (the mirror, in M. H. Abram's classic analogy), but as creative, idiosyncratic expression (the lamp). Art was transformed into something fundamentally more than mere technical skill, and artists became those individuals who found ways to communicate, to express, what others may have only intuited.[34] Art was now about one's heroic, artistic vision—and it was profoundly gendered.

A male artist took for granted a sanctioned individuality and creative agency that provided him with "creative relevance and authority," but as a young poet who happened to be a woman, Portal was acutely aware that her individual autonomy as an artist was far from given.[35] Western art was full of women as models, muses, and sirens, but rarely—if ever—as artists. Women inspired artists; they were not themselves agents capable of independently creating art. For literary women, access to such a radical, unquestioned individuality and the coveted creative authority it entailed would be "one of the many wonders of their self-invention as modernists."[36] Years before she dreamed of revolutionary politics, Portal first discovered her heroic agency by unleashing her own creative imagination, a task requiring a Promethean effort. For even when women managed to create art, their creative artistic authority was limited, since Peruvians had only a few set models for what female art might be. While literary Lima imagined male poets as dynamic, they imagined female poets— poetesses—as static and melancholic interiorities.

Reviewing her prizewinning "Nocturnes" in the first critique of her poetry, the colorful bohemian man of letters Ladislao Meza announced that
Portal had "brought a new sentiment" to Peruvian poetry.[37] Her "soul filled
with sadness" lacked "the happiness of youth," which was why, he concludes, "her verses have such a strange force, the gray of the landscapes
that she paints for us, the somber, almost tragic, color of the *retablos interiores* that she offers us in her compositions." Meza singled out these retablos interiores, these interior dioramas or altar scenes, as the central theme
of Portal's verses; she wrote poetry reflecting her interior affective landscape. Closely descended from "the static *tableau vivant*" of "the performing woman as an object of contemplation or inspiration that populated
late-nineteenth-century Spanish American *modernismo*," a "retablo" is a
paradigmatic static preromantic mirror.[38] Artificial and constructed, retablos are staged representations of action, scenes frozen in time, usually
religious scenes representing femininity around traditional images of the
Virgin Mary.

"She gives herself in her verses," Meza continued approvingly. The sadness and vulnerability in her verses legitimized her as an artist because it
proved her to be an authentic rendition of herself, or at least an authentic
rendition of what male critics imagined was the melancholic female retablo interior, the female self. Portal, Meza imagined, did not have to spend
"days and days" constructing elaborate poems because her verses sprang
forth organically and authentically from her melancholic feelings, unim-
peded by either formal training or her conscious effort to belabor or perfect them.

These were not casual metaphors. In Portal's reviews of other female
poets like the Chilean Gabriela Mistral and the Argentine Alfonsina Storni,
she also relied on definitions of femininity and womanhood strikingly
similar to the static retablos interiores that others used to understand her,
writing reviews dependent on superficial ascriptions of "melancholy" and
understandings reifying the many traditional implications of the retablo
metaphor, such as the "defined and not confusable embossment of the
female soul."[39] The twenty-two-year-old Portal would look at other female
poets and see a static melancholia that never had to be explained because
she and her world assumed it was immutable.

Although meant as an admiring critique, when Meza's poetic imagination settled on the metaphor of a retablo interior to describe Portal's inner

world, it imprisoned her, limiting her agency by implying her inner worlds were static and carefully staged representations, and that her mind was a mirror capable of faithfully reflecting the world, but not of creating new things for it. To escape her entrapment in a womanhood defined by the males around her, Portal needed a way to expand her vision of women, to explicitly conceive of female internal subjectivity as an active agent, capable not just of rational, critical thought but also of dynamic transformations and tremendous power.

"Shards of Love" documents two fraught, conflictive years she experienced as an emotional roller coaster of tremendous power that could never be adequately represented by a metaphor as static as a retablo and that demanded a new framework and language to translate raw lived experience to the rarefied page. The repertoire of fluid metaphors she developed for these poems to represent her feelings about her mother and motherhood now allowed her to see herself and her own inner world and self as rushing, as forceful, as powerful. She could start crafting what literary critics identified as her "signature authorial voice cloaked in rhetoric of vanguard dynamism."[40]

In "Prayer," Portal, hopelessly conflicted, had both bemoaned and celebrated her self and her curiosity, her audacity, her rashness and rebelliousness. "I want to be straight as an arrow and advance in life / without wavering in the path, curious and rash / like channeled water, like forceless wind," she had prayed. Now, a few years later, Portal was still conflicted, although not hopelessly. Her crazy, boundless heart would not be channeled, tamed, or directed. The levy she had been praying for strength to reinforce had definitely burst. While she was still ambivalent—would always be ambivalent—she was no longer overwhelmed or paralyzed. She had found a way to move forward, move in her world with the unthinking privileged agency of men, climbing over her fears that she would then never be a full woman and mother. Her inescapable ambivalence was another price to pay for her public writing life, and eventually, for revolution.

"Shards of Love" was Portal's tortured, conflicted reflection on women's structural conditions. Published years later in Costa Rica, this series was often hard to track down and rarely analyzed; these poems were difficult and troubling. But in these poems, Portal began feeling out a solution to the predicament the orphaned lettered women of Lima were all collectively living, a solution built on finding ways to turn down their internal

policing enough to adopt a masculine psychological orientation, to feel
enough like a man to act with his agency, a female masculine orientation
neither available nor recognized as a social type in 1920s Lima. Developing these themes fully also meant developing an unflinching self-
awareness and a scorching, radical, unforgiving honesty where Portal hides
nothing, not her faults or her vulnerabilities, from herself or from her
readers.

Basing Portal's literary importance in the twenties on popularizing vanguardia poetic techniques, literary critics miss her thematic contributions,
the emerging tendrils of a profoundly feminist philosophical vision
grounded in liberating an oppressed female psychology. In these poems,
Portal emerges as an authentic new type of voice, not because she celebrates vanguard literary techniques, but because she begins to develop
these themes by sidestepping Lima decente's respectability politics, resist-
ing being collapsed into simple binary categories: if she is public, she is
indecent; if she is audacious, she is rebellious; if she does not self-abnegate,
she is not a woman.

And what of Portal's mother? Later in life, Portal muted her own feelings
of maternal disaffiliation. "I learned many things from her," Portal concluded. "Her silent cry, her strength, her pride. She wasn't one to talk
much, she preferred to let others speak." Portal assured that "my mother
strongly supported my ideas. Never, never did she reproach me for anything." Well aware of her second-wave feminist audience reading this later
interview, it makes sense that Portal would want to downplay her emotional struggles and highlight her political triumphs, a public representation of self leaving little room for references to her private struggles with
her mother. But Portal assures us too vehemently that her mother "never,
never" reproached her for anything. Perhaps Portal continued to worry a
great deal, maybe even all the time, about how her mother saw and felt
about her behavior. In her unpublished memoirs, she still insisted that her
mother ultimately supported her, but also reflected more frankly: "I know
I made her suffer much, but she never complained. During my long ab-
sences, she always waited for my return. She waited. While her years consumed themselves."[41]

And what of her daughter, Gloria? Giving birth to Gloria catalyzed
Portal's desire to rebuild her relationship with her own mother while

introducing the new threat of losing herself in the overwhelming responsibility of being a mother or in traditional domestic obligations. Just as the prospect of her dissolution in her mother's worldview had tormented her before, the new great love of her life, Gloria, now threatened a similar, terrifying loss of self in another. "Nothing more than give birth after birth, not that. Be a housewife, take care of the husband, day after day, nothing more than that, no! The woman finishes there: in nothing, in a totally anonymous being." Portal now saw a stark and clear choice before her. She could lose herself in child-rearing and service to her husband—the self-abnegation Lima mandated for mothers and women, that defined them as mothers and women even as they fell into domestic anonymity. Or she could choose herself, her crazy, boundless heart, "the other thing . . . the other thing that gushed from my being, that was my way, my vocation."[42] There was something boundless about Magda Portal. Before Federico, before Gloria, the conditions limiting her freedom had been her natal family's descent into poverty and her society's rigid code of gendered decency. Now she confronted the ultimate structural limit to human freedom: maternity. A demure, decent woman would embrace motherhood and its self-abnegations. When Portal didn't, what became of her? A woman who rejected motherhood was proud, haughty; a woman who did not demur could command. If Portal appropriated and inhabited a masculine viewpoint to reject her oppression, if she affiliated with young men, winning entry into a band of brothers, she became something else, an unwomanly woman, a woman who could pick up a gun. She had once prayed to be "straight as an arrow to advance in life," hoping to convince herself to hew tightly to Catholic norms of behavior. Later she would find that unwavering rectitude, and it would advance her in life, but it was a different life of revolutionary dreams.

Portal made her choice. She had "various abortions." Did she have these before or after her marriage? We cannot know from the available sources. After her marriage, after careful deliberation, she concluded that she "never wanted to have more children." She convinced a friendly medical doctor to perform an illegal operation and sterilize her: "I was very young and the doctor asked me, 'But you won't want to have more children later?' 'No, doctor.' It appears that my tone was decisive." Gloria would be Portal's only child; Nature's painful, complicated, but ultimately generative gift.

CHAPTER THREE

Family Affairs

A FTER A YEAR-LONG ABSENCE during which she gave birth, Portal reappeared on the Limeñan literary scene in 1924, now married to Federico Bolaños. A young woman from a precarious family starting a new life with a new husband—this was as happy an ending as Limeñans expected. Did tongues wag about the circuitous route Portal took to reach it? In the curious timeline of her love affair and marriage, Portal became pregnant, carried the child, traveled with Bolaños to Huancayo for her third trimester, then returned to Lima to give birth in November, only marrying Bolaños in a Catholic ceremony at the end of July 1924, eight months after the birth of their daughter.

Do I choose Bolaños or my mother? This was the choice facing Portal. She chose her mother when she returned from Huancayo to give birth in Lima, with her mother by her side, fortifying that maternal bond. But now she had to make the same choice again. With an infant, would she choose Bolaños or choose to stay in her mother's home? Respectability, decency, Catholic morality—the forces pushing her toward marriage were so strong as to be inexorable; yet the eight months between Gloria's birth and their marriage suggests ambivalence. Bolaños's feelings for Portal were strong and constant enough to take her home to Huancayo and to marry her months after the birth of their child. Did Portal leave because she found living in her mother's home with a newborn unbearable? Was Portal's heart inconstant? Ambivalence continued gnawing at her. Increasingly approaching her world with a masculine orientation, Portal was feeling her agency, her charisma, her force, her will.

Magda Portal with Serafín Delmar and Gloria in Mexico City, late 1920s.
Courtesy estate of Magda Portal, Rocío Revolledo Pareja, and
Penn State University Press.

Motherhood, Portal had started to see, threatened to smother her in a "tapestry of large and small sacrifices." By illicitly sterilizing herself, making Gloria her only child and, in Lima's eyes, robbing her husband of his patriarchal right to his future progeny, she had definitively thrown that tapestry off, but not before becoming a wife and mother. Portal now turned to pursuing her own happiness by combining family life with her artistic commitments as a *vanguardia* poet. Portal's marriage would not repeat Doña Rosa's "intimate tragedies"; she would not be her mother. Instead, she would forge a new kind of modern marriage. Everyone in Peru, not just Portal, recognized that traditional marriage was a sacrifice for women, a suffering that needed to be borne. As Larriva de Llona pronounced, "Marriage is a cross to bear, it is said and it should be added: especially for the woman." The matriarch's final biting words of wisdom crystallized women's predicament: "Love is . . . only an episode in the life of a man—or many episodes, I would add—while for a woman it is *la vida entera*, the whole of life."[1]

Like other young modernist women, Portal strove to refashion marriage into a more progressive institution defined as an emotional partnership joining man and wife together in a larger intellectual project. Anchoring their modern marriage, the young couple jointly edited Peru's first self-consciously *vanguardia* literary review, *Flechas*, which ambitiously announced itself as the "organ of the modern literary orientations and of the new intellectual values of Peru."[2] Portal's happy ending was to have both family and letters. Could a bohemian husband, a bohemian New Marriage based on companionship, now temper the harshest edges of traditional marriage?

The "Poetry of the Home"

By the late nineteenth century, generations of Peruvian literary women had criticized traditional marriages, especially the arranged marriages orchestrated to serve family goals instead of individual emotional needs. Female novelists began writing about expecting love in marriage, recasting marriage into an affair of the heart, as "an end to satisfy individual expectations." In Mercedes Cabello de Carbonera's 1889 novel *Blanca Sol*, the title character concluded that "marriage without love was nothing but prostitution sanctioned by society, or else the ridiculous in action, like her marriage was ridiculous . . . a constant torture in her heart."[3] Female social and medical reformers insisted traditional marriage, practical unions without love, led to emotional damage, and they trumpeted the emotional and psychological benefits of a new form of marriage, one in which the woman was the "compañera, the companion, of the man." In early-twentieth-century North Atlantic cities, the rising middle classes who increasingly emphasized emotion over economy dreamed of taking their marriages one step further. Sophisticated people now also wanted to share their innermost thoughts in companionate marriages "imbued with psychological significance." The ultimate arena for that communion, that rich mutual psychological understanding, was the marriage bed. More than procreation, more than physical pleasure, sex was becoming the "preeminent form of companionship."[4]

At least it was in Bloomsbury and Greenwich Village. In Lima, still so cloistered and conservative, it is not clear how much of this new thinking animated even the most radical of young new bohemians. While many of Portal's poems were about sex, she rarely used the word "*amor*," romantic love; it was not one of her key words, and unlike Larriva de Llona, she did not use "amor" to mean sex. "Amor" did not seem to drive her own story; marrying Bolaños months after the birth of their child suggests their relationship was not a passionate, romantic love.

Lima's lettered women, discontented with marriage, had proposed marriage with love as a new model. The young modern women of Portal's generation took a further step in reimagining their own marriages: they would base their unions on love and ground them on a shared intellectual project, sharing the life of the mind as well as the life of the heart. Did Portal buy into this modified model, the affective definitions of a new marriage? She knew she did not want to be reduced to child-rearing and caring for the home; she clearly wanted a companionship of the mind. What was the "constant torture of her heart?" Marriage without love or marriage?

Dreams of marriages based on both an affective connection and an intellectual commitment, however, had not yet changed the circumstances of actual marriages. In the first three decades of the twentieth century, in 75 percent of Limeñan marriages husbands were at least ten years older than their wives, indicating that for the majority, "marriage did not unite equals" but was still driven by more pragmatic concerns.[5] In this, the Bolaños-Portal union did more closely match the companionate ideal.

Bolaños was only four years older, and both came from middle-class families headed by women. Like Portal, the three Bolaños brothers had come from a childhood marked by poverty. Their father had also died when the boys were very young, and their widowed mother, a schoolteacher, had difficulty supporting her three boys. Things were precarious enough that before he was twenty years old, the middle brother had resorted to smuggling alcohol. A regional capital in the central Andean region, Huancayo, with its sun and Andean vistas, felt very far from Lima's foggy, damp coast, but at about 300 kilometers (189 miles) from Lima, it was close enough to keep abreast of national and international currents. Before coming to Lima, the two younger Bolaños brothers had led a small "Huancayo Bohemia," for which the youngest brother had edited a poetry magazine.[6] The four shared similar backgrounds, similar loves of poetry, and, with the two younger brothers, Portal also shared a penchant toward self-invention and conscious self-construction. She had once thrown off her given names to reimagine herself as Magda Portal. Federico's two younger brothers also cast off their names, fashioning pseudonyms they would keep for the rest of their lives: the middle child, Reynaldo, became Serafín Delmar; the youngest, Óscar, became Julián Petrovick.

Together, the Bolaños brothers and Portal launched their new poetry magazine, *Flechas*, which demanded "spiritual renovation," promising the "ardor" of their literary mission would sweep away the "conservative old age" and "mental filth" of Lima's literary landscape and "topple the false values" floating "over the backs of the rabble, like cadavers in the sea." In their second issue, their language became even more defiant. "Attacks by the penned filth" mattered absolutely nothing to them, nor, perhaps more to the point, would the "silence of the lettered mummies." For all those who criticized and ignored them, they would "prescribe one thing only: the self-guillotine."[7]

What attack inspired such violent passion? Later critics wondered if *Flechas* may not "have been wholly received with applause because of its audacity."[8] But it was not all that audacious. Although the magazine proclaimed itself a vanguardia project, the purifying force of a redeeming youth, it did not actually feature revolutionary *vanguardista* poets or poetry. Classifying the dizzying array of periodicals emerging during the 1920s, Luis Alberto Sánchez lumped *Flechas* with other publications by provincials rather than touting it as a harbinger of the vanguardia.

Flechas's most controversial characteristic was instead its aggressive iconoclasm, and its most distinctive aspect was just how fully the magazine was the couple's exclusive vehicle. Their communal language referred to Bolaños and Portal, not a broader generational voice. They wrote the criticism and the literary reviews and contributed their own poems. This was unusual for the Latin American vanguardia; as a continental phenomenon, its members overwhelmingly preferred working in small groups or collectives, the pattern José Carlos Mariátegui would follow for *Amauta*. "This type of monopoly" was so striking it "suggests a restriction on the contributors or the absence of a group who could support the magazine."[9]

Flechas was, in fact, a family affair, a vanity project of four young, now related poets, isolated from their larger literary landscape. Their magazine failed to take root not because of its strident iconoclastic tone, or its advocacy of avant-garde literary trends, but because they were socially isolated in a literary scene worried about the growing influence of provincianos. Having married into this drama of regional identity, Portal was drawn ever closer to their furious fights. Isolated, with few allies, they lashed out. Even as they kept asserting their importance as serious vanguardistas, *Flechas* was dismissed as just one of many minor provincial efforts.

The Bolaños brothers and Portal were forging forward without the support of the networks nourishing similar vanguardia projects elsewhere, and it was Portal's energy propelling them. Their literary efforts, however, were not the sum total of their married life—they were a young family, after all, that needed to be housed, clothed, and fed, tasks that encroached on the time they could devote to their life of the mind. Peruvians liked to consider those domestic obligations another kind of art, a "poetry of the home."

It was this poetry of the home that Lastenia Larriva de Llona dissected and presented to her sons and granddaughters in her book, whose subtitle, "Psychology of the Woman," made clear that domestic happiness depended on women reconciling their romantic illusions to a much more severe reality. Young *limeñas* had few role models outside their immediate families. Larriva de Llona's book was a series of private letters she had written for her own family that she only published later. Young male Reformistas had begun saluting sympathetic teachers and public intellectuals willing to advocate for them by proclaiming them Maestros de Juventud, or Teachers of Youth. In such an anemic landscape, Larriva de Llona was, in many ways, the Maestra de Juventud to which Portal and other young women were supposed to turn. But while Maestros de Juventud encouraged their young male devotees to rebel against political and educational institutions, this Maestra de Juventud demanded instead that young women hew to the most traditional norms governing feminine behavior: principally, the "poetry of the home."

This "poetry of the home" was about more than cleaning, cooking, and rearing children. Larriva de Llona, for one, did not shy away from the hard truths facing women. Women were responsible for domestic happiness, both the practical tasks of labor reproduction as well as the household's emotional needs. A happy marriage depended on a woman who "civilized the male, making him a companion, a compañero," by, among other things, enforcing his temperance.[10] Women were to make their home so pleasant a refuge that their husbands would not want to stray. Women had both the responsibility and possibility of keeping men happy at home if they were virtuous. In the logic of the "poetry of the home," an unfaithful man pointed to a problem at home—an unvirtuous woman failing at the sacred duty of sustaining a pleasing domestic life.

A few lone critics dared to differ. "The defense of the poetry of the home is, in reality, a defense of the servitude of women," José Carlos Mariátegui, Lima's preeminent bohemian intellectual, railed. "Instead of making the role of women noble and dignifying, it diminishes and decreases it. A woman is more than a mother and a female, just as the man is more than a male."[11] If there was one marriage that could hope to embody the companionate ideal and its promises, it was Mariátegui's marriage to Anna Chiappe, an Italian woman he had met during his European exile. Renowned for their love and devotion to each other, Mariátegui and Chiappe protected a treasured intimacy, even speaking to each other exclusively in Italian, the language of their courtship. Every evening, Mariátegui held salons that became bohemian Lima's center of gravity and displayed their domestic arrangements to the gathered artists and intellectuals, salons where "sometimes, for a few instants, Anita entered, and said one or two phrases with her Italian accent, so musical, and left. The little children and the domestic attentions reclaimed her."[12]

Those who attended those famous salons all concurred that Chiappe was an exemplary wife and mother, and some also asserted that she was Mariátegui's intellectual partner. César Miró remembered that Chiappe "was not only Mariátegui's wife and the mother of his children, but his closest collaborator, the friend, the compañera, the indispensable woman."[13] "The most admirable [thing] about Anita," Miró remembered, was her absence-in-presence, her "constant presence at Mariátegui's side, how she moved among us unnoticed," and how she inculcated patriarchal values in her children, "giving them a direction, a profession, and cultivating in them a respect for the memory of their father" after Mariátegui's death. And in fact, memories where participants recalled Chiappe in terms of her absence—for instance, ending these evening tertulias by calling Mariátegui inside—were more common. When Chiappe did appear, all agreed that childcare and household duties commanded her attention and she did not participate in the conversations. At their most egregious, Mariátegui's male collaborators remembered her "next to him, attending to him, spoiling him . . , *la buena hada morena*," the brown-skinned good fairy, "with eyes of Etruscan wine, found one day by him in the old Italian land and afterward attached, *prendida*, to his destiny, to receive in exchange for her love and self-abnegation ten times more in soul than what was missing in body."[14]

Lima's lettered women looked to this marriage hoping to see a shared life of the heart and of the mind, a relationship based on companionship and anchored in joint intellectual projects. If they were honest with themselves, however, they recognized how completely domestic concerns, the "poetry of the home," came to define Chiappe, and admitted even this exemplary model was not the answer to their collective predicament. While Chiappe's domestic labor and economic contributions critically supported Mariátegui's work, it was just that—not a joint collaboration, but instead the supporting role of the buena hada morena.

The poetry of the home was threatened primarily by women's psychological orientation, particularly that of women who refused to adopt the mantle of adulthood, which in women meant self-abnegation and sacrifice. Larriva de Llona was most concerned with any behaviors hinting at female infidelity, especially *coquetería*, devoting an entire chapter to it in her advice to her daughters. Reducing this term entirely to the English translation of "flirting" is problematic, especially given that two years earlier Portal herself had toggled between the two terms "coquetear" and "*flirtear*," creating a Spanish neologism "flirteo" and using it as a related but not synonymous word.[15] Limeñans defined "*coqueteos*" and "coquetería" as indecorous posturing; it did not necessarily include explicit flirting or scandalous sexual advances. For Larriva de Llona, coquetería was "a certain studied affectation in one's manners and adornments," and in women it meant more precisely "the behavior of a woman who, because of her vanity, seeks to please many."[16] This two-part definition allowed traditional Lima to accept a demure version of coquetería in unmarried women as a necessary behavior crucial for elite sociability.

Larriva de Llona recognized that coquetería was the only weapon—she even calls it a science—unmarried women could deploy in a society that left women little agency in romantic relationships and thus "obliged her by divine and human law to a passive mode of existence." But instead of questioning how her society constrained women's agency, Larriva de Llona naturalized it, arguing that women's "nature" disposed them toward coquetería, because "the desire to please is innate in women." And this innate desire was strongest as a young woman waited to be courted and married, as she was forced to "wait an indefinite length of time, and sometimes in vain, [for] that anxiously-awaited moment" when she would find "the being predestined to complete hers."[17] And the stakes were tremendously high, as a young woman's marriage in a world without divorce determined her physical and emotional well-being for her entire life and established her social status and that of her children. In this all-important dance, an unmarried woman's only way to "replace initiative in love," and perhaps influence her fate, was a demure and tasteful coquetería, a "desire to please" her potential suitors.

The second definition, "the behavior of a woman who, because of her vanity, seeks to please many," however, made this same coquetería "criminal" behavior in married women. In women who had already achieved the ultimate goal of a husband, coquetería became an aggressive act and "one of the most repugnant vices." A woman who practiced it "irremissibly loses the love of her husband, the respect of her children, and even the esteem of those who solicit her favors," who "shortly throw them in her face." Recalling the internal judge of their conscience, Larriva de Llona wonders: "How do married women who permit themselves such criminal coqueterías manage to drown [the judge's] shout and keep it from impeding them by tormenting them in the midst of their guilty madnesses?"[18]

An unmarried woman could—and should—discreetly practice a demure and graceful coquetería as she was courted and wed; but once married, a woman had an obligation to please one man exclusively. This was the lesson in the story of a young newlywed couple in which María Jesús Alvarado, the founder of Peru's first women's organization, Evolución Femenina, described how the husband brutally attacked his wife "after the tertulias." "More than once he played the dentist" with his "strong fists" because his wife had "forgotten that she was no longer at a stage for coqueteos." After several days recuperating from "her strong toothache" and seeking medical help for her damaged teeth, the wife returned to daily life singing the praises of her husband's generosity for showering her with clothing and jewels after the attack. Alvarado, Lima's most notorious feminist, holds up this husband as a positive example. "Look here, then, how advantageous it is to have a fine and gentlemanly husband who commits a violent act, although exasperated for a just reason," but who "soon returns to offer his consort the considerations she deserves for bearing his name."[19] Everyone, from elite matriarchs like Larriva de Llona to Lima's few avowed feminists, subscribed to the politics of respectability dictated by the "poetry of the home." And if coquetería ever led to adultery, the consequences could include severe legal punishments in addition to moral censure. While infidelity was morally wrong for both men and women, the consequences for each differed dramatically: where men committed a misdemeanor, women sinned unpardonably. A woman's infidelity caused dishonor, ridicule, and shame.

In early-twentieth-century Lima, "jealousy . . . was much better founded in women. But the woman must be silent and suffer in silence, but not with the airs of a victim, she must pretend she does not know," she must "try to not inspire sympathy. . . . Additionally, the woman must try to attract her husband again with every possible means," Larriva de Llona advised.[20] Observers often assumed wives were responsible for their husbands' violent jealousy and abuse; independent of blame, all assumed it fell on women to fix the problem and find a way to keep their husbands from straying. This resigned recognition of the way the world worked paints another, darker layer to the "intimate tragedies" of middle-class life and the domestic violence both Peruvian men and women did not just tolerate but justified. Marriage, Larriva de Llona concluded, was a field of "unknown heroisms that occur in tight quarters, surrounded by four walls, and which Fame does not make known. They are realized in the quotidian small battles of existence, and there are no medals or crosses of honor."[21]

Late in life, Portal shared a similar realism, confessing that she "fell in love various times. Love is in all of my verses. But love has a time, and that time is brief. . . . I'm a little romantic, I believed that love had to last forever. But that is not true: love ends."[22] Her young marriage was failing and with it their magazine. The couple published the final three issues of *Flechas* as a single number on December 10, 1924. It had survived for six issues, appearing sporadically for six weeks.

Portal remembered those times as "such sad episodes." All we know for certain is that Portal abandoned her husband, left Lima, and traveled to Bolivia sometime in late 1925. She almost never talked about this, stressing only that "I did not travel with [Bolaños]. I traveled with my daughter."[23] Yet, violating everything the "poetry of the home" valued and held dear, Portal and Gloria did travel with a male companion: Federico's little brother, Serafín Delmar.

Inherently and Irredeemably Indecent

When Magda Portal left Lima for Bolivia with her one-year-old daughter and her brother-in-law, she destroyed any chance she may have had to redeem the scandal of her illegitimate pregnancy and birth by bowing to the "poetry of the home" in her marriage to Federico Bolaños. Of all the ways to escape an unhappy marriage, she chose the one with the highest possible personal price, the one least comprehensible to decent Lima, the one most certain to brand her forever as scandalous: inherently and irredeemably indecent. Unhappy marriages happened; wives left husbands. But in those unhappy circumstances, women returned to their natal homes. Portal could have abandoned Bolaños and returned to her mother's home. Or she could have left her infant daughter with her husband, or her mother. But running away with Delmar and Gloria precipitated a traumatic crisis of an order of magnitude higher than simply running away with another man; it not only annihilated her bond with her husband but also the fraternal bond between the two brothers. What drove such an inexplicable "guilty madness"?

Eliding the entire question of how her marriage ended, Portal only revealed that "my loves, my marriage . . . they are episodes in my life that I wish to forget even though they exist, the whole world knows about them, but I want them not to exist because they were weights for me."[24] Should we read this literally? Portal wanted to forget that her loves and her marriage even happened to her; these relationships did not complete her, as more romantically minded Limeñans might sigh. Instead, they weighed her down, weighed down her charisma, her force, her will, her power. Portal now had the necessary agency to think of both Bolaños and the structure of marriage as weights.

It is not difficult to imagine how high emotions may have run in an insular world created by four young poets, two of them a young couple with an infant, three of them brothers making their way in a hostile capital, piloting their weapon of choice, a literary journal. Portal, leveraging her growing influence as a prizewinning poet, selected Delmar as one of Peru's promising new poets. By late 1924, Delmar was also now *Flechas*'s secretary, highlighting just how insular, how fully their magazine was a family affair.[25] In what would prove to be their last issue, Portal published a poem in December 1924 entitled "Prayer to the Sea/*Oración al Mar*," likely a reference to Serafín Delmar, whose pseudonym meant Angel of the Sea. The poem began with a longing genderless voice. "This pain and this desire to travel / oh Mar! / This desire to surrender myself / to your rude and magnificent adventure / happy and sad." It ended with a desire for surrender: "Oh Mar / and rest / a long day / in your open arms / like a docile alga / at the mercy of the dance of your waves."[26]

After *Oración al Mar* appeared in December of 1924, Portal published only three poems in 1925, all in the March/April edition of the *Mercurio Peruano*, an elite literary review that represented literature's old guard, the camp *Flechas*, as the self-anointed avant-garde, wanted to destroy. She composed one of these poems, "Miracle Lives," in a conventional *modernista* style, choosing the most traditional second-person plural form, giving the poem a highly traditional, even anachronistic formality, suggesting her commitment to vanguardia iconoclasm was not absolute. While the readership of the *Mercurio Peruano* would have recognized the poetic form as conventional and familiar, the sexual subject matter was bracing in its audacious imagery. In the poem, a female voice appraises the masculine lives around her and entreats them to satisfy her thirsts. "Lives, mashed like red vineyards / in my Cup / I want to drink you," she began. The poem makes constant reference to her Cup, her Glass, and ends with a putative plea that reads more as a command: "My insatiable Cup / of dry lips / waits for you, oh vineyards / For your juices / she reserves [herself] fully / come to pour yourselves."[27]

"Miracle Lives" harbors multiple inversions. There is the shocking contrast of the audacious sexual theme clothed in the most traditional language and poetic style. Portal's sexual allusions are so explicit that respectable Peruvians would have considered them vulgar and indecent. This was a bolder assertion of her masculine orientation in a world where "initiative in love," to use Larriva de Llona's phrase, was an exclusively male prerogative. In a striking inversion of modernista ideas about poetic inspiration, Portal also transformed the men around her into the muses for her female-gendered poetic voice. Perhaps most importantly, this poem is not just explicit but unabashedly aggressive. Other female poets writing at this time tended to focus violence inward, against themselves and their own feelings. The Uruguayan Delmira Agustini, in her poem "Nocturne," for instance, identifies herself with a paradigmatic modernista symbol, a swan, but inverts the familiar image into an "errant swan of the bloody trails / . . . staining the lakes and taking flight," directing violence inward, against the poetic I.[28] In stark contrast, Portal's poem directs its aggression outward to the male lives around her that she yearns to consume.

In its aggressive female sexual agency, "Miracle Lives" pushed coquetería so far it tipped into something else entirely—the female voice is not trying to attract men to her so much as setting out to hunt for herself. For the readers of *Mercurio Peruano,* an elite magazine with national reach, this poem, in which a female poetic voice demanded that multiple men crush their lives for her pleasure, trumpeted Portal's rejection of life with only one man as unfulfilling. Portal had traveled a significant psychological distance and now openly challenged Peru's sexual double standard in her poetry. Four years earlier in "Prayer," female sexual agency was an unspeakable, perhaps unthinkable, terrifying sin from which she had prayed to be free. Two years earlier, in "Nocturnes," it was a temptation she could not resist, although her ambivalence about it rendered her immobile. Now, in "Miracle Lives," her sexual agency was neither a sin nor a temptation, it was a demand. In this poem, Portal asserted and demanded a personal sexual liberty more radical than anything the most militant feminists in Lima would advance. Portal's poetry reflected exactly the kind of aggressive sexual freedom from which bourgeois feminists worked so hard to distance themselves. And yet, in one of the stanzas, Portal commands the male lives "squeezed in my Glass / . . . to saturate the mouth / of open lips / that is my heart." It was just one reference, a small gesture toward modesty, but it allowed a part of Portal to assert that this was not just about sex but about love, though this ambivalent fig leaf could not disguise the poem's unabashed sexual aggression.

In May 1925, Portal published a second strongly positive review of Delmar's poetry in the much more popular magazine *Variedades*. Portal's enthusiastic reviews for Delmar's poetry, however, were about more than literature. Combined with her flirtatious poetic references to Delmar, and her increasingly explicit sexual poetry, they established a public relationship Lima would have considered a criminal, aggressive "guilty madness." Portal was now a married woman, and yet she was repeatedly, publicly rendering attention to another man. Such illicit coqueterías did not depend on actual adulterous sex, just on married women turning their attention to any man other than their husbands, on anything other than their homes. How did her husband, Federico, feel about this increasingly public airing of potentially scandalous, and for him, humiliating, details?

Sometime in 1925 Portal moved further to challenge the sexual double standard not just in poetry, but in life. Serafín Delmar "was very relaxed, an excellent poet, and committed to ideological questions"; based on his long-standing personal friendship with Portal, her first biographer discreetly observed that it can "not be denied that Serafín felt an attraction toward Magda."[29] Who advanced first? Was Portal flexing her growing agency into a forbidden sexual realm, once again the siren Loreley? Was she pulled toward Serafín or pushed away from Federico?

"That man was a weight, cowardly, lacking in personality, and so jealous," Portal remembered of Federico.[30] Piecing together Portal's scattered half-veiled references, we find her accusing her husband of jealousy and a violent temper, and her family suggesting to her sympathetic biographer that Bolaños's jealousy culminated in physical abuse. Given what we know about marriage and gender relations in Lima at that time, it is noteworthy that Portal's allegations against her husband revolve around his jealousy and that she never accuses him of infidelity, suggesting he was emotionally and sexually committed to their relationship. What was Bolaños jealous of? In the world they lived in, Bolaños had every right to be jealous of his wife's wandering attentions; even Lima's most staunch feminists would have believed him to be within his rights. Since we know how the story ends, we may first assume that he is jealous of the attentions Portal paid Delmar. But Portal was not just any wife—she was a prizewinning poet.

"The happiest unions were ones where the husband was intellectually superior to the woman," Larriva de Llona clucked.[31] While young modernist women dreamed of more egalitarian marriages, did this hold true, when the rubber met the road, for young bohemian men? Could Bolaños have chafed, knowing that in this relationship, he was not the only or the better poet? Was he jealous of who Portal was becoming, as a poet and a person?

Emotions ran high not just between Federico and Magda; Federico and Serafín were not as close as we might think. Delmar's childhood was haunted by what one of his literary critics has called the "inexorable authoritarianism of the older brother."[32] Echoes of this fear can be found in several of Delmar's later short stories. In a recurrent setting, an older brother ruthlessly and brutally punishes a middle brother for infractions involving losing or filching small coins or treats in a poverty-stricken home in a small town in the Andean highlands. The scenes of violence are vividly described, or perhaps remembered. They take place in a garden; the older brother uses a belt; he beats him viciously until blood flows. The mother, while distraught, seems to have abdicated all responsibility for maintaining family discipline to the older brother. The only ray of hope is a younger brother, who comforts the poor, beaten boy. "Juan was terrified of school," Delmar narrates in one of these stories. It was the "same macabre terror he felt for his older brother who played father in the house."[33] If these short stories were actually drawn from Delmar's childhood experiences, then he and Portal shared an even closer bond: a shared experience of chafing under Federico's attempts at enforcing patriarchal control. Their home was a cauldron bubbling over with high emotion: the stresses of a new family with an infant, a long-standing fraternal resentment, the pressure of a professional failure in their dying review, and the audacity of a young woman flexing her agency, her new and hard-fought psychological liberation. Portal had discovered she did not have the "innate desire to please" that Lima assumed of feminine character. Instead, she found power in doing what she was not supposed to do, in flexing her phenotypic beauty, playing the siren, and attracting men. In another facet of her emerging female masculine orientation, she was groping for ways to use the few weapons given women in this time and place to reverse gendered power dynamics and achieve equality.

Federico did attempt to assert his patriarchal rights, if not over her, then over their daughter. Portal's half sister reported that after Portal left him for his brother, Federico gave Gloria as an orphan to a family in the mountains of Huancayo. Was this an exercise of his patriarchal privilege, or an attempt to force Portal back into their failing marriage? "There was a moment when he robbed my daughter, and I then had to go with a revolver to reclaim her. I was willing to kill if they did not give her to me," Portal recalled. She found Gloria, recovering from scarlet fever, and rescued her with the help of a local prefect.[34] Larriva de Llona had warned that the repugnant woman, "drunk on her ire," converted her "home into the theater of the most reprovable scenes," but not even she could have imagined a scenario where a woman raised a gun to challenge her husband's wishes.[35]

Confronting motherhood and marriage, Portal had learned that even when everything in her society told her to, she was not one to sacrifice herself for her husband or to submit to an institution that collapsed the meaning of female life to a woman's ability to "weave sacrifices, large and small" to ensure the happiness of others. "I can bear the tutelage of neither man nor home," she categorically asserted toward the end of her life.[36] At heart, Portal found both motherhood and marriage to be prisons. That lesson learned, Portal had also learned what she was capable of, that she could break with every norm trying to constrain her behavior and her freedom, and that when called to, she could wield violence, she could pick up a gun. Serafín Delmar was her escape from Federico and also from the institution of marriage that had grown torturous, weighing her down.

But rereading Portal's poems and turning again to her later interviews, we are struck by her literal truthfulness. While she leaves out many important details, she never denies the chronology we have reconstructed. And rereading "Miracle Lives," it is noteworthy how literally the female poetic voice presents her sexual yearning. By so explicitly detailing her desires, Portal aimed to purposefully cut through artifice and pretension, the social niceties making female romantic initiative impossible. Her subsequent flight to Bolivia and the hardships such a drastic and dramatic move entailed were thus also a conscious choice for sincerity, for radical honesty. After her feelings for Federico cooled, and after her efforts at marriage proved unsatisfying, she refused to live in a stultifying status quo and instead chose to be sincere to her feelings for Delmar. And in a final riposte to traditional Lima, she announced her intention and its rationale in the most literal way available to her—her published verses. Portal was forging one of her characteristic postures: fearless authenticity and radical honesty. Portal would always be curious; audacious; fearlessly, scorchingly, radically honest; she would be unusually self-aware, and she would not posture.

Portal almost never talked about these events. Radical honesty was also about living with ambivalence, recognizing her pangs of regret, without repudiating the acts themselves. In interviews later in life, Portal always explained her flight to Bolivia without mentioning Federico Bolaños, instead explaining it as a political necessity. Her refusal to talk about Federico at all, literally writing him out of her history, suggests a deeper wound than just a romantic failure. Portal knew the consequences of her actions, how this "inexplicable guilty madness" would blow up their families. "Maternal love is the primary, the strongest of instincts in almost all female creatures; but in the woman, it is also pride and happiness and glory. That is why a more monstrous being is inconceivable, cannot be conceived, than a bad mother," Larriva de Llona intoned.[37] In not talking about Federico, Portal was also not talking about the kind of mother she was—one who chose her own happiness over her daughter's emotional and social stability and over the kind of mother her culture told her she had to be. Portal did what she had to do but was honest enough with herself to recognize her ambivalence, the part of her that wanted to be "good" and conform.

We have no other news of Federico Bolaños until he published a poem titled "The Man without Love" in December 1925, his likely response to the terrible blow of his wife and child leaving him for his brother, in which he wrenchingly portrays a pathetic man who has lost his love. "There goes / the old Prince / of the passion of Love / biting the lime off the walls / breaking his hands / finger bone by finger bone." In the poem, the pathos derives not just from the depth of the "old Prince's" suffering but also from the fact that he once enjoyed love and that he himself is partly responsible for his loss, leaving him "today with his forehead in the dust / and not yet finished swallowing his heart." But perhaps the ultimate humiliation and insult was how his youngest brother completed the betrayal, for Portal and Delmar also kept the allegiance of the youngest brother, Julián Petrovick, who would follow them into the ranks of APRA. Portal and Delmar erased the last tangible evidence of Federico when they effectively rewrote Gloria's paternity. In their public circles, Portal and Delmar passed Gloria off as their own child; she became "Gloria Delmar Portal."[38]

It must have seemed strange to those privy to the scandalous contours of this story how completely Federico renounced whatever claim he felt he had to Portal, his daughter, and his birth family—for he just drops away; he "disappears as a writer, as a poet, as a brother, and as a husband."[39] If he were the man Portal hints he was, a violent and abusive aspiring patriarch, then it seems unlikely and surprising that he would so quietly choose to accept this erasure and just disappear, instead of asserting his patriarchal privilege. In the end, their new modern marriage proved a surprising inversion of how Larriva de Llona and Lima believed the world worked. Portal chose to leave their marriage behind as one in a series of loves, as an unhappy episode she could choose to ignore and erase, while for Bolaños, his love for Portal proved to be the end of his private happiness and public presence, "la vida entera."

APRA rally in Trujillo, 1946. Courtesy estate of Magda Portal,
Rocío Revolledo Pareja.

Part II

The Dream of Revolution

Aprista cell in Mexico. *From left*: Mexican General Genaro Amezcua, Emiliano Zapata's ex-minister of Finance; Serafín Delmar; Esteban Pavletich; Mexican general Carlos Martines del Campo; Magda Portal with Gloria; Haya de la Torre; and Carlos Manuel Cox. Courtesy estate of Magda Portal, Rocío Revolledo Pareja, and Penn State University Press.

CHAPTER FOUR

Red Paths

IN HER 1926 SHORT STORY "The Wind," Magda Portal imagined Christ incarnated as Lenin—with a compañera. "Pale and agitated with great premonitions," his compañera "impels" Christ-Lenin "toward the struggle with more ardor," and together through "entire nights of destructive and constructive insomnias, they grabbed the picks of liberty and demolished the palaces." At his Last Supper, Christ-Lenin faces no Judas, and instead distributes "the bread of Liberty and the wine of happiness" to workers, fulfilling the utopian redistributive dream of the meek inheriting the earth. The story jumps to Leningrad, to Christ-Lenin's tomb, from where Christ smiles at finally seeing "the dream he had twenty centuries ago" catch fire and blaze.[1]

The story's potent and scandalous equivalencies between Christ and Lenin fulfilled the iconoclastic promise of the book of revolutionary short stories it opened, Portal's first: *El derecho de matar* (The right to kill), which she cowrote with Delmar and published in La Paz, Bolivia. Much like *Flechas*, in *El derecho de matar* Portal embraced a new collaborative project designed to cement her personal relationship with her compañero. But this new project added something she had never shared with Delmar's brother Federico. Having escaped Federico when they fled Lima, they were both now falling for a greater romance, one shared by many in the twentieth century: the dream of revolution. As Portal moved into this world enamored of vanguard revolutionary politics, her own political energy moved outward, from changing her life to changing the world, from transforming herself to transforming the world's powers and structures.

Their path forward, however, was far from clear. Unlike North Atlantic cities, Lima lacked anything we would recognize today as a political party. There was no way to be political other than the centuries-old process of patronage and courting the strongest caudillo in the room. Yet, besieged by their shared yearning for revolution, Portal and Delmar groped for a way to be political, to be revolutionary in this modern age. While their dreams would propel them to jump immediately to the maximalist language of tyrannicide, these same dreams were their first steps toward exploring the world of seductive politics, a journey that would lead them to the politics of mass electoral parties, the politics of APRA.

Bolivia

For the first six months of 1926, Magda Portal and Serafín Delmar lived in La Paz, Bolivia's capital, with her daughter, Gloria. They had arrived by January, when Portal published a short story and an essay in a Bolivian literary magazine.[2] Like Lima, La Paz also had a bubbling, if smaller, scene of increasingly radicalized students and laborers, and Portal and Delmar dove right in, helping them publish a radical newspaper, *Bandera Roja* (Red flag). But the principal fruit of their Bolivian period was *El derecho de matar*, which opened with an appropriately iconoclastic vanguardia warning: "Dangerous for literature's bourgeois!" But while *El derecho de matar* gestured toward their earlier literary iconoclasm, their attention had shifted decisively to new political concerns that completely dominated these short stories, which were drenched in a new language of class exploitation. Where before they had tried to demolish literary idols, now Portal and Delmar plunged into a world where they imagined everyone was starting to dream of the ultimate iconoclasm, the promise to overthrow everything: revolution.

In her previous work, Portal had referenced other Peruvian literary figures almost exclusively; now she wrote stories in which the only named individuals were Christ, Lenin, the famous French iconoclast and pacifist Henri Barbusse, the fictional character Sacha Yegulev, and a generic "Sigmund." This new focus was so abrupt, so new, and so total as to suggest an exhilarating new world had opened up to them in the books they read in La Paz, or perhaps in the liberty they now had to publish as they willed, as they were no longer in Lima or under Federico. In his 1911 novel *Sashka*

Zhegulev, the prerevolution Russian author Leonid Andreyev reworked a real-life story of a social bandit to "show the lengths to which young Russians felt they had to go in order to set things right." This novel was very popular in Spanish, and a leading Spanish novelist remembered how it "above all, profoundly affected the Spanish intellectual youth . . . who lost sleep over the heroic and adventurous youth of Sacha."[3] Much like her Spanish peers, Portal turned to this touchstone literary figure, identifying with the story's cry for revolutionary social change, certainly, but also the romantic pathos in its ill-fated heroic figure, who remained steadfast to his ideals only to be brutally betrayed by opportunists.

El derecho de matar contained fifteen short stories, eight authored by Portal and seven by Delmar; his stories totaled twenty pages to Portal's cumulative page total of thirty. In all the stories, representative types such as miserable and exploited slaves or workers eventually explode with violence after their radicalization. Portal's new understanding and enthusiasm for the international revolutionary struggle mostly consisted of an uncritical apotheosis of Lenin and the Russian Revolution read through New Testament verses stressing social justice. On the whole, the pieces eschew character and plot development, and instead read like rudimentary attempts at revolutionary propaganda meant to inspire anticapitalist outrage. Many of Delmar's stories, especially his one-page fragments, strove to evoke a sense of outrage but had no recognizable structure, characters, or plot. Portal, for her part, developed her stories more fully and made her pieces more comprehensible by offering other references, drawing especially from the New Testament to compensate for minimal narrative structure.

Within this new political framework, Portal continued thinking about female sexual agency and marriage. In "The Smile of Christ," Portal depicted Christ considering the past, which led an adulterous woman to betray her husband, contextualizing her crime. "The husband was a brutal and coarse man. Daily tasks made him hungry and sleepy. Once one was satisfied, he slept. And his caress for his wife was always like a beast's claws. The young woman was consumed by solitude, like an abandoned flower. But the harmonious and beautiful lover came, and sang to her youth. And something in her depths cried a shout so loud that it covered every other voice. It was like the golden bugle of the Sun, which makes Earth tremble when it announces itself. And she loved. And men said: 'Sin!'"[4]

In Catholic folk tradition, the alleged adulteress was widely assumed to be a prostitute. Portal's portrayal, however, does not depict a woman who sins out of presumed economic necessity, a reading that would have echoed the other stories' denunciations of economic exploitation. Instead, Portal described a woman who betrays her marital bonds because of her own feelings—her loathing for her husband, her loneliness and yearning for a compañero, and her infatuation with a new lover. Portal's outrageous reading of a well-known parable justified adultery based on personal emotions.

Portal depicted women who were more than muses, inspirations to action, or companions. In "The Wind," Christ's compañera propels him forward; she is an engine, a cheerleader, and a whip. The story does not suggest all women should take on such roles, but these are exceptional women, called to act by greater forces. Portal contributed almost two-thirds of *El derecho de matar*, significantly more than her compañero, and her stories shape the project, providing its cumulative energy, including the all-important rallying cry at the end. Portal's progression in depicting women and her oversized contribution to their book suggests that what had begun as a collaborative project, both in their art and in their personal life, was slowly evolving into something more than a coequal partnership. Later, Portal asserted she played the dominant role in her relationship with Delmar and guided his ideological education.[5]

But if she explored female agency in stories like "The Wind," in other stories she continued outlining her ambivalence about motherhood and other structural limits to women's freedom. In the March 16, 1923, issue of *Mundial*, eight months before she herself gave birth, Portal had published a short story titled "The Strange One" in which a woman experienced pregnancy as "Nature defeating her." The woman, however, discovered a new internal will in rejecting her child. "No! One more protest in the innumerable, useless protests of many centuries. One more cry in the millenarian stream of tears. And maybe one more child for the mother-jail [*madre-cárcel*]. For what? For the first time she felt an unknown force that fluttered in her cerebral caverns. Will." Upon the child's birth, the woman throws the newborn into a muddy pit to drown, and "thus the Earth heard one fewer lament."[6]

Now, three years later in her *Derecho de matar* story "Violet Circles," Portal depicted a pregnant woman who "truly believed she carried in her womb all the pain of humanity," whose pregnancy tortured her "like a fist that penetrates a rock." When she gives birth to a girl, she examines her curiously and sets out with no clear direction. She reaches the orphanage and turns away; at a river, after watching it for some time, she throws the child into the water. As the poems ends, Portal identified the woman for the first and only time as a "MOTHER, . . . bathed in indifference."[7]

Thematically, both "The Strange One" and "Violet Circles" narrate pregnancy and childbirth as profoundly negative experiences, and both ultimately culminate in infanticide at the hands of the mother. But "Violet Circles" injects more ambivalence in the woman's hesitant, dazed wanderings and specifies political explanations for killing her infant. "The Strange One" leaves it unclear why the woman kills her child—the female protagonist concludes her soul-searching with a simple phrase: "She wanted to be generous." But generous to whom? The evocative compound word "madre-cárcel" suggested the focus was the woman's suffering and betrays considerable anxiety about maternity's limits on women's freedom. In contrast, "Violet Circles" explicitly details the economic and political conditions driving the mother to kill her child when the woman rejects the orphanage as an "incubator of slaves and assassins." In "The Strange One," the woman discovers her will and uses it to kill an infant who would serve as her jailer, who would imprison the woman in the madre-cárcel. Three years later in Bolivia, Portal's protagonist killed her child to ensure the infant escapes capitalist exploitation. Portal had displaced her individual anxiety about maternity and its limits on her freedom to a more collective predicament of poverty and class as limits on the freedom of workers, and she resolved both predicaments in a maximalist language of infanticide. This was still, of course, in the realm of fantasy: Gloria was alive and well. But Portal was working something out.

These *Derecho de matar* stories show us Portal in the midst of a transformation. *Flechas* had showcased Portal's poetry, a genre she had excelled in and in which she had won a prestigious prize. *El derecho de matar*, however, was an unfamiliar genre, and her stories, critics agree, were not very good. They were important for Portal's own intellectual trajectory, however, because they added political radicalism to her aesthetic radicalism. Portal herself would later characterize *El derecho de matar* as an exercise in rhetorically "killing" the entire world, suggesting that she considered it hyperbolic, and critics have joined her in dismissing this Bolivian period as an excessively romantic, juvenile political radicalism.[8] But though crude and underworked, these stories marked Portal's efforts to imagine new ideological frameworks. The choice for sincerity in her personal life had mandated escaping her marriage and frankness about her feelings and desires. In Bolivia, this same drive for sincerity and radical honesty led her to proclaim herself a political revolutionary just as definitively as she had proclaimed herself a gender rebel by abandoning her husband in Lima.

Their joint choice for sincerity explains why Portal and Delmar chose to publish these stories under their own names, even when the book espoused a political violence that would inevitably brand them as political troublemakers. While *El derecho de matar* boasted that it was "dangerous for literature's bourgeois," the poetas gran señores were likely not as troubled as Leguía's repressive forces. At the 1923 Juegos Florales, Portal had not been involved in any political attack, however symbolic, against Leguía; now, just a little over two years later, she and Delmar threw *El derecho de matar* as a literary bomb in the face of an exploitive system personified in the figure of Augusto Leguía.

Taking authorial responsibility for such provocative work was potentially reckless, and professional revolutionaries might have taken care to sign with a pseudonym. Their attributable political activities and sympathies would, in fact, prove costly. Portal later explained how the Bolivian police deported them back to Peru, where the Leguía government promptly incarcerated them, after *El derecho de matar* "caused quite a commotion."[9] While no evidence of their incarceration has been found, something may have happened. When they returned to Lima in 1926, they published a reference to a "protest against the insult of the government of hernando siles [*sic*] against the compañero Delmar" they received from abroad.[10]

But taking an irrevocable public step was precisely what *El derecho de matar* was designed to do; Portal and Delmar were throwing down a gauntlet. Their book testified to how they understood at that time what being a revolutionary meant. In its pages, Portal presented herself as what she thought a revolutionary should be; in a sense, she was rehearsing the revolutionary she wanted to become. With only literary examples as models, Lenin and the Russian Revolution serve as powerful touchstones invoking revolution—as does the social justice implicit in the Jesus story. But this was also the beginning of their revolutionary education—they were reading, they were dreaming, they were projecting themselves into a revolutionary drama they may have first encountered draped in Russian but which they now set in America, in Peru. Given their lack of political experience, it is not surprising that the vision they crafted of revolution as provocation was disconnected from real-world conditions. Nonetheless, we cannot dismiss the seriousness of their act. Portal strove to write herself into the revolutionary history of her time; one of her stories was titled simply "1914." Critics who dismiss this book for its literary shortcomings miss the fact that Portal and Delmar meant this as a political—as a revolutionary—manifesto. *El derecho de matar* was their revolutionary pact cementing them in another joint project. Even then, in 1926, it was a risky madness almost certain to fail; but it was nonetheless courageous and audacious. It was also a necessary risk to establish who they wished to be politically and perhaps to begin catching the attention of fellow travelers. Narrating why she left Bolivia, Portal recalled: "My group was forced to return to Peru. Peruvian police in civilian clothes escorted us to the border."[11] Who else was in this group? And this risk—as opposed to their literary risks and their magazines—would be the risk to actually bear fruit.

In her personal life, Portal had committed the inexplicable "guilty madness" of leaving her husband and running away to another country with her brother-in-law and daughter. *El derecho de matar* was a parallel irrevocable action in her political life, meant to launch her on a path whose ultimate goal was revolution. She had once prayed for strength to resist the temptations of her young flesh with Catholic rectitude and focus. Now she was clearing another path for her strength of will, her rectitude, and single-minded focus. And in this red path to revolution, her answer to Peru's collective predicament was also a maximalist one as unthinkable as infanticide and perhaps surging from a similar realm of fantasy: tyrannicide.

One of the most important parts of any manifesto is the rousing end, the call to arms. *El derecho de matar* ended with one of Portal's stories, "Red Paths," which began dramatically: "Sigmo came from Russia."[12] After traveling throughout the world, Sigmo was born again in America, with a birthmark of a cross on his forehead, in "the land of a nameless tyrant," whom Peruvians would have easily identified with Leguía, given the story's additional details. Once in this unnamed Peru, Sigmo throws himself into the revolutionary struggle, exhorting workers to rise up against the tyrant, trying to shame them into action by attacking their masculinity. "'Compañeros,' he screamed into the stupefied silence of the workers, 'I call you to the grand meeting tomorrow. If you are cowards, I [alone] will shout my protest against the war and against tyranny. I wait for the MEN.'" At the meeting, the plan calls for another revolutionary, identified only as the "hero," to throw bombs into the tyrant's caravan. Once he throws the bombs and all is madness, the delirious crowd marches to the Presidential Palace, with Sigmo leading the human wave, screaming "'Down with tyranny, long live liberty!'" One of "the tyrant's slaves" fires at Sigmo, hitting him squarely on his cross birthmark, and he falls on his back, his arms spread wide, crucified. But his death does not stop the multitude, who continue toward the palace, "without stopping to watch the HERO, who in the serenity of death held in his lips—as if it was the name of the mother—the word bathed in blood and happiness / LIBERTY."

Lima

Magda Portal, her daughter, Gloria, and Serafín Delmar lived in Bolivia for about six to eight months, returning to Lima around June or July of 1926.[13] The new couple resumed their life in Lima with surprising ease. They would remain in the Peruvian capital for only one year, but it would prove very productive, both artistically and politically. While they had publicly claimed a revolutionary identity with *El derecho de matar*, they had yet to gain much actual political experience. Artistically, Portal entered into a heated debate over vanguardia aesthetics in the pages of José Carlos Mariátegui's new project, *Amauta*, the defining magazine of the artistic and political Left in 1920s Peru. Mariátegui's publishing workshop Minerva edited and released her first volume of poetry titled *Una esperanza y el mar* (A hope and the sea).[14] Portal and Delmar, finally abandoning the artistic project as a *compañerismo* ideal, gathered a small editorial group of the young poets *Flechas* had published two years earlier to publish another vanguardia literary review. Similarly, the political project Portal had first launched with only Delmar at her side would open its doors to others. In their first taste of mass action in Lima's *Amauta* milieu, they would recraft their understandings of politics and revolution, searching to move beyond provocation.

Politically, Lima was nothing like Mexico City or Buenos Aires. There were no political parties or clandestine movements; there were no Communist cells. As a leading conservative explained, Lima's "political parties ought not to be taken seriously," as they were "abstract nouns, inconsistent and ephemeral personal groupings."[15] Instead, Lima bubbled with social, labor, and cultural agitation, often directed by militant anarcho-syndicalists and increasingly captivated by European and Soviet events. For Lima's young intellectuals and artists, life revolved around Mariátegui, the most prominent bohemian intellectual still left in Lima. He returned from his European exile in March 1923, just months before the poet César Vallejo fled Peru for Europe in June and before Haya's forced exile later that year in October. But Mariátegui was more than just the last remaining intellectual of his stature; he was universally beloved by Lima's progressive intellectual youth. His deteriorating body, growing ever frailer, belied his powerful intellectual gifts and attractive personality; Portal remembered him as a "tireless conversationalist, half teacher, half capturer of those of us who frequented him, workers, miners, campesinos, students, intellectuals."[16]

Another young intellectual, recalling him in her eighties, still insisted that Mariátegui was not "just an unerasable memory" but a daily presence—still—in her life. It "was impossible to be near him and not be influenced. . . . His personality emanated sweetness." His young acolytes took turns pushing his wheelchair, and "when he went out to give a lecture, hundreds of people made way so he could pass and he would blush." Mariátegui "had a phrase, a word for every person, to encourage them, to direct them, to guide them. It was incredible how he remembered everyone, the sick child, the harvest, the problems, the aspirations. He was profoundly human, profoundly interested in the problems of every and each one."[17] While pulling out all the hagiographic and nostalgic threads shot through these memories is difficult, especially given the tragic circumstances of Mariátegui's illness, his influence on an intellectual field left vacant of other strong figures cannot be underestimated.

Portal's friendship with Mariátegui flourished after her return from Bolivia; she joined Mariátegui's group because, she remembered later, "it was the best there was. . . . He held me in high esteem, he was very generous, very likable. I listened to him with interest and said that it was worth hearing him."[18] Portal chose physical metaphors to underline the inevitability of his influence; she grew close to Mariátegui "almost by a physical force, since he was then like the strongest and most intimate pole of attraction of the moment." Their attraction was not political, because "none of them, of us, had a defined ideology, but we had the desire to learn Mariátegui's vital word."[19]

Back in Lima for around four months, in October of 1926, Portal and Delmar gathered a small editorial board, including Delmar's younger brother, Julián Petrovick, to publish their own vanguardia, "supra-cosmopolitan" literary magazine, whose title changed every issue: *Trampolín/Hangar/Rascacielos/Timonel*.[20] Printed on large sheets of colored paper folded into fourths, meant to catch the eye and appear innovative, the magazine attracted considerable attention, according to Portal, and contributions "rained" on the small editorial board that collaboratively wrote and published the small review. This "magazine of four names" abandoned the coeditor model of her previous efforts, exchanging the artistic project as the foundation for a companionate marriage model for the more common small-group editorial board.

Portal edited the first and last issue, and she used this new platform to publicize *El derecho de matar* and to continue their old attacks on Lima's literary community in the never-settled regional antagonisms against the capital. Although projected to be a monthly publication, this magazine, like *Flechas* before it, failed to take root and only survived for four issues. Instead, during this year in Lima, Portal found her widest audience in the pages of *Amauta*, where she published several poems and entered into a heated debate over vanguardia aesthetics with Miguel Ángel Urquieta.

In a book review, Urquieta had attacked vanguardia poetry as pseudo-leftist posturing. Portal retorted that vanguardia poetry delivered authentic leftist political advances and that she and other vanguardia poets were "soldiers of the Social Revolution." Ultimately, Urquieta argued that politically ambitious leftists like Portal and Haya should purge false leftists from their ranks while their movement was young, and he pleaded for doctrine and discipline. "The new art today is nothing but a game of words, of images, of concepts, and even of ideas, sometimes. A type of literary Mah Jong. But to play with these things, one must study, discipline the brain, work it."[21]

In this debate, Portal continued courting a public profile by engaging in an exchange many would have considered unfeminine in its combativeness. Her fame in Lima's literary circles had rested on her early adoption of vanguardia poetry, but her polemic with Urquieta showed her moving toward something else. As she felt her way toward a conception of art as inherently political, as a potent arm in the social struggles of the age, Portal became an early bellwether of the social realism in poetry that would draw other Peruvian poets away from the vanguardia. For Portal, art now had a double mission: "BEAUTY and LIFE," and in this formulation LIFE equaled politics, which in turn equaled social revolution. Her public profile before Bolivia had rested entirely on poetry and journalism. This polemic revealed that her peers now primarily saw her public persona through a political lens and considered her a strident leftist, even if she herself was always careful to specify that at this time she had no formal political commitments, just nebulous identifications with the plight of the working class.

Most interestingly, her disdain for the influence of the past on art suggested a broader personality orientation committed to never looking back on painful life episodes, one way of dealing with, of sequestering away, the shame that might otherwise have paralyzed her. "Of all the futurist doctrine, that with which I most agree is that which assassinates the past and memory," that which is feeble and has concluded, that which "we grasp at with illusions to sustain our balance in life," she wrote. Portal's own balance in life had been disturbed, of course, by personal choices violating the norms of traditional Lima. Her evocative phrasing—"assassinates the past and memory"—makes it clear that this is not just about forgetting, but about violently erasing as a point of principle. The past was "a putrefying cadaver that we must incinerate every moment so as not to contaminate us. There are no lessons from yesterday, only the realities of today," she continued. Her violent imagery—"incinerate at every moment"—reveals the strong emotional impulse behind this putative aesthetic ideology, and suggests how exhausting this constant vigilant excising of the past must have been. But it was crucial work, for a moment's lapse meant the past, with its painful lessons and shameful memories, was ever ready to spring back and "contaminate" her presentist orientation, the difficult choices of today. Portal now asserted, as a point of principle, a radical future-centered ideology that was a perfect fit for an aspiring revolutionary, one allowing for the rejection of middle-class comforts and approval of the utopian promise, however fleeting, of the future: "All of life is a Present with its arms open to Tomorrow."[22]

Portal's other political activities included collaborating with Mariátegui's multiple publishing efforts, including *Labor*, a magazine aimed at the working class, and a working-class printing press. With Mariátegui, already in a wheelchair, and a dozen other students and intellectuals, she celebrated a proletarian outing, the Fiesta de la Planta, where they "passed a day of fraternal company, colored with speeches, poems, and music." *Amauta* published a picture of Portal reciting a poem there, and she published an additional poem in the January 1927 *Boletín* of the popular university, now edited by Mariátegui.[23]

The Leguía regime, however, did not intend to tolerate any revival of the student-led agitation of 1921 to 1923, and it viewed such political activity with growing suspicion. On June 8, 1927, Portal and dozens of other students and intellectuals associated with *Amauta* were rounded up as part of a "Communist plot." Portal was one of two women apprehended, and until the end of her life, she remembered the headline of Peru's newspaper of record, *El Comercio,* that day: "Two Women Implicated in the 'Communist Plot.'" "We were the first [women] to be singled out as subversives," Portal proudly remembered.[24]

While they must have recognized the political danger they were in, their capture nonetheless came as a bracing shock for the young intellectuals in Mariátegui's circle. "Our arrest and subsequent deportation took us completely by surprise. Only days before, we had been with Mariátegui at his house planning an issue of the labor magazine that he directed." The Leguía regime hustled Portal and a small group onto a ship, and in her second trip away from Peru, Portal was deported. "The so-called Communist plot took us to Cuba."[25]

Mexico

Magda Portal could still recite that headline nearly fifty years later because her exile was a critical milestone establishing her as politically dangerous, something very hard for women to achieve. Portal had become a revolutionary worth expelling, although not for clandestine revolutionary politics so much as for social justice agitation. Cuba, however, would prove only a temporary stop. Politically suspect on arrival, the exiles saw their situation grow even more precarious when the Gerardo Machado regime discovered a "Communist plot" of its own. After only forty-seven days on the island, Portal, Delmar, and the small group of exiled Peruvians escaped to Mexico. Mexico had just emerged from a generation of war and violence, but the country was full of excitement and hope, a revolutionary success story busy reimagining and rebuilding itself. For young

Latin American militants with revolutionary ambitions, there was no more exciting place to be than Mexico City, the center of Latin American revolutionary activity, the stage where political thinkers like José Vasconcelos and artists like Diego Rivera, Frida Kahlo, and Tina Modotti were making their mark.

Portal, "intensely curious to learn about the Mexico of the triumphant revolution," fondly remembered it as a "hospitable country," a respite from political harassment, where "we enjoyed the solidarity of the Mexicans."[26] Her politics were still mostly unformed, she tells us; her ideas were "only impulses of solidarity toward the working class. . . . Mexico was my baptism of knowledge and social ideas, because I did not know anything about anything. I was only a poet." But in Mexico, ironically, Portal started to recognize the influence of race and "began to discover the indigenous people of Peru and America, the most underprivileged and least appreciated beings, perhaps only comparable to the Russian peasants before their revolution."[27]

Four months after settling in Mexico City, Portal met Haya again as he returned from his European studies, and their "long conversations" would eventually lead to the founding of APRA.[28] "Night after night, Haya conversed with us, the newly born Apristas . . . under a Mexican sky," Portal remembered. "Haya went straight to the point, illustrating, motivating, clearing up confusions, clarifying many things that until then had been obscure to more of us in the group and to me in particular."[29] In 1923, Haya had left Peru as a student leader, although already at age twenty-eight, he pushed everyone's definition of "youth," and "student." The man who now met his Peruvian colleagues was a promising regional figure who had studied in London, traveled throughout Europe, and visited the Soviet Union, soaking up ideas and impressing intellectuals, both potential patrons and his own peers, at every stop with his charisma, energy, and, some thought, overly grandiose ambitions. But even the disillusioned conceded that Haya exuded "an almost juvenile gaiety, fresh, warm, contagious. . . . He was charming and brilliant; he made each person he talked with feel specially loved, apart from the others."[30]

Haya's personality at this time and his life as a young political exile emerge from the extensive correspondence between him and Anna Melissa Graves (1875–1964), a writer, teacher, world traveler, and pacifist internationalist whom Haya befriended in Peru before his exile. Graves became Haya's principal patron, heavily financing his eight years of travels in the United States, Europe, and the USSR. She also facilitated his correspondence with those still in Peru and translated texts until his own English improved.[31] Quite a bit older and much more familiar with global progressive political efforts than the young Haya, Graves introduced him and vouched for him to her network and guided his publishing efforts, steering him to particular journals. The contacts and credentials she provided to Haya were as important as her money.

Their relationship developed into one of utmost importance and annoyance to Haya, who understood Graves's financial and political patronage with maternal metaphors. He signed his early letters "Your son," addressing her as "My dear mother Annie" or "My dear second mother." "You are a true mother to me," he wrote in 1923, "and every day I feel more respect and love for you. I receive your advice with love. I need it. You must tell me everything you think and everything you want because I am a good submissive son."[32]

A maternal relationship, however, was a double-edged sword: while it allowed Haya to receive her money and help, it also implied he was subject to her maternal guidance. He needed her money, but he was humiliated and dishonored when others learned of her help. He repeatedly asked her to destroy their correspondence, and in one letter marked "Private," he complained: "When you sent me money the last time, I had to answer to many people who asked 'and the check?' It seems that it was like an event."[33] The public knowledge of his financial dependence became a question of dignity. When Graves arranged to send money for his travels to England, he refused. "I will not go to England on charity—you are mistaken. I will not go like that! . . . I would sacrifice everything for you except my dignity."[34] He did take her money, but publicly claimed he traveled on a scholarship.

Graves was also not above using her patronage as a weapon in an effort to control Haya. When she opposed his trip to the Soviet Union, Haya spat: "It is not necessary that you write me everywhere on this earth telling me that 'you won't give me more money because you think that it does my character no good,' because I have never asked for that money and I would prefer to die before accepting another cent having not paid you back." He would assert the same to his parents and his other political patrons to "whom you have written accusing me of loving luxury."[35] Haya's heated language and frequent use of all caps as emphasis conveyed the tone of a pouting adolescent. He flaunted his loneliness and illness, melodramatically dwelled on his potential death, and equated Graves's financial aid with slavery. These emotional attacks, these attempts to solicit guilt, reinforced the reigning dynamic in their relationship of a mother and an increasingly rebellious son.

As Haya developed as a thinker and political activist through his travels, studies, and writings, he sought to redefine their relationship with the more democratic vocabulary of friendship. Ultimately, what chafed the most was not Graves's political "guidance," steering him away from Communism and toward a pacifism he considered unworkable, but her repeated interventions in his private life. She corresponded with his family in Trujillo, and Haya resented her attempts to bring him closer to his mother. She reviewed his receipts and complained about his spending, which she feared was careless, frivolous, and irresponsible. Graves also "advised" him about his friendships, and even suggested repeatedly whom he should marry. Haya's mother had worried about his traveling to the Soviet Union in part because, she revealed in a letter to Graves, it was a "country disintegrating in revolt of . . . libertines."[36] In Moscow a year later in 1925, Haya received an accusatory postcard from Graves: "When you say you cannot give me a son's love, you must remember that without a mother's love for you my giving and your receiving would be impossible without loss of respect for you." He shot back: "You are rigth. I cannot accept your conditions. I shall never love you like a mother. . . . I canot read more [of] your insults. That is a farce and after your investigation about my internal life and your recriminations. . . . I must ask you not more interference in my life."[37] Haya had originally typed, and then crossed out, "sexual life," suggesting that at least in private, Haya's homosexuality was a troubling suspicion to maternal figures in his life.

But such whispers did not hamper Haya's success in mobilizing his peers. "Haya found our presence in the Mexican capital to be quite useful as a way of validating his political ambitions," Portal remembered. "All of us who were in the initial group were very young, and none of us had a university degree. However, Haya told us that he was not interested in degrees. He didn't have any either."[38]

After announcing APRA as an anti-imperialist movement in 1924, Haya built his political ideas on his evolving understanding of Marxism-Leninism and watched how the mass politics of an emerging European Fascism mobilized, organized, and inspired. APRA was in many ways his "American" response to the Comintern, a continental movement with separate local, national sections, each addressing their individual national problems in "Minimum Programs" while all working toward their continental agenda and its five touchstone goals, their shared "Maximum Program."

Socialism, Haya argued as he looked at the American continent, was not yet possible for the "Indoamerican" republics, his neologism capturing the indigenista zeitgeist yearning to transform indigenous peoples and cultures from the obstacles to progress positivists assumed they were into the foundation of new and valorized national cultures. Appropriated from the influential Mexican indigenista thinker, José Vasconcelos, "Indoamerica" also emphasized how separate the Latin American experience was from Europe's.[39]

Europe would never work as a template or an answer for Latin America. Latin America had neither enough local capital to build their own economies nor an industrial proletariat large enough to lead a revolution. Indoamerica was so far behind that its primary mode of production was still a feudalism that no longer existed in Europe, where the forces of capitalism had swept it away. Their different realities demanded different political answers. To develop economically, Haya concluded, there was no choice but to play with fire and rely on foreign—imperialist—capital, even though they knew foreign capital would inevitably try to exploit Latin America both economically and politically. Lacking a revolutionary proletariat, Haya argued that true revolutionary potential lay in the middle class, because it was the most exploited, caught between the demands of both foreign capital and Peru's feudal class. Thus, although foreign imperialism was necessary, a strong, interventionist "anti-imperialist" state needed to control it, channeling its productive economic forces, while softening its negative impact on the nation's fragile middle and popular classes. The political base for this anti-imperialist state was a cross-class alliance of urban middle-class sectors and intellectuals with the working class, an alliance Haya called the "manual and intellectual laborers."[40]

Haya, Portal, and Delmar were among the handful of Peruvian exiles who drafted and signed a plan of action on January 22, 1928. If any one document can be considered the founding text of APRA as a political party with concrete goals and not just an anti-imperialist movement, it is this

Plan de México, which "solemnly declared before the Peruvian people, America, and the world" a revolution of liberation against the Leguía regime, internal feudalism, and foreign imperialism."[41] The agent of this liberation would be a nationalist revolutionary party, which would apply APRA's larger anti-imperialist and broadly Socialist tenets in Peru.

The plan touched on questions of national politics and economy, offering general principles instead of detailed programs. It declared APRA to be both a political and a military organization and Peru's only legitimate revolutionary group, and Haya as the party's "founder and supreme chief." It declared the Leguía regime illegitimate, proposed itself as the ideological base for a future Peruvian Constitution, and promised that the Peruvian struggle heralded a new age of similar revolutions of liberation in all Latin American countries. Economically, the plan promised a radical transformation in broad strokes, attacking Peru's landed oligarchy, advocating for the nationalization of wealth, promising to devolve all land to working people, and setting as a guiding model "the admirable agrarian system of the Incas, which affirmed in the community or *ayllu* the base of national agrarian life." It committed the party to fight for working people, broadly defined to include everyone from the middle classes, intellectual workers, military personnel, and all who "suffer exploitation." They addressed issues that had animated their activism in both the university and as provincianos. Their Reformista roots informed their promise of free access to a secular education, from grade school to the university level. They also promised "to radically reorganize the national political system" to end the "hateful centralism" keeping the provinces "totally subjugated, politically and economically," to Lima.

The plan also looked ahead to what its future civic society promised. All "Indoamerican men and women" who adhered to the plan's principles "are considered citizens with the right to be soldiers of the movement and servants to the cause." Their care to specify that women were eligible to be "soldiers of the movement" was a noteworthy and unusual invitation for women to participate, especially given the martial language of "soldier." Even more striking was their explicit recognition of women as citizens in their movement and in their "Peru after victory." Since female citizenship sprang from allegiance to their revolutionary principles, their language implicitly promised women the rights and obligations of citizenship, including female suffrage.

While it offered no action plan, the Plan de México was clear on one thing: it was the young exiles' "historical duty to undertake the revolution under very strict conditions of discipline and efficacy." The days of reckless provocation were over. In this new era, these young leaders had decided that only party discipline and hierarchy would allow them to reach their utopian goal with the least possible suffering, thus saving "the blood and energy" of the Peruvian people.

In the plan's conclusion, the signatories affirmed: "We solemnly protest before the Peruvian people, to fight until the end to obtain its integral emancipation, stripped of every personal interest and resolved to any sacrifice to reach the triumph of our cause." This soaring language seems appropriate for an occasion in which the participants have just formally and publicly declared war on the political regime, economic interests, and social history of their country. For Magda Portal, however, this solemn pledge was much more than flowery language. In Mexico, she would publicly enact this vow, stripping herself of every personal interest and resolving to sacrifice anything to reach the triumph of their cause, proving to her Aprista colleagues, and to herself, that she was a worthy comrade.

Her memories of this time foreground her position as the only woman in the founding group, the only woman present at their ceremonies and initiations. "I founded the Aprista Party with a very small group, with no more than just twelve people. We founded the party by candlelight. . . . There were no other women at that ceremony, not even the compañeros' women entered," she remembered.[42] The anecdote Portal most often narrated from these months in Mexico, however, focused less on gender and instead told the story of a dramatic choice, and perhaps of an induction, explaining how and why she put poetry aside to focus on revolutionary doctrine, the "less lyrical" subject of socioeconomics.[43]

She narrated the first and most widely known version of this story in an anecdote structuring the action around herself and Haya. "Haya told me: 'You cannot continue to write poetry. Now you have to study Political Economy.' I started to study. I remember that I was speaking with some friends one day in front of a river. I took my book *Ánima absorta* [Consumed spirit], and I ripped it all, and I watched later how the river took the pieces. . . . At heart, I felt torn, but I had taken the decision. 'I have to study, Haya told us we have to study.'"[44]

Reading this dramatic anecdote, the Peruvian literary critic Daniel Mathews Carmelino argues that Haya convinced Portal that "if she wants to have a social impact she must stop writing." Haya commands her obedience in part because he has metaphorically stepped in as Portal's "adopted father." Another Peruvian exile in this small group, Esteban Pavletich, described himself during this time as an "orphan," and Mathews Carmelino wonders how much more terrible this alienating dislocation must have been for Portal, "who dragged her orphanhood with her since the age of five," and for whom exile then becomes her "second orphanhood." Her relationship with Haya gives Portal needed security, allowing her to jettison all responsibilities. Portal "renounced her search" for meaning "to give all the responsibility to Haya, who installed himself as guide to her feelings and who offers her a security that up to that point she did not have, he offers her a faith, and makes her a participant in a collectivity." Commanding her to stop writing poetry, Haya thus becomes the "castrating father whom one obeys without possible debate," a father whose directions "determine existence," establishing what she can and cannot do.[45]

Mathews Carmelino insightfully turns to the psychological relationships in play, the emotional needs that might have been driving the actions of these young exiles. However, in his analysis, Haya becomes a grander-than-life figure, a historical character with super agency, capable of intuiting Portal's emotional needs and fulfilling them to his own best benefit. The story, of course, was more complicated.

Haya was not a father, and this relationship was not a hierarchical bond between the two of them fraught with patriarchal tensions and expectations. Instead, Haya was the brightest star in a constellation of brothers, and Portal's emotional satisfactions derived not from her relationship with any particular one, but from joining the collectivity as a comrade. And in fact, Mathews Carmelino points us to a poem Portal authored, "Grito," which instead of yearning for a father, yearns for a brother searched for after "scratching in every corner." Reading her collected poems to date, Portal's yearning was couched not in paternal but instead in maternal terms.

Fundamentally, Mathews Carmelino's reading presents Portal as vulnerable, emotionally and socially weak; it assumes she narrates a transparent act of compliance with orders from an inarguably greater authority. Haya terrorizes her into action, and using the language of the castrating father implicitly positions her as male, as the son in the oedipal drama Mathews Carmelino has constructed, and which prevents him from considering this her narration of a transformative free choice she willingly undertakes.

Portal was not in Haya's thrall. She certainly considered "Haya the best of the group, brilliant, no one reached his level, he created differences, confronted everyone, and we all knew it."[46] But while she held Haya in the highest esteem, she characterized their relationship at this point as "very fraternal, we addressed each other informally, *nos tuteábamos.*"[47] Even if the Peruvian exiles understood their sudden dislocation and isolation in suggestive terms like "orphanhood," within this group, Portal was not socially weak or vulnerable. On the contrary, Portal stressed that her colleagues held her in high regard, and her history in Lima's literary circles added to her prestige in their eyes. "For them I was an attainment, because I had a few prizes and I was known as a combative poetess," with a strong inflection on "combative." In addition to her 1923 Juegos Florales prize, the municipality of Lima had just awarded her latest work of poetry, *Una esperanza y el mar,* another prize. The other exiles, in fact, designated her by consensus the committee's general secretary, due in large part to her public profile as a recognized poet.[48]

We see this power more clearly in a second, more detailed version of the same story. "But I was bringing along poetry," Portal begins. "This is what Haya said to me, in no uncertain terms: 'If you want to be involved in politics, you must give up poetry.' I didn't hesitate. Ipso facto I replied, 'If my poetry is an obstacle, I'll have no more to do with it.' And so it was. One afternoon on a picnic in the country with all the group present, I took a copy of my first collection of poetry, *Ánima absorta,* out of my handbag. Standing on a bridge over a little stream, I tore it up—to the astonishment of a good friend of mine, Esteban Pauletich [sic]. I ripped it to shreds and threw it into the water, which carried it away."[49]

Portal felt "tremendous emotion" about throwing her poems away. "The emotion of someone losing something beloved, but not losing it forever, not irreparably. If it had been, I would have burst into tears. But I didn't. I simply tore up the book, and we went on talking. But people looked to me as if to say, 'What have you done, what is going on?' It was my way of answering to a new attitude, that of social struggle, of commitment."[50]

This version presents the event as Portal's conscious choice to dedicate herself to their shared political struggle. Haya does not force her to renounce her poetry, but he frames her poetry as a frivolous hobby, as one of the "personal interests" they had all taken a solemn oath to strip, to abandon, to ensure their focus and discipline. That is why she specifies that "if her poetry is an obstacle," she would not hesitate to renounce it. Once she takes the decision, narrated here as a personal one whose contours the witnesses are not privy to and do not really understand, she continues her conversation, refusing to cry and demonstrating to herself that she was not responding "like a woman."

In a final version of this key anecdote in her life narrative, Portal wrote in her unpublished memoirs that Haya told her both "jokingly and seriously" to stop writing verses and dedicate herself to studying economics. "I am a passionate and vehement being," she explained, "and for all that poetry was a part of me, I decided to take Haya's invitation, and one afternoon, in an outing in the country, I took the original draft of my first book, *Ánima absorta*, that I had with me, and without much fuss, I destroyed it page by page," throwing it into the river's rapid current, as her friends looked at her both surprised and concerned.[51] Here, the evolution is complete: Portal takes Haya's comments, both in jest and in earnest, as an invitation to full commitment and perhaps fuller affiliation. Certainly, everyone there watching the torn paper drift away knew Haya's fiery temperament often led him to take issue with those around him. But among them all, only Portal felt the need to perform her new affiliation so literally, proving her commitment and ability.

This ritual she enacted and then narrated until the end of her life became an important fulcrum in her life history as she understood it. She became a revolutionary that afternoon; this is where she narrated her story in the classic outlines of twentieth-century Latin American revolutionary affiliation, where heroic revolutionaries discover their agency in a "transcendental moment of choice." Analyzing the later revolutionary narratives of the Argentine Che Guevara and the Guatemalan Mario Payeras, María Josefina Saldaña-Portillo finds that these leaders represent becoming revolutionaries as a process of "revelation, transformation, and transcendence," an "epochal conversion experience" resulting in "the epistemic death" of who they had been before.[52] Like their stories, casting her poetry into the river became a revolutionary rebirth and a baptism into the Aprista community for Portal.

As much as this was the birth of a new, revolutionary self, it was also an "epistemic death" freeing Portal from her previous painful life story. While Portal may have destroyed some poems, her first biographer believes it was most likely because they were deeply personal pieces revealing intimate feelings about her relationship with Federico Bolaños and Gloria's birth, which did not fit well into Portal's new aesthetic orientation toward a politically committed poetry.[53] In her retelling, Portal specifies that she cast away the original drafts of her book *Ánima absorta*. Now something else, something other than the emotional firestorms of intense first love and its consequences, consumed her spirit, her energies, her commitment. It raised her profile in the eyes of her APRA comrades. In a 1929 letter, Haya describes the Mexican Apristas as "the most capable group, the most extraordinarily strong and sincere group we have. Like them, Magda Portal is made of steel. With them I would go to the ends of the earth."[54]

The Caribbean

The choice Portal made that day by the river did not entail her abandoning her writing so much as dedicating herself to rigorous immersion in revolutionary doctrine, especially the political economy that the party would need her to understand and transmit. After two years in Mexico, Portal launched herself on a tour of the Caribbean to mobilize and raise APRA's profile. She missed the sea, she revealed in her unpublished memoirs, and she was anxious to start acting on her new Aprista commitments.[55] Were there other reasons pushing her forth on this ambitious quest? She traveled only with Gloria—what of Delmar? In a March 1929 letter, Haya revealed that Esteban Pavletich was now "another little poet against me," since Haya had opposed Pavletich's attempts to woo Portal from Delmar. While Portal "remains on good terms with me," Haya explained, Pavletich "hates me. Del Mar wants to kill Pavletich," and the Mexican Apristas sent Pavletich to the Yucatán. Haya believed Magda would travel to Havana to meet up with Pavletich. Years later, Pavletich confirmed that he had long admired Portal since their university days in Lima and that "the life they enjoyed in Mexico was very free in their personal relations and that, in truth, he had fallen in love with Magda and tried to take her from Serafín."[56]

Portal traveled to Puerto Rico, Cuba, Santo Domingo, and Colombia, meeting with young militants everywhere and giving conferences on political topics, such as U.S. imperialism and the Mexican Revolution, but also on art, poetry, and the role of women. Her well-publicized travels throughout the region made a lasting impression, as attested to by the voluminous scrapbook of press clippings following Portal, which a Sra. Angélica de Enausquin kept for fifty years until she deposited it at the UT Benson Library in 1980.[57] A Puerto Rican journalist, for whom Portal embodied "the perfect type of the woman of the future," cast her in the masculine role of sower of men. Portal sowed "in the freshly dug furrow of inquisitive youth, the seed of a new way of feeling, a new way of thought, a new mode of action. . . . More than a poet of revolutionary art, more than a forceful essayist, more than a personality in emotional tension," he concluded, Portal was "a force in action, a trembling fount of dynamism, a liquid metal in continuous fusion."[58]

Arriving in Santo Domingo in August of 1929, she met a group of exiled Venezuelan students who hoped to launch an invasion and revolutionary insurrection against the Venezuelan leader Juan Vicente Gómez. Portal gave a conference on "yankee imperialism" and struck up a "friendly camaraderie" with the Venezuelan student exiles and, in particular, with their short and stocky leader, Rómulo Betancourt.[59]

Portal was Betancourt's first personal contact with APRA, and she made an enormously positive impression on him. At this stage in his political career, Betancourt was considered a bit of a provocateur himself, and witnesses recounted how his anti-imperialism reached comical extremes when he insisted on translating English names, particularly the United Fruit Company, into Spanish. Betancourt found in APRA the best channel for this anti-imperialism, his principal political concern. He was also deeply attracted to the Peruvians' proven success in connecting with the popular classes, especially through the popular universities. Betancourt left Santo Domingo as an Aprista. He traveled next to Costa Rica, where, when arguing over the Cuban Communist Julio Antonio Mella's scathing critique "What Is APRA?," Betancourt so fervently defended APRA that the debate turned ugly and ended in a fistfight.[60] Though Betancourt was throwing in with the fledgling APRA, the most powerful sanction for revolutionary change remained the surging Soviet Union. Haya had ultimately turned from the Soviets and Communism, but he still derived influence and prestige from his travels to the USSR. Increasingly, Latin American revolutionaries faced a choice.

Portal mentored Betancourt's political education along the same path she had cleared from revolutionary provocateur to disciplined party comrade. In a letter, Betancourt "thanked Magdita for having awakened in me the desire for a revolutionary education. Today I am convinced that it is not enough to be a Jacobin and be prepared to give one's life for an ideal at any hour, but instead that one needs defined ideological directives, qualifications, a solid base of thinking to make an interesting and lasting work."[61] Portal and Delmar stressed the importance of discipline, doctrine, and sustained effort over "hysterical" acts of provocation.[62] Strong emotions bound Betancourt to Portal and Delmar. Delmar's letter ends by reminding Betancourt that "you know that if you come to Peru you come to your *patria* and to the side of your Aprista brothers who love and respect you," and that Magda "remembers you like a sister. We always speak of you to the compañeros." Betancourt asked Portal to write the colophon to his first political publication, a short book he coauthored in 1929 on the 1928 Venezuelan student protests, demonstrating her influence on him, his respect for her, and how Portal had become a political patron worth courting among the radicalized Latin American youth.

In these letters, the advice Portal and Delmar passed along was from their own experience and self-criticism, marking the distance they had traveled along their own Red Paths. Portal had grown since writing *El derecho de matar*. She was now certain that the difference between being a rebel and a revolutionary was neither the vehemence of her passion nor the strength of her ideas, but her disciplined focus, her ability to transform that energy and those ideas into organized, consciously directed action instead of scattershot provocation. This was the most important transition in her political life and in that of her revolutionary fellow travelers.

Another marker of Portal's change and growth was her evolution on one of her key themes, maternity. Emotionally, Portal's writing on motherhood had progressed from indifference to sadness, and now reached for an anger-fed triumphalism, transforming her anxiety and deep ambivalence about the gendered responsibilities of childcare into a potent political rhetoric. In 1929, *Amauta* published another of Portal's poems dealing with motherhood. "The Child" begins with a strikingly unhappy image. "Like that—crucified by Life / [she] awoke one morning."[63] The poem attacks the exploitative conditions of work in "the implacable workshop," and the misery of the home of the poor, "where we lack everything / even the light / that penetrates timidly / through the dirty windows." But this poem, the second in a two-poem series titled "Two Proletarian Poems for the Compañeros of Vitarte," does not narrate an infanticide, but is instead a celebration of hope. "Since then / for the wound of her womb / which sketched her face / and transformed her body / with the lines of maternity / and brought her the present / of a child / a new happiness—also unknown / awoke in their life.—/ A deaf happiness." In this poem, the child becomes a new dawn and an invitation for a new existence for the mother, one unmistakably marked by politics. "Emptied completely into him, she would not be herself anymore. / The life that remained ahead / she now owed / to the little one with no name / . . . And then she did see the pain of the struggle / the now daily anguish of the entire factory / that never gives enough to satisfy hunger." The poem ends with the woman realizing her child is a call to arms. "He was a flag / she would defend him pressed against her breast! / Because of him she knew tears / in her worker's heart grew / rebellion."

Portal had now come to deploy the themes of pregnancy and childbirth for political ends. Three years after Bolivia, Portal employed these same themes as explicit propaganda, dedicated to Lima's most highly organized workers. In this last poem, the child not only survives but comes to stand for the proletariat and a new society, impelling the mother toward political action to end their exploitation. "The Child" is a utopian imagining where workers launch themselves into the political struggle to redeem their children's future. Portal had achieved this final triumphalist political maternity after struggling for years writing pieces that instead viewed pregnancy and motherhood with deep ambivalence, if not dread.

Portal's final stop on this Caribbean tour was Costa Rica, where she received an unexpected letter from Mariátegui, telling her he had founded the Peruvian Socialist Party and asking her to join them. Mariátegui had broken with Haya in a bitter exchange over the Plan de México, considering such an explicit declaration of war against the regime reckless. Now, everyone read in public declarations what his private correspondents already knew, just how egotistical, spiteful, and ruthless Haya could be. Mariátegui, he stabbed, was guilty of "excessive intellectualism," "mental masturbations," "tropical illusions and absurd sentimentalisms." He even attacked Mariátegui's physical disability—frail, trapped in a wheelchair, Mariátegui "cringes from the idea of action" and would never lead a revolution.[64] The Plan de México marked the moment when the Peruvian Left split into the groups that would form APRA and Mariátegui's Socialist Party, dividing a community of young militants into separate paths that would grow increasingly antagonistic as they evolved into the non-Communist and the Communist revolutionary Lefts.

Portal wrote back, breaking the news that she had already committed to APRA. These young intellectuals were all choosing paths and making choices. Haya, from his distant post in exile, and Mariátegui, one of the last of their numbers still remaining in Lima, had only imperfect and delayed knowledge of how their efforts were persuading and recruiting potential followers from the small pool of promising youth militants. In essence, these two leaders were fighting over Portal. But Portal also had a choice to make. Between the two leaders, Portal explained much later, she chose Haya and his vision because he had a more formal architecture for a new social and political movement. Mariátegui's salons, in contrast, were intellectual exercises that rarely reached ideological conclusions. Mariátegui hoped to gather the Peruvian exiles, most of whom had been his friends and had cut their teeth in those inspiring if inconclusive salons, to settle the political questions that had split the leftist youth between him and Haya. They might be able to do it in early 1930, in Santiago de Chile, he wrote Portal. "I know that you will always be where duty calls you."[65]

Eager to participate in what everyone could already see would prove to be the most important gathering of the Peruvian leftists of her generation, Portal called on friends to forge a Costa Rican passport for her and boarded a ship; she was delayed for a week in Panama, and her dire economic situation forced her to sell some of her books to make ends meet—most painfully, a beautiful set of the works of José Martí, a gift from friends in Cuba. When she finally arrived in Santiago, she found the Chilean government expecting her and the other exiles. They were all accused of conspiring against the government and jailed. After promising not to cause any trouble, they were quickly released; Portal was imprisoned for a total of eight days. Sadly, it was all for naught—Mariátegui died in April of 1930, never having regained his strength to leave Lima.

Now reunited with many of her Aprista colleagues in Chile after her solitary efforts touring the Caribbean, Portal was, at thirty years old, one of the most visible women in Latin America, both as a poet and as a political commentator. In the previous seven years, the young woman reporter tramping through Lima's streets had won prizes for her verses, and her nebulous identification with working-class intellectual circles had branded her a Communist conspirator dangerous enough to be thrown out of Peru. She had lived in revolutionary Mexico and traveled throughout the Caribbean. She had made several wrenching and incomprehensible choices for most young women of her time, place, and class: to have a child out of wedlock, to leave her first husband for his brother, to leave perhaps her first love—writing and poetry—for politics. She had become Magda Portal, a signature political organizer and leader for one of the most compelling political projects remaining to the young leftists of her generation: APRA.

CHAPTER FIVE

Woman with a Gun

MAGDA PORTAL WAS NO longer, in her words, "just a poet," but one of Peru's most visible young revolutionaries. In 1923, dancing precariously between publicity and notoriety, she had avoided the Juegos Florales stage, choosing not to publicly declaim her winning entries about a sexual relationship while visibly pregnant and unmarried. Now, seven years later, she fully embraced a different notoriety as a woman revolutionary. She had undergone years of emotional struggle to break free from traditional notions of middle-class decency, culminating in running away from her husband with his younger brother, Serafín Delmar, who now traveled with her as her revolutionary compañero, presented as the father of her daughter, Gloria. While painful, those transgressions, and the process of emotional struggle and separation they triggered, had burned away enough of her desire, her need to conform to gendered decency and its demands that women be pleasing, demure, passive, self-abnegated. Ultimately, that painful struggle had been necessary to let her conceive of herself as a potent revolutionary asset and to imagine herself—finally—as the most militant of her band of brothers, fully affiliated into the fraternity of revolutionaries that was APRA.

Building APRA for Peru's 1931 election, Portal led grueling campaign tours to the provinces, where, she remembered, "we gave ourselves completely to our . . . proselytizing actions . . . in all corners of the country. That was how I first came to know all of Peru."[1] In practice, this meant endless speeches and rallies to crowds "disconcerted by the novelty of our presence and our words."[2] Every time they stepped on stage, they enacted Aprista promises of class alliance and new political opportunities for

APRA family tree, *Últimas Noticias*,
January 18, 1932. Courtesy Magda Portal
Papers, Benson Latin American Collection,
University of Texas at Austin.

workers, provincials, and women. Provincial audiences had never seen
national politicians among them before, nor had they ever heard of an
ideology quite like APRA's. In truth, they had probably never heard any
ideology, since politics had always been presented as a scuffle between
people and personalities, not ideas and doctrines.

One day on this whistle-stop tour, the Apristas entered a bursting theater,
with workers crammed into the upper sections above the local *señores* arrayed more comfortably below. "We entered in a mortal silence, nobody
applauded, they were enemies," Portal vividly recalled, "and I had to close
the act." The audience was inclined against the Apristas from both the
Right and the Socialist Left: "You could feel that the people burned with
fury." She directly addressed the cheaper upper deck about their economic
exploitation. "I spoke for a long time. I don't know how long, I believe more

than forty minutes. . . . It's curious," she noted, using her preferred phrase to underscore important details, that "none of the speeches were applauded. But for me, at the end, they gave me an ovation, and opened the way for me."[3]

Another success in another theater for Portal. At the 1923 Juegos Florales, others had applauded Portal's silence, her refusal to step forward, as something it was not, as a political statement against Leguía. Now, proselytizing in the provinces, she succeeded by taking the stage and speaking forcefully, steered by astute political instincts and powered by the strength of a full-throttle political personality. She had become, to herself and those around her, both an Aprista woman revolutionary and a revolutionary woman in Peruvian history.

Leaving town, the Aprista campaigners ominously discovered that someone had sabotaged their car by letting the air out of the tires. Such a malicious act launched them into dangerous and uncertain territory—was it a warning or a first strike? With few options, they climbed into a new truck, whose driver suddenly pulled over, claiming there was a problem. It was about 6:00 P.M., with night falling.

While the men climbed out to inspect the damage, Portal waited inside. Six men approached, saying, "*A quien queremos conocer es a ésa, a la Magda Portal*" (The one we want to meet is that one, that Magda Portal). Their use of the article "*la*" to describe her was unmistakable—an aggressive and pejorative objectification. Instead of ignoring their brutish hail, Portal, "thinking they were friends who did not know how to express themselves better," opened the door and jumped out. "That was so very curious," she remembered, using her characteristic expression. "As it was a little chilly, I had my hands in my pockets. 'I am Magda Portal,' I told them." They left without saying anything, "as if they had been frightened. Maybe they thought I was armed?" Portal mused.

Telling the story later, she confessed that at the time she was "disconcerted," especially when she realized they had only one revolver among them all. Her hapless Aprista brothers, dutifully inspecting their broken vehicle, proved unable to protect the group; even though one of them actually had a firearm, they were "frightened tremendously." Later, she framed this episode more explicitly as one of mortal danger: "There was a group that wanted to kill me but that did not dare because they thought I had a revolver in the pocket of my overcoat, where I had my hands."[4] In both versions, Portal presented herself as the hero; these anecdotes were meant to prove she was always, even when only huddling for warmth, the woman with a gun.

Her Aprista brothers-in-arms surely breathed easier that night after their narrow escape, but their relief was inevitably tinged with anxiety. APRA was still a small, intimate world, little more than a handful of leaders who had bonded during their days as student militants and in exile from Leguía's Peru. Portal's comrades must have known the stories about her past swirling around her, even—or perhaps especially—the torrid tale of how she brandished a gun against her husband and ran away with his little brother. If this woman could raise a gun to her own husband, were there any limits to the threat she could pose?

Portal's anecdote also hinted at the increasing stakes at play when women began participating in the nation's political life. In a country where women could not yet vote, Portal was creating new templates for women in public life that caused considerable anxiety among traditional leaders. In the conservative southern city of Arequipa, "the priests prevented the women from attending" their APRA rally, Portal recalled, though the priests themselves "were in the front row." Perhaps the priests were rightly worried, as "groups of women who had been attracted by my presence and who had never intervened in political matters before" followed her and joined APRA, Portal observed, satisfied.[5]

"As a woman who knew how to speak, who knew how to express herself, which many women almost did not know how to do, at least in those environments . . . the enemies came to hear what I had to say." Curious crowds of both friends and foes focused on APRA's female headliner, since, as Portal noted, "this had never been seen before, as women had always been relegated to domestic functions." Far from a symbolic presence, Portal was one of the party's highest leaders. Everyone who came could see she had left domestic functions far behind. Portal believed she was "unquestionably" the "central figure" in these provincial Aprista campaigns, which made her "suddenly more" than other leaders "wherever I went."[6]

The novelty of Portal's gender being "out of place"—not just as a woman but as a female leader—in these public fora attracted Aprista converts from all quarters. Reporting from a small village two years later, the Aprista press captured what they felt Portal represented. "An elderly Indian, even though ignorant of Spanish, understanding the liberating meaning of the

Aprista message, threw himself to enfold our compañera Magda tightly in his millenarian and emancipated arms," they gushed, seeing "in the eyes of this compañera the sincerity and the truth for which our indigenous Andean has clamored for so long."[7]

What "sincerity and truth" burned in Portal's eyes? She was certain and unwavering in her revolutionary Aprista convictions. But it was also the fevered excitement of watching APRA's ideas catch fire, as thousands flocked to their rallies, joined the party, and planned to vote for Haya in the upcoming October 1931 elections. In the dramatic year ahead, Portal and Delmar would be central protagonists in the Aprista leadership that mobilized a mass movement and shepherded their emerging party through unprecedented events in Peruvian political history, including Peru's first modern presidential election. Those not caught up in the Aprista tornado of revolutionary dreams and outsized expectations might well have seen the fire in Portal's eyes as that of the romantic, the deluded, or the fanatic. Who were these petty-bourgeois, half-failed students and theoretically confused radicals, many just recently returned to Peru after years of absence, to think they could burst so suddenly and convincingly onto the Peruvian scene? But elbowing in as a lead player in the political drama unfolding over Peru, Magda Portal burned with a sense of her own heroic agency, with the certainty of her personal importance to their shared cause, and with the joy of finally fully unleashing in all its strength what she would later describe as "her own human personality, never expressed, never understood, capable of great and noble actions."[8]

A Dream Becomes a Movement

In August 1930, the eleven years of Leguía's government ended in a military coup, sharing the fate of other Latin American governments hit hard by the Great Depression, which pummeled export-dependent societies the world over. Peru was particularly vulnerable to these global economic earthquakes because during Leguía's tenure, its economy had shifted from depending on agricultural products like sugar, cotton, and wool produced by a national elite to mineral exports, including petroleum, copper, and silver, extracted and owned primarily by foreign capital. Additionally, Leguía's preferred mode of economic growth had been courting foreign debt, especially from the United States, which by the 1920s had overtaken Great

Britain as the country's largest foreign investor. During Leguía's *oncenio*, Peru's external public debt skyrocketed from $12 million in 1919 to $124 million in 1931. This gush of dollars repaid old debts, expanded the bureaucracy, increased middle-sector employment (especially in Lima), placated the army, and built massive public works projects. The Great Depression abruptly shut off this tap of dollars, just as Peru's export earnings plummeted 71 percent between 1928 and 1933.[9]

As the regime's economic foundation crumbled under his feet and military coups threatened neighboring governments in Argentina and Bolivia, Leguía struggled to stay in power. A coup seemed to many "a foregone conclusion," with rumors in Lima focusing not on its possibility, but on who would lead it.[10] The first popular demonstration against Leguía erupted on July 14, 1930, in a Bastille Day celebration at a movie theater he rather cluelessly attended. As the Bastille was stormed on screen, people, "protected by the shadow of the movie theater," stood up and shouted "Down with the tyrant!" and "Long live liberty!" As the theater operators hurriedly turned on the lights, Leguía left, with the horses of his regimental escort slipping on the asphalt while pursuing the audience chasing and harassing the president.[11]

But in the end, it wasn't angry movie spectators who brought the regime down. In the southern department of Arequipa, a recently promoted lieutenant colonel named Luis Miguel Sánchez Cerro had been conspiring to overthrow the government since receiving command of one of Arequipa's army units just months before.[12] Sánchez Cerro was forty-one years old, short and slight, weighing just over 110 pounds, and nicknamed El Negro for the angular, indigenous features and dark skin that testified to his racial background as a mestizo. On August 25, he launched his uprising, which quickly spread to other southern regions. Unable to muster the support necessary to match his opponent, Leguía stepped down, and Sánchez Cerro triumphantly entered Lima a few days later, where he was greeted as the "Hero of Arequipa" by the largest public demonstration in Peruvian history, all the more impressive for being spontaneous.[13] Luis Alberto Sánchez, lost among the crowd, remembered Sánchez Cerro, still wearing his military campaign outfit and surrounded by his troops. The young Limeñan seemed most struck, however, by the lieutenant colonel's large, toothy smile, "like an orangutan," and his "ugly laugh" ringing out from his "vehicle spiked with machine guns" pointing out toward the crowd.[14]

Sánchez Cerro quickly capitalized on his popularity as a liberator and a mestizo man of the people and moved to alleviate the worst suffering caused by the Great Depression. He gained loads of goodwill from the most marginalized citizens by abolishing Leguía's forced labor program, which had conscripted thousands to construct the new roads connecting Lima to the provinces. Within three weeks of taking command, he ordered Lima's police stations to distribute food to the destitute, unsurprisingly making him wildly popular among the city's poor. But no one confused Sánchez Cerro's populist moves with a progressive political agenda. By nature a political conservative, he surrounded himself with equally conservative members of Lima's political elite who had chafed under Leguía's attack on the old political parties.

After this military coup, Haya ordered all the members of the Aprista cells in Paris, Berlin, Santiago, Buenos Aires, and La Paz to return to Peru, legally or clandestinely, to begin building a mass party and to prepare for his return. When Leguía fell, Portal was in neighboring Chile, where she had traveled to attend Mariátegui's ill-fated summit, with Serafín Delmar; her daughter, Gloria; and Serafín's brother, Julián Petrovick. In September of 1930, they were among the first Apristas to return to the country, which left them responsible for much of the party activity in Peru. On September 20, a group of about fifty, mostly students, professionals, and workers from the UPGP, the party's popular university, founded the Peruvian section of APRA in Lima.[15] Among the fifty, only Portal and Delmar were part of the core leadership who had also signed the 1928 Plan de México.

The returning Aprista exiles faced many obstacles. In the words of Fredrick Pike, they had earned a reputation "as dangerous fanatics filled with a sense of their own importance and disinclined to share command with those who had not suffered at the hands of the 'tyrant' Leguía and had not undergone the moral purification of exile."[16] With "absolutely no capital," they met where they could, often in private homes, sometimes in Portal's apartment.[17] They faced increasingly severe government repression and had set before themselves a Herculean task: to build a viable political party, recruit party members and voters, prepare political platforms and plans for governing, coordinate and campaign for the October 1931 election, and launch a mass movement to change Peru's politics and society. What they would manage to achieve would amaze even the most optimistic among them. As Sánchez noted, any one of these tasks should have taken years and required considerable financial resources. Only two factors explained to him and his Aprista compañeros what they had nonetheless achieved: *fe y juventud*, faith and youth.[18]

The leaders were all very young, all under forty, with the youngest a mere twenty-five years old. Antenor Orrego was the eldest at thirty-eight; Haya and Arturo Sabroso were about thirty-six; Manuel Seoane, Luis Alberto Sánchez, and Portal were about thirty; Carlos Manuel Cox was about twenty-eight; and Luis Heysen and Serafín Delmar were about twenty-seven.[19] Their shared youth and experience of exile made this small group capable of both imagining the impossible and of launching themselves on an audacious attempt to remake their world. And it was this audacity that was one of their strongest political assets, winning them "tremendous national political attention" and putting "APRA at the very centre of Peru's political imagination."[20]

In this first frenzy of Aprista activity, Portal, Delmar, and Petrovick focused on organization and propaganda. Both Delmar and Petrovick served as high-level propaganda leaders, helping the new party host Rómulo Betancourt, who appeared in Lima as a "compañero Aprista" in early October and was warmly greeted by his Aprista brethren, if not by the Sánchez Cerro government, which impeded their public presentations.[21] Portal and the Bolaños brothers directed the movement's first publication of doctrine and propaganda, a weekly magazine simply titled *APRA*, which debuted in October. The three wrote articles for almost every issue, and undoubtedly wrote many of the unattributed articles.

Portal felt free to write broadly about the most pressing political issues facing her party and Peru, including the current political situation, Aprista leaders and their history, imperialism's economic effects, APRA's doctrinal differences with Communism, key elements of Peru's social struggle, and the political situation in other Latin American countries. She even wrote partisan stories for children. As one of APRA's most prominent leaders, she addressed all key political and party debates, a task she relished. Even though she was careful to distance APRA from their Communist adversaries on the Left, Sánchez Cerro and their adversaries on the Right heard both parties talking the same language, asking the same dangerous questions, and posing essentially the same threat against Peru's traditional power structures.

The efforts of the Peruvian APRA section intensified after two other key leaders returned from exile, coincidentally on the same day, November 17, 1930: Carlos Manuel Cox (on a ship from Mexico) and Manuel Seoane (arriving overland from Buenos Aires). Their timing was unfortunate. By November's end, Sánchez Cerro moved to suppress all emerging opposition. APRA was added to the government's target list, which until then had centered more on supporters of the fallen Leguía, who himself languished, sick, in prison.

Between the founding of APRA's Peruvian section and the renewed government repression, the young Apristas had only sixty-six days of relative liberty in which to begin organizing.[22] After working just six days for the cause, Cox was thrown in jail on November 23. *APRA's* seventh issue appeared on November 27, after which the government shut it down. Seoane sought asylum in the Chilean Embassy and then left the country. As the noose tightened and the summer heat grew oppressive, Delmar worried that Portal, Petrovick, and he would have to join the other leaders in exile abroad.[23] With *APRA* closed, Portal turned to international journals such as *Repertorio Americano* to update continental allies about APRA.[24] As Petrovick recalled six months later, the half dozen key Apristas still free in Lima had to work doubly hard to maintain their organizing momentum: "We ourselves had to take to the street to distribute our pamphlets. We ourselves had to transport our propaganda papers to the provinces. We were the thought and the action."[25]

According to Sánchez, the repression was meant to "behead" the emerging Aprista movement, to pursue APRA's top leaders and not "the second-line leaders or the rank and file," and he specified that the government "did not touch" Portal or Delmar, thus implying that they were at best second-tier leaders.[26] Portal, Delmar, and Petrovick, however, were critically important leaders, especially since their magazine was the only vehicle for Aprista doctrine, publicity, and propaganda, and since Cox and Seoane were only able to work for the cause for days—literally. This subtle belittlement irked Portal, who emphasized later that "when we founded the Aprista Party in Peru, we founded it with a small group that grew as the exiles returned. Therefore I have had the privilege of always having been a member of the national executive committee. I have never been rank and file. I have been a leader since I was a founder. They could not belittle me [or demote me (*rebajar*)] in any way."[27]

Sánchez Cerro moved to establish himself as the leading contender for the 1931 presidential election, announcing that he would campaign while still holding executive power. The specter of Sánchez Cerro controlling the election from his perch at the Presidential Palace appalled Peru's elite, but the lieutenant colonel was adamant, reputedly claiming that he "would not step down from power even if I was asked to do so by my mother standing naked."[28] However, other powerful military sectors shared the elite's distaste for such a power grab. In January 1931, more military unrest erupted in Arequipa, this time against the "Hero of Arequipa" himself. By late February, Sánchez Cerro could no longer control the forces lining up against him, and on March 1 he resigned and headed off to Europe in self-imposed exile, planning to return soon to campaign for the presidency. With Sánchez Cerro's "Government of Six Months" over, a junta of leading military and civilian men took over as caretakers until Peru elected a new president later that year. The junta rolled back the repression against Apristas, who now had seven months to campaign for an election with the highest possible stakes, including congressional delegates who would also serve as members of a constitutional assembly to rewrite Peru's constitution, and the sweetest prize: the country's presidency.

These seven heady months were probably among the most exciting in Portal's life. They certainly were for Luis Alberto Sánchez, who characterized them as "perhaps the most intense" of his life in his memoirs almost forty years later. "We lived saturated with idealism. . . . Life appeared unreal."[29] Events happened so quickly now that they tripped over themselves. The young Apristas officially registered the Peruvian APRA section as a political party and established formal headquarters in a large, old-fashioned *casona* with three patios, where they organized meetings and held debates, assemblies, and lectures, some given by Portal.[30] On March 10, the weekly *APRA* reappeared, with Delmar as editor. Two months later, on May 16, with "100 soles of capital and a million hopes," Seoane and Sánchez founded *La Tribuna*, the Aprista daily newspaper, which faithfully chronicled the efforts of Portal and other leaders as they mobilized their party.[31]

Portal's official duties in the party's central executive committee included working with Petrovick in the all-important "Organizing Section," for which they displayed, according to a proud Delmar, a particular talent: "They turned out to be magnificent organizers."[32] This was why Portal organized so many traveling propaganda tours, during which Delmar stayed in Lima, fully devoted to publishing *APRA*. He never appears in the photos Portal kept documenting her campaign travels, although some show that her daughter occasionally joined her. These tours, Portal explained later, aimed to "get closer to the people and speak to them face-to-face, many times with translators in the native language and with the attitude of comradeship [*compañerismo*], not of ordering or command." Given the party's limited funds, they scraped these trips together: Portal would organize a committee, and these new Apristas would in turn gather the funds to pay for her passage for the next trip.[33] It was, after all, the height of the Great Depression, and no one had any money. Haya moaned that "the greatest enemy of Aprismo is our poverty." Sánchez and Seoane were "earning" about 50 cents a day for editing *La Tribuna*, which essentially paid only for their transportation around the city.[34] The party was so poor, in fact, that it would *charge* adherents to attend their rallies. That their forces nonetheless came out in the thousands was a source of great pride for Apristas, who challenged other parties to assemble similar numbers "without pay, without pisco, and without suborning promises."[35]

Ultimately, these exhausting months of travel and work must have been exciting and thrilling for Portal because now most of her exiled brothers were back and the party was sweeping in adherents at a dizzying pace. *La Tribuna* began with a circulation of five thousand and grew to ten thousand and then again to thirty-five thousand.[36] In June, Delmar excitedly reported to Betancourt that APRA now had twenty thousand registered party members in Lima alone, and 180 organizing committees and fourteen newspapers in the rest of the country.[37] "APRA," Portal wrote in early July, "is like an uncontainable wave that comes taking everything, rolling up everything, in spite of all the obstacles—the innumerable obstacles—that the reactionary opposition plants in its way."[38] Of course, it took work to make the party grow so precipitously, to turn their dream into a movement. The days and the nights spent in feverish activity until three or four in the morning passed in such a blur of exhausting activity that Portal tried amphetamines to fuel her past her body's physical limits.[39]

Apristas gathered in regional party congresses all over the country to "hammer out" a campaign platform.[40] In June, for about a month, around one hundred Apristas gathered at the Department of Lima's Regional Party Congress, where, in meeting after meeting, they tackled broad social questions like the "humiliating despotism" of the ruling classes toward poorer people or analyzed why "women submitted to the medieval concept of their physical and psychological inferiority."[41] Portal lobbied aggressively at this regional congress to demand radical social changes in their platform. Writing to *Repertorio Americano*, Portal described her "amazement" at how eagerly people responded to APRA's message. "I have never felt a more profound revolutionary emotion than during our Aprista Congress. . . . We have worked entire days, hours and hours, without fatigue showing in the eyes of these brave workers" whose "rough" yet "sincere" words sent "chills . . . down our spines."[42] For Apristas, these regional congresses proved their party was attentive to provincial concerns, inclusive, and democratic.

Portal and her party now demanded civil divorce among other expanded legal and civil rights for women. Women attending the June Lima APRA congress proposed an easily approved plan for expanded rights, including political rights like suffrage and the right to hold office, and civil rights like equality of rights in marriage, legal equality of illegitimate children, access to free education through the university level, social legislation to guarantee salary parity, protection for laboring children, and social and maternity security. Some of their demands were broader in scope, including fixed rent laws, subsidized government housing, and demands for the secularization of women's hospitals and prisons.[43] As the APRA's Women's Section's national leader, Portal shepherded the party's platform on women's rights at the congress and also addressed women's roles in the party in her doctrinal and propaganda writings.[44]

These months were also deeply fulfilling personally. She had made so many painful choices in the previous ten years to achieve precisely this outcome: her tumultuous personal relationships with her mother, husband, and lovers; turning her back on her society's notions of female decency; even discarding her own poetry for revolutionary politics. They were all elements she had chosen freely, if painfully, in the hopes of achieving something just like this moment. Somewhat ironically, one of Sánchez Cerro's decrees from his short-lived "Government of Six Months" officially established civil marriage and divorce and literally marked this transition. On May 19, 1931, a Limeñan judge granted Portal's request for a legal divorce from Federico Bolaños, accepting her claims that Bolaños had "abandoned their home more than five years ago," but ignoring how she herself had left their home with another man.[45] Portal took full advantage of a new right that Peru's deeply patriarchal society had long denied, and that many in this Catholic country abhorred, to tie up this loose end from her past, which suggests that this legality made a real-world difference to her. She did not, however, legally marry Delmar. Now, in 1931, professionally, politically, and personally, Magda Portal had reached her highest realization as a free being.

APRA, "the Uncontainable Wave"

The presidential campaign entered into its most intense period with the Peruvian winter. Sánchez Cerro returned to Peru on July 3, 1931, and Haya followed a few days later, arriving in Peru on July 12 after years of exile.[46] For the next month and a half, both men waged a brutal campaign. Sánchez Cerro ran on the Partido Unión Revolucionario (UR) ticket, a party hastily created by conservative backers and right-wing nationalists, who saw in him a way to regain power.[47] The UR moved quickly to try to make up for APRA's "ground game" advantage, given its head start of several months.

In a significant break with the political past, "the popular masses played a major role in national politics for the first time in Peruvian history" in this 1931 campaign, the country's first truly modern political campaign.[48] The Leguía regime had relentlessly attacked the country's established political parties. With older parties discredited and dispersed, emerging parties like the UR and APRA could realistically contest for the presidency. The October 1931 elections were also the first allowing expanded suffrage, with compulsory voting for all literate males aged twenty-one to sixty, and establishing a more transparent election infrastructure, including voter registration and the secret ballot.[49] This election was the first truly national one in Peru's history, with both candidates campaigning extensively in the provinces, which, as Portal remembered, had never happened before.[50]

Even if his party had been hastily erected for him, Sánchez Cerro proved a formidable candidate. The lieutenant colonel, well known in Peru as the "Hero of Arequipa" for overthrowing Leguía, inspired a fervent working-class following. In contrast, Haya had been exiled for years and could expect to be dimly remembered primarily for leading the charge against the consecration of the nation to the Sacred Heart of Jesus in 1923, a double-edged association that his opponents quickly used to label him as rabidly anti-Catholic. "An extraordinarily gifted orator," Sánchez Cerro presented himself quite successfully as "above all a straightforward man of action." His short five- to ten-minute speeches explicitly rejected complicated ideas: "You must not fill your speeches with phrases that might be very beautiful for the university but that the people do not understand," he once instructed his personal secretary.[51]

Like many closely contested political races, the campaign's heightened emotional environment generated on both sides an intense personal dislike of their opponents and ugly prejudices against each other's adherents. Soon, slurs escalated into coordinated campaigns of vicious propaganda, which in turn built swiftly into a climate ripe for violence. Aprista leaders were targeted, especially in the staunchly conservative and pro–Sánchez Cerro south: in June, Luis E. Heysen was "almost crucified" during a riot in Cuzco, and a few weeks later Carlos Manuel Cox would nearly be killed during a campaign stop in Arequipa.[52]

On both sides, the violence filtered down to the rank and file. Some acts seemed like pranks taken too far, as when a group broke into APRA headquarters to destroy a portrait of Haya. But there was more than childish violence lurking. Young militants went about mundane campaign chores carrying guns. Sánchez reported that in mid-August, a group of Sánchez Cerro supporters, "carefully intoxicated, armed, and paid," attacked two Aprista youths busy pasting party propaganda on a city wall, who, "brimming over with enthusiasm and courage," responded in kind. At least one person fell, wounded in the crossfire. The constant undercurrent of danger and the threat of physical violence and gunplay created its own excitement. "We had to go about with a pistol in our belt," Sánchez insisted. "Assaults and threats were commonplace."[53] In Lima, twenty Sánchez Cerro supporters were killed, often "gunned down from cars in Chicago gang-land style."[54] To try to control the violence, APRA formed a "Discipline Section" charged with safeguarding leaders and ensuring order and discipline among its own partisans during party functions.

Even as the two sides increasingly polarized the Peruvian population, their political programs did not seem insurmountably opposed. Even for key protagonists, after the hottest political passions of what would prove to be "sixteen tragic months" of near civil war cooled, their similarities seemed much more salient than their differences. "Luis Alberto, we were so wrong to misunderstand each other thirty-five years ago," lamented Carlos Sayán Álvarez, a spokesman for Sánchez Cerro in 1931 who twenty years later would lead the country's Supreme Court. "Nothing serious divided us; we could have reconciled almost all our discrepancies; we did not have to hate each other; we belonged to the same generation. Why were we so senseless and why did we cause our country so much harm?"[55]

Apristas, however, saw any similarity in the two party programs as a dangerous political fraud meant to confuse potentially well-meaning voters seeking transformative change. In the depths of the Great Depression, Apristas believed that the UR platform was designed to deceive poor voters into believing that Sánchez Cerro would carry out anticapitalist measures, addressing their immediate economic needs. Apristas looked at the UR's elite backers and scoffed at the idea that Sánchez Cerro would carry out these campaign promises; they feared that any economic half measures he might take would only stymie the social and economic revolution needed to deal with the country's inequalities. The UR declared that new lands should be opened so that every farmer could own his fields; Apristas wanted redistributed land expropriated from powerful landlords. The UR advocated state ownership of public utilities; Apristas insisted on nationalizing Peru's industries, including the all-important mining industry.[56]

The distance between the futures promised by these two parties was further magnified by the differences their followers perceived in their political personalities. Apristas saw themselves as more democratic and contrasted how their regional party congresses drafted the national party plan to how only a handful of right-wing elites dictated the UR's plan, flirting with a proto-Fascist right-wing nationalism.[57] Apristas believed their party and its young leaders represented the future, whereas the UR represented the political remnants of the old, corrupt oligarchy. Apristas saw their party as an "uncontainable wave," a generational party of youth that would long outlast their opponents and whose time to lead had only just arrived as their opponents' squandered time in power was finally receding. When a woman supporting Sánchez Cerro challenged Haya, he shot back: "That's fine, Señora," and pointing to the infant in her arms, continued, "but your child will be an Aprista. You defend the past, Señora, we defend your child's future. You cheer your candidate, but [your child] will be one of ours."[58]

Perhaps the most striking political difference between the UR and APRA, in both style and substance, was the degree to which APRA was "deeply concerned with" developing a complex, elaborate, and coherent political ideology, not just to differentiate themselves from other parties but also because they had larger ambitions to create a new, freestanding, American-born, non-Communist, leftist doctrine. This developing ideology did not just serve the party elite's intellectual needs. It also—perhaps surprisingly, given how often rank-and-file adherents admitted that such ideas confused them—comforted working-class party sympathizers. The very "beautiful university phrases" that Sánchez Cerro dismissed reinforced the rank and file's confidence in the elite leadership. The emerging Aprista ideology, presented by their leaders in public speeches and published both in periodicals like *APRA* and *La Tribuna* and in popular pamphlet editions available to the party faithful for just a few cents, "gave individual Apristas a sense of political identity" beyond individual candidates with which to adhere.[59]

During this campaign period, then, Portal found herself deeply immersed in the most important areas of APRA Party life: the domestic organization efforts needed to build the party and mobilize voters; the outreach to other Latin American leftist allies; and in her writings in *APRA* and other international journals, the shaping of the emerging ideology that her party saw as its most distinctive feature and that it believed would create a continental political doctrine. We can capture the scope and impact of her party work by following her through August and September of 1931, the campaign's last two months.

August began with the publication of Portal's letter to *Repertorio Americano* on the success of the Lima regional party congress in late June.[60] Other good news arrived from the north, where a group of women in Chancay, where Portal had organized an Aprista section three months earlier, had organized a "Conversatorio Magda Portal" in her honor to "spread Aprista culture in the working masses."[61] Portal had little time to bask in these successes, however, as she was fully immersed in the party's first national congress in Lima, where Julián Petrovick reported on APRA's national organizing efforts. He pointed the audience to *APRA*'s latest issue, where they could consult the Organizing Section's proposals for party organization, helpfully clarified by a complicated flowchart. As a member of that section and Petrovick's close collaborator, Portal must have been involved in imagining the contours of this future party structure. Petro-vick also announced that they had organizing committees in every Peruvian department, in 80 percent of the provinces, and in 30 percent of the districts, for a total of five hundred committees and fifty thousand inscribed party members, including two thousand women, a "revealing detail of the realism and greatness of our professed ideals, because when the women, traditionally prejudiced and reactionary, affiliate with a party, it is because that party's doctrine has penetrated profoundly in the national soul."[62] Given the constraints on women's political participation, including their lack of suffrage, it is not surprising that 96 percent of APRA's members were men. When Portal surveyed these new women members, she focused not on their numbers but instead on what their Aprista affiliation said about their character and desire to make a difference; these were women "who aspire to be a compañera at the side of men and not a toy of pleasure."[63]

However, this national party congress, which was charged with crafting APRA's Minimum Program, a plan addressing Peruvian national problems meant to serve as the party's campaign platform, would not match the unqualified success of the earlier regional Lima Department gathering. Portal and Delmar had been working on parts of the Minimum Program for months; Delmar had sent a draft to Betancourt six months earlier, in December 1930.[64] Portal remembered the national party congress as "daring" because it advocated social reforms, including women's civil rights, that had "never before been a part of a political party." But while the congress drafted a revolutionary program, Haya balked at it. It was too radical. "Consequently," Portal finished, "we had to regain our reason, and leave the great ideas and their possible actions for the future. Those of us who were there, those of us who had written" the Minimum Program, "were disappointed, but we were not the majority."[65] This was Portal's first substantial defeat in the party. At this critical juncture, every decision was now being reevaluated with an eye toward electoral victory.

Yet even if Portal felt that the national party congress and the APRA Minimum Program did not fully live up to her revolutionary expectations, like all Apristas, she must have been immensely proud of the process itself. This national congress, and the many smaller regional ones that flowed into it, incarnated the Apristas' vision of themselves as Peru's first modern and national political party. Haya would later write: "For the first time in our political history . . . a presidential candidate of a party receives, and does not give, a program"; Aprista leaders were "only the political inter-preters of a technical program and the spokesmen of the people strictly controlled by the masses of the party they represent."[66]

With Haya arriving to campaign in Lima on August 15, there was little time to brood over opportunities missed at the national congress. Portal published two pieces in *APRA* as part of the presidential campaign: a ret-rospective on Sánchez Cerro's coup a year earlier that attacked his qualifi-cations, and a piece lauding Haya's entrance as the start of a new era in the country's politics.[67] The Women's Section that she led also organized a large rally to greet Haya upon his arrival to Lima where Portal was the first to speak.[68]

As August turned into September, Portal was given more responsibili-ties as the PAP's secretary of Exterior Affairs, which charged her with dis-seminating this emerging political doctrine to leftist allies throughout Latin America, a critical responsibility given APRA's continentalist ambi-tions. She began publishing a column in *APRA* titled "Panorama de América," in which she reviewed regional current events and politics.[69] Portal also found time to keep up with her own reading; *APRA* began running a book review section, which on September 8 featured an un-signed review of the famous Russian revolutionary and feminist leader Alexandra Kollontai's *The New Woman and Sexual Morality*.[70]

As the party added thousands of new members, it became increasingly important to find ways to welcome, socialize, and integrate them into their new "Aprista family." The same September 8 issue of *APRA* featured a new series introducing the growing rank-and-file membership to their leader-ship. "Reporting on Our Leaders" was a written questionnaire answered by top party leaders that ran regularly for a year and a half, eventually re-porting on thirteen leaders. Each "report" was accompanied by a sketched portrait (a photograph, in the last installment), literally allowing new ad-herents to put a face to a name. On September 23, 1931, Portal became the third leader profiled, after only Carlos Manuel Cox, the party's general sec-retary, and Manuel Seoane, Haya's second-in-command.[71] On the page opposite Portal's profile, readers found rave reviews of her recently pub-lished pamphlet of political analysis, "The Aprista Party on the Current Moment," which summarized a lecture that she had given at the party headquarters.[72]

In mid-September, *La Tribuna* reported on the "magnificent reception" hosted by an Aprista women's organizing committee in Lima in Portal's honor. "Deeply touched" by "the strenuous and prolonged" cheering of the welcoming crowd, Portal accepted a bouquet of flowers from two little girls, one dressed in the colors of the Peruvian flag and the other in red, the color of APRA's banner. Portal's "beautiful improvised speech" focused on her pleasure at seeing the growing ranks of women joining the party, literally performed at this rally in these two young girls who embodied the Aprista future, representing both the Peruvian youth constituting the party's uncontainable wave and the young girls who would grow into future Magda Portals. This meeting also doubled as an election rally, with four other male leaders, including Seoane, highlighting Portal's achievements and making the party's pitch for the upcoming elections. To conclude, they sang the national and party anthems and excitedly cheered for the party, the Aprista woman, and Haya.[73]

Portal was also called upon to whip up Aprista enthusiasm at one of the party's largest collective functions yet, an August 23, 1931, rally to formally present its recently ratified Minimum Program. Something between thirty and forty thousand people crowded into Lima's Plaza de Acho, a giant venue that had been the capital's principal bullring. The party leadership was thrilled with the large crowds, given the short notice and the modest admission fee. Filling the Plaza de Acho was the physical manifestation of how their dream had now become an unstoppable movement. "When the Aprista Party began its political labors in Peru . . . our members fit perfectly and comfortably in any normal room," they marveled. "We told ourselves, some smiling, some hyperbolically, that very soon we would need the Plaza de Toros for our rallies." Now only that Plaza de Acho could fit "the thousands and thousands of citizens who would come to hear the words of our leaders."[74] Portal was the third of five leaders they had crowded to hear, and they roared their approval of her speech on the role of women in the party with "great shows of enthusiasm." After her, the poet Alberto Hidalgo read a short poem, and then Haya swept in for the main event, a three-hour speech detailing APRA's Minimum Program.

The Minimum Program Haya presented cemented the two foundational pillars APRA would campaign on for the next forty years: an economic vision organized around Peru's role in a global economy and creating an active technocratic state that would intervene to ensure rapid economic and social change.[75] Nonetheless, careful listeners among the delirious crowd heard Haya subtly but unmistakably moderating their stridency, assuaging their suspicious opponents. They were anti-imperialists, of course, but "we are not enemies of foreign capital." Apristas would be willing to work with everybody: "We open our arms to all those who want to discuss our ideas." In fact, the U.S. ambassador believed the United States had "little to fear" in an Aprista victory, which might bring in "an excellent and beneficient [*sic*] administration of strongly liberal tendencies."[76]

Is there any way to capture how Magda Portal must have felt that night? How euphoric, intoxicated, self-realized, literally incredulous? The party was perfecting the staging of a captivating rally, adroitly orchestrating symbolism, ritual, and stagecraft into a collective experience meant to move adherents, but that staging must have been even more potent for the leaders, who watched it all happen from above the fray, as if by magic and at their command. Their rallies began with young party activists marching into the arena with the party flag, a gold circular "Indo-America" on a red background. The crowd sang the party anthem, the "Aprista Marseillaise," and other party songs, and then tens of thousands burst into rhythmic clapping: three rapid bursts, pause, repeat. The clapping continued, joined by the honking of horns from nearby cars: Clap, clap, clap; pause. Clap, clap, clap. This triplet rhythm accompanied thousands of voices chanting: SEA-SAP; SEA-SAP, the acronym for "*Sólo el aprismo salvará al Perú*" (Only Aprismo will save Peru).[77]

The Aprista press reported that the "classic APRA sign" of waving their handkerchiefs was not enough for the crowd to express their collective identity. "Without another way of exteriorizing their joy, the Apristas invented another greeting of profound significance: waving their voter registrations in the air to show that every conscientious citizen was registered and had his identity card ready for the moment when he could give his vote that no one could then deny."[78] How must Portal have felt seeing that ocean of voter registrations waving at her? She could not vote; and even if she was speaking to these tens of thousands of men about women, this spontaneous "show of joy" reinforced that she was not speaking to women. She was literally one in thirty thousand, and this ocean of men had gathered to hear her, to applaud her—in essence, to follow her as a leader in this new political movement that less than two years earlier had been the dream of only a handful.

"Sixteen Tragic Months"

The election on Sunday, October 11, 1931, ran smoothly, with few problems and none of the violence that characterized the last weeks of campaigning. The initial unofficial tally gave Haya the lead, validating Aprista dreams of electoral triumph. But this initial joy disintegrated into disbelief eight days after the election, as the results showed Sánchez Cerro overtaking the Aprista leader.[79] As Haya appeared to lose key balloting locations in Lima, Aprista disbelief quickly turned to suspicion and anger. After all, just three days before the election, APRA had designed their final campaign event to showcase their electoral strength. Lifting their voter registrations high in the air, Aprista partisans had marched through Lima's streets in groups of ten, every hundredth group carrying a sign to mark the thousand Aprista votes that had just marched by.[80] The party had counted thirty-four thousand Limeñan votes for Haya that day, and now they were being asked to believe that their candidate had only garnered twenty-seven thousand votes. This election was starting to appear to them as just another rigged contest, no different from every other election in which money, power, and brute force had determined the winner. Their suspicions were heightened as Sánchez Cerro began openly implying that he would take power by force of arms if his "rightful" victory were denied.[81]

When the final results were announced almost two months after election day, they reported that Haya had lost the presidency, winning 36 percent of the vote. Yet even if they had lost the presidency, by electing 16 percent of the representation to the next Congress (23 of the 145 delegates), APRA had achieved a surprising influence on Peru's national politics in a very short time, which was "no small achievement." Haya had arrived in Peru just months before the election as "a relative unknown [who] could not hope to match the fame and popularity of his opponent. . . . Indeed, the humblest shepherd had probably heard of the exploits of the macho mestizo lieutenant colonel who had brought down the once powerful Leguía."[82] APRA fell short in part because it faced a fundamental demographic disadvantage: the groups with which the party's appeal was strongest were not as large as those more inclined toward Sánchez Cerro. Even though some Aprista scholarship maintains to this day that the election was fraudulent, the consensus after almost eighty years of scrutiny is that Sánchez Cerro won with 152,062 votes to Haya's 106,007 in a clean election.[83] The 1931 election laid out the pattern for the next thirty years: APRA would win around a third of the vote, sweeping the north and showing strength in coastal areas, but never really convincing the majority indigenous south.[84]

Apristas sincerely believed that they had been cheated out of a historic victory. They had seen just how rapidly their growing numbers and huge rallies had sprung into being, as if by the force of their will alone. They were awash with a euphoric sense of their own agency as they witnessed what they believed to be their remaking of their political world. Combined with the country's history of fraudulent elections and Apristas' certainty that Sánchez Cerro would stop at nothing to recapture the presidency, fraud was the only explanation that made any sense, and party leaders forced a review of the election results.

Some leaders undoubtedly recognized the tactical advantages of publicly denouncing the election's honesty, allowing them to continue asserting "the party's manufactured aura of invincibility" and that it spoke for the majority of Peruvians. It could also create just enough uncertainty about Sánchez Cerro's victory to justify overthrowing the "illegitimate" government.[85] But for the most committed partisans on the ground who had dedicated the past year to building their party and channeling its explosive growth, such cynical calculations no doubt paled before a powerful sense of having been wronged and a growing rage against the "tyrant" who had engineered their loss.

Menacing threats of political violence intensified in Lima. Party militants were attacked. In the early-morning hours of November 25, a vehicle sped away into the night after shooting and wounding Seoane, on his way to the offices of *La Tribuna* after catching a late movie. In retaliation, armed Apristas attacked a group of Sánchezcerristas, leaving several dead.[86] Aprista leaders like Portal were certain Sánchez Cerro was orchestrating the violence. "As opposed to Aprismo, which never uttered a single threat against" its opponents, Portal wrote several months after the election, Sánchez Cerro "ordered the persecution of Apristas, thus fulfilling his promise, made in all of his political speeches, of exterminating the Party of the People."[87] Other leaders agreed: Luis Alberto Sánchez attended one of Sánchez Cerro's campaign rallies and left believing APRA's opponent promised a "civil war" against the Apristas should he win the presidency. "This is not a normal struggle," Haya diagnosed. "We are facing a social war, and the loser will be brought up against the wall."[88] Extermination, civil war, summary execution: facing what they believed to be such an existential threat from Sánchez Cerro, who they feared aimed at nothing less than a total liquidation of their party, some Aprista leaders started approaching sympathetic army officers to plan a military coup.[89]

Publicly, APRA challenged the incoming Sánchez Cerro government with "uncompromising opposition at every turn." They moved to block the inauguration itself, scheduled for December 8. A week before the planned ceremony, a band of Apristas cut electricity to Lima, hoping to provide cover for a military uprising. Miscommunication allowed government troops to easily suppress this and other small uprisings throughout Peru. Having failed in their first insurrectionary attempts against the government, Apristas were left with little but the symbolic refusal to attend the inauguration.[90]

That same day, just hours after his bitter opponent was triumphantly inaugurated as president of Peru, Haya spoke at the APRA Party headquarters in Trujillo, the northern city of his birth where the party enjoyed its most fervent support. He spoke extemporaneously, without notes, and for perhaps ten minutes, but it was one of the most important speeches he was to ever deliver. Haya had no plans to deliver a traditional concession speech. Instead, this "Sermon on the Mount" became a counterinauguration assuring Apristas that they were "not lost" and setting forth as a central party tenet a refusal to recognize Sánchez Cerro's government as lawful. Sánchez Cerro might now have the brute power to command, Haya charged, but not the legitimacy to govern, which remained with APRA. "I affirm that we are stronger than ever," Haya thundered, "because to govern is not to command, to abuse, to turn power into a stage for all the inferior passions, into an instrument of vengeance, into a gallows for liberties. To govern is to guide, to educate, to provide an example, to redeem. . . . They might command, but we will continue to govern."[91]

Haya counseled Aprista militants to "wait" for their chance at power. After all, he intoned, Aprismo was "like a religion of justice" and "a perennial and tenacious battle." Ultimately, the "Sermon on the Mount" was not a call to man the barricades so much as a dark prophecy of a wave of government repression that would crash over APRA, whose partisans would be called to embrace martyrdom. The hours ahead would be punishing.

"More Aprista blood will run, our martyrology will add to its immortal list, terror will begin its opprobrious task once again, but Aprismo will sink deeper each time into the consciousness of the people," he pledged. The upcoming trials would allow Apristas, both leaders and rank and file, to prove "our faith, our energy, our revolutionary spirit, our unfainting decision as builders of the New Peru." Scholars have even characterized the "Sermon on the Mount" as a "prophecy of immolation."[92]

But it was more than a dark promise. Haya's speech came to be known as the "Sermon on the Mount" because, just as its biblical namesake established Jesus's criteria for what a good Christian should be, it starkly laid out the duties now facing Apristas, detailing not just what they should do but even how they should feel during the coming trials ahead. "Whoever in this worrisome hour of immediate somber expectations for us feels intimidated or short of strength is not an Aprista. We do not want in the party Apristas who doubt their cause or doubt themselves in the moments of danger. We do not want cowards. We do not want traitors. And to be a traitor in this hour is not only to be the Judas who sells us out, but also the coward who takes a step back."[93]

The "Sermon on the Mount" began building an almost religious attachment to the party in its most fervent militants. Haya transformed his ultimate aims: denied formal political power, APRA would rely even more on its vision of itself as more than a political party and as a larger crusade, a moralizing force by which "our discipline, our organization, our unity, our absolute personal disinterest" become means to educate Peru's people, politics, and society; an education "absolutely necessary in a people like ours who have always lacked the healthy example of eminent leaders," Haya wrote a few months later. "We consider the moralizing of the country as important as the task of its material reorganization."[94] The "Sermon on the Mount" was APRA's clarion call to the struggle ahead, which would prove to be sixteen years of active Aprista military conspiracies against multiple Peruvian governments.[95]

For his part, Sánchez Cerro, the man of action, was not going to sit idly by while Aprista elements conspired to overthrow his regime. He purged the military, especially the Navy and the Civil Guard, where APRA had the most success, and prepared an anti-Aprista patriotic study guide for soldiers.[96] On Christmas Eve, 1931, police attacked the Trujillo APRA Party headquarters, wounding several party members gathered to enjoy a "fraternal Christmas hot chocolate," in what Portal and other Apristas charged was an assassination attempt on Haya.[97] Sánchez Cerro forced emergency powers through Congress that gave him more leeway in pursuing his opposition, and by early January 1932, he had established "virtual martial law." As the repression against him and his party intensified, Haya secretly escaped from Trujillo to Lima, where he tried to gather allies. He called on the U.S. embassy, and over tea with the ambassador and his wife, persuaded the diplomat that he was no Communist. In fact, the ambassador mused, it seemed to him that Haya wanted to build a purely Fascist party. Haya explained away aggressions against Sánchez Cerro as little plots resulting from a split in Aprista leadership that he had resolved by expanding the party's executive committee to dilute this radical revolutionary wing. What Haya wanted, the ambassador reported, was for APRA to be a loyal opposition in the British mold.[98] Haya had in fact called a meeting where the entire Comité Ejecutivo Nacional (CEN; National Executive Committee) leadership resigned and passed into a less-visible second line of command, leaving a "provisional" new leadership committee made up entirely of workers.[99] While expanding the highest leadership may have diluted the strength of the most strident voices, it also protected the party's original founders and intellectual leadership.

Sánchez Cerro continued targeting all party institutions and leaders, closed both the popular universities, and, on February 15, *La Tribuna*, which began publishing a daily clandestine edition the very next day.[100] To inculcate patriotism and fight the perceived internationalist Aprista threat, the government required public schools to use Peru's national emblem and to sing the national anthem. The archbishop required churches and private religious institutions to fly the national flag on holidays as a sign of patriotism and an attack on APRA.[101] Most spectacularly, at around 2:00 A.M. on February 18, police forces stormed the Congress and arrested fifteen APRA congressmen, including Luis Alberto Sánchez, who was pounding away on a denunciation of the attack on his typewriter up until the second when the police dragged him away.[102] APRA's entire congressional delegation was exiled, with the majority sent to Panama.

Portal and Delmar found themselves entangled with the Sánchez Cerro government when it moved against the magazine that Delmar edited, *APRA*. Cited for printing articles prohibited by the emergency law, the periodical was fined 200 soles by the government. Delmar chose to go to prison instead of having the party pay the fine, and he asked the members who had begun a collection for him to donate the funds to the party instead to help the families of those wounded in the December attacks in Trujillo.[103] During Delmar's twenty days in jail, Portal acted as *APRA's* editor, loudly denouncing the repression against the periodical and Delmar. By March, Haya himself was driven underground.[104]

On Sunday, March 6, as Sánchez Cerro left Mass at the Miraflores Cathedral, a well-dressed nineteen-year-old man walked up and shot him, gravely wounding him. The president was rushed to the hospital in critical condition, as he had been shot perilously close to his heart and his hemorrhaging wound could not be staunched.[105] Police hauled the young would-be assassin, José Melgar, who had survived a shot to the head, into custody. Based on Melgar's information, police charged Juan Seoane with giving Melgar the pistol he had used. Juan Seoane was a respected Limeñan judge, who also happened to be both Melgar's cousin and the brother of Manuel Seoane, the currently exiled Aprista congressman, founder of *La Tribuna*, and Haya's most trusted first lieutenant. The police arrested Delmar again, on charges of having previous knowledge of the attack and not informing the authorities.[106]

Melgar claimed that he had told Delmar about his planned "tyrannicide" fifteen days before, but that Delmar had not believed him. During another interrogation, however, Melgar changed his story, claiming Delmar had both known about and agreed to the plan. He had declared his plans to Delmar, Seoane, and Magda Portal in Delmar's home. Only Delmar and Juan Seoane knew who would form the next Aprista government, Melgar believed. Even though he was a civilian, Delmar was rushed through a court martial a few days later. Delmar testified that Melgar had come to his house on February 5, declaring that "somebody" had to kill the president. Suspecting that Melgar meant himself, Delmar told the young man that any such "somebody," should they be a member of the APRA Party, should renounce their political affiliation before acting. Delmar's testimony was not a viable defense, since it confirmed the charges against him that he had failed to inform the authorities about a suspected threat against the president. In essence, Delmar stood at his court-martial and flatly admitted his role in this conspiracy, acknowledging his steadfast revolutionary convictions.

Other Aprista leaders decried Melgar's attack as a lamentable individual action. Writing from exile in Colombia, Manuel Seoane characterized Melgar as "the young fanatic, illuminated, generous but in error," and insisted that "our party repudiates the personal attack as a political method. . . . Spilled blood is not enough to provoke an authentic transformation."[107] In an address written from hiding to the Peruvian nation a few weeks after the assassination attempt, as the full force of the Sánchez Cerro government crashed over them, Haya distanced himself and the party from Melgar's actions, assuring Peruvians that APRA was a revolutionary force—but "not in the catastrophic sense of a coup from the barracks, a riot, or anarchy"—that believed it was "possible to be a revolutionary and make a revolution without recurring to violence."[108]

In contrast, Delmar and Portal defended Melgar's attack, refusing to repudiate or even sugarcoat what they felt was an ugly reality of revolution: that "tyrants" do not willingly step down and that revolutions often—if not always—depended on violence. Writing three months later in *Repertorio Americano*, Portal embraced the Miraflores attack as "that admirable gesture that any dispassionate observer of our history could characterize as an explosion of Peruvian consciousness."[109] Melgar was a "young Aprista whose pain from being persecuted filled him with a holy hate," and who could "justify his gesture before history as the desperate and proud protest of a generation that [the government] intended to baselessly destroy." Later in life, Portal revealed that, sitting with her, Delmar, and Juan Seoane around her kitchen table, Melgar had told them that a "tyrannicide" against Sánchez Cerro was necessary.[110] When asked by a newspaper fifty years after that fateful March if this assassination attempt meant that in its beginnings, APRA had challenged the oligarchy with anarchist methods, Portal replied curtly: The attack "means that violence was the sign of the times. . . . The youths who attempted [assassinations] against the representatives of the dominant sectors assumed responsibility for their acts without mentioning the party. That was a heroic gesture proper to the difficult moments that were lived."[111]

Given Portal's and Delmar's precarious position as highly visible party leaders still in Lima, their choice not to distance themselves from Melgar seems misguided and naïve, prizing revolutionary consistency over the potential tactical advantages of distancing themselves from the attempted assassination. Portal and Delmar were now living the drama of revolutionary "tyrannicide" that they had deliriously outlined six years earlier in *El derecho de matar*. Now they were no longer protagonists; Melgar cast himself as the "hero" in the real-life version of the "Red Paths" short story, a young man ready to lead the way to a revolutionary future and to drench the path with blood, both the tyrant's and his own, if necessary—the two meanings suggested by the title. With the rest of the highest leadership exiled or forced into hiding, any young "hero" looking to strike against the growing repression could turn only to Delmar and Portal. When Melgar did so, he found leaders who did not counsel that such an assassination was "barbarous and useless," as did Seoane, or that revolution could eschew violence, as did Haya. Instead, Melgar found two leaders who adhered to the highest standard that Haya had called them to two months earlier in his "Sermon on the Mount." No matter the personal cost, when presented with an opportunity to strike against their enemy, Delmar and Portal would not be "the cowards who take a step back."

The personal costs were very high. There was little glory in the real-life version of "Red Paths." The assassination had failed, the "tyrant" lived on, and his government grew stronger and more repressive. APRA was declared illegal; its publications were shuttered; its leaders exiled, jailed, or driven underground; and rich bounties were offered for their heads.[112] This very nearly successful assassination attempt further intensified the authorities' repression and their desire to completely destroy APRA. Arresting Delmar and Juan Seoane was the government's attempt to ensure that the two most prominent periodicals in the Aprista propaganda infrastructure never reemerged.[113] Melgar and Seoane were sentenced to death, but their sentence was commuted to life in prison two months later. For his part, Serafín Delmar, in prison since March 6, 1932, was sentenced to remain there for another twenty years.

Forced into hiding, Portal was the only one of her family—both her immediate domestic and revolutionary ones—to escape prison. Julián Petrovick soon joined his brother Delmar in the political prisoners section in Lima's primary prison, and Petrovick's compañera and their daughter were taken to the Santo Tomás Women's Prison. Portal was able to write to Delmar at least once during this period, describing how "the noose was tightening and that people were afraid." For his putatively free compañera, Delmar noted sadly, all of Lima and Peru were "just one great prison."[114]

Portal would spend the next year living underground, "one of the police's most wanted prey," remembered Manuel Seoane.[115] When she recounted these years later, Portal made no mention of Delmar's fate or of their role in the Miraflores attack. "Each time the party decided to undertake one of its attempts [*intentonas*] at revolution, we would fall again into illegality. I remember that when Sánchez Cerro came to power the violence intensified," she stated. "It was a barbarous persecution. . . . He said 'those Communists—because for him the whole world was Communist—I'm going to squash them like cockroaches.'"[116]

APRA had not had the time or resources to develop the infrastructure necessary for such a period of repression. "We lived from one day to the next," Portal recalled. In one particularly memorable incident when a potential safe house fell through, disguised in a Salvation Army uniform, she was forced to huddle for the night in a pond on the outskirts of Miraflores, separated only by some thin wire from a ring of angry dogs "barking like crazy." Her compañeros retrieved her and tried to hide her in their own neighborhood, but "a good snitch" warned them by saying, "'I won't ask you who has arrived, but you get her out of here before six this morning; if not, I have to turn you in.'" With their second hideout compromised, Portal turned to a "half-rich aunt" who lived nearby, where Portal was accepted, even though she arrived while her aunt's birthday party was in full swing. Portal hid there for three months. Even if APRA's infrastructure for this clandestine period was rudimentary, the fact that Portal remained hidden for three months with a relative suggests that Sánchez Cerro's dragnet was also not that sophisticated. Manuel Seoane remembered how, during one of her escapes, Portal was wounded when the car she was fleeing in crashed: "In the middle of the confusion and the pain, she represses her physical impairment and without losing her serenity, takes another car to escape the police."[117]

Her exciting escape stories, however, never mention the fate of her own mother or her eight-year-old daughter, facing a future with a father in prison and a mother in hiding. When her daughter was forced underground, Doña Rosa had to "change houses, sometimes every fifteen days, to escape the police, because they would come and they would take everything from her, they robbed the books, the letters. That's how I lost all of my correspondence," Portal lamented.[118] We don't know if Gloria was ever with Portal during this year or who looked after the child. Portal smuggled at least one letter to Delmar reporting that Gloria was in hiding and being pursued by the police.[119] There were allegations that the police tried to pressure the eight-year-old girl to reveal her mother's where-abouts. Exiled in Panama, Luis Alberto Sánchez reported receiving news that Portal was in hiding, "and that in reprisal, they captured Gloria and they tortured her in such a manner that the little one has suffered a broken arm."[120] A few weeks later, Portal's sisters and mother, in whose house APRA hid the secret party printing press, were thrown in prison for six months, in another attempt to flush out Portal.[121]

During her year in the Aprista underground, Portal wrote poetry, some-thing that the last few years of furious political activity had made impos-sible, and continued as the party's secretary of the Exterior, refuting opponents and thanking allies for their solidarity in the regional press.[122] Among APRA's regional allies, few rallied harder in support of the belea-guered APRA than Rómulo Betancourt. During Peru's 1931 presidential contest, he wrote tirelessly in support of Haya, both in public venues and in private correspondence with his own growing regional network of dis-sident youth. As suspicions of "rightist deviations" made Haya a more po-larizing figure among the continent's Left, Betancourt continued to defend Haya's personal and anti-imperialist credentials, although he confessed to his closest confidants that his solidarity had little to do with Aprista ideol-ogy, which he himself didn't really understand.[123]

Betancourt's close group of Venezuelan comrades, exiled in Colombia, were concerned that Betancourt would follow a similar rightist turn, and they pressured him to distance himself from APRA. Colombia also shel-tered Manuel Seoane, and the younger Venezuelans did not like what they heard from him. Slowly, Betancourt also came to believe that centrist po-sitions that he had assumed were tactical actually revealed APRA's funda-mental principles. His Venezuelan comrades "sent me documents: reports of Manuel Seoane, verbal declarations of what he had told them. . . . Faced with this pile of testimonies, and even more so, faced with the open atti-tude of reproval of my compañeros," Betancourt explained, "my discipline left me no choice but to adopt an attitude of reserve with Aprismo."[124] In May 1932, finally convinced that he could no longer support it, Betancourt "closed his Aprista chapter."

It was more than Seoane of course. APRA had first been imagined as a continental anti-imperialist political movement, but it was now in all but name fully subsumed within Peruvian national politics. There was no time, energy, money, or people to keep the international torch burning. When Betancourt returned to Costa Rica, he found the APRA chapter there "dead," and he instead joined the Communist Party, which had also founded a popular university and focused on anti-imperialism, Betancourt's two most important political concerns.[125] But Haya continued insisting on APRA's internationalist reach and exaggerated Aprista influence on other Latin American leftist movements. Haya publicly claimed that Betancourt had told him that the 1929 Falke expedition, an ill-planned, easily defeated military invasion against the Venezuelan president Juan Vicente Gómez that landed hundreds of Venezuelan students in prison, was an Aprista undertaking. "Haya's lies" infuriated Betancourt, who was "steaming" at his misappropriation of Venezuelan efforts and the unflattering light in which the claim cast Betancourt.

To his worried Venezuelan comrades, Betancourt explained that his attachment to APRA was really his personal attachment to Portal and Delmar. "I allowed myself to be guided by my love for Magda and Serafín, in whose honesty I believe."[126] Ironically, Betancourt had to distance himself from Portal and Delmar because he had learned their lesson too well: professional revolutionaries cannot afford to have personal feelings interfering with discipline. Betancourt tried to maintain a warm personal relationship, writing to them as his "dear siblings" and offering what help he could at this terrible hour with Delmar in prison and Portal in hiding.[127] But even their friendship was not enough to keep Betancourt from closing his Aprista chapter at the insistence of his comrades who rallied so strongly against "those terrible Aprista boys."[128]

Portal's year underground must have entailed fear and terrible loneliness. Her revolutionary life that just a year earlier had allowed her to feel for the first time fully realized as a human being had transformed into a painful test of her revolutionary convictions. With her party comrades in prison, in exile, or also forced into hiding, they had all entered the period of trial that Haya had promised them was coming in the "Sermon on the Mount." Without her daughter and her compañero, without her mother and her sisters, her family life was shattered. Delmar's imprisonment, in particular, must have anguished Portal. Delmar was one of the few political prisoners who could expect never to be visited, since everyone he loved was either already in jail or in hiding. His fellow prisoner Juan Seoane recalled the heartbreaking occasion when Delmar passed him a simple wristwatch, hoping Seoane could find a way to give it to Portal. "It was a poor wristwatch that will go now like a last caress of the poet lover, like a last embrace of the revolutionary compañero."[129]

While they could not comfort each other in person, left with only simple personal possessions to caress, they could turn to their poetry. Delmar's poems from this time still burned with revolutionary fervor. In one, dated February 1933 and titled simply "Haya de la Torre," he detailed the sacrifices necessary for the painful birth of the revolution he still devotedly awaited and wholeheartedly expected. "The Man arrived, / and with him the victory of the people—/ founded / oh, upon so many painful defeats! / We all love him / because he is just and humane. / His life is the life of all, / and in his teachings / is the collective love / that uplifts the Nation. / His voice guides us / to the struggle for the land / and to the song that will redeem us. / . . . / The dead do not return—/ But when they fall for social justice / they are made perennial in the soul of the people. / The jails are other tombs of pain, / but the truth cannot be assassinated, / she arrives like a dawn / in the arms of the Man."[130]

Delmar's poem vividly showcased the larger-than-life messianic role that Haya was assuming for Aprista partisans. Haya is the Christ figure who, with his enlightened teachings and advanced personality, will literally bring the new revolutionary tomorrow in his arms. The poem recognizes, however, that this "victory of the people," while inevitable, can only come after much sacrifice. It is "founded / oh! upon so many painful defeats!," catalyzed by the blood of the Aprista martyrs who trade their physical presence among the living for a more enduring and more meaningful existence "in the soul of the people." For Delmar, this revolutionary creed is a truth no violence can destroy; contrary to Sánchezcerrismo, the Aprista truth "cannot be assassinated."

In "The Lima Penitentiary," a poem dated November 1932, Portal explored similar themes of revolution and sacrifice, although she focused more on her private sadness and loneliness: "and you—compañero Aprista—/ walled in a cell / I think about your solitude: the creaking of the closing bars, / commanding voices—taciturn faces filled with hate, / and silence, silence . . . / We are the galley slaves of this new crusade, / generation condemned to bear on its shoulders / this culminating stage of History / I think about your cold and narrow cell / with a double coldness:

a physical cold and that of my absence—/ compañero Aprista—/ peace was not made for us / who, moreover, are poets. / And our youth / like a tree laden with fruit? / Let's toast it to the Revolution / whose dawn already illuminates the landscapes of America."[131]

Portal's evocative, almost wistful images, casting them both as "galley slaves" of the revolution, painfully spelled out the price she felt they were paying as the shock troops of the Aprista revolution. This was the less glamorous side of becoming a woman revolutionary and a revolutionary woman. The final positive image of a successful revolution dawning over Latin America echoes Delmar's imagery and makes this poem still, in essence, revolutionary. While not a triumphant anthem, it reaffirmed Portal's acceptance of the personal sacrifices needed to bring the Aprista tomorrow. "I belong to a party that does not know how to plead for clemency, but that instead accepts its responsibility with serenity," wrote Manuel Seoane, confronting a sacrifice of his own as he informed the Peruvian government that he was willing to return from exile and stand in for his brother if Juan's death sentence for his role in the Miraflores assassination attempt was not commuted.[132] Like her Aprista brothers, Magda Portal understood that the burden of their redemptive sacrifice and martyrdom was required in the struggle for the "New Peru," as promised by Haya in APRA's "Sermon on the Mount." Their pain was their badge. She was the woman who had chosen to pick up the gun. She would not shrink from its responsibilities; she would bear its consequences.

CHAPTER SIX

Dream of a New Woman

E ARLY ON A WINTER morning in July 1932, just months after the attempted assassination on Sánchez Cerro, residents of the northern city of Trujillo spilled into the streets celebrating. Crowds gathered at the city's symbolic center, the Plaza de Armas, where a band playing APRA songs caroused around the square, as photographers took pictures of the young men with rifles at the center of the commotion, commissioned by the young fighters to commemorate this day and its unexpected military victory. In the early morning hours, a group of Aprista militants had surprised the military barracks on the edge of town and wrested control of its installations and arms cache. Trujillo, the birthplace of Haya and the beating heart of Aprista support in Peru, was celebrating the anxiously awaited eruption of the Aprista revolution, bringing with it the promise of a new Aprista tomorrow and an end to the tyranny of Sánchez Cerro.[1]

An unusual humming sound was the only warning the spontaneous party had that something was wrong. Suddenly, airplanes flew over the city center, dropping bombs on the unsuspecting crowd. The first bomb exploded in the Plaza de Armas itself, spewing a screaming panic amid overturned food carts and killing "a number of people."[2] The bombs kept falling, hitting nonmilitary targets: private homes, even the city hospital. Planes dived to just one hundred meters above the city, strafing buildings and people. Almost six years before air strikes decimated the Basque city of Guernica, Sánchez Cerro had sent airplanes to terrorize Trujillo.

Fighting back against the threat from above, Aprista insurgents aimed rifles at the diving planes; a pair of sisters climbed a roof to shoot at the attacking planes so enthusiastically that their comrades warned them to

Magda Portal with Apristas in Cuzco, 1933. Courtesy estate of Magda Portal,
Rocío Revolledo Pareja, and Magda Portal Papers, Benson Latin American
Collection, University of Texas at Austin.

save ammunition. Aprista women organized themselves to provision their
fighters, collecting food and cooking collective meals.[3] Others, like Haya's
cousin Marcela Pinillos Ganoza, traded on their aristocratic background
to serve as unsuspected liaisons between Apristas and subverted military
officers.[4] Perhaps the best example of Trujillo's women fighters, however,
was a young woman named María Luisa Obregón Sarmiento.

Just twenty-three years old, Obregón was a seamstress who, after starting in the party's youth organization, had spent the last year climbing up
the provincial Women's Section of Trujillo's growing APRA Party.[5] A
"strong, healthy, very charismatic" mestiza, Obregón had fully dedicated
her life to APRA, and like national leaders such as Magda Portal during
these "heroic years," "her life was her work and her party, nothing else
came between her [and the party] or had meaning for her." Trujillo's July
Revolution was this young Aprista militant's proving ground. She was the
only woman among the dozens who charged and captured the military
barracks early that morning. Afterward, they hid their newly won military
spoils in her house and toasted their victory with hot tea her mother
prepared.

But she would be remembered by her Trujillo comrades for her actions during the next few days, as the city moved to defend itself from the advancing government onslaught. Obregón was everywhere. On July 9 and 10, she presided over the preparation of communal meals and the distribution of goods throughout the city. She nursed wounded Apristas, giving the hurt "strength and courage, and also recognizing the fallen compañeros," important commemorative work for a party that already drew spectacular strength from its growing list of martyrs. She launched herself into the thick of combat. As government troops advanced on Trujillo, armed with a rifle, she held a group of advancing soldiers at bay for almost half an hour by herself. When Aprista reinforcements reached her position, she "categorically refused" to leave her rifle and retreat to safety. "She could fight as well as any man and she had just demonstrated it," an Aprista journalist explained. Government troops "would have to kill her first before entering the city."[6] Later, as government troops overran their position and her Aprista comrades shook her by the shoulders telling her to run, she refused and kept shooting. It was for such spectacular acts of courage that her male compañeros publicly praised her bravery under fire.[7]

But the defenses young Apristas like Obregón could provide proved sadly insufficient against Sánchez Cerro's advancing troops. After reestablishing military control and breaking Aprista defenses, they condemned Obregón to death for her role in the stillborn rebellion. She fled Trujillo on July 11, hiding for months working at a restaurant in a nearby small town, where her mother visited her, clandestinely smuggling in Aprista propaganda.

Obregón's notoriety was local, restricted to the area around Trujillo. Hiding in the Aprista underground in Lima, Portal was unaware of Obregón's individual exploits in battle, but she was keenly aware of the critical part women played in the bloody events of Trujillo. In 1933, as a member of the Aprista collective League of Revolutionary Writers of Peru, Portal published a collection of revolutionary poems and stories that included the Aprista poet Juan José Lora's "Song to the Compañeras": "You are everything, everything, compañeras, Ready / for the voices of command and for whatever mission! / (In Trujillo, Aprista women were seen / reaching for rifles, handing out munitions) / . . . / Revolutionary [passion] that by work and grace / of APRA, be the Worker's fatherland / and where no other aristocracy will exist / than your beauty of flowering Aprista."[8]

Portal would do more than celebrate in poetry the role women like Obregón played in Trujillo. For Portal, having been bloodied in battle made Aprista women into full partners in revolution, and the violent events of July 1932 became pivotal points in her argument for affiliating women into APRA and its revolutionary dreams. Women and men could join as compañeros in the Aprista struggle, Portal contended, and their collaborative experience as a partisan Aprista couple would reimagine and re-create domestic life and the Peruvian future, liberating it from the gender prejudices inherited from the Spanish colonial past. Building on age-old notions in Western political tradition linking citizenship with military service, Portal argued that by picking up rifles and risking their lives against the Sánchez Cerro government, women like Obregón had become full Aprista comrades in arms, full Aprista citizens, and the vanguard of the new Peruvian woman Portal herself had modeled.

The Return of "Our Powerful and Creative 'Collective Madness'"

Two months before the Trujillo Revolution, on May 6, 1932, the government finally flushed Haya out of his underground hiding place in Lima. For about two and a half months, Haya had eluded the government by hiding in a private home, where he "read, wrote, and pulled the invisible strings of his persecuted party," from a second-floor bedroom.[9] He was arrested for subverting public order and thrown in jail to await trial for fomenting insurrection. For more than a year, Haya was caged in the same prison cell that had held his old nemesis, Augusto Leguía—double bars, double lock, windows bricked in. Holes in the ceiling allowed guards to watch his every move, and his captors promised that if he ever turned off the light bulb over his head, even to sleep, they would leave him in darkness forever.

While Haya waited in jail, rumors ran wild, vividly detailing the tortures he was suffering and whispering darkly of his execution at any moment.[10] In Trujillo, Haya's birthplace, such rumors anguished many Apristas, who believed that now that Sánchez Cerro had Haya in his power, he would finish the job his police had botched on Christmas Eve in 1931. That night, the Trujillo APRA had organized a *chocolate popular* at the party headquarters to celebrate Christmas. Planning to attend, but delayed while waiting for his parents to return from midnight Mass, Haya sent a message to headquarters. Seeing the leader's car, and believing that Haya had arrived, Trujillo police burst into the building shooting, Apristas reported, and killed six party members; the police officially admitted to three dead and five wounded. Apristas considered this the government's first organized violent attack against their party, and it frightened many of them enough to believe that Sánchez Cerro, having already tried to assassinate Haya once, would not respect his life in prison.

Aprista plans had been in the works for several months to launch a military uprising from Trujillo to try—again—to overthrow Sánchez Cerro. The plans called for a sympathetic military officer, Col. Gustavo Jiménez, to return to Peru from exile in Chile and lead subverted troops against the government. Col. Jiménez, nicknamed "The Fox," was a crucial national player: as the most important military man in the 1931 junta that had steered the country through the election, he had commanded the critically important garrison in Lima, and he and Sánchez Cerro were bitter adversaries.[11] The planned uprising, however, had been postponed, and Col. Jiménez did not arrive in Peru as scheduled. As Haya languished in prison back in Lima, a "hot-tempered, charismatic union organizer" named Manuel Barreta, nicknamed "The Buffalo," took matters into his own hands.[12] Fearing for Haya's life, and deeply skeptical of ceding control of the revolution to national military officers, he decided to act when he learned that the barracks' weapons were to be moved.[13] Against the orders of the Trujillo PAP, he led a group of armed Apristas against the local army barracks in the early hours of July 7, 1932. After four hours of battle, the garrison fell to Aprista rebels, who turned it over, as well as its arms cache and the city government, to Haya's younger brother, Agustín. They locked many of the defeated government defenders in cells that hours before had held Aprista prisoners.

The young militants on the ground probably had only a vague idea of the national Aprista revolutionary strategy calling for a coordinated wave of simultaneous local rebellions all over Peru to force the government to disperse its forces. Trujillo was to play a central part in this plan, but it had pulled its trigger too early, and other Aprista regional leaders were unprepared and unwilling to launch their own local rebellions. This premature attack in Trujillo, while locally successfully, doomed the national conspiracy. The government branded the revolt as "apro-Communist," and analysts at the U.S. embassy agreed: the insurrection was "absolutely and unequivocally bolshevik and Communist." While the more moderate Haya might be a "parlor bolshevik," his lieutenants were "dangerous characters, absolutely unscrupulous and without honor, and in some cases fanatical."[14]

When only a few nearby cities followed Trujillo's lead in rebellion, Sánchez Cerro was free to concentrate the full force and fury of his attack against the northern region.[15] "Determined to stamp out this trouble as far as it is humanly possible," the president handpicked his best officers, all "hard-boiled" men who were "efficient, talk little, and waste no time."[16] Two days after their initial attack on the city barracks, it was clear that the northern Aprista rebels stood alone and that government troops would arrive at any moment in overwhelming numbers.

Agustín Haya de la Torre and other leaders herded the Aprista insurgents to the countryside to begin a guerrilla campaign, but not all followed. Right before government troops stormed the city, around sixty of the prisoners the Apristas had taken just days before—police, army officers, and civilians—were murdered in prison, almost certainly by rogue Aprista elements. When Sánchez Cerro's subsecretary investigated the site of the killings, he described a gruesome scene, "a real cannibal's feast." He had "seen the wound through which they removed the heart of the commander. . . . The rest of the assassinated had their testicles cut off and each body has a thousand wounds," he claimed. "I am horrified by this much evil." Official military autopsies did not document any mutilations.[17] Such spectacular allegations, however, would become entrenched in the Peruvian imagination and color the government's and the military's view of APRA for generations.

After the city fell, the women who had organized days earlier to feed the Aprista insurgents now secretly smuggled food and supplies to the Apristas who had managed to escape and whom the government ferociously hunted down. APRA's purported inhuman crimes against the government prisoners were used to explain and excuse the brutality of the "enraged" government troops who immediately shot most captured Apristas and arrested hundreds of suspected rebels.[18] Trujillo would be severely punished for launching this sputtering attempt at revolution. "Every effort is being made to thoroughly terrorize Trujillo by wholesale execution," U.S. embassy analysts reported. "Three courts-martial are functioning for what are called the '*gente de figuración*' [the people who matter], while the common rebels or rebel suspects are turned over to the firing squad without the benefit of trial. Practically all Trujillo is Aprista, and this opportunity to eliminate the more prominent ones is not being lost."[19]

A military panel condemned any suspect whose trigger finger or shoulder showed evidence they had recently fired a weapon, and Sánchez Cerro's troops shot hundreds—some claim thousands—in the nearby ruins of the pre-Columbian capital city of the Chimú people, Chan Chan. The government massacre quickly matched and then surpassed any Aprista brutality, as they shot Apristas for days against the ruin's walls, leaving them unburied and abandoned to the scavengers and packs of starving dogs who took over the ruins. When any one patch of ground was too crowded with dead bodies, the government troops turned to another wall in this warren of pre-Columbian walls. The nightly killings at Chan Chan did not stop until military authorities in the city received a written plea from the city's women, begging them to stop the violence, perhaps suggesting to the commanders that their violence against Trujillo's "apro-Communists" was becoming public enough to prove a liability.[20]

The intense air attacks also continued long past the point where the Apristas posed any credible military threat. Impressed with the "efficient performance of the aviation during this revolt," the U.S. embassy noted that "the planes have done exceptionally good work," since "aside from dropping bombs," the planes proved "extremely useful" for their "moral effect on the ignorant Indians and for locating rebel bands." The aviators tasked with bombing civilians were more troubled than their superiors, describing the officer who bombed the Plaza Mayor as "a very reckless sort of person," and blaming that bomb for causing the Apristas to murder their prisoners in reprisal. When ordered to bomb the entire city the next day, "they declined to do so in view of the large number of casualties that would surely ensue, and limited themselves to flying low over the city and shooting with machine guns at various groups of rebels."[21]

The carnage of this aborted revolution in Trujillo, however, was not limited to the fifty to sixty police and army prisoners executed by Aprista rebels, or the one thousand Trujillo civilians caught in the crossfire, or the uncounted Apristas shot at Chan Chan, with wildly varying estimates running anywhere from one thousand to as many as five thousand. The entire country felt the political repercussions. Sánchez Cerro arrested more than seven hundred civilians in Lima and over two hundred in Cuzco. In a meeting with Lima's leading lights, he pushed them to fire all their Aprista employees, which, given that "most of the employees in the Lima business houses are Apristas," seemed unlikely.[22]

The bloody atrocities at Trujillo seared APRA in many military minds as their implacable enemy. APRA's ability to enforce discipline on their adherents, and their mobilization of middle- and working-class sectors, where the party essentially competed for the same men the armed forces needed as foot soldiers, already made APRA suspect and dangerous to the military. Trujillo, however, made a neat and easy lesson to drill the evils of aprismo into generations of Peruvian cadets, and for the next forty years, the armed services commemorated the "Trujillo Massacre."[23] The executions at Chan Chan similarly further radicalized Apristas. The figure of "The Buffalo" was transformed into a glorious, if ill-fated, Aprista militant of action. The party named its soldiers, members of its defense brigades, Búfalos in his honor and composed a party anthem commemorating him, "The March of the Buffalos." For Apristas, the violence, the death, and the brutal defeat of Trujillo became the "most important event that transformed secular loyalty into near-religious allegiance."[24]

As the country digested the aftermath of the Trujillo uprising—APRA's most advanced attempt yet at a military insurrection—regional events in the Amazonian department of Loreto took over the national scene.[25] In 1922, Leguía had signed a treaty with neighboring Colombia ceding 4,000 square miles on their shared border called Leticia, after a nearby town. Now, ten years later, on September 1, 1932, Peruvian settlers reclaimed the lost land and, surprising the government back in Lima, Peruvian soldiers stationed nearby supported the settlers, touching off a border conflict with Colombia. While Sánchez Cerro initially believed he could exploit this conflict to bolster his own popularity, the military situation soon soured. In February of 1933, the festering conflict broke out in armed battle, severing diplomatic relations between the two countries, and making a major war a frightening possibility. As the stakes escalated, Sánchez Cerro called back the Peruvian ambassador to Great Britain, Gen. Óscar R. Benavides, to take control of the country's military effort.

On April 30, 1933, just days after recalling Benavides, Sánchez Cerro was reviewing thousands of newly conscripted troops assembled at a racetrack in Lima, when an unknown Aprista in his early twenties shot him. The president was once again rushed to the hospital, but this time he did not survive. Neither did the young assassin, shot thirteen times and sliced through with bayonets by the president's security detail.[26] For Magda Portal, this assassination was "an act of supreme justice" that "liberated" the country from Sánchez Cerro.[27] Juan Seoane, still in prison for his own connection to the first failed assassination attempt a year earlier, eulogized the young assassin as "the cry of the people . . . who casts his life like a coin in exchange for Liberty. Chocolate-vendor, terrorist, redeemer."[28] For APRA's highest political leaders, however, this "act of supreme justice" was an unexpected surprise. Immediately attributed to APRA, the president's assassination just as quickly jeopardized Haya's life in prison.

Since Peru had no vice president, the Congress quickly named the newly arrived Benavides, who had served as president before for a year and a half in 1914 and 1915, to finish the four remaining years of Sánchez Cerro's term. More important than his previous experience, however, was the general feeling that Benavides was the only national figure who might be able to govern the fractured country. A personal friend of the Colombian president, he defused the Leticia conflict, and after averting that war, turned to face the thornier problem of Peru's simmering civil war.

Benavides called for a period of Paz y Concordia (Peace and Harmony). He met with Haya personally three times to hammer out what this might look like.[29] The Apristas wanted a general amnesty for all of their prisoners and the reinstitution of their exiled congressional deputies. For Benavides, however, a general amnesty was politically impossible, since Aprista prisoners included not just Delmar and the other two men jailed for the first attempt on Sánchez Cerro's life, but also hundreds implicated in multiple Aprista attempts at military insurrection, including the "excesses of Trujillo." He refused to reseat the party's congressional delegation, but agreed to hold another congressional election quickly to fill the empty seats. The new president lifted martial law in early May, declared a partial political amnesty, and released many Aprista leaders. On August 10, 1933, he personally released Haya from prison. Benavides did not formally legalize APRA; neither did he rescind the "Emergency Law," which he chose to keep, as Luis Alberto Sánchez noted wryly, as "a loaded pistol in his desk drawer, ready to be fired as the situation demanded."[30] The president nonetheless did not actively repress APRA's efforts, and the party was for all intents and purposes free once again to begin mobilizing and campaigning for the congressional elections Benavides promised were just around the corner.[31]

Three months later, on November 12, 1933, APRA held another massive rally in Lima's ancient bull ring, the Plaza de Acho. This was a grand event to reintroduce the party, now legal once again, to the nation's political landscape and to prove that the party had not been broken by the repression of the sixteen tragic months and still commanded the fervent allegiance of thousands of people. Before the thirty-two thousand people they claimed to have gathered, APRA introduced new elements to their already spectacular political theater, most notably the "Búfalos," an honor guard of young uniformed militants named after the tragic instigator of the Trujillo Revolution, which now served as an armed escort for the entrance of the party leaders.[32] When Haya finally took the stage before the delirious crowd, he recalled how "I always smiled in the solitude of my cell when I learned that a reactionary newspaper said that the strength and enthusiasm of Aprismo in the hours before the election was a 'collective madness.' Here we are again, seeing the resurgence of our powerful and creative 'collective madness.'"[33]

Magda Portal, like other party leaders, dived headfirst into another period of frenzied party organization. Things were, of course, quite different this time. Personally, this was no longer a period of revolutionary excitement shared with her comrade in arms, Serafín Delmar, who was not part of the political amnesty and still languished in prison. Collectively, the APRA Party had also changed. The failed attempts to take power by force of arms and the repression they had suffered had honed them into a different, sharper institution. They had always focused on party discipline, but now they elevated discipline to their highest value and restructured their party into a "vertical organization" concentrating ever more power with Haya and the party's National Executive Committee, the CEN, which became "both the PAP's directing apparatus and a shadow Peruvian government."[34] The Apristas named section leaders "national secretaries," and their sections "ministries," and these ministries began preparing for an Aprista transition to power. Heading the Secretaría Femenina, the Aprista Women's Section, Portal was one of these twenty shadow ministers.

The structure of the CEN at this moment of rebirth in 1933 is a telling snapshot of how the Aprista leadership regarded their party and the contours of the political world of which they dreamed. Eight ministries oversaw different aspects of national governance: Culture, Economy, Interior, Defense, Exterior, Labor, Politics, and Social Assistance. A ninth Regional Ministry of the North, the only geographical region with its own dedicated ministry, highlights the prominence given to the party's historical heartland, but also suggests a myopic short-sightedness in not targeting other regions of lukewarm support, particularly the South. There were five ministries dedicated to internal APRA Party governance: Proceedings, Discipline, Propaganda, Press, and Organizing. Two other ministries oversaw the technical tools Apristas believed necessary for modern governance: Statistics and Technology. Finally, four separate ministries focused on the needs of particular social groups: Cooperatives, Women, Labor Unions, and Indigenous and Campesino Affairs, underscoring the role the party envisioned for women, organized workers, and indigenous peasants—groups whose political needs had been either long ignored or actively suppressed.[35]

The party revealed its best vision of itself in the roster called to head these twenty ministries and serve as APRA's national leaders. A lavishly illustrated supplement in the first issue of the newly resurrected *APRA* magazine, surely meant to be torn out, kept, and perhaps even displayed, featured photographs of all twenty secretaries and their subsecretaries. Of the forty leaders, there were twenty-three professionals, five *empleados* (white-collar employees) or *comerciantes* (shopkeepers), eleven workers, and one military officer. Workers represented just shy of 30 percent of the leadership, indicating more than token representation. Perhaps even more tellingly, there were seven ministries in which the worker was the secretary, and a professional, empleado, or comerciante was his immediate subordinate, the subsecretary. The prominent role of these workers in the commanding heights of the party leadership presented the party's utopian vision of itself as the seamless union of intellectual and manual workers. Of the forty leaders, three were women, including one female worker—another way the party leadership was visibly different from traditional Peruvian politics.[36]

One of the first things the CEN did was found the Atahualpa Cooperative Press, a dedicated Aprista press designated as the "only authorized press" for APRA Party doctrine, political analysis, historical documents, or more literary efforts like essays and theater.[37] Atahualpa was the primary star in an expanded constellation of Aprista outreach and propaganda efforts, a key part of what Sánchez characterized as the party's "intense campaign to spread their principles" after emerging from the catacombs. This campaign included material outreach efforts aimed at improving the condition of the Aprista faithful, like opening a communal kitchen and a public medical clinic. It also included a full-on assault of propaganda and doctrinal outreach: they resurrected the daily newspaper *La Tribuna* and the monthly magazine *APRA*, as well as the popular universities, now almost exclusively focused on partisan instruction. To these, the party added a second newspaper, *Trinchera Aprista*, a propaganda seminar titled "Túpac Amaru," and, of course, the Atahualpa Cooperative Press.[38]

The editor of Atahualpa was Magda Portal, and in that role she was tasked with "carefully revising" all the works submitted to the press to ensure they were "absolutely guaranteed" to be in line with Aprista doctrine. Published at the lowest possible cost to make their titles accessible to the rank and file, the works were intended to be bound together to create readers' own "Aprista library." And, in fact, that is precisely what the most devoted members did, as evidenced by the texts that Ricardo Luna Vega collected, bound into eleven separate volumes, and eventually donated to the archives of the Institute of Peruvian Studies in Lima.

What did it mean to Portal to be appointed as Atahualpa's editor? Perhaps of all her responsibilities, this one demonstrates the confidence that Haya and the party leadership had in Portal and the high esteem in which they held her. Since Atahualpa was the only authorized APRA press, Portal was, in essence, the gatekeeper and steward of the party's evolving doctrine. This was a position of great trust within the highest national leadership in a party that valued such ideological foundations above most other things, and at a historical moment when the party was consolidating their structure and doctrine into an emerging orthodoxy.

Portal also continued her literary efforts as the main engine behind a writing collective called the League of Revolutionary Writers of Peru, along with Delmar, Julián Petrovick, and other notable talents such as Alberto Hidalgo and Ciro Alegría. But her most important publishing efforts now were not aesthetic literary pieces, but instead political doctrine that she published at Atahualpa. Her most visible effort was a short book titled *Hacia la mujer nueva* (Toward the new woman), in which Portal developed her own emerging ideas about women's political participation and outlined how Peruvian women would need to transform, both at the collective level of social organization and at the individual level of personalities, to undertake their new public responsibilities.

By the end of 1933, then, Magda Portal was an increasingly visible source of energy and authority in the reemerging APRA Party, with public duties that included heading a ministry in the CEN, at a moment of increasing structural centralization. Her diverse intellectual roles included editing Atahualpa, the party's new doctrinal press; leading the effort in the League of Revolutionary Writers; giving conferences and teaching at the popular university; and publishing the most developed party position on women's political participation in both APRA and Peru's public life.[39]

Hacia la mujer nueva

After the "sixteen tragic months" of the Sánchez Cerro repression, APRA's reemergence represented a precious second chance for Apristas to start over, to rebuild, to reimagine themselves and their party. By late 1933, APRA mobilized again, more battle-hardened and propelled forward by the Trujillo martyrs and the brutal repression they had suffered. Portal grabbed this chance to reimagine the Aprista position on "the woman question," and *Hacia la mujer nueva* forcefully asserted women's claims to citizenship in the party and in Peru. Portal was trying to systematize Aprista doctrine on the role of women's political participation for Aprista men and for Peru. Part of being an Aprista meant aspiring to a more progressive position on "the woman question," but what did that mean? Unlike their shared assumptions about economic issues or international relations, Apristas shared no central idea, no tenet, no doctrine that showed them how to get to where they felt they needed to stand.

The *APRA* magazine series "Reporting on Our Leaders," which ran from September 1931 through January of 1932, paraded the leadership's many nuances of opinion on this "woman question." It was important to them: the interview always ended by asking, "Tell us your thoughts on the role of the woman in the Aprista renovation"; no other demographic or social issue merited its own dedicated question. For Portal and the leaders closest to her, the Aprista woman was "the compañera of the man on this journey to popular justice." Delmar had gone as far as musing that women might even give more to the revolution. "The woman demands the same rights and imposes on herself the same obligations. At times, she is superior to the man."[40] For her part, Portal believed women represented "a magnificent contribution" when they understood that the "Aprista struggle wishes to demand the totality of her rights, integrating her at the side of the male as a compañera, not as an inferior entity."[41] Petrovick argued that women were "a great factor" for the Aprista cause, "not only as cooperators" but also because realizing their own emancipation was a crucial objective in its own right.[42]

But there were also more traditional answers. Luis E. Heysen told *APRA* readers that the role of the woman in the struggle should be that of "the mother, girlfriend, and admirable wife, like that of the compañera and friend in all the hours in the Aprista day."[43] Several keywords repeatedly emerge in these interviews: women as collaborators, as cooperators, and as compañeras, that is, companions and comrades. The leadership was confused, however, about the nuances of meaning of words like "compañera." For Heysen, a compañera was a traditional female companion, there to support a man "in all the hours in the Aprista day." For leaders like Delmar and Portal, however, the word held a deeper reservoir of meaning implying equality between men and women, who were not "inferior entities."

Heysen is a good place to start to understand the leadership's confused yet aspirational thinking on women in their revolution and in public life more broadly. A national leader who had joined Haya's efforts while they were both students volunteering at the popular university in 1923, Heysen was exiled to Argentina in December of 1924. Returning to Peru in 1931, he was well known to the rank and file in part for spending his last weeks in Argentina as a political prisoner, along with Manuel Seoane—a rough experience the Peruvian Aprista press avidly followed. After the electoral loss to Sánchez Cerro, Heysen was elected to the Parliament and was one of the twenty-three congressmen deported in early 1932. During APRA's time in the "catacombs" during the Sánchez Cerro government, Heysen served as the party's clandestine general secretary. When APRA reemerged in 1933, Heysen was a member of the CEN, the secretary of the party's Ministry of Technology.[44]

Even though his answer to his 1931 interview envisioned the Aprista woman as little more than a man's auxiliary companion and caretaker,

Heysen often returned to the woman question, yet his ideas on the role of women were confused and contradictory. Like other Apristas, Heysen was proud of the fact that they were the first, and in the early 1930s, the only, politicians demanding women's civil rights. "Our postulates of equality have no limits or exclusions," he stressed. APRA "will be inflexible until we obtain the electoral collaboration of women and their own liberation from the feudal yoke" of traditional marriage. But he immediately contradicted himself by claiming Apristas agreed with the Spanish philosopher José Ortega y Gasset that "WOMEN NEED TO COLLABORATE NOT BY ADMINISTRATING THE ELECTORAL VOTE, BUT BY ADMINISTRATING THEIR WELL-AIMED SMILES."[45] A few months later, and once seated in the Parliament hashing out the country's new constitution, Heysen and the minority Aprista delegation justified limiting women's suffrage. While APRA struggled to achieve "the transformation of the Biblical rib into a citizen," Heysen explained, they would only "recognize the right to vote for women who work in the home, in the factory, or in the fields and for the women who study and who think. . . . We differ with those who want to give citizenship to the society girl, whose unemployment exposes her to suffer strange influences, if you will, clerical" influences.[46] Ultimately, agency here rested on the party that would wrest women from the Catholic Church and transform them from "Biblical ribs" into citizens, starting with the few trusted women they felt were already ideologically prepared to support APRA.

Three months after his "Reporting on Our Leaders" interview, Heysen was in the northern city of Chiclayo, commemorating Haya's cousin and Aprista leader Marcella Pinillos Ganoza and bringing an APRA crowd to its feet in a series of "deafening ovations." The title of his speech, reproduced in a large, blazing red, bold-face-type headline in the *APRA* magazine, was "The Rebellion of the Woman." As Peru, "disturbed, agitates to find its salvation," Heysen proclaimed, "we contemplate today the woman shooting at her past . . . that has impeded her from taking manly attitudes and positions." The vivid and violent image of women shooting at the traditions holding them back thrilled the Aprista audience to their feet. Ultimately, Heysen's shooting woman was not an individual militant struggling alone, a woman who pushed into politics with a masculinist orientation, but instead a woman who entered the masculine arena of political action by collaborating with, "welding" herself to, Aprista men, to jointly struggle for their political goals. Nonetheless, the portrait he painted was a far cry from the constant companion suggested in his interview three months earlier, the patient, passive wife or mother whose only role is to support her Aprista man. This new, rebellious woman, Heysen asserted, left behind traditional feminine frivolity to launch herself into the masculine world of political action. The Aprista woman *"does not affiliate with the Peruvian Aprista Party to speculate with loves, nor to speculate with figments of the imagination, with fashion or with rouge; but instead, simply to join together and liberate our country."* [47]

Of course, everything had changed in the three months separating Heysen's interview from this high-voltage speech. In that theater in November, Heysen was whipping up a committed partisan crowd as Sánchez Cerro was being declared victor in the national elections, a crowd certain that only electoral fraud could explain this devastating turn of events. In one of the night's biggest applause lines, Heysen explicitly fanned the flames of this Aprista outrage. "Napoleon said, 'Let's sheathe the ballot boxes and let the bayonets talk,'" he roared. Their opponents "are pushing us in the country to impose the voice of the bayonets and of the people, united against fraud. (Clamorous ovation.)" As the political landscape turned so rapidly against them, Aprista leaders like Heysen prepared for their uncertain political future by feverishly rallying everybody, including women. [48]

But Heysen also spun a long, complicated, and puzzling argument supporting changes in women's traditional roles. Since World War I, he contended, the world's most advanced economies had industrialized and transitioned from a patriarchy to a matriarchy, where "the woman is everything." This jargon was important to him and his Aprista listeners—the transcript carefully bolded "patriarchy" and "matriarchy." Another example of the "advanced doctrine" that the Aprista rank and file expected to hear, but not fully understand, from their leaders, such jargon marked the leadership's advanced education in the latest social and political theories, even if the leaders did not understand or communicate these ideas effectively.

But it also pointed to the lack of coherence in the leadership's ideas on women. Earlier that same month, Portal explained that women's oppression was an artifact of an exploitative economic system rather than male prejudice and that it would only change by addressing the exploitative nature of society's economic base. [49] Heysen's pronouncements that women's rights had already triumphed in the most advanced capitalist societies, which had demonstrably not vanquished economic exploitation, contradicted Portal's contention that women's inequality was an artifact of an exploitative economic system.

Heysen was also still falling back on common gendered understandings denigrating women, attacking the party's enemies by feminizing them, calling their political maneuvers the "acts of their little feminine hands." In an article published eight months earlier, Portal had argued that the male Aprista partisan, "because of the mere fact of being Aprista," had transcended his conservative worldview "and considers the woman on a level of human dignity equal to his."[50] Portal was trying to teach her Aprista brethren that if they treated their wives as inferiors, they were not Apristas. At this public celebration of a female Aprista leader in Trujillo, Heysen's gendered insults made it harder to accept Portal's assertion that Aprista men's advanced consciousness allowed them—by definition—to transcend male prejudices.

Heysen proved that sympathetic leaders who wished for women's active political participation, who urged women to join APRA and shoot at their traditional past, still nonetheless struggled for doctrinal coherence and relied on "reactionary" attitudes about women. It was clear their doctrine on the volatile "woman's question" needed to be directly addressed, developed in detail, codified, explained, and used to instruct the rest of the leadership and the party rank and file.

Four primary themes emerged in Portal's thinking on the "women question." First, she stressed women's rights should be achieved through collaboration with men and not through divisive or antagonistic means. Second, she argued that the goal of women's liberation was not a limited juridical one like suffrage, but instead a sweeping psychological liberation in individual women that would then lead to an egalitarian society and culture. Third, Portal thought this psychological liberation could not be legislated or "given" to women; women had to fight for it themselves, and APRA partisan activity was the only viable arena for their struggle. Finally, Portal promised that the payoff would be, in the long term, the success of APRA's revolutionary program and a better society; in the short term, these psychologically liberated vanguard women would enjoy a full affiliation with their male Aprista peers, allowing them to transcend the culturally imposed limits on women's public and private lives. These four foundational ideas reflected what Portal believed was her lived experience; in her thinking, she led the vanguard of exceptional Aprista women who would spearhead APRA's collaborative revolutionary project and then bring the fruits of expanded rights to all Peruvian women.

In 1931, in the first flush of Aprista mobilization, Portal had promised that "Aprismo presents for women the rehabilitation of all her social, juridical, political, civil, and cultural rights." Such sweeping language implied profound and potentially terrifying changes, but Portal stressed that achieving women's civil rights depended not on antagonism between the sexes, much less open conflict, but instead on collaboration. "The Aprista woman," she assured, "does not pretend to conquer her rights through an open battle against the man . . . but instead she comes to collaborate with her compañero."[51] This collaborative strategy depended on male Aprista compañeros welcoming the new Aprista woman, not on Aprista women defying, forcing, or demanding anything from them.

Universal female suffrage, she warned, would only ensure a conservative electoral victory, since politically unenlightened women could not see that APRA was a vote for women's rights and their interests. "Women are not capable of exercising their political rights without the influence of the Catholic home, the convent, and the confessional," she diagnosed. Instead of narrow, formal, legal rights like suffrage, the fight was for far more sweeping changes. The "real goal of the revolutionary woman, of the modern woman" was "the equalizing of all the orders, for the defense of her human personality before the capitalist struggle, for her expanded education, both free and free of charge, for laws that protect her as a woman, as a mother, as a worker."[52] "Equalizing all the orders" would then lead to the vote for women, not the other way around. Just as Catholicism directed the will of traditional women, Portal argued that female citizens could only be trained by APRA, which would educate them about their actual interests.

Now, in 1933, with the experience of the "tragic sixteen months" behind her and her party, Portal took the ideas she had introduced in the heady days of 1931 further. Though only two years later, the repression Apristas had endured had changed everything. "Women of today, much more resolute than those of the first Aprista era, *because they now have experience*, are the vanguard of the revolutionary movement in Peru," she explained. Women now knew that they were "neither useless nor decorative, that they signify contribution, effort, and conscious action" and would no longer be content to be left behind in the life of either APRA or the nation.[53]

In *Hacia la mujer nueva*, Portal presented women's liberation as fundamentally a psychological process, demanding a complete transformation of individual psychologies and traditional gender norms. "Aprismo is a revolution," she proclaimed, "more total" for women, since it "rips" them "from a spiritual state and a social situation" into one completely different and opposed to how they had lived before. This Aprista revolution was "the violent opening of a prison" and the releasing of "its astonished inhabitants toward a vast and limitless field, toward a full and complete light and liberty," she promised. "Wrapped in the old medieval spirit that still survives [even] after a hundred years of [a] democratic republic, the woman suddenly enters, without stumbling, into an era of liberty. She is shown what will be the path to take, a path with no other travelers, where she has to walk alone, valiantly free [*valientemente libre*]."[54]

This utopian future of freedom as individual agents offered much more than formal civil rights; it offered essentially psychological rewards— rewards of the self. Women would be able to "breathe deeply the air of liberty" and fully develop and manifest their "never expressed, never understood" human personality "in all its strength, capable of great and noble actions." It promised women an expanded sense of self-worth. "The definitive Aprista woman," Portal assured, "will be sure of herself," a woman "who has taken a path of heroic struggle and who through this means has begun to enjoy rights never before known to her."[55]

What Portal meant by releasing women's personalities was making them less timid. "Her proverbial timidity has secluded the virtues of her true personality in the farthest corners of her spirit," her unconscious. But that personality was still there. Releasing this new personality, this "great creative force within her," from its prison of inhibition and forging a new sense of self necessarily meant targeting the family and home, where personalities were formed. In essence, Portal's vision of the Aprista revolution was a new social consciousness creating not just a New Woman and a New Man, but also a New Home, "*un nuevo hogar*."[56]

This domestic world of home and reproduction sustained by women's labor was the prime arena where conflict between men and women was likely to arise. Portal could not avoid addressing such domestic duties, especially since critics were already raising the specter of broken homes should APRA gain power, arguing that women, "tied to new duties and anxious for new achievements," would abandon "their feminine instinct" and their obligations as mothers. "Nothing was further from the truth," Portal assured her readers, contending that any domestic dislocations would be a transitionary phase lasting only until "Aprismo has triumphed and at last imposes its creed of justice and fraternity." In truth, she argued, the Peruvian home was already in a sorry state, "disunited and demoralized because of the errors and the prejudices that have made of the woman an inferior slave and the man a despot," and buffeted by new economic conditions forcing women to abandon "the home, her center" for "the factory, the office, the workshops." The new Aprista home, in contrast, would be "a cultured home, materially and spiritually sound . . . founded on a base of mutual respect between the man and woman." By definition, she insisted, such a future ideal home could only strengthen the "family nucleus . . . , since the woman will no longer be just the demure female, happy in her inferiority, the doll of the salon or the poor domestic, stuck in routine and with no other incentives."[57]

Such an explicit emphasis on motherhood and maternal obligations strengthened traditional definitions of women and "women's duties," and Portal explicitly defined motherhood as the base of authentic femininity and womanhood.[58] And yet, this maternal definition of women gave the party, like other progressive movements elsewhere, the justification for advancing protective labor demands that considerably improved the daily conditions of working women. In addition to equalizing the rights between men and women, including wage parity, the party would also "legislate taking into consideration those natural circumstances that make the economic struggle more difficult for women, especially maternity . . . in this way liberating her from one of her most anguished cares."[59] The Women's Section had submitted to the First Party Congress such protective demands, including shorter hours for unhealthy or heavy work, prohibitions against child labor for school-age children, protections for nursing women at work, and maternity insurance and pensions.

Portal's definition of motherhood was so expansive that it actually exploded conventional assumptions about women's roles and the preparation these required. Aprismo, she contended, wanted "mother" to mean not just bearing and physically caring for children, but also psychologically forging a child's personality, creating in them "feelings and virtues capable of making each child a free and dignified man or woman," a child "who indignity, corruption, servility . . . can never make prey." To do this, she would need to "dedicate special care to penetrate in every corner of the current Aprista home, with the goal of weeding out from it all the bad, all the wrong that still remains, product of the old education, . . . of female misery and indolence—and to plant, with the great happiness of a spiritual awakening, education, physical and moral strength."[60]

This new woman was also responsible for educating and cultivating a new modern personality in her husband, "showing him that she joined him to form a family and not to serve him as a domestic, on an inferior plane, since both are given the same attributes of intelligence and both need to divide the duties of building their happiness and forming healthy children, molded into superior spirits by their example and dedication."[61] To do all this, Portal's expansive definition of motherhood demanded dramatically improved educational access for girls and women. For Portal, Aprismo and the APRA Party mediated the ideal balance between what she argued was women's central and essential role as mothers and the psychological transformations necessary for women to fully flourish as human beings. The party would teach women how to recognize their own conditions and interests and would educate and train them for public life, loosening their ties to tradition and families and their repressive expectations, which tied them "in conditions of semislavery."[62]

The utopian future Portal sketched for women here was not a collective one, but instead a classically liberal future of possibility for autonomous individuals. It was a proving ground where every individual woman tested her mettle among others, all now equal in opportunity. The revolutionary challenge was that in Peruvian society, women had never gained the individual rights and privileges promised by liberalism. If anything, the bargain struck in Peru's transition from colony to republic in the nineteenth century had further sacrificed women's civil rights by expanding men's legal powers over them in the domestic sphere.[63]

The personality Portal assumed all women possessed was a fully formed, heroic agency; yet somehow, it was trapped and cornered, cowered by the weight of the colonial patriarchy suppressing it. Did all women have such a will to action hiding in the corners, or was this heroic agency an exceptional quality in all humans, male and female? If women did possess such a suppressed willful agent already developed, would it be so easily cowed? More troubling, women alone bore the sweeping task of transforming society's gender organization and individual psychologies. The process of liberating themselves was as important, if not more so, than any formal rights women gained. Neither men nor APRA could hand women their civil rights as "yet another gift of the man."[64]

Portal's analysis of women's liberation was intently focused on individual will as the agent for change. Women's collective struggle, she proposed, would arise spontaneously as thousands—perhaps millions—of individual women launched their personal and individual battles to protect their own interests. For Portal, the agent of struggle was always either the individual woman, engaged in a lonely and difficult struggle, or the enlightened partisan couple. This couple, however, was only possible because of the women who emancipated themselves and then additionally educated their compañeros. This was a striking deviation from other Aprista strategies for liberation from oppression. In the fight against capitalist exploitation, for instance, neither Portal not APRA advocated that workers should struggle individually against their bosses, but they had long fought to organize and coordinate collective action to address workers' demands. Portal's choice to focus so intently on individual will underestimated the structural barriers to women's participation in public life that collective action was designed to breach. The pendulum of agency in her analysis swings between two extremes: a woman's supreme act of individual will as the engine for her psychological transformation and the tutelary role of the APRA Party in making women conscious of their rights and how to struggle for them.

Portal's guidance for her fellow party compañeras, and ultimately her fellow countrywomen, reflected her own understanding of how she had joined and risen within the party and in Peru's political arena, achieving some measure of equality with men. She underestimated, however, how impossible these instructions would prove to other women. Although later in life Portal seemed acutely aware of her own exceptionalism, she assumed that other women could—and should—be able to summon forth, and sustain, the immense act of will, the unflagging commitment necessary to reject such ingrained traditional gender expectations and be willing to bear the pain of the consequent sacrifices.

When Portal began to project into the future, instead of using her past experience as a template or model, her instructions started to show significant discordance with even her exceptional example. When she described the ideal Aprista woman and her relationship to her male partner, her children, and her home, she described an ideal she herself never achieved. Portal had already suffered through the emotional trauma of leaving her husband to instead forge a companionate marriage at the side of Delmar. But the rigors and dangers of clandestine revolutionary militancy ensured that they could not create the ideal Aprista home that her daughter, Gloria, needed or that APRA prescribed as a necessary building block for a new Peru.

The collaborative strategy she advocated also closed off potential avenues for achieving women's rights. By assigning the Aprista woman the task of transforming her compañero, Portal placed an inordinately larger burden on women and left no clues for how to proceed should men fail to live up to her revolutionary ideals. Portal depended on men's acceptance of an emancipated woman as a collaborative partner. During this transition period from the old decadent order to the new Aprista future, both men and women were still burdened by traditional mentalities. Nonetheless, Portal charges women, whom she has argued are not psychologically whole because of the burdens of patriarchal colonialism, with both the superior task of will necessary to overcome and break free from their traditional mentality and then the additional task of helping their compañeros rid themselves of their traditional mindset. What was the men's task of psychological liberation?

While Portal had not fully reconciled all the tensions inherent in her ideas, she also had other goals in *Hacia la mujer nueva*. She was compiling and writing a history of women in APRA, rescuing and defending their heroic contributions. Portal listed every incident of Aprista women being persecuted by the Sánchez Cerro government and every political action and danger undertaken by female party militants from 1931 to 1933.[65] She carefully footnoted her references and compiled a documentary appendix that collected her own essays from 1931 on the role of women with other letters, petitions, and communiqués issued by Aprista women from 1931 to 1933. She was creating an archetype: the heroic revolutionary Aprista woman, a model to inspire and mobilize other women and to serve as an example to Aprista men of women's contributions in their shared revolutionary struggle. Ultimately, of course, the book itself signals a lack, a need to describe an APRA with women already fully affiliated. She titles the book *"Toward [Hacia] the New Woman,"* and this is her aspirational vision of what her party can become and her map guiding APRA toward that change so it could then transform people and institutions to achieve her radical vision.

Hacia la mujer nueva was well received by others in the high leadership. Manuel Seoane, writing two years later, echoed some of the book's key ideas: women "must collaborate with their masculine compañeros" while "at the same time, to be efficient in the struggle, they have to demand their specific claims. The first task imposes a political duty of collaboration, and Magda Portal carries it out *abnegadamente* [self-abnegatingly]."[66] In April of 1934, Haya sent Portal a short note about *Hacia la mujer nueva*: "Compañera Magda: It would please me very much to speak with you about your pamphlet, which is very interesting," he began. But Haya wanted more. "In addition, since you don't let yourself be seen—sometimes I fear you will become a nun—I want to speak with you of many other things. *Tu viejo,* V.R."[67] No one could fault Portal for lack of dedication or half-hearted revolutionary commitment. Was this the only thing keeping her away, cloistering her affections from Haya and their other compañeros in the leadership? The tone in this fleeting note is unmistakable—he missed her.

Toward Citizenship: Compañeros Apristas

"The Aprista woman," Portal wrote in *Hacia la mujer nueva*, "must propagate her ideas of liberation and justice without foregrounding hostility toward men or attributing to them a manifest perversity or intolerance toward women. She understands that the mentality of the men of the past—a semifeudal mentality that still influences the present—has been molded by a now decaying historical era."[68] This reasoning made clear that individual men were not at fault for their retrograde "colonial" ideas. With this clear-eyed assessment, Portal recognized men's hostility toward women's rights, and proposed collaboration instead of overt antagonism as the political way forward to achieve them nonetheless. Certain that women could only conquer liberation and citizenship by participating in the nation's politics from within the party ranks, she made the first order of business finding ways to affiliate women into the community of Aprista men.

Portal understood her own entrance into the Aprista leadership in the 1920s as part and parcel of the camaraderie they all shared in Lima's bohemian circles. A mutual trust and friendship among people who spend time together, this camaraderie was a social identity, and its primary inflection was friendship. But such camaraderie was no longer an avenue for other women to join the party—that moment was gone, both for Lima and for a now-maturing APRA. In 1920s Lima, this bohemian camaraderie brought these slightly out-of-place provincials together, provided them emotional and practical support in a cold and distant capital, and allowed them to show each other an affection that might otherwise be suspect. They bonded in part by excluding women. But for Portal, this same camaraderie marked her as different, made her different, from other women. As this group of young men brought her deeper into their homosocial fold, she felt increasingly distant, even alienated, from other women and from feminine traits.

Within this circle of friends, Portal was one of the earliest leaders and a powerful recruiter for the Aprista cause. The small group of men Portal coalesced around her became some of APRA's most important and tireless organizers, most notably, the two younger Bolaños brothers, Serafín Delmar and Julián Petrovick. In 1931, remembering how he joined APRA, Petrovick listed "reading books on the social questions, the movement of the 23rd of May in 1923, the work of the UPGPs, and the friendship that I struck with the c. [compañera] Magda Portal, as the reasons that "made me decide to enroll in the ranks of Aprismo."[69] Portal walked among these young militants as an example of the changes liberated women could effect in the men in their lives, living proof of her revolutionary ideas. Portal's promise of the New Woman rang true within this circle of bohemian camaraderie, and the Bolaños brothers' own leadership in the party testified to Portal's power as the emancipated woman who had liberated herself and then liberated the men in her life, inducting them into the Aprista struggle. Other leaders considered them a tight clique, bound by their intimate personal relationships and their close political collaboration; Sánchez remembers that he and his group in the leadership referred, somewhat dismissively, to the three as the "Serafines."[70] From the brothers' testimony, however, the "Portales" more aptly captured the truth. Among these bohemian companions, Portal was the *mujer nueva*, a leader, even the female equivalent of Haya.

But Sánchez's testimony also hints at the limits inherent in affiliation through such bohemian camaraderie, which depended on maintaining the mutual trust and friendship that had brought them together in the first place. As time passed, and as these young men transformed from provincial university students composing poems and dreaming of revolution into actual militants organizing a political party, inevitable personality conflicts and professional jealousies began eating away at their camaraderie. Sánchez, for instance, explicitly accused Portal, Delmar, and Petrovick of being jealous of him. The "Serafines," Sánchez sniffed, had turned themselves inside out trying to block him from joining the party, claiming that he was too closely affiliated with Leguía. Jealousy and envy, however, went both ways. Petrovick was also Haya's personal secretary and enjoyed additional access to their leader, and the rivalry between their two publications, *La Tribuna* and *APRA*, undoubtedly exacerbated nascent jealousies.[71] Sánchez repeatedly calls *La Tribuna*, which he had founded and edited, "the living word of the party," and in his multiple books, both personal memoirs and works he wrote as "APRA's court historian"—descriptive, deep, rich works full of details including street addresses, exact dates, and even people's outfits—he "neglects" to mention the influential magazine *APRA* or Portal's role as editor of Atahualpa.[72] If the ties binding Portal and the men who created and led APRA had only remained this bohemian camaraderie, a collective friendship where her primary identity among them was being the "girl among the boys," she would always remain the one apart, the easiest to pick out, and the first to be dismissed.

Another more promising avenue for affiliating women into APRA was becoming an Aprista compañera. "Compañero," the Apristas' favored term for a member of their partisan community, literally meant companion, but much like the usage of "comrade" among Communists, this appellation called forth an entire world. It conjured the Aprista imagined and beloved community, connoting a basically egalitarian partisan affiliation, where hierarchy was based on ability and merit, with opportunities open to all. In their writings and letters, Apristas used "compañero/a" as a title of address, like Petrovick did when referring to "c. Magda." In colloquial Spanish, however, "compañera" could also mean conjugal partner, and a sexual relationship was inherent in its definition. Compañera Aprista, then, was an identity seething with a living tension: equal partisan companion on the one hand, and on the other, a sexual partner, a wife or mistress. As opposed to camaraderie, the principal inflection of compañera was a partner, one half of a dyad. Open to definition was what type of partner: a sexual and political partnership of equals or the traditional model of marriage, with women cast as subservient, auxiliary, essentially as domestic servants.

As she navigated among the slippery nuances of meaning of "compañera," Portal underscored the potential meanings of "companion" to erase the lived experience of wife as vassal. A woman was "man's collaborator, not his slave, compañera in the broad spiritual meaning of the word," Portal explains in *Hacia la mujer nueva*. The agent of struggle was not individual men, but instead the human couple. Focused on her own liberation, a woman's disciplined and revolutionary activity would "raise her to the higher plane—spiritually and materially—from which she will be able to fully realize her destiny, at the side of her male compañero, also free of prejudices, who understands and respects her in everything she is worth." As half of this couple, the Aprista woman would gain equality with her partner through their cooperative struggle in APRA's revolution. "Fighting at the side of man, she becomes his equal," she promised.[73]

By constantly modifying "compañero" with "male," Portal calls forth meaning beyond sexual partner, which would otherwise be understood. The phrase "male compañero" makes sense only within a larger collectivity of Aprista comrades. This formulation made women's affiliation into APRA not just possible but critically necessary, since the triumphant agent of struggle was now neither man nor woman, but instead the enlightened and politically conscious Aprista couple. In Portal's vision, this new Aprista couple constituted a new type of affective and political relationship, a partnership in which romantic and political affiliation were woven so tightly together as to be indistinguishable, and which would ultimately serve as the foundation of a new home, family, and nation—all now healthier, more egalitarian, more psychologically free.

At its purest, the promise of compañeros Apristas as partisan couples added sex's combustible energy to their revolutionary and political commitment, a potent combination that politically committed couples had tried to harness elsewhere: in revolutionary Mexico, Republican Spain, Soviet Russia. This ideal of the partisan couple combined two of the most electrifying forces of the age: sex and politics. And once again, Magda Portal was its living example.

In November of 1933, an Aprista poet named Aurelio Martínez wrote a poem titled "*mujer nueva* [new woman]," inextricably entwining his fascination with Portal as the New Woman, the epitome of a female revolutionary, with sexual attraction. The poem celebrates the carnal strength and power of the rural Andean landscape, and reads as an unmistakable sexual invitation for Portal, the "revolutionary woman, woman of destiny": "revolutionary woman / now that you walk my new world / I feel my nerves become lightning / and that this vile flesh quickens / . . . / revolutionary magda / strong woman / woman of destiny / magda / magda guide of american femininity / here is my ande / the racial apu that never dies / . . . / revolutionary magda / let us climb to the highest peak / of these mountains that have vanquished centuries / here is the mountain night / . . . / what epic sensation / will run through our bodies / . . . / revolutionary magda / take in the wings of your fighting soul / the geographic force / and the universal vitality / of my ande and my titikaka / . . . / apra is the red flag / that we all wave / because it is the crackling cry of our race."[74]

The multiple layers of romantic identification in this poem captured the Aprista horizon of possibility in 1933: the New Woman, radically emancipated politically, but mostly sexually; the redefinition of indigeneity from a backward force sabotaging modernity to a powerful, eternal landscape of possibility; and APRA as the vehicle of revolutionary politics that would midwife that glittering future. Portal saved a photographic souvenir of herself in traditional Quechua garb, posed in front of Cuzco's Incan walls over the party slogan "Only Aprismo will save Peru," attesting to her own identification with these three powerful dreams.

Martínez, the young Aprista poet, most likely met Portal as she toured southern Peru in late 1933, mustering support for the elections to replace APRA's lost congressional seats that Benavides kept assuring them would soon be held, a grueling two months in hostile territory where Aprista support was at best lukewarm. She traveled with the union leader Arturo Sabroso, and together they incarnated a new possibility as political leaders unlike any their audiences had ever imagined: a woman and a labor leader.[75]

For poets like Martínez, Portal was the walking example of the revolutionary woman, the representation of APRA and the ideal projected sexual partner for the indigenous south, alluded to in the poem as "the

Magda Portal posing in Cuzco, December 1933. Courtesy estate
of Magda Portal, Rocío Revolledo Pareja.

universal vitality / of my ande and my titikaka." Of course, since Portal's own compañero Aprista, Serafín Delmar, languished in prison, the sexual charge animating the poem was, presumably, in this case misdirected. Yet, Portal included this poem in an Atahualpa edition of Aprista revolutionary art, a pamphlet that Delmar also contributed to and no doubt read. What did he feel as he read these thinly veiled carnal invitations his compañera inspired? Later, in her 1956 novelistic memoir *La trampa* (The trap), Portal's alter ego agonized over how she was slandered as unfaithful to her imprisoned partner.[76] The dark side to supercharging revolutionary commitment with sexual energy was negotiating the jealousy that such intimate relationships inspired.

This model of the partisan couple never took root among other national leaders who all built much more traditional marriages and families, and in practice lived lives in which their consorts conformed to traditional expectations of Peruvian femininity. Rarely political, these women were the "*damas Apristas*," the Aprista ladies, whose roles in the party were social and auxiliary. The exception was Haya, who never married. But this did not mean he eschewed traditional models of marriage, as his young cousin, the provincial Aprista leader Marcela Pinillos Ganoza, the same young woman who had risked her safety in the Trujillo uprising and whom Heysen had celebrated in his rousing speech on the rebellion of the woman, learned. In 1936, she was "saved" from an uncertain future of Aprista militancy when she met and married an immigrant "Swiss Adonis," who "entered her life at a crucial moment because most probably if she had matured in the youth leadership of the Apra Party, she would have immolated herself for her cousin Víctor Raúl." Marcela attempted to reenter party life after marriage, but "her cousin and leader retired her with a strict decision: 'Marcela, you get out of politics and dedicate yourself to your husband,' he told her categorically. For Haya de la Torre there were no half measures: it was the party or the family, so he sent her home. . . . In the end, her momentum had to cede before party discipline."[77]

But others in these northern hotbeds of Aprista militancy may have lived lives as partisan couples, combining both interests instead of choosing between "party or family." María Luisa Obregón, who had so valiantly carried arms for APRA during the ill-fated winter days of the Trujillo Revolution, emerged from her months underground and continued her rapid rise in the provincial party leadership, with her "persistent labor, enthusiasm . . . vitality, knowledge, and charismatic youth." Returning one November night in 1933 from a secret APRA meeting, she was killed in a car accident. The three thousand Aprista mourners at her funeral remembered her as "an authentic example of Aprista womanhood, all enthusiasm, all faith, all bravery and self-abnegation," who "died as every Aprista should: fulfilling their duty." Provincial party leaders laid her to rest with a prayer that repeatedly eulogized her as: "C. Luisa Obregón: Aprista virgin par excellence, pure, self-abnegating, brave, and fervent." Luisa was buried next to the remains of a Domingo Navarrete T., "with whom," it was lyrically noted, "she maintains a permanent dialogue to continue strengthening the ranks of the party from the infinite, from the other side of the stars."[78] Was Domingo her Aprista compañero?

Affiliating through partisan coupling carried existential dangers, since each person's political tasks meant the risks of prison and death were real and constant. But as society and even their beloved partisan community found it too difficult to foreground modern meanings of compañera as an equal partisan, reflected in the egalitarian companions these partisan couples aspired to be, the meaning of the term too readily collapsed back into the ancient one of wife and vassal. What seems like a striking contrast—commemorating a partisan woman-at-arms as a pure, self-abnegating Aprista virgin and then burying her next to a partisan lover and comrade—also reflected the tension within APRA between a radical political orientation that included women's emancipation from a repressive sexual morality on the one hand, and on the other, a focus on disciplined morality as the foundation for the renovating politics Peru so desperately needed. The 1934 Code of Conduct for the Aprista Youth Federation (Federación Aprista Juvenil; FAJ), which opened with "Aprista youth: Prepare yourself for action and not for pleasure: this is your law," explicitly repressed "sensuality." Four of its first five commandments focused on disciplining sexual energy.[79] Norm no. 1 set the tone by ominously warning young Apristas that "the major tyrant you need to combat is within yourself: sensuality," and the second cautioned the ambitious that "the man who wishes to command others must first learn to command himself." "Don't waste your vitality," Norm no. 39 admonished: "Restrain sensuality. Reserve your sexual energies. The strength of your children tomorrow depends on your continence and health today. Condemn *donjuanismo*. If you feel sexually attracted to a youth of the opposite sex, do not permit it to translate into external manifestations of a morbid and destructive sensuality. Dignify your feeling, elevate it, use it as a lever to propel your spiritual perfection, converting it into a fountain of collaboration and a stimulus for <u>your</u> *fajista* <u>work</u>."[80]

"There is no different morality in private and political life," according to Norm no. 4, and Norm no. 5 spelled out what loyalty meant: "Be loyal to your party, be loyal to your affections, be loyal to your friends, be loyal to your wife and your children, because there is no excusable treason in love, or in marriage, or in brotherhood, or in friendship. Treason is one unitary thing, and wherever it is practiced, [therein] lies the germ of the traitor who tomorrow can be disloyal to his Fatherland, to his cause, and to his party."[81] From the perspective of Magda Portal, or perhaps María Luisa Obregón, such an Aprista morality could add another brick to the wall built by Catholic morality that repressed women's sexuality. But for the majority of young male Aprista recruits, these attempts to sublimate and redirect their sexual energy created a safer harbor for rank-and-file women to participate in party life. Manuel Seoane, for instance, predicting in his 1931 *APRA* interview that the role of women in the Aprista struggle "will be decisive," mused that men's "sentimentalism or our sensuality impedes us from learning the springs of constructive energy of which the woman is capable. I have had many loyal [female] comrades, especially among the Argentine Russian Jews."[82] In these interviews where the leaders introduced themselves to the rank and file, he is the only one to describe women as comrades (*camaradas*).

"Comrade" was also another meaning of the word "compañero," and it pointed to a final route to full affiliation in the party. While also calling forth the collective Aprista experience, the primary inflection in comradeship was a political identity born from fighting back to back, shedding blood, and sharing sacrifice. Comrades are brothers in arms who need not even share ideological convictions, "just" the experience of battle. In her own experience affiliating with the Aprista leadership, Portal had cycled through bohemian camaraderie and partisan coupling. But only comradeship had the potential to transcend entrenched gender hierarchies. Bohemian camaraderie sidestepped the issue—Portal became one of the boys, but the "boys" category remained unchallenged. In a partisan coupling, the constant and irresolvable struggle was asserting the egalitarian partisan identity over the assumed subservient wife or mistress. But a comrade could literally blow those categories apart.

In another case of such a "discovery of comradeship," a generation of young European intellectuals dissolved the unbreachable barriers of a rigid class society in the comradeship of the Great War's trenches. Comradeship was not friendship, but was instead described by contemporaries as "'a sort of splendid carelessness . . . holding us together.'"[83] It did not depend on either companionship born from physical proximity or a shared affinity for each other's company, but instead on the transformative experience of communal trial by fire. Its power could "be properly appreciated only when placed against the background of a society that divided people by putting up unbreachable ramparts of language, dress, and education." In the trenches, comradeship bridged the social chasm between the laboring classes and the elites who perceived the lower orders "not as individual human beings but as creatures deliberately designed to serve those above them—or alternatively, as members of a grey mass whose growing demands were to be feared and resisted."[84] In those trenches, these comrades discovered the nation in each other.

The social construction of gender, of what men and women could and should do, similarly divided men and women in Peru's middle and upper classes. Comradeship fundamentally transcended these categories in the collective life-and-death experience of battle, a human drama so powerful it erased—if only for the moments of fire—foundational social hierarchies and distinctions. Once experienced, that transcendence cast those same human distinctions as both artificial and stultifying.

Tellingly, in her *APRA* interview introducing her to the Aprista rank and file, Portal chose a terrifying combat experience as the event that "left the greatest emotion in your spirit." While exiled in Mexico a few years earlier, Portal revealed she had traveled from Jalapa to Mexico City, "in open battle and in an armor-plated train, expecting attacks from the rebels hidden in the hills. When the train reached a certain sector of the road, I then had the great emotion of being in the volley of a mock battle. Because I did not know it was a simulacrum, I had the full feeling of the assault."[85] Portal did not yearn for literal battle but to share its equivalent emotional experience to thus transcend gendered exclusion and fully assimilate with her male peers in the APRA leadership. The ultimate desire this story expressed is not blood but comradeship.

A week earlier, Manuel Seoane had answered the same question with a very different kind of anecdote revolving around the compassion and aid

of friends and allies, recounting a touching story of his Argentine comrades starting a collection to help him and Heysen get to Santiago once
the Argentine government deported them to the Chilean border. Both Portal's and Seoane's anecdotes highlight, in their way, what they saw as the
collaborative experience of being an Aprista, of being a member of their
partisan beloved community. For Seoane, that community was brothers
coming to one's aid. For Portal, it was proving she had already survived
the rigors of combat. Experiencing this human drama—this Aprista
drama—in the flesh was particularly important for Portal, because it distinguished her from other women whose revolutionary commitments were
dismissed by men as little more than romantic and literary affectations.
Listing her revolutionary credentials, allies like Rómulo Betancourt
stressed how Portal's "revolutionary passion, the anxiety to cooperate as a
soldier in the ranks of the cause of social justice . . . have not been literary
themes" for her. Betancourt counted off Portal's many political persecutions and near escapes, contrasting all of these "small and large tragedies
she has lived in her own flesh" with the literary fantasies other women enjoyed from the safety of their couch, as they read about romantic and distant revolutionary struggles, like the Russian Revolution.[86]

It is worth noting that none of the Aprista high leadership, male or female, had experienced open warfare yet when they answered these interviews, and they built their comradeship on a shared political repression
culminating in exile. This, of course, all changed after the 1931 campaign,
and especially after the Trujillo Revolution in July 1932, when women's experiences in conflict transformed Portal's yearning for comradeship into
reality. Like most Western political projects since the French Revolution,
APRA's ideology explicitly predicated citizenship on the willingness to
fight and die for the nation. As members of a political movement built on
expanding social justice, Apristas understood their struggle for the rights
of Peruvians to be their sacred raison d'être. But "it is just as sacred a patriotic duty to guard and defend Peru's soil without reservations. . . . Every
citizen must prepare themselves without exception to be a soldier of Peru
for the defense of its sovereignty and its rights as a Nation."[87] Pointing to
Aprista women who had defied the government and faced repression, especially those who carried arms in Trujillo, Portal argued that by their service to Peru through the proxy body of APRA, these women had earned
citizenship for all women. Years later, in 1946, in what became her second

history of women in the party, Portal stressed the physical costs women suffered for the party during these years and their transformative experience into comrades. Aprista women "suffered their baptism of blood" at the Christmas Eve attack on Trujillo in 1931, when they behaved "self-abnegatingly and heroically," suffering "bullet wounds, mistreatment, and prison" themselves.[88] During the sixteen tragic months of persecution, Aprista women proved themselves as "active and discreet militants," Portal recounted, as they "carried munitions to the trenches, collected the bodies at night from the ditches of Chan Chan, and healed the wounded" during the Trujillo uprising.

"The sixteen months of the sanchecerrato are, then, the trial by fire for the compañeras of the party," Portal concluded, when women bore "the maximum, suffering many times greater than their strengths. The persecution, the separation from loved ones, the insecurity, the hunger, the misery, and the prison cell become common for Aprista women," who, she noted somberly, became Peru's first female political prisoners.[89] Portal extended her definition of militancy to include women who risked repression by organizing Aprista social assistance brigades and by staffing logistical positions and serving as messengers, an "indispensable contact for coordinating party activities." Women, she pointed out, played critical roles in producing and distributing clandestine Aprista propaganda. In fact, the fevered repression that fell upon Aprista men, Portal argues, ensured that the party's very survival depended on such women's "auxiliary" work, which became the work of the party itself. She also included as party martyrs the women left behind when Apristas were thrown in jail, the wives and mothers who "for years suffered their Calvary . . . wounded in their deepest heart." Through it all, Portal noted proudly, "not a single mother surrendered, not a single wife snitched, not a single sister was weak under threat of torture."[90]

Aprista women, then, "like men, fulfilled their role, each in their place. And the Aprista women did not suffer fewer persecutions, prisons, or tortures"; they were "the true martyrs of this era of great and supreme sacrifices."[91] Portal did not need to say out loud what her partisan audiences all remembered: that she herself had led and carried out all these tasks. "With hundreds of compañeras and thousands of compañeros in prison," Seoane remembered in 1935, she "organizes social aid for prisoners, solicits moral support from foreign groups, writes manifestos, flyers.

Takes part in conspiracies. Leaves for and returns from extremely dangerous missions dodging dangers."[92]

The almost obligatory praising of women as *abnegadas*, self-abnegating,
hinted at how women could expand their expected selflessness to encompass
a larger national family. Like the Aprista emphasis on disciplined morality, relying on self-abnegation as a framework for understanding women
presented both obstacles and opportunities. In Peru, articulating women
as self-abnegating was particularly well suited to an Aprista political culture of sacrifice and martyrdom, suggesting another entrance for women
to participate in party life while still inhabiting a foundational feminine
archetype. The same traits used to laud a woman's total and self-sacrificing
devotion to her home and children could be shifted to focus not just on her
family but now also on her larger Aprista and Peruvian home and family
through the work of the APRA Party.

The institution these Aprista comrades entered was essentially an army,
dependent on their discipline and respect for hierarchy, as Norm no. 20 in
the FAJ Code of Conduct reminded them. "Remember always that since
the Aprista Party is an organization of STRUGGLE, the most severe discipline and the most strict command hierarchy needs to be observed and
respected."[93] While the partisan struggle could be a space of women's
emancipation through the transformative experience of comradeship, it
was always fragile because Peruvians understood discipline and hierarchy
in racial and gendered terms. Transformative comradeship, where everything, including entrenched gender norms, was at stake and could be
sacrificed in the utopian struggle, was perhaps possible within a small
circle, in a face-to-face community of brothers in arms or quixotic exiles
in the trenches against unthinkable odds. As the Apristas transitioned
into a mass movement, their growing organization increasingly relied on
discipline and hierarchy taught through familiar patriarchal models.
Norm 10: "Unity is the secret behind the strength of your great party. You,
as a fajista, cannot forget at any moment that you are an Aprista and that
the members of the Party of the People are your older brothers."[94] Relying
on family metaphors reinforced patriarchal assumptions about how
people should behave—how younger and older brothers relate to each
other, or how to understand Haya as the benevolent father. Such patriarchal social relations, and the absence of familiar metaphors with active

models for women, threatened to completely collapse the emancipatory space of genderless comrades.

The frantic months in 1933 and 1934 would prove to be, in Seoane's evocative phrase, "a period of semidemocratic vacations," neatly capturing both how Benavides deftly kept both democratic and authoritarian hopes alive, and how Apristas recognized this period of quasi-legality as transient, a fleeting moment of relief before their reality as the persecuted party crashed back down.[95] Repression, prison, and a return to the catacombs loomed more fearfully every day as the national political situation rapidly got away from the Apristas and Benavides found Peace and Harmony increasingly untenable. On the Left, APRA had never considered conciliation after emerging from its years in the catacombs, and it immediately prepared for "new hostilities with the government. . . . Although . . . within the limits of constitutional tolerance for a democratic state in tranquil times," historians judged, APRA's politics of confrontation were "grave provocations in the explosive Peruvian atmosphere of 1933 and 1934."[96] On the Right, the Revolutionary Union, Sánchez Cerro's old party, was now explicitly steering toward Fascism and growing increasingly violent at Benavides's policy of conciliation. Between May and November of 1933, Benavides had to dissolve the Sánchezcerrista cabinet he had inherited, face down an army revolt, and arrest Revolutionary Union partisans for plotting his assassination.[97] Increasingly loath to let either the leftist Apristas or the Fascist Right into Congress, Benavides kept postponing the congressional elections.

In January 1934, a labor strike caused government repression against APRA to spike, and Seoane was forced once again to flee into exile.[98] A few months later, in October 1934, Haya was aboard an airplane that suffered a mysterious "accident." Although he emerged unharmed, this was all the proof APRA needed that Benavides was trying to kill their leader. When Benavides postponed congressional elections for the sixth time a month later, Aprista patience broke. On November 26, 1934, another Aprista rebellion broke out, but it fizzled after a few days. Benavides captured almost one thousand Apristas in retaliation. Haya escaped to the Aprista underground once again, assuming the nom de guerre of Pachacutec, "Earthshaker," the most important Inca emperor, and naming his principal hiding place Incahuasi, House of the Inca. He would remain there for ten years.[99]

"Mostly aware" of the upcoming Aprista assault, Benavides's forces captured Portal the night before the revolt, on November 25.[100] "Nobody has been able to see her," Seoane complained. "Any exchange of words with her is forbidden. Her mother, her sisters cannot see her. Not even Gloria . . . can stretch her little arms to her. Nothing, nothing. It is ferocious vengeance, total, feral, primitive, loaded with hate."[101] She was sentenced to prison for five hundred days or to a fine of 5,000 soles, a cruel joke for Seoane: "5,000 soles for her, who many times did not have anything to eat, or [for] the party cornered by persecution?" She would spend the next sixteenth months, from November 1934 through February 1936, imprisoned in Lima's Santo Tomás convent, which also served as the prison for women.

With Haya underground; Seoane exiled abroad; Sánchez, Cox, and others deported to Chile, Portal was the highest-ranking Aprista leader imprisoned in Peru. Six months into her prison term, in May 1935, Antonio Miró Quesada, one of South America's leading journalists, who ran the country's most prestigious and anti-Aprista newspaper, *El Comercio*, was assassinated walking in downtown Lima with his wife. A young Aprista militant named Carlos Steer had walked up to them and shot Miró Quesada in the back. His wife threw herself at the young assassin, who then shot and killed her. Steer turned the gun on himself, but survived two shots to the head and was hauled off to prison. This horrifying attack on one of Peru's most elite families "would never be forgotten," and branded Apristas as "terrorists and assassins."[102]

For Portal's Aprista brethren underground and exiled abroad, this new assassination made her safety in prison a key concern. In letters crossing the Andes to their respective exiles in Argentina and Chile, Seoane and Sánchez rallied their solidarity machine to secure Portal's release, since they feared she ran the "risk of being assassinated."[103] Their efforts culminated in a dedicated special issue of the Argentine magazine *Claridad*. Organized by Seoane from Buenos Aires, *Magda Portal: Su vida y su obra* (The life and work of Magda Portal) had as its goal "diffusing Magda Portal's personality and intensifying the protest for the imprisonment she suffers."[104] After a short biographical sketch, the magazine gathered profiles and poems, including one by Delmar, as well as some of Portal's own poems and partisan essays. Haya, Sánchez, and Seoane all contributed profiles. It was these *Claridad* profiles, "dedicated to exalt[ing Portal's] intellectual and revolutionary personality," that first recast events earlier in her life, starting with the 1923 Juegos Florales, to make her the best example of a revolutionary woman.

In prison, Portal was "not alone: 4 walls / and portraits. Victor Raúl, my daughter / and someone else who I no longer know /—he has left alone, as he came—."[105] In letters written nearly a year into her term, Portal put on a brave face: "In any case, prison is serving me well. One learns, meditates, sees the world in perspective. Contact with the people of a level below that of the masses, the delinquent or abnormal women, is also an experience. And for those of us who know how to observe, it is much like school." Portal faced prison as another Aprista organizational challenge, assigning the other prisoners daily chores and access to showers, teaching them to read and write, and composing songs and short plays for them to perform. Many things remained uncertain. "I don't know when I will be released," she confided in her correspondence. "They have indicated five hundred days, but they are not confirmed. I know that in many Latin American countries they are working for my freedom, with no results yet. I don't know if I will have to leave the country when I leave prison, but I am sure that if things don't change, the threat of a new prison term will continue weighing on me."[106]

In prison, Portal wrote a poem to Seoane, "Message for Manuel," documenting how her suffering in prison brought her closer to his suffering in exile, deepening their affective bond far beyond the possibilities of bohemian camaraderie. Politics and ideology are nowhere to be found in this poem; there is no triumphalist revolutionary ending. Instead, it is a study of Portal's and Seoane's two-fold suffering: the actual pain of deprivation, of imprisonment and exile, and the pain and rage of their impotence in the face of each others' suffering. "Brother, I am thinking / how your wound must hurt you / I am thinking here / with my hands tied behind my back / unable to do anything. / . . . / I don't know how to tell you that it hurts me /—I guard my words so much!—/ tell you that within me, in my entrails / like the fire of a wound / your silent tears burn / I would like to speak to you of hope / like we talk of heaven for those who die / like we paint children magical paradises / to fool their anxieties / of adventures and such / but everything is so fragile / so ungraspable and false, / so childish for us / who are now so grown / that I prefer to tell you, break every distance / and come to be a little silent with me / side by side and facing / this pain / not shunning it, strong, / tasting all of its flavor / bitter and acid."[107]

In Europe, "comradeship arose out of the sharing of a common danger and a common disillusion that was 'beyond all hope,' . . . sharpened by the enjoyment of common pleasures and by a sense of alienation from those left behind—those who had not been there, who had not seen the horrors, who had not experienced the fear of dying and the relief of survival, and who therefore would never understand the looks on the survivors' faces."[108] This is the disillusion and alienation animating Portal's poem, where hope is a foolish fairy tale told to soothe frightened children, undignified for these two mature revolutionaries, "who are now so grown." Their emotional recourse is not escaping to comforting fantasies, but instead sharing—savoring—the "bitter and acid flavor" of the pain that was the price of their revolutionary commitment and that only comrades could understand. "I understand you, I / why even say it? / this is like the sky is blue / and the sea deep / and your tragedy brings cold to my being / as it does to you yourself / . . . / I, who today also suffer, without caring /—anonymous pains—/ small beasts who entwine in my soul / to break my faith that raises its mast / in the emptiness of this sky, / I tell you, / of your pain and mine / let's make one only; / and like facing a river / whose origin we don't know / let's watch it flow since everything passes. / Maybe your heart and mine / perturbed and anxious for the struggle / will at last find their peace!"[109]

Seoane was not a poet. But in his Argentine exile, writing his profile of Portal for *Claridad,* he also captured some of the emotional depth of Portal's message to him. "So, when she is imprisoned and I suffer this impotent liberty that disgraces and shames me as a man," he wrote, "I have wanted to pen these hurried lines of a memory that is not a judgment, nor elegy, but merely a moving foreshortening of a true revolutionary, of a new woman in this Latin America full of antiquated defects."[110]

SUPLEMENTO No. 2

Ultimas
canciones
del
F. D. N.

Cancionero Radial

PRECIO:
15 CTS.

Director del «Suplemento» C. R.: M. Ascencio   Lima, 18 de Junio de 1945.

MAGDA PORTAL

La mujer luchadora incansable del
Partido Aprista Peruano.

Magda Portal in 1945, *Cancionero Radial*, "PAP's Untiring Woman Fighter," June 18, 1945. Courtesy estate of Magda Portal, Rocío Revolledo Pareja.

Part III

Demolitions

Magda Portal and Gloria in Buenos Aires, 1939. Courtesy estate of
Magda Portal, Rocío Revolledo Pareja, and Penn State University Press.

CHAPTER SEVEN

Almost within Grasp

PORTAL WAS FREED FROM prison in February of 1936, a month shy of completing her term. No one was really sure why she had been freed early, though it was rumored that José Gálvez, the judge at the Juegos Florales thirteen years earlier and now the ambassador to Colombia, had flexed his influence.[1] While technically free, Portal was reportedly under surveillance, and, writing her thanks to her compañeros in Chile for their support while in prison, she confessed: "If I were to be entirely sincere with you, I would tell you all that my freedom does not make me entirely happy. Even though it is extremely limited, for many reasons, it hurts me to be free alone, here where all of ours—leaders and militants—are either underground or imprisoned."[2]

Presidential elections were to be held that year, and though Haya was running, the Apristas had no faith in the electoral system and plotted with the Bolivian president, promising the landlocked nation support for a Pacific port in exchange for arms and aid in overthrowing Benavides. Once again, however, Benavides learned of the conspiracy and disqualified Haya's candidacy, forced Congress to annul the election and extend his own term for three years, and then promptly dissolved Congress and governed as a dictator until December of 1939.[3] Portal kept a low profile in Peru for these three years. In January 1939, using falsified passports, she and Gloria finally escaped to Buenos Aires, where Manuel Seoane met her at the train station.[4] With no work or other ties in Argentina, she crossed the Andes to join the Aprista exiles in Chile, arriving in Santiago in November 1939.

Tests of Aprista Faith

The Chilean Popular Front, in power since 1937, had brought the Socialist Party of Chile, the Partido Socialista de Chile, or PS, into the governing coalition and now welcomed the exiled Peruvian Apristas. Chile sheltered the largest community of Aprista exiles abroad, and Portal, Seoane, and Luis Alberto Sánchez were its top three leaders: Sánchez was their titular head, and Portal headed their Culture Section and took over as the interim Press and Propaganda secretary from an overwhelmed Seoane.[5]

The Peruvian Apristas and the Chilean Socialists had a long and intertwined history—they considered each other kindred parties, both part of a larger family of Latin American radical reformist projects that also included Betancourt's Acción Democrática in Venezuela. Founded in 1933, the Chilean PS was more Marxist in orientation, but like APRA, it was a multiclass alliance of middle and working classes arrayed against the national oligarchy and international imperialists, and both stressed democracy, nationalism, and state intervention to promote industry and welfare. These two leftist parties from these Pacific neighbors were the closest of sisters, and had long looked to each other for aid and inspiration. APRA was the older sister, the strongest foreign influence on the Chilean PS.

By the late 1930s, the Latin American political landscape shifted dramatically as the resource demands of World War II and geopolitical realignments created new spaces and possibilities unimaginable only a few years earlier, best demonstrated by the expanded negotiating space Lázaro Cárdenas found when nationalizing Mexico's oil reserves and realizing a long-standing nationalist dream. Latin American countries in the early 1940s tolerated democracies that acknowledged, if not always worked to meet, the demands of labor—a marked difference from the wave of authoritarian regimes that swept through the hemisphere after the Great Depression. Peru and Chile experienced this "mid-decade opening to mass politics" as a window of opportunity for their largest leftist political parties, APRA and the Socialists respectively.[6]

While Peruvian Apristas, Chilean Socialists, and the Venezuelan Adecos (sympathizers of Acción Democrática, or AD) were all able to share in national power in this postwar climate, the contours of possibility for each were quite different. Looking at Peru with Chilean eyes, their experience

in the PS gave Seoane, Sánchez, and Portal an overly optimistic orientation, making it easier to misread their situation and keep agitating for an
ideological purity impossible in a Peruvian context where APRA, as the
leftist mass party, was still politically persecuted and remained embattled
by entrenched political and economic interests.

In addition to reuniting her with her Aprista brethren in a political environment that welcomed their leftist orientation, Chile became a harbor
for Portal's personal life, providing increasing stability for her and her battered family. The Aprista exiles in Chile were technically on borrowed
time: Haya had recalled them in an April 1939 letter with orders for everyone under fifty and not ill to return to Peru within the year to rejoin the
national political struggle. But the exiles, many blaming their modest economic circumstances, trickled back only slowly.[7] Portal planned to stay in
Chile to finish Gloria's education and remained for almost six years.[8]

Portal's political work in Santiago revolved around the extensive network of leftist allies she had cultivated since the late 1920s. She affiliated
with the Chilean PS, befriending its rising star, Salvador Allende. She
maintained a vibrant correspondence with her old friend Rómulo Betancourt, who was rising to the commanding heights of Venezuelan public
life. In 1940, together they organized a Congress of Latin American Popular
Democratic Parties, which she cared enough about to call "our Congress."[9] Although it came about through the initiative of the Chilean PS,
and was cosponsored by Betancourt's Acción Democrática Party and
APRA, the congress was "dominated by Aprista doctrines."[10] To this international group of similar-minded politicians, Portal, the only named
Peruvian delegate, was the face of APRA.[11]

During World War II, as Peru basked in a "period of unity and tranquility" buoyed by an export boom driven by the war's insatiable demands,
APRA further toned down its anti-imperialist rhetoric. World War II only
strengthened the United States' role in Latin America, and the Allied victory made the U.S. "brand of liberal democracy and capitalism indisputably
hegemonic in the hemisphere."[12] Latin American popular movements, inherently suspicious of U.S. imperialism before the war, had to further adjust
themselves to the United States and its expanding power and influence.

Haya had built his regional bona fides on just such an anti-imperialism.
Nonetheless, even from the 1930s, he had started warming to the United
States. In the early 1940s, far from being adversarial, Haya now hoped to

leverage U.S. democratic sentiment to strike against his Peruvian political enemies, and "vainly lobbied" the U.S. government to pressure Peru to return full rights to APRA as "part of the Allies' international crusade against 'totalitarianism.'" After 1941, the neighboring PS leadership also became "increasingly social democratic and friendly to the U.S.," and followed APRA in moderating their anti-imperialist rhetoric, arguing that "'democratic imperialism' was preferable to 'totalitarian imperialism.'"[13]

From their distant exile in Santiago, Portal and other Aprista leaders grew increasingly concerned about Haya, who was entering his fifth year of clandestinity, hiding in Incahuasi, surrounded by advisors they deeply mistrusted. The Chilean group strongly disagreed with Haya's downplaying of key party principles, complaining about his substitution of "democratic Interamericanism without empire" for "anti-imperialism," which they considered a nonnegotiable foundational Aprista principle. But even more than ideas, the exiled leadership complained about the party's increasing authoritarian tone, which they attributed to Haya's "forced cloister" that led him to over rely on new advisors who "assaulted" him with "captious rumors." Sánchez went so far as enlisting Betancourt to meet with Haya on a swing through Peru in 1939. Betancourt, Sánchez wrote Haya, very much wanted to relate the lessons from his own three-year experience as a clandestine party chief in Venezuela. "Much of the news he received in hiding had been false or deformed," Sánchez told Haya, and Betancourt grew to appreciate the "dose of reason" that the Venezuelan exiles in Colombia provided, and came to see that "a prejudicial group that maintained understandable but sterile jealousies with the others had formed around him in hiding."[14]

Old-guard Apristas felt ignored. "We receive letters frequently here from the cc. [compañeros] saying attention is not paid to them," Sánchez complained to Haya in 1939, and the Chilean group similarly felt that "for five years, our own opinion has been systematically devalued." The leaders in exile were not being kept informed of internal party affairs, much less consulted about key decisions, and yet they remained as signatories on Aprista declarations. This infuriated Sánchez, who repeatedly complained to Haya about this in 1939 and 1943, stressing that it made them feel used, that the party was democratic and consultative in name only, and that Haya's will was the only one that mattered. They all understood the need for a public party line, of course, but the leadership in exile needed to be kept apprised of what was actually happening, unlike the time Sánchez opened the pages of *El Comercio* to learn key details about an Aprista revolt, "even though I was supposedly to take charge of the government."[15]

In criticizing APRA's lack of internal democracy, Sánchez "insisted on calling on our long-standing friendship and our sincere compañerismo, which he did not "believe consists of always saying yes . . . of complicit silences or unappealable denials." For this group of friends turned political leaders, part of the problem was the inherent confusion of writing to Haya as both a long-standing friend and as their ultimate political chief. This was a critical moment, and APRA faced many serious problems, as Sánchez's long letters analyzing the delicate national and international situations attested. But for Sánchez, their "primordial task" was confronting head-on the mistrust, the "lack of faith" that APRA now engendered. "We have come to elicit a systematic distrust," and the dominant question in his conversations with people of every type was "'But, can the word of the party be trusted?' I don't know if they tell you that, even though I referred to it in one of our conversations in Lima, but this prejudice handicaps us terribly. We have to reconquer the confidence of our following, at whatever cost."[16] When Haya ignored Sánchez's impassioned letter for two months, he wrote again, reiterating that the party had to "reconquer the faith in our capacity to fulfill our word. From every sector affirmations arrive that we are the most disloyal people in the world."[17]

For Sánchez, the situation was getting desperate enough that he threatened to leave APRA. "If we don't return to our fraternal and democratic habits of consulting among us," he concluded, "I feel myself more and more distant from the party, and I come to see triumph as a liberation, not because it would be the realization of so many blunt dreams, but instead to say the formal good-bye, since the clear outline of the intimate good-bye begins to emerge in my will and my feelings."[18]

Like Sánchez, Portal also wrote Haya a private letter on June 20, 1941, to voice her growing concerns about his role as an international leader and the disconnect between the efforts of Apristas in Peru and those exiled abroad. She complained that the "congress of Aprista initiative, of Aprista achievements and Aprista solutions" she had organized "was given so little importance" by the party in Lima. Stressing her "irreducible anti-imperialism," Portal conceded that Latin America could not elude U.S. influence and argued that Haya was the only regional leader capable of resuscitating a "new Indoamerican politics" that would allow the region to reach an understanding with the United States, preventing "the slavery of the Indoamerican countries in a near future."[19]

But to forge this new politics, she argued, Haya needed to leave Peru, where Aprista politics had become hopelessly mired and was no longer inspiring allies abroad. "Abroad, [Apristas'] focus on their victims, prisoners, etc., is becoming tired. We have exhausted the plaintive tone," she diagnosed. Apristas' never-ending focus on martyrdom and personal sacrifice was tiring not just once and future allies, but even leaders like Portal, who was slowly rebuilding her personal life after years of perennial sacrifice and martyrdom. "Don't you think that there is enough sacrifice for now?" she asked Haya. "It is human to think that there should be a limit to every pain, and Peruvians have already sacrificed a lot for the party. Except for a few leaders—a few!—the rest do not want to continue sacrificing themselves. It is both human and politic that you consider this side of the problem."[20]

Haya's response immediately opened on the offensive. Portal's Chilean congress, he accused, got so little press because of terrible information, received late. Instead of serving as proof of her efforts, the congress proved the opposite to Haya: Why weren't they working on a second one? Why were they shrinking from their duty as Aprista exiles to be continental apostles? The letter implicitly attacked Portal and explicitly named Sánchez and Seoane for not mobilizing internationally. The exiles, Haya fumed, ignored his proposal to set out on "Aprista pilgrimages" throughout the region. When high-ranking leaders did campaign, they failed to meet Haya's standards: Sánchez had "gone a few times to Argentina, Uruguay, and Bolivia but without the apostolic rhythm of a frank surrender to a crusade that would be a great success." Seoane, "a great orator, . . . has a sufficient base for a magnificent and successful campaign. What keeps you all in Chile?" If she had "thought for five minutes," he explained angrily, she would see clearly that his leaving Peru is precisely what the Right wanted him to do. Her letter made him, and not the enemy, culpable for the persecution. He refused to leave. He was fine in his hiding: uncomfortable, but with a "profound interior life" and certain of his path and his duty.[21]

This exchange rang in Portal's ears for years. Attacking his exiled Aprista generals for not working hard enough to mobilize international allies, Haya refused to recognize that this was exactly what Portal's Congress of Latin American Popular Democratic Parties was. For Portal, it was self-evident that APRA would be better served if its top leader left his "profound interior life," nurtured in perpetual martyrdom, and did such outreach himself. His refusal to leave the labyrinth of the Aprista underground in Peru left her and other leaders to serve as the face of the party, and she was certain it was harming APRA's international reputation.

But what Portal focused on when recalling Haya's response nearly forty years later was his "ferocious" tone and his perpetual emphasis on his personal suffering and sacrifice. Portal had been working closely with Haya for fifteen years and knew his personality as well as any other party intimate; his reflexive defensive reaction should have come as little surprise. Her own letter was, if not "ferocious," very blunt in its probing when she demanded why Haya did not step up to a larger continentalist role. "Is it because you don't have faith in yourself? Is it that you think you might fail?"[22] Such provocative questions suggest the personal tone of a trusted family member, that of the intimate allowed—at least at one time—such liberties.

When Haya dismissed her criticism by arguing that her own suffering and sacrifice for the party was never enough, that her time in prison could never match his own suffering, she saw him resorting, true to form, to the "plaintive tone" she had argued was alienating APRA from its regional leftist allies. Working in Santiago, Portal was starting to question how much sacrifice, how much suffering, was too much to bear for their revolutionary cause. If Haya's "profound interior life" kept him certain of his revolutionary duty, Portal's own personal circumstances were changing. In 1942, Serafín Delmar was finally released from prison in Peru and joined Portal and their daughter, Gloria, in Chile. For the first time in ten years, Portal's family was once again complete.

Haya was not wrong, on one level—he could not know what the Chilean exiles were doing and feeling, as much as they tried to stay abreast of each other with letters flying between Haya's secret hideaway and Santiago. Neither could the Chilean group ever really know what Haya was going through. These were seasoned politicians with more than one stint in the underground; they all knew that such conflict between leaders who stayed hidden in the country and those who toiled from exile abroad was inherent in clandestine politics. But knowing that did not erase the power of the emotions among them, nor the enduring intensity of their psychological bonds.

The central question was the nature of APRA. Was it a doctrine, a set of ideas and policies that, once modified or violated, undermined the Aprista raison d'être? Their constant reference to "Aprista faith" suggests it was more. The essence of APRA for the highest leadership was both the tight social connection, the fictive kinship, or what Haya termed the "memory and infrastructure of a community of a womb" combined with what another Peruvian observer would later call Haya's "palace of ideas," a philosophy meant to provide answers to every problem of private and public life.[23] But this meant APRA was so sweeping, so abstract, so not focused on policies and politics, the nitty-gritty of actual governing, that it had tripped a wire from politics into a life orientation, what they understood as the many-layered "Aprista faith" some now questioned. Their intense emotional investment in such bonds was driving Haya and his exiled generals to actions neither rational nor legible to those on the outside who were not privy to their shared "palace of ideas" and its associated feelings.

Portal may have felt Haya's letter as such a "ferocious attack" that she remembered it to the end of her days, but it was par for the course in his correspondence with other generals in exile. His reply to Sánchez was, if anything, more brutal, full of personal attacks designed to slice like razors, the long association between the two men mined for the most painful ammunition. After ignoring Sánchez for two months, a deafening silence in a correspondence that at times saw several letters exchanged in a week, Haya's bitter, furious letter stretched for seven typed pages. Sánchez's "provocative" letters proved his "unmistakable acrimony and arrogant disdain toward us and our efforts," his critiques were "unjust and absurd," and his "deformed vision of our movement" was "constructed" from his "powerful imagination." Sánchez's latest book is "the worst I have read from you," due to "the same defect that your critics . . . point to in your literary work (and forgive me): haste, superficiality, etc., that seems to me to [also] be your fundamental defect in the political order." Haya, who claimed to be no poet, nonetheless spun a powerful rhythm by interjecting such a parenthetical "(and forgive me)" after seven separate attacks on Sánchez's character and abilities, emphasizing instead of cushioning each blow. Haya tore at even the oldest scabs, accusing Sánchez of being a Leguista, and explaining Sánchez's spiritual distancing as a product of his being "uprooted, and because you are a man of *Letras* and of Lima who admits no errors," reminding Sánchez that he was never part of the original provincial nucleus at the heart of their movement and implying that his education in the humanities made him a rigid intellectual instead of a man of action.[24]

Explicitly addressing Sánchez's threat of breaking with the party, Haya saw this as a shameful crisis of faith. "Announcing that you are leaving in the hour of triumph and that you already feel unattached shows a crisis of faith so typical of intellectuals in these disconcerting times. . . . I know that there is an abyss between your sensibility and mine," Haya continued. "Only the faith in Aprismo has joined us. I neither understand nor have made the life that you understand and make. I have always said that one of the best demonstrations of the cohesive force of Aprismo is the case of our long-standing compañerismo, given that we are so different. As you know, other than Aprista faith, we have shared no other bond. But for me, Aprismo is as strong a solder of differences as the memory or infrastructure of the community of a shared womb. So, if you lose the faith and break the ties, what's left? I have felt the same way in your attitude toward Manolo [Seoane]. I feel it now with you. . . . Only Aprista faith ties me to people, and I don't change it like a shirt."[25]

An aside "explaining" Sánchez's motives hints at reasons for Haya's vitriol. "To this must be added—and how disagreeable it is to allude to it, given that it is a family matter of those I hate to get mixed up in," Haya spat, "the open and in-house campaign of your Señora wife against the party, against me personally, and against everything that our movement refers to." Sánchez's social-climbing wife was leading him astray, notoriously "repeating everywhere" that " 'the government does not want to deal with Haya, but with another . . . ,' and if this phrase was not so well known for being birthed by the flights of fancy from Santiago, I would not emphasize it. But so it is."[26] Haya accused the Aprista exiles in Santiago of trying to displace him. Every critique that Sánchez launched about the direction of the party, every doubt raised about a political decision, Haya now interpreted as both an attack on him as a person and on his perhaps no longer inevitable role as chief of their movement.

Portal's Chilean interlude ended in 1945, when the exiled leadership returned to Peru as a new democratic opening legalized APRA as the principal force in a center-left electoral coalition. Just weeks before Portal's planned departure for Peru, Betancourt entreated her to come join him in Venezuela, "if your residence in Peru proves unfeasible."[27] With her capacity and ability, Betancourt urged, they could build something special in Venezuela. Betancourt's offer must have been tantalizing: the trajectory of his political project was promising, as the latest incarnation of Betancourt's political party, christened Acción Democrática (Democratic Action) in 1941, was now also part of a center-left coalition, a key player negotiating for presidential power.

Betancourt mobilized shared friendships to try to persuade her. Betancourt and his wife really wanted her to join them, one friend pressed in a letter sent just a week after Betancourt's. She would find an interesting political situation, a group of true friends, and might she be interested in editing a magazine? Traveling with Betancourt throughout the Venezuelan countryside, he reported Acción Democrática was "already a surprising organization for so little time, and there is this also: it is a fraternity of friends throughout the country, like the first days of La Reforma, like the beginning of Aprismo."[28]

And it was this additional promise of comradeship that must have been most tempting. Working in Venezuela offered the additional benefit of affective ties to replace those thinning among her Peruvian brothers in arms. "Besides, my spirit would find your friendship, your fraternal company very pleasing. The solitary intimacy of public life is tragic," Betancourt revealed. "I always have at my side that gift that life gave me of my wife and little girl. But I am always desirous of the nearness of other close affections. It is not easy to satisfy that desire when one holds certain positions. Brotherly resentment is so many times hiding behind the friendly embrace."[29]

Portal faced a choice: she could continue working for social justice, surrounded by fraternal comrades whose affection was authentic and proven, but in Venezuela. Her exchanges with Haya were already revealing increasing ideological and strategic discrepancies and, perhaps just as— or more—importantly, a straining personal relationship, what Betancourt called "brotherly resentments," and what the leadership in exile experienced in their inflammatory letters between Santiago and Incahuasi. Haya's letters were so vicious, so personal, it is hard to imagine the exiles sharing them or commiserating over their ill treatment; they likely suffered alone. The tenor of the correspondence on both sides reflects their searing intimacy. Yet she was not so alienated from APRA and her comrades to turn away from it; when she embarked from Chile, she left for Peru. Among the last of the exiles from Chile to return, Portal arrived in Lima in May 1945, just four days after receiving her entrance visa.[30]

But she traveled alone, with only her daughter in tow and Serafín Delmar staying behind. Years later, she revealed that she and Serafín had troubles from when he first arrived from Peru in 1942.[31] Upon his release, Serafín had received a letter from a mutual friend meant to encourage him as he faced the challenge of rebuilding his life after ten years in prison. "I need to tell you," their friend confided, "that you have an ideal and magnificent compañera who has known how to epically resist those ten long years."[32] Why did Serafín need such reassurance? Portal anxiously worried—if not anguished—about Serafín believing she was unfaithful to him during their decade apart. She would later write a revealing prison scene about a poet jailed for political crimes that begins by describing him as "a strange being. Someone has told him: 'your woman is cheating on you,' and he smiled. He always smiles. His smile is like his refuge. The years pass and the poet keeps smiling. His smile has almost become a tragic mask. When his wife and daughter come to visit him, he trembles. . . . Maybe because of her evasive gestures, he suspects some truth in those rumors . . . but he always smiles."[33]

Troubles in her relationship with Delmar become bad enough by December 1944 to appear in her own correspondence, when she wrote to an old Aprista friend living in Mexico, investigating the possibility of leaving Chile and moving to Mexico with Gloria. "How happy it made me, *hermana* Magda, to hear from you after so many years! But also what sadness to learn of your family troubles," he commiserated. "I don't know what faults we are paying for so dearly."[34]

Ironically, it was not her fidelity that brought the situation to a head. Walking into their apartment, Portal surprised Serafín in bed with one of her friends. "Shocked and desolate," her biographer and interviewer Kathleen Weaver explained, Portal broke with Serafín and refused to take him back, even as he "begged" her to forgive him, "insisting . . . it meant nothing to him." Portal refused to talk about the catastrophe when she returned to Peru, leaving Gloria to explain Serafín's absence to their family. Unhappy and bewildered, Serafín even wrote a long letter to Portal's mother, "imploring" her to intervene. No one could change Portal's mind, much to the dismay of her sister, who believed him to be "the great love" of

Portal's life.[35] He remained in Chile, dedicating himself to publishing the work he had written in prison and eventually going into business. He retreated from all literary and political public life, "as if he had felt a profound and incurable uneasiness with society and the world; he extinguished his voice and never published again ... apparently devoted to other tasks far from those of his restless and rebellious youth." He died in 1980.[36]

What happened? Weaver suggests Portal's "punitive" behavior in such a "brutal severance" shows how much Portal still cared for Serafín.[37] His efforts to reconcile certainly suggest he remained emotionally committed to her, but how committed did he remain to the revolutionary dream that had so long tied them together? Serafín was no longer motivated by political ideals, and his decade in Peru's prisons, an endless series of nightmarish trials that formed the basis of his last books, had beaten out whatever Aprista faith he once had. Perhaps he had no interest in returning to Peru to be either a party public figure or even an Aprista decorative figurehead— the martyred poet. He must also have known that Portal, a stranger in many ways to him after their decade of separation, could not be happy building a life with someone as profoundly disillusioned as he was. In their life together, he had always been the junior partner, swept up into the delirium of their—her—revolutionary dream. Did her dream of revolution, her politics, matter more than love? Was this Serafín's way out?

Once back in Peru, Portal received a letter from a friend in Santiago. "I beg you to be brave. . . . Serafín appears to have married that slut [*mujerzuela*]," the painful letter began. "People who told me believe that I should not tell you, but I believe it is my duty to tell you," to prepare Portal in case a friend, such as Salvador Allende, would mention it in passing. "I understand the pain, the anguish and desperation that this causes you, but don't forget that you have duties with Gloria and that you must overcome this moment of such bitterness," her friend counseled.[38]

The news was couched so gingerly as to give the impression that Portal was still devastated by her break with Serafín. Perhaps. Delmar's rapid remarriage suggests that his affair, despite his assurances that it "meant nothing," was more than a passing fling. Portal's portrait of him as the smiling poet is therefore surprisingly sympathetic; she was honest enough to shine a light on her own "evasive gestures" marking the growing distance between them that they would prove unable to bridge once Serafín was finally released. While her friend in Santiago may have felt the need to tiptoe around the news, perhaps Serafín's affair and remarriage became a painful but ultimately useful way out of a companionate marriage of poets, of compañeros Apristas, which after ten long years had seemed once again finally within reach, but which instead definitely collapsed. Musing at the end of her life about how "love has a time and that time is brief. . . . Love ends, even friendship ends," Portal was reflecting not just on her ill-fated marriage to Federico Bolaños, but also on her partisan coupling with his brother.[39]

APRA's Triumphant Return

APRA returned to legality to share national power as the foundation of the broad center-left National Democratic Front coalition. In this alliance, Haya agreed not to run for the presidency in the 1945 elections and instead to endorse José Bustamante y Rivero, who agreed to legalize APRA and share power. APRA's massive electoral support propelled Bustamante to victory with two-thirds of the vote. Bustamante legalized APRA as the Partido del Pueblo (Party of the People); the party had changed names in order to steer clear of a constitutional prohibition against international parties. Haya's judgment in choosing a political alliance over an insurrectionary revolutionary gambit yielded spectacular dividends when APRA won a commanding congressional majority.[40]

Later, critics on the Left would indict APRA's political effectiveness for not achieving programs on anti-imperialism, agrarian reform, or economic planning; in this reading, APRA became the "substantially less successful" Latin American midcentury populist project, especially compared to neighboring Argentina and Brazil.[41] However, APRA leveraged their congressional power to move their social and economic agenda forward. On the new administration's very first day, the Aprista congressional block passed a bill freeing political prisoners and reestablishing freedom of speech and of the press. Politically, the coalition advanced Aprista planks, including strengthening industrialization, taxing wealthy exporters, favoring the urban middle class and workers, and building housing and schools. Sharing power, APRA delivered. Their legislative achievements focused on education, where they extended primary education to the entire population, floating a loan to build schools throughout Peru;

passed a university reform law; and increased education spending from 9 to 15 percent of the national budget. They sponsored several bills to raise the standard of living through public spending on social welfare and public works, passed legislation favoring labor unions and adding cost-of-living wage adjustments, and ensured that government mediation of labor disputes was squarely pro-labor.[42]

Apristas roughly modeled this "planned democracy" on the New Deal, and those in the National Democratic Front "saw themselves as the victors over the oligarchy and as the bearers of the triumphant banner of democracy."[43] They were not wrong. Although relations between top Apristas and their opponents "were so cordial" in the first four months of this power sharing that a high-level counselor "was moved to remark that this was a class reunion rather than a class struggle," outside observers recognized the profound democratic challenge that APRA represented in national politics. The charge d'affaires at the U.S. embassy looked at Peru and saw "no other American republic where the old elite is so secure in its power, where the country is still so completely controlled by so few," with only "some seventy families, more or less," still controlling 90 percent of the wealth not in foreign hands. "In this picture," he argued, APRA "represents as much of a social revolution as did the French Revolution."[44]

Peru's National Democratic Front shared the broad contours of other leftist, reformist coalitions in post-1945 Latin America such as the Chilean Popular Front. But such center-left coalitions were not the only order of the day, and other leftist parties moved quicker on their own, bypassing coalitions and power sharing with conservatives. In Venezuela, Betancourt's AD joined a military coup of young officers in October 1945. The following three years—dubbed the "Trienio Adeco"—were "three years of boisterous, dramatic," radical political reform, and Betancourt soon maneuvered into the top leadership spot of the Revolutionary Governing Junta. He changed the petroleum law to give the government an unprecedented half of oil revenues, forced foreign oil companies to help diversify and develop Venezuelan industry by requiring them to invest in nonextractive industries, and created a new constitution focused on social welfare. Government oil revenues doubled, primary school enrollment quadrupled, and the Trienio turned its attention to land reform and the plight of the peasantry.[45]

On his way to congratulate Betancourt on taking power in 1945, Salvador Allende, now a Chilean senator and the general secretary of the PS, stopped in Peru to visit his Aprista allies. Standing before Peru's Parliament, he celebrated the Apristas' victory as part of their center-left coalition, seeing in their ascension "the tide of democracy, economic liberty, and social justice rolling over Latin America in the wake of WWII."[46] These sibling parties, APRA, PS, and AD, and their leaders, entwined by years of shared hardship and exile, considered themselves an inevitable wave of mass democratization in Latin America, the long-awaited national political incarnation of the "American hour" they had all dreamed of years before. And these same cohorts—onetime students and Reformistas, sometimes revolutionaries and exiles, longtime friends and allies, were shepherding the democratic masses into power and finally leading their countries to the promised democratic future.

Portal's role and influence in APRA had never been stronger. Six months after her arrival in 1945, she was named the secretary of the Women's Training Unit, Comando de Capacitación Femenina, making her once again the only woman among the twenty members of the new APRA National Executive Committee, or CEN. Once again, she traveled throughout the country, organizing sub–Comandos Femeninos and kick-starting literacy campaigns for adult women.[47] As a woman, she could neither vote nor stand for election, but there was talk in the party of her as a potential ambassador to Mexico, one of the country's most important and visible diplomatic posts; and her friends in Santiago hoped to see her named ambassador to Chile.[48]

Portal was just as dedicated to the party as she had ever been. To celebrate her forty-sixth birthday, Aprista friends collected a gift of almost 6,000 soles, which they gave her along with a commemorative album signed by dozens of comrades and forwarded with an effusive handwritten note by Haya. She donated the funds to the party, keeping only the album.[49] "Frankly, I don't know how to thank you, in the name of the party, for the nobility of your gesture," Haya thanked her. "It is an attitude of great Aprista quality for which we will always be thankful. It gives the exact measure of your Aprismo, and believe me that it is something truly pleasing to realize that the promise that we all saw, one day now long ago, is today once again reaffirmed."[50]

Portal and her fellow Apristas also proudly followed Haya's growing international profile. Finally free to travel, Haya spent most of 1946 on the road, racking up four honorary doctorates in neighboring countries and

accepting presidential invitations to visit Colombia, Venezuela, and Guatemala.[51] Such a presidential tour in all but name must have been particularly inspiring and rejuvenating. While Haya did not yet hold a formal post
in the Peruvian government, he traveled as an elder brother to this regional
cohort of peers who after long years of struggle and sacrifice were finally
reaching their due positions of responsibility leading their countries. Haya
no doubt assumed that his turn to receive the presidential sash was not
long in coming.

APRA was now a mature party, a senior partner in the governing coalition. Taking stock of what APRA had become and what it had achieved
almost twenty years after the Plan de México, Apristas could count on
commanding about a third of the vote in any national election, although
their electoral strength remained concentrated on the coast and in the
north, especially the important export-oriented sugar-producing coast, the
home region of Haya and many other founding leaders.[52] Demographi-
cally, they were still strong with organized labor and urban liberal-leaning
middle sectors like white-collar employees and teachers, especially in Lima.

Who did APRA speak for when it considered itself the voice of the
people? Certainly, it spoke for Peru's middle-class actors who played such
a pivotal role in Haya's ideology, which considered them the agents of progress and whose structural complaints, such as the favored position of
foreign capital, were shared by most of APRA's high leadership, almost
all middle-class children themselves.[53] Its influence over labor was more
political and tactical. In the early thirties, the Communists, APRA's main
political competition, pushed hard for a confrontation with the state to has-
ten a revolutionary crisis. The resulting state repression scarred and disillusioned the labor movement. Moving quickly, APRA seized the opportunity to defeat its Communist rivals and consolidate its influence over labor
by stressing its anti-Communism.[54] But even if it revealed its tactical maneuvering in securing control over labor, its nationalist vision resonated
more broadly throughout the country than its electoral showing suggested.
Recent scholarship has expanded our understanding of APRA's strength
and appeal, pushing back against the notion that its message utterly failed
to resonate in the southern sierra, which was economically cut off from
international markets and populated mostly with indigenous peasants,
with only anemic middle sectors. In provinces as different as highland Ayacucho to the south and the steamy jungles of northeastern Amazonas,

APRA appealed to liberal-leaning local elites, even if the party failed to carry provincial elections. These local elites were inspired by APRA's nationalist vision and considered Aprista demands for decentralization from Lima and regional inclusion as their best chance to integrate into the modern nation-state as full partners, with access to the fruits of that modernization.[55]

Like any lasting political movement, APRA's ideas and programs evolved with changing conditions, although Apristas were still defined by "first principle" positions—anti-imperialism, the necessary constructive role of the state in the economy, and the need for profound economic redistribution. But while APRA prided itself on its "modern" doctrine, in the final analysis, it was not ideas that bound Apristas together or that provided the emotional texture of being an Aprista and that, in the end, most distinguished APRA and ensured its survival and vitality. From the start, Apristas shared a broadly "populist" orientation—the "us against them" mentality that assumed they were the vehicle for the "people's" furious will against the oligarchical elites who had so long oppressed them. And more than the nuts and bolts of any of the plans that they might read about in *La Tribuna*, Apristas strengthened their collective identity and solidarity in everyday practice when they ate at party cafeterias, took their children to party medical clinics, played in party recreational leagues, and gathered in their mass rallies for collective extravaganzas of quasi-religious fervor.

A "street-level" snapshot of Aprista life in this postwar period showed a well-oiled machine organizing large swaths of members' daily lives. Politically, APRA recruited and trained people in every sector and at every stage of life, with organizations for youth, women, labor, and professionals. Portal's work for the Comando Femenino was part of this larger Aprista strategy concentrating on "constructing efficient mass organizations," which included consolidating control over Communists in labor unions, gaining control of student movements at the national university, and extending control into secondary and even elementary schools by organizing teachers.[56] APRA aimed to organize all facets of social life, not just explicitly political sectors. Once recruited, new Apristas were inducted and integrated into party life with elaborate and carefully scripted ceremonies and rituals drawing heavily from European mass politics. The party reassured its rapidly growing rank and file that expertly prepared leaders were at the helm with long and detailed expositions of party ideology and future plans for the nation. The party also tackled their affiliates' everyday material needs, providing everything from subsidized meals at Aprista cafeterias to free dental care at party headquarters.

APRA demanded the wholehearted allegiance of its faithful and boasted a feared political discipline, enforced by an Aprista Ministry of Defense, which established a Supreme Court of Discipline in 1946, an elaborate protocol to investigate, judge, and punish partisans who failed to carry out their duties or who deviated from Aprista behavioral norms. It reviewed more than fifty cases, mostly for dereliction of duty, but also for embezzlement, fraud, abuse of authority, hoarding, debts, cases against sexual honor, corruption, extortion, and other acts condemned by law or by the Code of Conduct of the Aprista Youth Federation.[57] According to Portal, the Comando Femenino also had a special discipline section for complaints against party members who abused their wives.[58]

The years of illegality had focused the party into a highly structured and vertical organization, and now, operating in the open, it retained that hierarchy and discipline that had made it so effective. Aprista congressmen, for instance, deposited an undated and signed letter of resignation with Haya, ensuring his political control over their partisan bloc. The U.S. embassy reported that APRA had adopted the Communist practice of "the levy on . . . the salaries of party members in public office. Although the practice may not be widespread, there are those who claim to have given the party their entire salary, receiving in return enough to live on."[59]

Jockeying for power in the unfamiliar field of legal electoral politics, however, APRA was overconfident of its own powers and underestimated its opponents. Apristas were not as aggressive as their enemies on the Right who adroitly maneuvered to make the Apristas appear to be perpetual aggressors. Opponents decried clandestine Aprista paramilitary "discipline" groups that advanced party interests with plausibly deniable sabotage and violence, from street brawls to assassinations. For instance, in April of 1946, conservative women demonstrated against the high cost of living and the government's inability to deal with chronic shortages. Peru's export-driven economy, which had boomed in the immediate postwar period, was deteriorating as Europe got back on its feet and as the price of imports increased. With inflation rising, the cost of living had increased 60 percent in the three years from 1944 to 1947.[60] The Aprista leadership, expecting that the demonstration would also attract men rallied by the anti-Aprista press, mustered the Comando Femenino to challenge the conservatives and sent additional Aprista male "defenders." Apristas gleefully recalled how they won the day and dunked the organizer of the conservative women's rally in a fountain.[61] The humorous image of a high-society lady sputtering in the fountain gives the affair the veneer of a student prank, but for a U.S. embassy analyst, the confrontation was an "Aprista terrorist tactic" of targeting protesting women and nearby offices, including that of an anti-Aprista newspaper.[62]

The apex of Portal's reinvigorated political life was organizing and hosting the First National Convention of Aprista Women in November 1946, where her power to convoke, organize, and mobilize women from all over Peru demonstrated her strength within the party. For eight days, they gathered for intensive classes on Aprista doctrine, discussions that surely extended into the evenings they spent housed in the homes of party militants.[63] Portal opened this national convention with an inaugural address synthesizing women's participation in the party over the past twenty years. Published as "La mujer en el Partido del Pueblo" (The woman in the Party of the People) in 1946, this was Portal's effort to reclaim women's party activities into a legible political (as opposed to solely auxiliary) history. She gathered evidence from questionnaires congress participants filled out about their partisan activities in the past fifteen years. Portal repeatedly read out long lists of names of female militants in an "honor roll of activism and sacrifice," fifteen arrested here, twenty there.[64] In addition to inscribing these women into the history of a party obsessed with sacrifice and martyrdom, Portal was organizing women's activism into a recognizable form of female comradeship—a community of compañeras Apristas, a band of sisters born out of shared struggle. This was important for the self-worth of women who could now recognize and celebrate themselves as part of a militant party with a storied history. This documented record of dangerous political activity also, Portal argued, entitled women to full and active citizenship within APRA. This history, once legible, proved women had suffered and sacrificed at the Aprista barricades.

Portal also now publicly raised doubts about the limits of human suffering and sacrifice for revolutionary ideals that she had first raised privately five years earlier when writing to Haya. Rhetorically passing the torch to the next generation of female Apristas, Portal focused on the suffering the first generation had endured, which she hoped had made possible the next generation's psychological freedom and their full and open participation in APRA. These younger women were "the ones who mark the rhythm to follow for the women of Peru and the ones who without a doubt will complete the ranks of the party with capability, dynamism, a spirit of work and responsibility, without anything or anyone pointing to them as inept elements, sure of themselves on the wide route that the party has cleared and for which those of us [women] who began this trajectory had to go through dramatic conditions, breaking the tangled and confusing [*enmarañada*] jungle of prejudices and injustices, wounding ourselves and protesting, and many times in complete spiritual orphanhood, misunderstood or turned away."[65]

This convention was the pinnacle of Portal's life as an Aprista, her "moment of greatest glory and triumph" in the party. In true Aprista fashion, the congress included a "warm and emotional" closing plenary session dramatizing Portal's role and influence. The room was "overcome with great emotion" when a delegate proposed a motion naming Portal "Teacher and Guide of the Peruvian Woman."[66] Delegates praised her character, her "strong personality," her labor over the past twenty-five years, and her "selfless efforts" and leadership to "emotional applause." "The emotion reached its climax" as the delegates stood, raised their arms, and "swore by the party, by the Jefe, and by Magda Portal to fight as one for the definitive triumph of our Great Party and for the revindications of women." Haya's private birthday note six months earlier confirmed how highly her brothers in the APRA leadership esteemed her for her "great Aprista quality" and nobility. With the strains of the "Aprista Marseillaise" that closed the ceremony still ringing in her ears, a "vividly touched" Portal had now also been publicly validated by her constituents, her Aprista compañeras, the women she had worked for years to mobilize, who had sworn by her to continue their fight for women's rights.

For Portal, however, the emotional highlight may have been watching her only child, her daughter Gloria, give a presentation on social work at an evening plenary session.[67] This was another, much more intimate validation, a vivid demonstration of how Aprista youth continued Portal's pioneering labor in APRA. It proved that Portal's example as a public

Magda Portal at First National Congress of Aprista Women, 1946. Courtesy estate of Magda Portal, Rocío Revolledo Pareja, and Magda Portal Papers, Benson Latin American Collection, University of Texas at Austin.

woman, her choice to continue as a partisan and visible leader, had found root in her own daughter, despite the unquestionable domestic sacrifice and suffering it had caused. This was the promise of the Aprista New Woman and New Home: Gloria was a young Aprista partisan leveraging a university education—something Portal's own mother was unable to provide to her—to better Peru. How must it have made Portal feel, watching her daughter on that stage, to know that she had birthed and reared the Aprista New Woman?

Haya, as the APRA chief, closed the weeklong convention with a speech on the "moral norms within the Aprista family," arguing that Aprismo "wants the rights of everyone to be respected in each home," and that the party's larger task was not just political but included creating a more expansive democratic code of conduct. Governing structures reflected domestic ones, and since "the first draft of the government is written in the Home," APRA had to expand from formal electoral politics to "reach into the Home, which is the embryo of the life of the State." Haya departed swiftly at the end of the speech because he was due at a benefit for the victims of a devastating earthquake that had hit the interior of the country only days before.

Nine days later, in an editorial titled "The Home and the State," the Aprista daily *La Tribuna* reviewed Haya's key points. "With his habitual eloquence," Haya reaffirmed that APRA had been the first movement to "give democracy its whole breadth, overcoming the prejudices of the superiority of one sex." Since the movement's foundation, women had "rights and tasks equal to those of men" in APRA and had "labored in all party ranks and shared in equal measure the punishments and sufferings during the times of persecution." The "energetic invocation of the c. Chief calling for the reign in the home of the harmony and respect characteristic of democracy," the editors explained, was rooted in his belief that Aprismo, "which fights against tyrants in the States, cannot conceive of tyrants at Home," or of "the man who calls himself a democrat in the streets, [but] who turns into a dictator in the Home." This understanding of gender roles is "a revolution perhaps deeper and more transcendent than that which might be realized in the world of political and social relations," and any new Aprista state "assumes new men and new women, with a modern and just spirit who have overcome the past." This Aprista future necessarily required "a very high criteria of responsibility," especially among men, "who until now have used and abused feudal and irresponsible customs."[68]

Later in life, Portal singled out this speech as a sour note, arguing that Haya fundamentally undermined her commemoration of women's contributions to APRA's political battles and her demands that the party more fully integrate women. Haya infuriated her with his deeply conservative and traditional view of women as keepers of the domestic sphere and the country's moral character. "He began to speak to the women of their duties," she remembered. "And what were these? The mother, the wife, the husband, the children, the home. 'Because you have no other function in life than the home, to improve the home, make the home your kingdom.' I was furious with what he was saying. 'Don't talk about that, don't you understand that is not what they want,' I whispered to him. Haya continued with a furious face and he went on and on until at last he finished and he marched off, almost violent." But, after this conflict, "it was extraordinary what happened next. Common women, campesinas, workers, some teachers, but all with a great desire to learn. I asked them what they wanted me to speak to them about, and one said, 'Of Marxism, compañera.' It was like a slap in Haya's face, I would not have expected it. But they wanted another type of speech from the chief of the party.... This was a lesson for me."[69]

The lesson Portal took from this experience was that even as Haya was retrenching into more traditional views on women, the Aprista female rank and file defied him, turning instead to her for lessons on Marx. But Portal's recollection was diametrically opposed to the tenor and intent of Haya's speech. Although it espoused some traditionally patriarchal language and imagery, including an unusual governing metaphor where the husband was the executive and the wife was the Parliament of the nuclear family, Haya's speech was far from reactionary. It was not very different from Portal's 1933 *Hacia la mujer nueva*, which also proposed an expanded role for the party within the home to educate more egalitarian citizens.[70]

Perhaps Portal was not the only one to misread Haya's speech, which may explain why the *La Tribuna* editors so carefully outlined why the c. chief focused on harmony in the home, reassuring readers that Haya's speech was not a reactionary turn to conventional gender expectations, but instead advocated for a revolutionary egalitarian transformation of domestic life. Portal's memories may not be able to tell us what Haya's motivations were in his speech, or what the gathered Aprista women heard and wanted from him, but they do tell us with crystal clarity what she herself wanted: a militant and radicalized rank and file who turned to her first for their ideological formation.

That was Portal's dream, but it was not shared by everyone, even those closest to her. What was Gloria's dream? Portal saw in her daughter a maturing political militant, a young Aprista ready to work for her party and the country. Gloria may have wanted that, but she also wanted other, more worldly things. She wanted her father—she had been deeply hurt by Portal's separation from Serafín a few years before.[71] She wanted a lover, and was involved in a love affair with a much older man connected to the party. Portal did not approve of this affair. Gloria must have known at least the broad outlines of her mother's youth; as she confronted her mother's disapproval, surely she wondered why she could not break the same norms of gendered decency. Perhaps Gloria even intuited that her mother had liberated her own personality by breaking such social norms. Why couldn't she?

Two months after the National Women's Congress, these pressures in Gloria's life boiled over. On January 3, 1947, in the flush of the hopes inspired by a new year, Gloria returned from university to their home, retreated to her bedroom, and shot herself in the heart. She was only twenty-three years old. She was found by her aunt, Portal's sister, who recalled how Magda "screamed and tore her hair," and "nearly went out of her mind and did not want to live."[72] The reasons for the suicide were not entirely clear. There was some family speculation that Gloria may have been traumatized by seeing her lover in the street that day with his pregnant wife, of whom she was unaware. In an interview late in life, Portal's sister suggested, after many decades of reflection, that Gloria may have been quite emotionally fragile at that point in her life. That Gloria did not leave any explanations for her actions only exacerbated Portal's anguish.

Gloria's suicide was the most unexpected and traumatic personal loss of Portal's life, and her family and closest confidants in the party were genuinely afraid that she might harm herself in her grief. Haya ordered a twenty-four-hour guard of Aprista women to accompany her for a week after Gloria's funeral. Portal had a "nervous collapse" and was too distraught to attend the graveside burial; her old friend and Aprista leader Carlos Manuel Cox spoke in the name of the family. The party insisted that condolences be sent only by post, as Portal needed "tranquility"; after a week in Lima accompanied only by her Aprista guards, she left for a month of solitude in southern Peru.[73]

A few poems that she wrote shortly after Gloria's suicide allude to her feelings of devastation, hopelessness, and despair. In "Sad Ballad," she wrote: "I do not know how to find myself / I am lost from myself / just at the moment in which you left / to live in my heart. / Your absence is a premonition of everything in me / solitude, breakdown, and defeat / and this zero hour without possibilities / without tomorrow or dawn."[74] What stands out in this poem is the sense of loss of self, the lack of a future or possibilities. With a single moment, impossible for any parent to imagine, Gloria's suicide took her daughter and the possibility of any future family life. It implicated her as a bad mother, torturing her for having devoted her time and energy to politics at the expense of everything else. Regretful echoes of this guilt came out at the end of her life. "They were twenty years of Aprista militancy. . . . I forgot even my home and my family and I was nothing except Aprista, which maybe was excessive, but that was how it was."[75] Portal confronted the terrifying truth that she was unable to understand those closest to her on their own terms—Serafín, her compañeras Apristas, Gloria. To create her creative artistic and political agency, Portal harnessed a great strength of will to a worldview, an imagination, that by definition was "habituated to evade or distort aspects of life." Her imagination, her canvas for conceiving the world and her place in it, had to be anchored not in a historical world, the world as it was in all its ugly limits, but instead in a dream world of future personal and political possibility. Even intellectually brilliant people were then "unable to see the world realistically or clearly," often failing "miserably in their attempts to provide reliable accounts of human existence."[76] Like Haya himself, Portal was married to her party and her dream of revolution, and she could not see Serafín or Gloria as human beings with their own stories when they deviated from the heroic outlines of Portal's life story as she understood it.

". . . Zero Hour without Possibilities"

Just four days after Gloria's suicide, Peru was rocked by another, much more public, death. On January 7, a green Buick carrying two people drove up to and assassinated Francisco Graña, the editor of the leading anti-Aprista newspaper, *La Prensa*. Political violence, including beatings, bombings, and even murders, had spiked in the months leading up to this event. Though APRA had suffered some of this violence, the party was widely blamed for killing the socially prominent and very popular Graña in an assassination that could not help but recall the murder of the editor of *El Comercio* a dozen years earlier by a young Aprista.[77] Graña's assassination unleashed "a national furor," and as allegations blaming APRA flew, the party mobilized everything it could to sway public opinion. *La Tribuna* trumpeted in screaming red headlines a reward for the killer donated by party members that grew by leaps and bounds every day, reaching more than 60,000 soles within a week, and offered the investigation full access to APRA archives.[78] As APRA scrambled to keep ahead of events, the party leadership appeared confused and bewildered about the best way forward.

The Graña case set off a cascade of political consequences and many self-inflicted wounds that would prove nothing short of devastating for APRA. In the first of what U.S. embassy analysts considered "a series of errors in judgment that in retrospect are little short of amazing," Haya withdrew the Aprista ministers from the government. More than a stupid error or miscalculation, Haya hoped the grandness of such a conciliatory gesture would prove APRA wanted to ensure no undue influence on any investigations. Ultimately, his move backfired; it failed to move any anti-Apristas and neutered APRA's ability to defend itself within the government. President Bustamante, perhaps sensing an opportunity to escape Haya's hold on their governing alliance, turned to one of APRA's fiercest enemies, General Manuel Odría, whom he quickly appointed minister of Government and Police, where his influence "slowly but inexorably" turned the government against APRA.[79]

Apristas seethed with frustration as the leadership's fumbling and miscalculations rapidly deteriorated their political position, hastening the crumbling of APRA's hard-won strength and influence. What for most Apristas was a partisan disaster could not have come at a worse time for Portal, still mad with grief only hours after Gloria's suicide. In the 1920s and 1930s, revolutionary militancy had helped Portal process and perhaps even heal from other, if not as devastating, personal traumas. If that failed, what could now help her escape—much less process—the pain and guilt associated with Gloria's suicide?

These were the many layers in her "zero hour without possibilities." As a young woman, Portal had once perceived Gloria's birth as a threat to her sense of self, opening the door to losing herself in the overwhelming responsibility of being a mother or in traditional domestic obligations. "Nothing more than give birth after birth, not that. Be a housewife, take care of the husband, day after day, nothing more than that, no! The woman finishes there: in nothing, in a totally anonymous being."[80] Portal perceived a clear opposition between losing herself in child-rearing and service to her husband—falling into domestic anonymity—and "the other thing . . . the other thing that gushed from my being, that was my way, my vocation." Ironically, Portal faced this terrifying loss of self not in the process of birthing and rearing Gloria, but in surviving her suicide, which sent her into a tailspin from which she "was lost from herself," unable to find her way back. In moments of personal crisis in the past, Portal had the comfort of knowing that her political work in APRA, "that something else," remained a meaningful, ready shelter. Her psychological refuge, her militancy in revolutionary politics, was crumbling around her when she needed it most.

Her compañeros, both in APRA and abroad, all mobilized to help Portal through this "zero hour without possibilities," building bridges to bring her back into her political life's work. On February 19, she flew to Caracas. Betancourt invited her and Luis Alberto Sánchez, now the rector of Lima's San Marcos University and the incarnation of Reformista success, to witness the transfer of power to the Adecos. AD had dramatically expanded the Venezuelan franchise, giving everyone the right to vote at eighteen— male or female. As the electorate exploded to 35 percent of the population, Venezuelans rewarded the Adecos with 70 percent of the vote in the 1946 Constituent Assembly elections, giving them control of Congress.[81]

While she was officially representing APRA, the trip's real agenda, of course, was to strengthen and encourage *her*, not just the relations between these two parties; to provide her solace as she visited with her old friends and allies in their moment of political triumph. Portal stayed for three months, touring the country with Betancourt, witnessing the success of the Adeco revolution, and, according to *La Tribuna*, "collaborating decisively in strengthening the ties joining these two great popular movements of Indoamerica."[82] While undoubtedly triumphant at Betancourt's and AD's successes, could she have helped comparing how efficiently and successfully AD maneuvered, how they adroitly handled their political situation, to APRA's stumbling back in Peru?

The political landscape had only soured further upon her return. Observers at the U.S. embassy documenting APRA's precipitous decline in the aftermath of the Graña assassination attributed it to "strategic errors" resulting from the party's "inexperience and the superior judgment and astuteness of its opposition." APRA's opponents were not a "loyal opposition" but were instead committed to blocking APRA at all costs, even though—or perhaps because—the Apristas genuinely represented a majority of the Peruvian electorate. The rumor was that when APRA's historical opponents had changed course to support their legalization in the 1945 election, they had "full confidence that Apra would make such a mess of things" that the Right would be shortly "called upon . . . to return to power as saviour[s]."[83] Looking ahead, APRA's opponents did everything they could to sabotage the Apristas and thwart their governing coalition, strategizing to prevent the "probable" 1951 election of Haya as president.[84] In essence, the party's opponents wagered that APRA, unsure how to maneuver in democratic waters, could be set up to fail, and its failure could be used as cover to wait out the growing regional and global pressures for democratic political change in the wake of the end of World War II. The Right painted Apristas as intransigent, undemocratic, inherently unstable, and violent, even as the Right proved more intransigent and considered every move first from its political potential to thwart the legislation, for which APRA had an overwhelming democratic mandate.

With a classic populist perspective, APRA believed it interpreted the needs of Peru's majority, and its opponents claimed the party believed this mandate trumped minority rights and liberties. This populist certainty, and their lack of experience governing or participating in legislative bodies demanding compromise, was their greatest disadvantage, clucked the Right. The structures and habits of mind that had been created and seared into the party DNA during its years in the catacombs, their enemies diagnosed, were exactly the opposite ones needed for the delicate compromises of such a fragile power sharing. The party could only compensate with its iron-clad discipline—Aprista legislators always followed the party line. When the Apristas passed legislation, the Right tarred their discipline as parliamentary thuggery, claiming they forced their measures through with little debate or compromise. The opposition would not allow Peru to fall into the clutches of what they called APRA's "dictatorship of Parliament."

As parliamentary opponents banded together to block the Apristas, they hit upon a winning strategy. APRA held the majority, but not enough for a quorum. With Congress scheduled to open for the new legislative session on July 28, 1947, the opposition unified all non-Aprista senators from the Left and the Right and boycotted the Senate. Unable to meet their quorum, the Senate, and therefore the Congress, could not function. As observers at the U.S. embassy noted, legally and constitutionally, "there was no question" that APRA was in the right and the boycotters in the wrong. "Nevertheless, the final result was that [the opposition] succeeded not only in persuading themselves, but also the President, the Administration, and practically all non-Apristas in the country that it was not they but Apra which was responsible for the Congressional impasse."[85]

The Right openly defied the democratic process to deny APRA the political forum of their greatest strength, Apristas complained. As Aprista frustration festered, they found no aid in President Bustamante, ostensibly their partner in their political coalition. As Seoane, now a senator and vice president of the Senate, bitterly observed, in joining the coalition,

Apristas believed they had elected Bustamante "captain of the team," but the president saw himself instead as the unaffiliated guardian of the political order, whose job was to "referee the game."[86] The Aprista leadership was at a loss as to how to deal with this unprecedented parliamentary strike blocking their democratic process. They floundered as they searched for a way to cut this Gordian knot and punch through this technical—but unbreachable—parliamentary obstacle.

Locked out of Congress, APRA turned to its historical strength, its rank-and-file organization, and planned a general strike for late August as a show of strength. The Aprista general strike, however, was "a dismal failure" that proved only that the Aprista-controlled labor confederations had little power over their subsidiary unions, and reinforced APRA's growing impotence instead of parading its strength. With the bitter taste of the failed general strike still in their mouths, the APRA leadership pounced on another opportunity to bolster its strength when a student strike broke out a month later in October. A young man died in the ensuing conflict, and hoping to rally the population by showcasing their opponents' brutality, APRA planned to parade the young Aprista martyr through the streets. The government, however, blocked their demonstration. In fact, according to U.S. embassy observers, APRA's role in this strike "succeeded as much as any single event that year in further alienating public opinion. . . . The turning of this strictly student affair into what was very obviously a political maneuver resulting in the death of a student turned the stomachs of many who had hitherto looked at least tolerantly on Apra."[87]

As APRA's increasingly drastic attempts to break the parliamentary strike foundered, the stymied Congress effectively stalled the entire political system, to Apristas' rapidly escalating frustration. There was no hope for legislative compromises on the country's long list of problems if the body could not even meet. Rising economic discontent—including labor unrest after years of repression, skyrocketing increases in the cost of living, and a growing tax burden on the agro-export elite—was also putting untenable pressure on a fragile political process that had only just emerged from over twenty years of undemocratic control. APRA bore the brunt of the political cost: unable to debate, much less pass, any additional legislation, it was widely blamed for their opponents' obstruction and wounded by the backlash to its mishandled attempts to leverage its popular strength to force open the Congress. As an observer at the U.S. embassy noted, "It has long been a saying in Peru—since long before the party reached power in 1945—that Apra frequently gets the ball but is never able to kick the goal. Apra was handed the ball in 1945. Now it has lost it, perhaps irretrievably." APRA, of course, was not the only loser. President Bustamante himself despaired of resolving the hopeless stalemate between the two forces he called "the sect" (APRA) and "the clan" (the oligarchical Right).[88] Nobody expected him to last out his term.

With the country's political structures paralyzed, and APRA sailing into uncharted political waters, Haya left the country in late January 1948 for an extended lecture tour of the United States. To casual observers, it seemed as if he was leaving the party without a helmsman at a time of great national political uncertainty. These were very dangerous times. Behind the scenes, a frustrated party leadership was conspiring with radicalized elements in the military to overthrow the government. The day before he left, Haya assured trusted party insiders that the plans for the insurrection were on track. "I'm leaving everything ready!" one remembered Haya saying. Haya told them to act as they saw fit to execute their revolutionary plans and explained that he was going abroad to secure international recognition for their future revolutionary government.[89]

Haya thus transferred responsibility to others for any mishaps while he lobbied for support in the United States for APRA in its national crisis. The planned insurrection sputtered and fell apart when the older generation of party leaders and the younger naval officers planning the military insurrection failed to cooperate, tussling over ultimate control. The next month, in a blistering radio address, President Bustamante announced he had uncovered an Aprista plot to overthrow the government. The president added three additional military officers to his cabinet and purged Apristas from the municipal councils they controlled.[90]

This was not the first time, nor would it be the last, that such an insurrectionary conspiracy failed because of lack of coordination, a further indictment for a political party that prided itself on its logistical organization and its professionalism, its very ability to get things done. A generous reading is that in this new age of legality, needing to be everything to all people, Haya had developed an "ambiguous, indeed vacillating and indecisive style of leadership."[91] Those not inclined to such a sympathetic view claimed Haya encouraged the militants spearheading revolutionary conspiracies only to withhold support at the crucial hour.

Teetering on this political precipice, the Second National APRA Party Congress opened in Lima on May 17, 1948—"a show of Apra's strength," believed the U.S. embassy, adding with a delicate gift for understatement, "at a time when its fortunes appeared to be at a rather low ebb."[92] For Portal, the congress was another high-profile opportunity to keep mobilizing women, one that promised Peruvian women "the certainty of acquiring the title and category of integral citizens" in the near future when APRA "controlled the machinery of the state." As the congress opened, she repeated this focus on citizenship and emancipation in rallies where she "brilliantly warned" that women had found in the party "an instrument of liberation from feudal burdens and prejudices," and her promises that Aprismo would allow women to claim their rights as citizens were enthusiastically applauded.[93]

For Haya, who returned only the day before it opened, the congress offered affective, emotional opportunities instead of policies or programs; it was an "opportunity to infuse" Apristas "with some of his never-flagging enthusiasm and optimism."[94] Haya's opening speech "analyzed at some length the vertical organization of the party, to prove that it was neither Fascist nor Communist but 'functional' and 'democratic' in intent and operation." The U.S. analyst believed this was a response to criticism launched by the anti-Aprista press, but Haya was just as surely addressing U.S. diplomatic audiences increasingly concerned about "totalitarianism." Outside observers were paying attention and reported that the congress "considered well over one thousand papers and resolutions, most of which were said to have been passed after 'free and democratic' discussions in committee and plenary sessions."[95]

However, there was a third, internal audience. As they watched the congressional strike grind into a second, excruciating year, disaffected Apristas, frustrated at the party's unsuccessful attempts to punch through this infuriating obstacle, were starting to buckle under the pressure and their rage at the party's impotence. Aprista ranks were agitated, many hoping APRA's deteriorating political situation would lead to a preemptive strike against the Bustamante government to beat a likely coup from the Right. Adding to this warlock's brew were increasingly vocal demands for more democracy in the workings of the party and a new political direction, especially from provincial parties and the Aprista youth wing.[96]

While flagging the dangers of an overly vertically organized party, their complaints were also the inevitable consequence of APRA's legality and mass popularity. New members flocking to their ranks made APRA powerful but also a target for opportunists. Juggling such growing pains, Aprista provincial forces were in dangerous disarray, with rumors flying about discontented rank-and-file members. At the congress, Apristas gossiped about provincial leaders building new factions to stop Bustamante, presumably to sidestep an ineffective national APRA leadership. In Cuzco and Trujillo, a dissident group calling themselves the *"auténticos"* had been elected as representatives to the national congress and were attacked by their putative Aprista brothers with "fists and bullets," annulling their election.[97] These disparate disaffected ranks heard Haya's commentary on party governance and internal democracy and thought he was placating them.

After two weeks of presenting, negotiating, and debating, the congress closed with a marathon plenary gathering on June 2, an all-night session of speeches and reports, which only ended at six in the morning. The main event that night, the congress's dramatic climax, was the contested election of the twenty-five members of the party's National Executive Committee, the CEN. Disaffected Apristas supported Seoane, who was running to be the CEN's secretary of Politics, the most powerful position after that of the maximum leader, which uncontestedly belonged to Haya. In the first two rounds of voting, Seoane overwhelmingly beat the "staunch conservative" Fernando León de Vivero, one of Haya's two closest confidants whose election promised no significant political change.[98] But in the final, definitive round that night, Seoane was elected national secretary of Government, leaving León de Vivero to be elected unanimously as the secretary of Politics.[99]

While some disaffected Apristas complained that "El Cachorro" had been outplayed, it is worth remembering that Seoane was an operator at the center of party power who, with his aristocratic background, was widely considered APRA's most presentable and "presidential" politician. We should not discount the possibility that the 1948 CEN election was a conciliatory deal, perhaps with Seoane himself as the architect, meant to paper over divisions in the leadership caused by their growing frustration at the untenable political situation. In a show of unity, the new CEN saw all of the male leaders who were considered potentially malcontented elected to secretary-level positions: Seoane to secretary of Government,

Carlos Manuel Cox to secretary of Control, and Luis Heysen to secretary of Discipline.

Portal was elected as one of two general subsecretaries, the honorific position right below the general secretary.[100] While this meant she no longer headed the Comando Femenino, such a high-level honor at the head of the new CEN reasserted her position in APRA and may have been a way to make a space for her, commensurate to her standing in the party, in light of personal circumstances that were distancing her from the everyday rough-and-tumble politics of this increasingly dire national situation. The other newly elected general subsecretary, Arturo Sabroso, had, three years earlier in 1945, been tried and found guilty by the APRA Discipline Section for acting too independently of the party in his work as a trade unionist.[101] The 1948 CEN election brought this party founder of such symbolic importance—the most visible working-class leader—back into the fold in a show of Aprista unity. Portal and Sabroso, who in the early thirties had braved hostile political settings campaigning together as the visible representations of just how inclusive, how different, how promising APRA was, now stood at the pinnacle of the party's hierarchy, ready to face the political hostilities of this day. A week after the congress ended, the new secretary of Capacitación Femenina, Portal's old office, held a celebration for her attended by hundreds of Apristas, in part a "democratic congratulations" for her election to this new post.[102]

Before they could hope to face their opponents, APRA needed to set its own house in order. Their agitated team was resorting to deus ex machina fantasies of revolutionary coups. In a game where all their previous moves had backfired, and each day seemed to be ever more impossible to win, APRA moved to silence, and perhaps to placate internal critics, shore up rank-and-file support, and present a unified face to the growing national political crisis eating at APRA's influence and threatening to thrust it back into illegality. Only days after APRA's party congress, the oligarchical Right tried to overthrow the government. The president's cabinet, almost all military men by now, pushed him to outlaw APRA and purge the Aprista congressmen to "solve" the congressional strike. When Bustamante refused, still hoping for a compromise solution, Gen. Odría led the military cabinet in resigning, disgusted with the failure to outlaw APRA and "cripple its conspiratorial efforts."[103] The government survived, for the moment, but all the action was moving off scene as secret conspiracies proliferated.

Odría quickly began organizing his own conspiracy against the government. In fact, by mid-1948, there were at least three different factions in the armed forces plotting to overthrow what they perceived as Bustamante's ineffectual rule. Odría led a faction allied with intensely anti-Aprista civilians; within the navy, an APRA-allied faction of radical junior officers and enlisted men led by Major Víctor Villanueva and Enrique Águila Pardo had been organizing since mid-1947; and finally, the former minister of War, General José del Carmen Marín, led a small faction of senior officers in the army favoring a "bloodless coup."[104] In early August, Marín approached Haya suggesting that in exchange for APRA's help, they would allow the party to compete in free elections after their coup. This option intrigued Haya, in part because it seemed less risky than launching a full-scale popular revolution with Major Villanueva. Yet, two months passed without Marín making any moves, and Major Villanueva's radical naval faction grew ever more desperate to act. Peru was a pressure cooker rocking at high heat, whistling furiously as the steam expanded, exploded, needing to escape.

CHAPTER EIGHT

Exits

JUST AFTER MIDNIGHT ON October 3, 1948, officers at Peru's Naval Base received telephone calls to report back to duty, only to find Aprista revolutionaries who surprised them and took them prisoner. In just two hours, the revolutionaries took command of the Naval Base, the Naval Academy, San Lorenzo Island, and every ship in the Callao port except the submarines. They distributed weapons to revolutionaries on land and raised the Aprista flag over their newly liberated areas. The lid had finally blown off: Major Villanueva's radical naval faction had launched a revolt in Callao, and another Aprista revolution had begun.[1]

The U.S. embassy estimated that two thousand Apristas joined the insurrection. On shore, armed Aprista Búfalos, the party's defense cadre, cut telephone service, and Aprista urban resistance included rifle fire and homemade bombs thrown from cars and planted in key locations throughout the city. In one hair-raising discovery, twenty-nine bombs were found in a hotel near the presidential palace.[2] Government authorities retook the central telephone exchange before serious damage to the capital's communications infrastructure was done, although the fuse of a homemade bomb had come within an inch of exploding before it burned out.[3]

However, Aprista elements in the other military branches—the air force, army, and civil guard—as well as some of the party's own paramilitary units, did not join the fighting as planned. Learning of the Callao revolt well in advance from multiple leaks, including an 11:00 P.M. phone call from a high-ranking APRA leader that same Saturday night, the Bustamante government mobilized immediately.[4] Government forces "pounded" the revolutionaries "into submission" with tanks and air attacks, losing

"Magda Portal, líder Aprista acusa al Apra,"
Semanario Peruano 1950, February 13, 1950.
Courtesy Magda Portal Papers,
Benson Latin American Collection,
University of Texas at Austin.

one F47 plane in a spectacular midair explosion. The revolutionaries who did raise arms did so ineffectively: in the Callao harbor, revolutionary ships shelled a nearby airfield, only to watch their shots fall harmlessly in the water. On shore, the government immediately instituted a curfew and patrolled Lima's main streets in a show of force, and, after outlawing APRA, swept through its party headquarters, newspapers, and radio stations.[5]

By 8:00 P.M. on Monday, October 4, it was all over. The Aprista revolutionaries on shore had surrendered, and sometime that night the revolutionary Aprista commander at sea was fatally shot.[6] The butcher's bill for the two bloody days included about fifty killed, two hundred wounded, and over one thousand taken prisoner, over eight hundred of those naval personnel, a devastating loss from which it would take the navy years to recover.

Though not involved, Magda Portal knew the strike was coming.[7] Recalling the events thirty-three years later, she described driving to the site with three of her party secretaries. "We wanted to know what was happening, because the gunfire was tremendous. We saw a truck leave with many bodies in it, and a few men standing. One of them recognized me and gestured to me (I can't forget it) that they had lost."[8]

The loss was total and more unbearable because it was not just APRA in shambles. In Venezuela, the Adecos were also racing too fast, and their "damn-the-torpedoes-full-speed-ahead strategy, by going too far, too fast, on too many fronts catalyzed a classic backlash mobilization, one aggravated by the U.S. Cold War desire for stable anticommunist regimes—particularly one in a major supplier of oil located in close proximity to the Panama Canal."[9] Fearing a looming crisis, AD worked harder still, pushing through a radical agrarian reform law in October 1948, just as their Aprista brethren were being pummeled. It proved too much, and a month later, the same military officers who had helped bring AD into power in 1945 overthrew them. Acción Democrática's exuberant Trienio was over, and Betancourt was forced, once again, into exile. Just as these Latin American mass-based political movements had ridden a global wave of democratic optimism into power in the wake of World War II, so now they were caught in the dangerous undertow of a congealing Cold War. By the early 1950s, governments throughout the region had turned sharply, abruptly to the Right. Popular movements were "eviscerated, defeated, and bankrupted," thereby "pulverizing" the hopes for social change kindled in the 1930s. Witnessing this catastrophe, the collapse of their generational dream, their American hour, a leading Aprista lamented: "The year 1948 was terrible for everyone. Some sinister hand had decided to crush our hearts, not only mine, not only those of the Apristas, but the hearts of all Latin Americans. Every day brought the announcement of another calamity."[10]

Sixteen Desolate Months

Callao was the most serious insurrection in Peru since the 1932 failed Aprista revolution in Trujillo. What had gone wrong? The party civilian leadership had known about and encouraged Major Villanueva's conspiratorial organizing for nearly a year, since November 1947.[11] However, they did not believe they had the civilian backing for an uprising. Major Villanueva's faction went ahead on their own based on their assessment of their strength in the military and betting that presenting the waffling leadership with a fait accompli would force the old guard's hand to publicly support the insurrection. Now faced with the mutiny, the party leadership had to make an immediate choice: support Major Villanueva's faction or withhold support and try to salvage what chances they might still have with Marín. Supporting the mutiny would mean praying Apristas would take to the streets in a full-scale insurrection with many casualties, which was far from a sure thing, given the recent failed 1947 general strike and their own temperature-taking of their civilian rank and file. The second option was becoming more illusory by the second, since Marín would certainly back down.

Callao was a rebellion the insurrectionists achieved against all odds, a revolutionary ember they had carefully nurtured and which sputtered to life only because they protected it from the Aprista high command's vacillations. When Aprista militants tried to fan the rebellion, the leadership instead stamped it out in what the mutineers saw as a callous betrayal of APRA's revolutionary aspirations. Writing nine years later in 1957, leading Aprista "Octoberists" defended themselves: they employed a power to initiate the revolution "expressly received from Haya," only to find that Aprista leaders "betrayed us at the decisive moment, denouncing the movement before the police."[12] The mutineers portrayed Haya as a general for the other side who oversaw events unfold from shore with binoculars and sent the mutinous officers orders to surrender. Top leaders first went to party locales claiming the revolution had been delayed, the insurrectionists complained bitterly, and then told others that it was all a Communist trick to destroy APRA. As Major Villanueva rallied Apristas to open a second front in Lima, militants were told that Aprista orders were to stay home, and that Major Villanueva had been bought by the government and had organized the rebellion to destroy the party.[13] In the Octoberists' reading, their revolution failed because of "sabotage, the demobilizing of the masses, and the counterorders" of the leadership, who "decisively aided Bustamante in squashing the Callao mutiny."[14]

The APRA leadership faced a different calculation when confronting what to them was not a revolution but a mutiny against their party leadership and against the elected government of which they constituted the largest part. They were a legal party now and could not support any insurrection unless they were absolutely certain of its success. As they frantically parsed through the scattered bits of information trickling in that night, unsure of what was actually happening and thinking through its implications on the fly, the pressure of such staggering stakes surely made the leaders cautious and hesitant. As the night unfolded, there were Apristas who believed the Callao revolt was an authentic revolution with a substantial chance for success. Aprista senators "met in the Congress building in anticipation of a victorious revolution and the transmission of the Presidency to Haya," only to be arrested.[15] Reportedly, on the eve of the revolt, high-ranking Apristas met to divide cabinet posts for a new Aprista government, postponing critical decisions amid their wrangling and disagreements.[16] Seeking asylum, Manuel Seoane told the Brazilian ambassador that the "uprising started without knowledge of top Apristas by hot-heads."[17] Fishing in troubled waters, President Bustamante later reported that Seoane himself had informed him on October 2 of the navy revolt in return for letting Seoane leave Peru.[18]

As the years passed, skeptical observers concluded that APRA leaders had decisively "aborted" the revolt quickly enough to keep the story under wraps from the public for years, in another example of the leadership's cynical exploitation of their rank-and-file's insurrectionary fervor.[19] Later Aprista histories would understand the events of what one leader called "the longest night of his life" as Major Villanueva's dooming any revolution with his premature and irresponsible forcing of the leadership's hand. Luis Alberto Sánchez maintained that Haya was surprised with the news in his bedroom at 5:00 A.M. on October 3 and knew nothing about it.[20] Much like the Trujillo Revolution sixteen years earlier, militants on the ground had pushed the insurrection forward too soon and too fast, caught the party leadership unprepared, forced it to play catch-up, and made impossible the official, responsible conspiracy scheduled for a week later.[21] Unlike the Trujillo Revolution, however, Callao's aborted Aprista revolution did not harden into a unified meaning for the party. Trujillo, despite— or perhaps because of—its failure, had forged APRA, while Callao shattered it, as different factions blamed each other for this latest devastating failure.

As the government smothered the Callao revolt, Haya and the top Aprista leadership met in secret to deal with the crisis. The young leader

Armando Villanueva remembered Portal as a "sentimental woman" whose "pleas" for the mutineers were cut off and silenced by Haya, the decisive leader determining a course of action with only two choices: organizing themselves or dying heroically. "'You have always been the one who at the last minute begins to give sermons and muddle everything,'" Villanueva remembered Haya accusing. "'There is no need to debate here. We need to know how we are going to react, how we organize ourselves, or how we die.' She stayed quiet."[22] Of course, the situation was actually the inverse: Portal was really demanding that the leadership support the insurrectionists and launch itself into an inescapably violent revolutionary situation, certainly not the action Peruvians expected from "sentimental women."

The starting question was how to support those in open rebellion, but as the military window slammed shut, it became what did the party owe the mutineers, its new martyrs? The party had faced similar questions in the past, during previous failed insurrections or when confronting what was owed the young assassins who killed for their interests, if not formally in APRA's name. Portal had consistently affirmed they owed these martyred compañeros a moral posture of support, especially if they failed. This was Portal's position in that last CEN meeting—she pleaded both to convince the leadership to support the mutineers and not to abandon them after their military failure, an impossible position for any legal party to take over any insurrectionary movement. Portal was one of the only leaders who contributed to a collection on behalf of Major Villanueva in the failure's aftermath.[23]

After squashing the revolt, President Bustamante moved quickly and arrested 1,127 people. But it was much too late for his government, as the Callao revolt convinced the armed forces he could not deal with APRA and alarmed military leaders by revealing insurrectionary factions within the military and threatening discipline.[24] APRA was now dangerous not because of its civilian partisan activities, but instead because it threatened the armed forces' morale and cohesion.

Within a month, Odría led a successful coup, placed Bustamente on an airplane to Argentina, and promptly outlawed both the APRA and the Communist Parties. The Right took command of Peru's politics for another generation, installing a military dictatorship and crushing APRA. Uncertain of how the new situation would play out, a U.S. naval attaché nervously observed that APRA was "equal in strength to the combined membership of all other political parties," and that Lima's working class responded to its outlawing with "surprise, despair, and bitterness."[25]

"Virtually all the Aprista leaders of any consequence" were hunted down, forced into another exile abroad, or driven underground, languishing in prison for months to await court-martial if captured.[26] As one of the party's two subsecretary generals, Portal was among the hundreds charged in the Callao revolutionary attempt. Another partisan friend had secured asylum for her at an embassy, which she declined.[27] Driven into hiding, she spent another sixteen months underground. We know nothing about the sixteen months from October 1948 until she remerged in early 1950. Instead of the heroic "sixteen tragic months" in the catacombs after the failed assassination attempt on Sánchez Cerro almost twenty years before, these latest months in hiding must have instead been sad, retrospective, increasingly bitter and enraging as she dissected what went wrong. There was nothing romantic, redeeming, or hopeful about the Aprista underground this time around, and Apristas stewed for months on how APRA had won the votes, had shared power, yet had still lost everything as Odría took the political winnings by force.

Odría decimated Peru's political landscape. He consolidated and legitimized his power through a scorched-earth campaign against all his political enemies, but first and always against APRA, committing his regime to its "total eradication" and literally trying to erase "all visible signs" of APRA. However, while appearing overwhelmingly victorious, his control was actually far more tenuous. After the first crushing blows against APRA, Odría believed and announced he had struck a devastating, fatal blow to his loathed enemy. Having spent most of its existence as a clandestine party, however, APRA's surviving militants regrouped underground. When signs of its survival emerged, like clandestine newspapers or graffiti trumpeting "APRA is Peace," they revealed Odría's regime as "both inefficient and foolish" and "totally in the dark" about its raison d'être—war against APRA.[28]

Especially in the provinces, where the national government had always struggled to consolidate power, government officials became paranoically, terrifyingly certain of APRA's strength, unity, and death-defying resilience and organization. State agents "began to indulge in the darkest fantasies about APRA," imagining it as all-powerful and that they were surrounded by crypto-Apristas. Government officials grew increasingly uncertain of their effectiveness and legitimacy as they imagined APRA growing into a daily, reified presence, a potent "anti-state."[29] Like the British usage of "shadow cabinet," APRA was the "shadow state," literally hiding in the shadows of clandestinity. Comforting to partisans, terrifying to opponents, everyone could feel its presence, waiting in the wings.

Odría's regime purged Peru's media of any positive reference to APRA and crafted "a new public sphere" where people could not express any sympathy, however innocuous, toward APRA. Anyone could report politically suspect friends, neighbors, or acquaintances, and people began carefully surveilling themselves, making it impossible for the government or Peruvians to trust any public truth claims.[30]

It was in this landscape that in December 1949, just over a year after the Callao mutiny and Odría's coup, Portal sent Odría her defense excoriating the Aprista leadership, and requested assurances for her freedom if she surrendered to a court-martial. Offering her "unbreakable decision to not intervene in any political question going forward," Portal wished only "to attend freely the cited trial and be able to categorically demonstrate my innocence." She solicited "the necessary guarantees, in order to reintegrate into a normal life and dedicate myself to my own private affairs."[31]

Like other key leaders such as Seoane, Portal had made a deal, reached an accommodation with Odría, and reclaimed agency in this new situation. In her unpublished memoirs, she recounts how she spent thirty days imprisoned awaiting the court-martial, during which she wrote *¿Quiénes traicionaron al pueblo?* (Who betrayed the people?), a scathing pamphlet accusing the high leadership of betraying Peru's revolutionary hopes.[32] Her decision to surrender and publicly detail her complaints with the party was an unexpected bomb that sent her compañeros into a demoralizing shock. In his prison diary, awaiting his own court-martial, her one-time comrade on the CEN, Armando Villanueva, called Portal's defense *"porquería"* (filthy trash).[33]

When Portal reemerged from the shadows of the Aprista underground in 1950, the Peruvian public had lived in Odría's dark discursive landscape for almost a year and a half. The massive court-martial trying more than two hundred people for the Callao mutiny dominated Peruvian politics. Portal's court-martial was held on February 10, 1950, at the El Potao Barracks in Lima.

Calmly escorted by police, Portal walked before a small audience of judges, guards, lawyers, and five others, presumably family members.[34] In another perhaps surprising concession to her pride and dignity, she dressed for the occasion, and the press breathlessly commented on her elegant silk suit, green glasses, and matching white purse and shoes. Although her lawyer had ably defended her against charges of treason, Portal read her own defense.[35] She stood before the court-martial and spoke for twenty-five minutes and "completely destroy[ed] what she had supported and predicated twenty years earlier," denouncing and attacking the party she had labored in for so long. Portal was, in the eyes of the press, "a new example, tired, beaten, and moving, of the political and ideological breakup of the party."[36]

Portal's public resignation and denunciation of APRA was only the latest in a genre grown increasingly familiar to Peruvians. The authorities "literally filled the airways and the newspapers" with formal renunciations of APRA affiliation and pledges of loyalty to the government. The very intensity of this "overwhelming barrage," however, precipitated yet another crisis when some of these performances proved, inevitably, to be just that: performances.[37] The Odría regime brutally chased down these false apostates.

Peruvians, including government officials, began to "lose faith" in public rejections of APRA. In this dangerous and duplicitous landscape, people could never prove their sincerity even when they tried to publicly renounce APRA and swear loyalty to the Odría regime. In fact, the government "came to view as suspect the very act of presenting oneself as loyal, to view anyone who presented him or herself in these terms as potentially subversive."[38] Portal was distinguished as being the highest-ranking Aprista leader to so declare herself, and she no doubt differentiated herself from the others in that she renounced APRA while not pledging allegiance to Odría—a distinction perhaps too nuanced for most to notice, although undoubtedly key to Portal's own understanding of her actions.

When Odría's regime failed to destroy APRA, its purported reason for being, the state found itself facing a skeptical audience. But Portal became a fortuitous new player to draft into its production. Her iconic visibility as the only female in the highest leadership made her instantly legible to Peruvians as an Aprista, perhaps second only to Haya himself. By providing discursive space for her within its otherwise antiseptic public sphere, the regime might capture the attention of a public that no longer trusted, or even really listened, to its truth claims, while simultaneously cultivating doubts and divisions within APRA itself. Portal was "proof that in the current hour, in illegality, Aprista cadres have not maintained their organization, their discipline, their unity. That the crisis continues. And that it deepens, until it reaches the highest ranks of its leadership," the press reported from her court-martial.[39] Portal's own motivations were undoubtedly more tangled. The deal liberated her from clandestinity, but she had to find a way to explain to the public, and perhaps to herself, her accommodation, her own betrayal of APRA and its emancipatory ideals to which she had dedicated her life.

Six weeks later, on March 22, the court-martial announced its verdict.[40] Of the 248 defendants tried, 238 were convicted, with sentences ranging from eighteen months in prison to the death penalty for a military officer convicted of murdering a superior. Aprista leaders under custody, including Carlos Manuel Cox and Luis Heysen, received the longest civilian sentences of three years' imprisonment. Portal and Sabroso, APRA's two subsecretary generals, were among the only ten acquittals. The court-martial decided that the year she had spent underground from 1948 to 1949 would count as time served.[41] Portal was a free woman.

Explaining the Exit: *¿Quiénes traicionaron al pueblo?*

In April of 1950, just weeks after her acquittal, Portal published her defense as *¿Quiénes traicionaron al pueblo?*, a pamphlet tracing Aprista political errors from 1945 to 1948 and condemning APRA as a deceiving shell of its former promise, all revolutionary bluster but no longer an authentically radical political alternative. Portal reserved her fiercest attacks for the leadership's failure to support the Callao mutineers, a betrayal where, in their "blind cowardice," they abandoned and denounced the rebellion, "allowing the police to corner the movement once begun."[42]

APRA's forced return to illegality after Callao turned internecine divisions into "grave wounds," Portal confirmed. "The people had been denied, abandoned, betrayed." In a sequence that just as surely reflected her own emotional progression in these second sixteen months underground, Portal detailed how "first the doubts, followed by suspicions and then the certainty that the high command had had much to do with the defeat and therefore the catastrophic fall of the party, preyed on the spirits of thousands of Apristas."[43]

But what struck one about her defense was not her analysis, but its scathing, seething, highly charged tone. It railed not against the party, or even all leaders, but pilloried Haya and the tight clique of insiders surrounding him. "Tired" after so many years of illegality, "in the autumn of their political vigor," they "aspired to enjoy a comfortable if bourgeois personal situation," she accused. Perhaps the leadership had at first disguised APRA as a centrist party of order instead of a revolutionary one for tactical advantage; the disguise, however, had now assimilated them.[44]

Her very public attack on the leadership is a puzzle, however, because she had previously explicitly dismissed resigning publicly to avoid harming APRA. On the eve of the ill-fated Callao rebellion, prepared to accept that any potential revolution would fail and disgusted with APRA's failure to effectively wield political power when in government, Portal promised an Aprista friend that when the coming revolution failed, she would definitively leave Peru but "would not harm the party" by resigning.[45] Sixteen months later, however, she resigned in the most public fashion possible by reading into the record and then publishing her blistering attack, clearly intending not just to harm the party, but to destroy it.

To explain this complete about-face, Portal turned to the power of ideas. In the late 1970s, looking back and narrating her own life, she stressed that ideological shifts alienated her from APRA and the leadership, explaining that she had been in "frank rebellion" ideologically against the party since 1945. "The Aprista Party formulated its social doctrine vaguely, without . . . defining its position on capitalism, and it came to identify with the higher class, it came to feel closer with those above than with those below. Then, it ceased being revolutionary. I left the party because of that," she explained, sidestepping that her public denunciation meant she left in the least revolutionary fashion possible.[46]

Just a few days after returning to Peru, Portal's disquiet grew, she wrote in ¿Quiénes traicionaron al pueblo?, when Haya took the stage at a massive rally on May 20, 1945, for what became known as the "Reunion Speech," where APRA reintroduced itself as a legal political party. Haya announced that APRA "had not come to take the riches from those who have them, but instead to create riches for those who do not." Observers considered this a minor modification meant to help APRA catch some of the energy of the postwar democratization wave, a small but necessary price to pay to participate in Peru's government. But Portal felt blindsided: Haya's speech "surprised everyone," and they realized it signaled the end to one of the party's bedrock principles: income redistribution and the Socialist realignment of the Peruvian economy.[47] As the leaders retreated from structural and economic explanations of imperialism, their new explanations appalled her. Her once revolutionary comrades now asserted that imperialism was an artifact of an "Indoamerican inferiority complex," dismissing the party's entire raison d'être in the twenties and thirties to an individual lack of psychological strength and denying the very existence, it seemed to her, of capitalist imperialism.[48]

Portal's alienation crested in 1948, she explained, identifying the Second National Party Congress as the moment when she broke with APRA, a meeting she now understood as an infuriating exercise in futility, a mere performance of an open debate that instead antidemocratically ratified a preordained conservative agenda and election. Her disaffection was evident, she claimed, in her dramatic storming out of the congress's plenary session in protest, in her refusal to attend the swearing-in ceremony for the new CEN, and in not renewing her party membership.[49] Defending herself before the court-martial, Portal recalled that "I remember that in one of the sessions I attended I got up and abandoned the room, a room larger than this one, and at the door I murmured, 'This party is on its way to Fascism!' . . . I was resentful, defrauded, and betrayed."[50]

In this reframing, the 1948 party congress became a critical point of disillusion.[51] Portal was livid because instead of addressing concerns about the direction of the party and its fidelity to revolutionary principles, leaders convinced provincial delegates that any frank discussion and potential policy about-faces would give their enemies additional ammunition in these dangerous times. This congress was charged with either modifying or reratifying the statutes and philosophy that had been crafted seventeen years earlier at their first national Aprista congress in 1931. When U.S. embassy analysts considered the governing program actually ratified in 1948, they found it illustrated "how little Apra's fundamental program has changed since 1931."[52] But in 1950, Portal argued that Aprista leaders pushed through their own reactionary program, ignoring the concerns of frustrated Apristas who believed the changes—including pulling back from redistributive economics and anti-imperialism—were betrayals of party first principles meant to placate the government and the oligarchy.[53] The leadership, she accused, sold off party first principles for access to the corrupting electoral process.

Portal claimed she did not attend most of this congress, and it would not be surprising that she kept her distance from such an intense partisan gathering held just over a year after Gloria's suicide. She did attend the plenary session for the election of the new CEN. Party leaders had assured frustrated Apristas that the committee revising the statutes and philosophy would make its recommendations then, leaving plenty of time for debate, she explained. According to Portal, the dissidents planned to argue against the increasingly conservative turn in party principles and elect a dissenting slate of leaders to the CEN, but they were blocked when the leadership schemed to elect León de Vivero over Seoane as the powerful secretary of Politics through parliamentary maneuvering. With the dissenting CEN leadership slate defeated, Portal and her allies still hoped to publicly debate changes in Aprista principles and ideology. But their carefully prepared speeches were never heard. The new statutes and philosophy were submitted and approved without debate after the leadership pushed through an ad hoc rule that, in Portal's words, "guillotined" discussion.

Portal's dramatic gesture of storming out, "followed by a great number of compañeras," was certainly one of the brightest displays in the political fireworks of the last plenary session.[54] But the ultimate motivation for her protest remains far from clear. Other leftist Aprista dissidents saw it as a blow struck for more internal democracy in the party, and a dissident manifesto recounted it as the "blocking" of "the valuable criticism of Magda Portal."[55] Party insiders read the move as a disruptive and selfish personalist gambit; it's worth noting that Portal later revealed that this was not the first time she had stormed out of party meetings.[56] Portal dismissed her new office as subsecretary general as a gilded muzzle: "a type of concession to impede me from making public declarations."[57] Recounting this episode later in life, Portal mused, "You know, a subsecretary is like a vice presidency. It has no function other than to replace."[58]

But ideas alone cannot explain the ferocity of her attack, or why she chose the most dramatic public showcase for her resignation, or to take the additional step of publishing it after the court-martial. The timing also demands explanation, especially since APRA's organizational shortcomings she denounced had been clear for years. The party had been failing to live up to its revolutionary rhetoric for decades, and Portal had found a way to remain in the leadership. "Some people ask me," Portal revealed later, "'Why didn't you leave earlier?' Because I couldn't, because I could not leave without fighting, without telling them anything, leave and go elsewhere. For the people, because I worried that the people would be disappointed so soon. I told myself: 'Well, I can be disappointed, but not the people.'" She could not resign before, she explained in 1950, because she wanted to avoid "a scandal, since the people and the youth still trusted the party and keeping in mind that my resignation could cause them serious harm."[59] Something happened in the second sixteen tragic months after Callao that made her quiet resignation impossible.

Previous biographers have seen her public attacks against APRA as a heroic stance, her "*j'accuse* moment."[60] U.S. embassy analysts saw not so much epic courage as tactical maneuvering, implicitly attributing her acquittal to Portal's renouncing "the party and all its works as 'reactionary' about a month previously in a widely publicized declaration," and Sabroso's acquittal to his "broken health and morale," which "cancelled him as a factor to be reckoned with."[61] But these two iconic Apristas, the party's most visible woman and its most visible worker and labor leader, who had stood for APRA's emancipatory social ideals from the very beginning, were both broken in health and morale, one just more visibly than the other.

Something much larger than ideology broke in Portal during these second tragic sixteen months. APRA had always been the vehicle for Portal's dream of revolution, a revolutionary aspiration that always encompassed more than formal politics and included an emancipatory sense of self, a liberated feminist personality. In 1947, with the suicide of her daughter, followed by APRA's political collapse after the Graña assassination, that dream of Aprista revolution began to crumble, and definitively collapsed with the leadership's failure to support the 1948 attempted revolution. During these second tragic sixteen months, Portal realized she lacked the psychological reserves necessary to throw herself once again into the abyss, as she had with such abandon when she was younger. While Haya might still enjoy a "profound interior life," making sacrifice for APRA not just tolerable but productive, she had nothing left to get her through this never-ending revolutionary night.

Facing a return to the catacombs, a return to a life of hiding, persecution, and such difficult sacrifice, would be psychologically trying even for militants in the best place of their lives, secure in their convictions and the certainty of their purpose. Portal was certainly not in that place, confronting multiple gaping, potentially fatally consuming wounds to her sense of self: the dissolution of her life with her revolutionary compañero, Serafín Delmar, now married to another woman in Chile; her daughter's suicide and the inescapable doubts implicating her and her life choices as a mother; and the crumbling of the Aprista political identity that formed the bedrock of her personality and self-worth that had sustained her for more than twenty years. She could not talk about the first two—Serafín's name never comes up in her later interviews, and, for the rest of her life, she could not stand anyone even mentioning her daughter's name.[62] But she could talk about the last, and the depth of feeling she poured into her attacks against the party leadership and Haya were in part a deflection of the anguish occasioned by the first two.

With the dream of Aprista revolution dying, Portal created a series of crises, starting at the 1948 party congress and continuing through her court-martial defense forcefully attacking the Aprista leadership, which set up a demolition of self and brought down the whole edifice of her public commitments. She burned every bridge in the most definitive way possible to what had in the past been her last and best refuge—APRA as a revolutionary dream. We could choose to understand this as a complete breakdown, but it was also self-preservation; she smashed through to create an exit ramp out of what was now revealed as a life of perpetual suffering. She created a possibility in her zero hour where none seemed possible. This was likely not calculated—rage may have been fueling her much more than reason. APRA would never lead the revolution. Suffering and sacrificing for it was suffering not for an end, but as a way of being. During these sixteen tragic months, underground and on the run, Portal realized she could no longer live this life, that the sacrifice had been too much, and that she needed to find a way out. Portal had reached the point Delmar had reached after ten years in Peru's prisons—the limit of her ability to suffer and sacrifice for her revolutionary dreams. Ultimately, this was not just an ideological and political break, but primarily a human tragedy.

As her closest political allies, the people who knew her best, struggled to understand her break with APRA, and especially her decision to attack the party leadership, they focused on the tragic dimensions of this larger personal crisis of faith. Betancourt, one of Portal's closest political friends since the late 1920s and now ex-president of Venezuela, wrote in a March 1950 letter to Luis Alberto Sánchez that her "spiritual crisis is one of the most tragic human spectacles that I have felt." For someone generally characterized as "difficult to deal with" because of his "egotistical, embittered, selfish nature," Sánchez was also surprisingly empathetic.[63] "My impression of Magda, after learning about her declarations [against the party] is that she has gone to pieces after a process of tragic exhaustion," he diagnosed. "I am neither surprised nor do I reproach her anything other than not knowing what she could bear." Ultimately, he saw her response as an unfortunately timed reaction based on her inherent heedlessness, the very same decisive heedlessness that had made her early life possible as an effective militant, organizer, and revolutionary. "But, she suffered much and she possesses a temperament that distanced her from friends and that makes her prone to an inapplicable extremism to which she rises at inopportune times."[64]

Betancourt's insightful use of "spiritual crisis" to describe Portal's crossroads captures the essence of her dilemma—Portal was in the clutches of a crisis of Aprista faith. A crisis of faith is much more than doubts—it is a crucible of terrifying clarity demanding resolution, compelling a choice. Portal had to either reconcile her doubts about APRA's revolutionary potential and the competency of its leadership or she had to abandon the faith. Among the highest leadership, Portal was neither the first, nor would she be the last, to confront such a crisis; perhaps Sánchez's uncharacteristic empathy was born in his own crisis, his own impulse to leave the party, documented in the bitter, angry letters he exchanged with Haya seven years earlier. This cohort was well into middle age, "in the autumn of their political vigor," in Portal's scathing but accurate assessment, the classic age for such moments of desolate reconsideration.[65] Reassessing what little they had achieved at tremendous personal costs, other leaders also plunged into a crisis of faith about what they saw as APRA's changing ideologies and structural shortcomings. Perhaps more to the point, these oldest, closest leaders also saw Haya displace them with a new guard, and the party definitively transition in these three years of legality from the work of a few to a mass political party. But these other leaders found a way to resolve this crisis and remain in the leadership and the party. Portal's own crisis was more complicated in that it was two-fold: the larger, shared crisis in APRA as an institution and possibility, and a more personal crisis of relations, of Aprista camaraderie and comradeship. She would not find her way back.

With APRA once again out of power, being in the APRA leadership was now not about policies or shared political, much less revolutionary, aspirations, as much as an affirmation of faith. This is how Haya understood the bond still holding the leadership together after almost twenty years. "We have never lacked for faith, the only bond capable of uniting" the high leadership. "And, for my part, I don't think I will ever lose faith. Before anything else, Aprismo has been, is, and will be a movement of faith. Faith in the ideals, faith in the cohesive power of those ideals, and faith in the men who support and don't give up on those ideals. Nothing remains once that faith is broken. It filled abysses among Apristas and it made us feel like compañeros of those with whom we never would have been, or ever were, friends. Aprista faith built bridges, tied bonds, straightened twists, and opened roads to Damascus. That is why it is fraternity and decision."[66]

But, perhaps, a dream of revolution without APRA survived. Portal's "extremism" now swung from APRA's most faithful militant to its opposite: its truth bearer and ultimately its destroyer. To resolve her crisis of faith in the Aprista revolution and therefore in herself, Portal cast herself as David to the leadership's Goliath. She forged a new revolutionary certainty in which she remained the only one faithful to the party's original leftist and revolutionary principles as others fell prey to the seductive temptations of bourgeois comforts, political power, and *yanqui* imperialism. During these cumulative crises, Portal determined that she believed first in principle, and not the party. She was still deeply invested—in love, really—with what she once was: a fully committed militant partisan. Arguing that the others in the APRA leadership betrayed their principles first allowed her to understand herself as the Aprista truth bearer, the principled hero who betrays a smaller, bankrupt Aprista faith to save the larger, authentic revolutionary faith. She did this for herself, to allow her to explain, understand, and defend to herself actions that just a few months earlier she believed unthinkable. Ultimately, she chose herself over the collective commitment, the "powerful, creative collective madness" she had shared with her Aprista compañeros.

This is what makes a quiet resignation impossible. Denouncing the party publicly was not just a tactic meant to save her own skin, as outside observers believed. To be the last remaining authentic revolutionary soldier in a field of impostors meant revealing APRA's duplicity to the naïve masses who still hung their revolutionary hopes on the party. "The political future of a people cannot be at the mercy of mendacious traffickers of their hope," Portal concluded.[67] Before Gloria's suicide, before the Graña debacle and the death spiral it instigated in the party, her disillusionment in APRA's failure to live up to her idealistic dreams was a personal betrayal, just another in the long list of sacrifices to bear in the hopes that APRA could still fundamentally change society in some revolutionary future. Now, as the very title of her attack made clear, *¿Quiénes traicionaron al pueblo?*, it had become a collective, national betrayal. All revolutionary potential in APRA was dead, and continuing to leave anyone believing otherwise was the type of opportunistic duplicity she had spent her life defining herself against.

This new role of truth bearer also cast her once again as a protagonist, as the vanguard visionary who saw through the dangerous revolutionary farce APRA had become. In a revealing moment in an end-of-life interview, Portal "explains" her break with APRA not by explaining anything, but instead by asserting that she had to pick a fight. "But in the end it had to be that way because I had to fight with them. In any case, in public. I had to resign publicly."[68] Picking this public fight became a psychological necessity for her, a claim to agency.

Portal's new public duty would be exposing the leadership's hypocrisy to the rank and file and redeeming the ideals of Aprismo by ultimately destroying the party itself. Writing in 1950, Portal revealed she "would feel doubly at fault if my silence fostered the continuation of the deception, the fraud, and the treason" of APRA's "false leaders."[69] But who were the false leaders? Could Portal have really seen herself as the Aprista truth bearer or was this just self-serving self-delusion? A constructive self-delusion, after all, is one of a revolutionary's sine qua non qualities. Nonetheless, glimmers of potential moral doubts bubble up when we recall how adamantly she refused to consider a public resignation before Callao, perhaps an unguarded aside she revealed in an end-of-life interview, or her explanations in a 1950 interview that she did not leave Peru even as her disaffection with APRA grew, although her "every intention was to go abroad," because some Aprista women "asked me to stay because my leaving would have been a blow to women."[70]

This revolutionary certainty ultimately came at great personal cost to herself, since it cast her from both the material and emotional embrace of the Apristas and from the larger regional network of leftist and anti-imperialist allies she had cultivated since the 1920s. But she now faced an audience larger than her brothers in politics. Nervous and fidgety in that 1950 interview, she had trouble breaking the ice with her interviewer. Not because of mistrust, he felt, but because of her "sense of responsibility. It is that History is the third person" in the room, "and she knows it."[71] But was this "History," personified in the gaze of her compatriots, judging her or judging APRA?

An Exit in Deed: Aprista Revisionism

A free and now unaffiliated woman who had demolished the revolutionary aspirations that had sustained her for over two decades, Portal had to rebuild her life. Although free to travel, she stayed in Peru with its toxic partisan landscape and painful memories. Breaking with APRA and escaping from the life of a revolutionary was a key life decision, perhaps the definitive turning moment in her life. The benefits of leaving APRA were worth the cost of facing an endless horizon of sacrifice and suffering for a political project that would never bring revolutionary change. Demolishing a foundation of her self-identity, however, necessarily meant finding something to fill the yawning vacuum it left. Had Portal made a mistake in choosing Haya over Mariátegui all those years ago and misjudged the revolutionary potential of APRA over other leftist alternatives?

For Portal, that new meaning was casting herself as the authentic soldier who remained faithful to revolutionary ideals and who tells truth to power, a position that allowed her a ready psychological defense to face down the chorus accusing her of treason. Portal stayed in Peru as the Aprista truth bearer. Perhaps this was part of her accommodation with the regime. In *¿Quiénes traicionaron al pueblo?*, she explained this accommodation to the world as the inevitable consequence of divergent ideas, even if her actions had more to do with her emotional or "spiritual" state. But her words—her ideas—were not enough. Portal had to prove, perhaps to Odría, perhaps to others, certainly to herself, that she was not a false apostate.

Attacking APRA was not a situational stance, a tactical position of convenience, but instead one of principle.

Having cast herself as the party's truth bearer, Portal found her task much harder in Odría's duplicitous political landscape, where no one could be sure where anyone truly stood. She launched herself into new projects to reach rank-and-file Apristas, hoping they believed the sincerity of her resignation and listened to her scathing critique of the leadership she was intent to prove was only deceiving them. Portal's campaign began by publishing her defense as *¿Quiénes traicionaron al pueblo?* three months after her court-martial.

In June 1950, just two months after her incendiary pamphlet appeared, Portal was elected president of a Third National Revisionist Congress of the Partido del Pueblo. A group of 145 dissident Apristas convened this revisionist congress as the open and frank debate about first principles and failed policies they had demanded from the 1948 Second National Party Congress, and as they mercilessly dissected APRA's shortcomings and failures, they enjoyed what Portal boasted was a "freedom of speech such as was never given in the great Aprista assemblies."[72] The dissidents dissolved the APRA Party, "deauthorizing" it as an authentic revolutionary political project. Haya was nothing but "a traitor, a mercenary sold to yanqui imperialism," and party organizations were *caudillista* groups whose only function was being "electoral agencies in search of personal benefit" instead of organizations working for any social good.[73]

The dissidents staked a higher moral position, refuting charges of treason against the party by claiming to be the most steadfast proponents of its lost revolutionary potential. "Accusations that we have been bought, that we are traitors, that we are apostates, will not take from us the right to declare our revolutionary truth," they promised.[74] In the three years of cogovernance between 1945 and 1948, when Bustamante denied Haya a political post commensurate with what his followers considered his stature, Apristas considered Haya Peru's "moral" president.[75] With a similar logic, the revisionists were now claiming themselves the "moral" remnants of a failed and corrupt APRA. As the elected president of this group, Portal was thus staking claim to being the "moral" head of APRA. Her Aprista credentials included her stature as a founding member of the party and her internal reputation as a long-standing militant from its radical left wing. Her renegade credentials, including her court-martial

Magda Portal, Frontispiece of *¿Quiénes traicionaron al pueblo?* (1950).
Courtesy estate of Magda Portal, Rocío Revolledo Pareja, and
Penn State University Press.

defense blasting the leadership and her subsequent publishing of *¿Quié-nes traicionaron al pueblo?*, were similarly unimpeachable. The frontis-piece to that pamphlet, which she had dedicated to "the Apristas of all Peru," was a photograph of her writing at her desk, identifying her as a founder of the Peruvian Aprista Party. She was a thinker at work, the anti-Haya, an alternate founder and theorist.

Ironically, as the Odría regime's fears about APRA's power burned at a fever pitch, within the party itself the spectacular failures of 1948 precipi-tated a series of internal crises about ideological direction and lack of democratic governance. Years later, in his memoirs, Luis Alberto Sán-chez outlined the two forces he saw trying to "divide Apra, unsuccess-fully and with much treachery," in the five years after October 1948. Portal was the "visible head" of one group, his language subtly denying her agency as a potential leader by assuming there was another power behind the throne.[76]

Sánchez could be forgiven for assuming that Portal was maneuvering to split the party and lead its more radicalized dissenting elements. Major

Víctor Villanueva, in fact, wrote Portal a long, searching letter trying to recruit her into his revolutionary Aprista splinter group.[77] But Portal did not join the Revolutionary Unit for which she had pleaded during Callao's agonizing end. Her refusal to join this revolutionary faction, or the Peruvian Communists, or even create her own revolutionary political option, makes it difficult to fully accept her words explaining—defending, justifying—her break as the full reason for her actions. Portal instead claimed she did not want to head a "neo-Aprista" faction. The hard truth, she argued, was that Aprismo was "historically liquidated," unsalvageable as a party, as a doctrine, and as a vehicle for emancipation and liberation. It would be either "naïve or malicious" to attempt to create a neo-Aprismo because Aprismo as doctrine and practice had collapsed into crass *caudillismo*, the dissidents asserted. "All Aprismo is Hayismo."[78]

Instead of the opening shot in a bid for leadership, this congress was Portal's eulogy to APRA as a revolutionary project, and she argued that neither APRA nor its doctrine *should* survive because both had proven they lacked the strength to lead the people to victory. Her closing speech carefully choreographed the bookend of her political career, announcing her "unbreakable decision to retire from militant action to return to my silent tasks of being a writer," ceding the stage to the youth best suited for the coming "labor that imposes all types of efforts and sacrifices. Like the good actresses, I am retiring in time, before it is too late, and as you can see, compañeros, I exit stage left."[79]

Portal was done; she was exiting politics, and the finality of her message conveyed her emotional state. But she exited only after ensuring everyone knew she was still a principled leftist. In her life narrative, when the young Apristas were just beginning to organize in Mexico in the late 1920s, she had once dramatically performed her full commitment to their shared revolutionary dream by publicly throwing her poetry into a river in front of her Aprista compañeros, boldly answering Haya's complaint that they needed political economists and not poets. Now, she publicly declared the inverse return: her exit from politics and a return to writing. This was also a parting shot against the other protagonist in that key life anecdote: Haya. Portal crafted her decision to leave the stage for a new generation into a barbed jab at an aging leader at the head of a party that had privileged the energy and regenerative vision of youth since its founding.

And it was youth who filled the revisionist ranks. José Fonkén, a young revisionist leader, claimed it was "in reality a youth movement," with "young people" composing 90 percent of its membership.[80] Half of the forty-four total signatories to the congress's concluding resolution "de-authorizing" APRA were youth leaders.[81] Notably, eleven, a quarter of the total signatories, were national-level leaders, six of whom had served as the national secretary of the party's youth wing. These young radical-ized revisionists did not pose an authentic threat to APRA, but their pub-lic rejection could be seen as a tragedy of lost leadership from the party's most promising youth.

Twenty-two of the signatories were also provincial-level leaders. Youth and provincials: the two most radicalized groups in the rank and file and the two most vocally dissenting groups at the 1948 Second National Party Congress. Their exit was a powerful repudiation to the leadership of a party that began as a vindication for provincials in Lima who thought of them-selves as the vanguard young modern leaders Peru needed. As the "moral" head of these revisionists, Portal stood at the front of the party's radical youth and provincial wing, the equivalent group to the Trujillo bohemi-ans who thirty years before had formed the nucleus of what became APRA. With the founding generation of APRA now all in their fifties, and Haya now fifty-five, they had had their chance and their time as militants had run its course, Portal implied. The final punch was the reminder that unlike Haya, Portal was leaving having kept faith with the party's founding ethos. For Portal, Aprista politics was a dead-end, not the dream of revolution.

But looking out over these young faces, Portal also knew that these were not her people. These youth romanticizing themselves as the equivalent of the Trujillo bohemians could just as easily be seen as opportunists upset at their own diminished career opportunities in a party now forced back into the shadows. While the dissidents clothed themselves in these heroic trappings, others saw only a sad affair—a pseudo-Aprista meeting Odría allowed only to pull Aprista schisms further apart.

This revisionist congress gave Portal a stage on which to reiterate and expand her attack on the leadership, hoping to reach a rank and file who still considered APRA and its leadership a revolutionary option. For Odría's regime, allowing this gathering exposed dissent within APRA and provided a venue and opportunity for promising—or simply ambitious—upcoming leaders to disaffiliate from the party. Some of these young, disaffected leaders took the next step, seeing this autopsy as a necessary prelude to organizing a new and authentically revolutionary political project, and convened a national organizing convention for a new revolutionary party.[82] Fonkén, an emerging dissident leader, clarified that "Magda Portal, whose brave position inspires our sympathies, is not a leader of our movement." She had "declared her decision to not intervene in politics; truthfully, we are sorry she does not form part of the movement."[83] But they thanked her for providing them with space in the magazine she was now publishing: *Tiempos.*

True to her plenary speech declaration, Portal returned to her "silent tasks of the writer" by founding a news magazine three months later. Portal dreamed of a "national magazine, unique in the genre, that fills a great gap in our journalism," one that would "foster political discussion that will clear the country's political climate, liberating it from the prejudices and taboos imprinted by the long years of a single militant political group's passionate propaganda."

At first glance, *Tiempos* bore a close resemblance to the first magazines in which she was published as a young journalist in the early 1920s, magazines like *Mundial* and *Variedades*: a large format, full of photographs, covering national and international news and cultural events. The back cover always featured a glamorous full-page photograph of a movie star. This was nothing like any of the magazines she had founded and edited before, which had focused either on vanguard poetry or partisan politics. With its mix of photography, news, celebrity entertainment, and cultural criticism, *Tiempos*, like midcentury middle-brow publications elsewhere, was trying to find a comfortable balance between culture and commerce.

But just below the celebrity photographs, *Tiempos* harbored a serious political purpose. With the bulk of its articles and cartoons devoted to criticizing APRA, any observer leafing through *Tiempos* would immediately recognize it as an anti-Aprista space of which the Odría regime no doubt approved. For instance, "Pachacutec's Offering," a cartoon published on August 9, 1950, was a biting depiction of a corpulent Haya as Pachacutec offering Peru as a gift to Uncle Sam. The caption was a 1946 quote in which Haya argues that Aprista ideas were good business for the United States, which the dissidents saw as a frank betrayal of the party's founding anti-imperialist principles.

While exposing Aprista duplicity was key to her role as truth bearer, Portal also wanted to show what could be possible in an open public sphere. In Odría's brutal dictatorship, of course, a genuinely democratic, much less revolutionary, public sphere was an impossible dream. But she still tried to foster an open political discussion in a weekly section titled "Neutral Ground," where Portal offered space in *Tiempos* to every political tendency. In her effort to appear politically impartial, she even published an Aprista attack from its underground press calling the dissidents (and naming Portal personally) "reptiles" and "a gang of scoundrels." Portal was painfully conscious of being dismissed as a partisan mouthpiece, by which she meant entirely anti-Aprista, with no positive purpose. She even refused to accept commercial advertisements for the first six issues of *Tiempos* until the magazine had proven its political independence and "demonstrated to the public that we were animated by a sincere spirit of service," which undoubtedly fueled rumors about her financial backing and the support Odría's regime may have provided.[84]

Tiempos was ultimately Portal's example of a public sphere, meant to enact what a democratic, open, and free conversation about politics might look like, much as the revisionist congress had enacted what the dissidents felt an open, genuinely democratic party congress should be like. Of course, since the principal political project in Peru was still the fractured remnants of the now verboten APRA, which could never publicly defend itself, this could never be considered a free, open theater for all ideas. Portal and other Aprista dissidents aired grievances and critiques they had harbored for years; they saw themselves as a critically necessary corrective. For the Peruvian public, who were not privy to those long-festering internal party divisions, their critiques were one-sided attacks, much to Odría's delight. As Aprista dissidents, both in Peru and abroad, turned to her magazine as a platform for their complaints, they aired all sorts of dirty laundry.

Dissecting their scandals and accusations in *Tiempos*, Apristas exposed their party as far from the unified, highly organized specter the Odría regime feared, revealing instead their spiteful, ineffective, and splintering groups. Allowing Portal to publish *Tiempos* publicized and hastened APRA's splintering into ever smaller bickering factions. This was a powerfully alienating aspect of Odría's turning Peruvian public life into a drama where people were constantly performing loyalty. People strategized alone, as solitary individuals, about how to convince one another of their anti-Aprista positions. "This new anticollective isolated people, separated them from one another, and turned each individual into a potential threat to all others."[85] Portal's own trajectory followed this same process of alienation: her dissent transitioned from the more collective effort of the revisionist congress to the more individual, atomized efforts of *Tiempos*. When she represented herself on the frontispiece of *¿Quiénes traicionaron al pueblo?*, it was not as part of a collective voice of dissent, but instead as a solitary individual at work.

As dissidents like Portal atomized their struggle, Odría won an important battle in splintering his potential opposition. In becoming a revolutionary, Portal had affectively affiliated into the brotherhood of Aprista leadership and the shared embrace of the revolutionary promise of Aprista collective identity and action, what Haya had once called their powerful "collective madness." This process was never easy for her as a woman in a patriarchal society that severely restricted female public roles, but she succeeded by affiliating with other marginalized groups like the provincial university students in the twenties, or by deploying rhetorical frameworks such as comradeship, and by working harder than anyone should have to in organizing the party. Now, losing the psychological sanctuary of her revolutionary ideal and recognizing her own limits for suffering as an end in itself instigated her affective *dis*affiliation from this "collective madness" that had been the touchstone of her emancipatory vision for more than twenty years. Her increasing atomization flowed from her disaffiliation.

The splintering of Aprista partisans who were once comrades was personal and bitter. A leader of the party's defense organization, Carlos Boado, published a letter in *Tiempos* accusing the leadership of making him take the fall for the Graña assassination. His Aprista friends, who still hoped to salvage his party position, exchanged letters dripping with the emotions raging behind the scenes.[86] "My plan and intent here have been the following," one strategized: "I knew of the letter that appeared in the dilapidated rag written by the doubly harlot Magda. Now, we were interested in yanking Boado from the claws of that pimp with one hand and slapping him with the other. We practically yanked the letter from him."[87] They plotted to release a second letter, ostensibly also written by Boado, disavowing the first, to repair Boado's reputation.

The rage fueling the ugly, sexualized insults in this bickering—with Portal as both harlot and pimp—was symptomatic of a life in Lima as an

Aprista apostate that was growing increasingly difficult for Portal. The "right to declare our revolutionary truth" carried a high price. Apristas furiously attacked Portal and others who started trickling, and then flooding, out from the party ranks. Remembering the "horrible" things said about her, Portal recalled: "The nicest thing they said was that I had sold myself, that Odría had given me I don't know how many thousands [of soles]. All of us who left the party in that era—we were many—we each had a price, and mine was one of the highest." One day, carrying home groceries, she ran into two Aprista women on the bus. "One of them said, 'The Traitor.' And I said, 'Yes, but carrying burdens, same as you.' 'Traitor,' they called me, then. I was simply a traitor."[88]

Portal's attempt at exposing the hard truths about APRA in *Tiempos* soon failed, and after a short run of eight numbers, Portal ceased publishing her magazine in November of 1950. Portal had alluded to difficulties in publishing the magazine, and surely both Aprista pressure and lack of commercial support must have weighed *Tiempos* down.[89] Just as certainly, Odría's regime had no long-term need for the more open public sphere Portal hoped to create. Who could have been Portal's imagined audience for the magazine? Would either the elite or the working class be interested in such a middle-brow, politically oriented magazine? *Tiempos* was the latest example of Portal's inability to see people as they were instead of how she wanted, or needed, to see them. Other Aprista leaders had shared this most necessary delusion in their party's heroic organizing phase—this was a key element of their shared Aprista faith—but Portal never evolved a way to step out of it to see either people, like Serafín or Gloria, or things and situations as they really were.

Nonetheless, she remained a target of Aprista threats and violence, hounded and harassed and even receiving death threats. Her ex-compañeras in the party warned her not to go about unescorted. Portal's sister recalled that once, a taxi driver told Portal that Haya had issued orders to the APRA-controlled taxi union that if they should pick her up, she should be taken to a deserted spot and beaten. " 'I may be an Aprista,' the driver told her, 'but I'm also a human being—Señora, don't take a taxi.' Magda took this warning seriously."[90]

Threats of violence also swirled around Portal. After breaking with the party and attacking them in print, Portal reported that the APRA leadership "wanted to kill me. But they did not kill me. They have always believed that I walked around armed." In the collective Aprista imagination, Portal had always been associated with violence. Now, however, they saw her as a dangerous and destructively violent woman representing an existential threat against APRA itself. Rumors abounded that she had founded a revisionist unit along with workers from *La Tribuna* with the goal of assassinating the leadership, including Haya.[91] There was no truth to these rumors, and it's worth noting that Haya's favorite charge against dissidents was that they were trying to kill him.

Portal spent a year attempting to broadcast the hard truth that APRA was little more than a revolutionary deception in Odría's ever-narrowing public sphere. As she realized there was no space possible, as that task grew increasingly futile, and as Aprista intimidation and harassment increased, she finally chose to leave Peru. In mid-1951, she traveled to Buenos Aires to work on her writing. When she arrived, however, her luggage with her treasured wardrobe and all her working drafts never appeared. In the last blow of what had proven to be five terrible years, she had lost "the unpublished intellectual work of more than twenty years," and was so despondent that she told friends she intended to give up writing.[92] By the next year, Portal found herself working as a secretary to try to make ends meet. Her personal life broken without repair; her political identity, influence, and dreams crushed; the drafts and materials of her literary and political work, carefully crafted over many years, lost in one stroke, Magda Portal now had to scramble for her very financial survival.

What was left? Looking back at the past five years, she worked valiantly to understand what had happened to her after she had taken what she believed to be a series of heroic, principled stances at a tremendous personal cost. But on bad days, did she look back and wonder about these definitive exits? Was she the Aprista truth bearer, or a sad figure presiding over a puppet congress of opportunists in her exit from APRA? Was her exit from politics protesting too much because she suspected another, more painful truth? Was *Tiempos*, founded in the hope of re-creating the success of her earlier journalism, just another dirty compromise? Why did the final decision to leave the country, to flee from Peru, have to result in the end of her writing life, with all her precious words lost? Was this really the way Magda Portal exited public life, she, Peru's woman revolutionary and the revolutionary woman in the history of Peru?

CHAPTER NINE

Personality Politics

IN JANUARY 1949, THREE months after the Callao disaster, Haya sought asylum at the Colombian embassy. The news hit the party "like a bucket of cold water." Many had believed Haya would continue leading the underground struggle as he had in previous periods of illegality.[1] Dumbstruck Apristas facing court-martial were shocked. One bitterly recalled Haya swearing they would "find my body thrown in the streets of Lima . . . before a new dictatorship is enthroned." Instead, what suffered the blow was the "Myth" of Haya as the leader who sacrificed all for the struggle and deserved to lead a party in which "the positions of honor" went to those who faced the greatest danger.[2] Haya plaintively insisted he had no choice. "I sought asylum with loathing," he said, only because "I was cast out from every possible refuge, and thrown from every house. . . . Nobody wanted to see me."[3] Among Apristas, "the prestige of the 'Jefe' was at the edge of the abyss."[4]

In the normal course of affairs, Haya could expect safe passage from the country as a political refugee, but Odría surprised everyone by declaring Haya a common criminal and demanding that the Colombians surrender him.[5] For Haya and the party's current high leadership, Odría's unexpected heavy hand was a gift from above. As the Peruvian government dug trenches around the embassy, barricaded the roads around the mission, and trained spotlights and machine guns on every door to prevent his escape, it allowed the aging leader, once again, to appear as the embattled underdog. With this wildly disproportionate response, Odría did Haya "the greatest favor of his life," a disillusioned Aprista complained, as the pathos of his new dilemma "drowned the contempt that his

Magda Portal and Haya de la Torre at APRA rally at Plaza del Acho, 1931.
Courtesy estate of Magda Portal, Rocío Revolledo Pareja, and Magda Portal
Papers, Benson Latin American Collection, University of Texas at Austin.

cowardice had made one feel."[6] Whatever disgust and disillusionment Apristas may have had with Haya's perceived complicity in the failures of October and his cowardice in its aftermath transformed into sympathy and righteous solidarity with their leader, unjustly held hostage by Odría. He would remain in the embassy for five years.

For the increasingly disenchanted Manuel Seoane, Haya's predicament was a particularly thorny problem. Once one of the party's more moderate leaders, Seoane was now, like Portal, visibly struggling to steer APRA to the Left, having battled for the influential CEN position of secretary of Politics, only to lose to Haya's favored candidate, León de Vivero. The conflicts between Seoane and León de Vivero were so bitter that *Tiempos* could speculate that León de Vivero had targeted Seoane for an assassination they could then blame on their enemies, hoping such a "Gaitanization" would rally the Aprista masses, like the 1948 assassination of the popular Colombian Liberal politician Jorge Eliécer Gaitan.[7] Learning of the plan through his own informants, Apristas whispered, Seoane was allegedly shaken enough to have asked the Bustamante government for a security detail.[8] Seoane may even have genuinely believed that he was targeted for assassination. Luis Alberto Sánchez confirmed that, safely in exile in Chile, Seoane told him he believed that the two of them were to be shot if the 1948 revolution had been successful, and that he blamed Haya and the CEN.[9]

Seoane had had enough. By February 1949, a month after Haya entered the Colombian embassy, Seoane had drafted his resignation from APRA and written Haya of his impending exit, which everyone understood would "indubitably" split the party. Apristas "begged" Seoane not to go public and convinced him to delay his resignation until after Haya's situation was normalized. Seoane had no way of knowing that Odría's intransigence would keep Haya in limbo for five years. When Haya was finally released in 1954, the heat of the crisis had passed and Seoane remained in the party as a revered founder and statesman. When Seoane died fourteen years later, his obituary in *La Tribuna* transformed this difficult period, a moment of crisis when Seoane almost broke with the party. "Víctor Raúl is in diplomatic asylum transformed into a prison. . . . The exiles organized around [Seoane] raise the struggle everywhere. New books, enriching the doctrine. Víctor Raúl left asylum and the elder brothers of the party embrace once again."[10] While it is not surprising that his Aprista obituary glossed over Seoane's period of disenchantment, it is notable how this interlude was presented and understood: Seoane is literally an APRA "elder brother," and anyone remembering the discord of those years could understand that while brothers might fight, they always embrace at the end.

Juxtaposing Portal's five dark years from 1948 through 1953 with Seoane's concurrent experience of dissidence lays bare the predicaments facing women in APRA and in revolutionary movements. Portal's denunciations against APRA gained so little traction precisely because of the gendered dynamics that characterized the long intimate history of personal relations within the high command. Haya was a master at deploying these affective ties to reach his political ends in ways not available to Portal, who could not leverage her "Aprista faith" to achieve her political and personal goals. Trapped within just one register in this Aprista politics of sentimentality, Portal had long been less effective in the party's internecine conflicts and was forced into a colder, stilted affect others read as an "extremism" that heightened her isolation and contributed to her increasing difference with other leaders.

A Portrait: Portal Writes Portal

With Haya stuck in the Colombian embassy and the party adrift, Apristas improvised with what they called a Postal Congress of Exiles, where they exchanged ideas in letters analyzing the failures since 1945 and proposing new directions going forward.[11] Seoane was elected secretary general of the Organizing Committee of Aprista Exiles and was considered APRA's "acting chief in exile," a title that overestimated the glamour of the position; unable to even afford a typist, Seoane had to type most of the circulars himself.[12] The First Postal Congress ran from January through March 1950, precisely when Portal was publicly attacking the leadership, first at her January court-martial and then again in April, when she published *¿Quiénes traicionaron al pueblo?* Politically, Seoane's congress hoped to reunite the party despite "the hate of the resentful or the panic of the escapists"; it affirmed the exiles' submission to party authority and expressed their solidarity with Haya in his embassy prison. But they also wanted to "defend internal democracy as a permanent norm of intraparty life" and lean toward ceasing cooperating with the United States.[13]

Of Seoane's "new books enriching the doctrine," none was more famous than a letter he wrote in 1952 in which he broke with the long-standing tradition of not publicly questioning Haya. He argued that APRA should not in the future enter into political alliances of opportunity, given the disastrous precedent of 1945 to 1948.[14] Seoane argued that Haya's "inter-Americanist" positions had been too cooperative with the United States. Politically, he said, Haya had retreated into the company of "a small clique of sycophantic intimates" and failed to confront the opportunists who personally profited from APRA's new influence.[15] It would become no secret that Seoane felt Haya had wasted his chances at the presidency, and most now believed he was "the spearhead of the opposition to Haya's continued leadership."[16] As he began maneuvering to become APRA's presidential candidate in place of Haya, Seoane denied that his letter was merely "a personalist maneuver" and explained that, while he did not "aspire to any charge or position," he would not "shun the duties imposed by the function that I perform."[17]

While Aprista revisionists dismissed the postal congresses as mere "surveys" and "a farce of the leadership to entertain the exiles," both the exiles and the dissidents were lobbing nearly identical attacks.[18] Portal's critique of APRA's failures during the 1945 to 1948 period was also based on the party's miscalculations in national and congressional strategy while railing against an authoritarian stranglehold of internal party governance. Ultimately, like Seoane, she blamed a small, increasingly removed circle in the high leadership. The putative leadership of the party, the CEN, had met only six times in the tumultuous two years between 1946 and 1948, and its role was only to be informed of decisions already taken by "a triumvirate" of Haya, Jorge Idiáquez, and León de Vivero.[19] Unaffiliated observers offered very similar readings.[20]

Both Seoane and Portal thus offered similar diagnoses for what ailed APRA and placed blame on its leadership. The Postal Congress of Aprista Exiles, the Revisionist Congress, and *Tiempos* were concurrent efforts to identify Aprista shortcomings: a reformist one from within led by Seoane and an indictment epitomized by Portal from outside the ranks. What was distinctive, of course, was her scorching tone—she was not critiquing to reform; she was attacking to destroy. To use Luis Alberto Sánchez's language, her "extremist personality" had found another "inopportune time" to strike now that the party was being persecuted.

By 1952, Seoane's moments of wavering allegiance to the party were three years behind him, and he assured his exiled compañeros that they had "definitively overcome" their period of dissension and advanced "a formal call to solidify our unity." "The initial solid cement of Aprista unity," Seoane underscored, "was the sincere affection that tied and ties the founders, with mutual personal consideration, without pettiness or betrayals."[21] This affection among the men of the highest Aprista leadership, this "solid cement of Aprista unity," was the currency that allowed Haya to bring Seoane back into the fold. But the magic did not work with Portal, whose political positions during these same years were in some ways the mirror images of Seoane's.

Can there be an explanation—other than personal idiosyncrasies and life events—for the vastly different outcomes of Portal's and Seoane's stories? For the Aprista old guard, personality explained everything. Luis Alberto Sánchez claimed that "personalist" divisions in the leadership first appeared at the 1948 Second National Party Congress, when "a new divergence became clear: that of Magda Portal, who left the congress dragging with her a considerable number of women." His comments suggested that Portal's critique was unexpected and implied that the women who allied with her did so because of the force of her coercive personality.[22] Sánchez did not outline what the divergence was actually about; after all, if it is just a personality conflict, it neither needs to, nor can it, be further explained.

Once Portal's alienation from the party was understood as a personalist drama, Apristas could dismiss her ideological concerns as incidental. They could also be conveniently resolved by her departure. "Personalist" meant that the conflicts were a consequence of personality and inappropriate ambition, not ideology, and thus epiphenomenal because they did not bear on matters of party doctrine. The personalist explanation blamed the chasm separating Portal from the leadership on her "extremism," not, as she alleged, on their changing principles. The personalist label also meant Portal's actions were by definition self-serving and selfish, if not traitorous. It made her a scapegoat for broader dissension while allowing the leadership to dismiss anyone who joined her and avoid dealing with messy ideological discrepancies. This logic was recognized by the young revisionist leaders still hoping to salvage a revolutionary project from the ashes of APRA. Assertions that Portal was their leader were "false and captious," José Fonkén complained, mere attempts to blame her for all revisionist dissension.[23]

Not only did personalist conflicts not need to be analyzed, decorum mandated that such distasteful topics be avoided. Haya was a master at eliding uncomfortable questions while explaining away things he would rather not directly address. Asked in a 1978 television interview if APRA had supported any conspiracies in the 1945 to 1948 period, he thundered: "That is false! . . . That is the product of the fevered imagination of APRA's opponents. There is no truth to that. We were loyal cooperators and loyal allies of the constituted government. I don't want to talk more about that, because I would have to approach the problem of personalities."[24]

Portal's "extremist personality" thus became something more than a personal characteristic—it became an explanation acceptable to other male leaders and even, perhaps, to Portal herself. This was revealed when Portal dissected her public personality in her 1956 book *La trampa*. This novel-memoir ostensibly explored the case of Carlos Steer, a young militant manipulated by APRA cadres into assassinating the director of Lima's leading newspaper, *El Comercio*—a sensational crime for which he languished in jail for decades. But as the text switches between first-person perspectives, it becomes Portal's extended portrait of what APRA, as well as she and its other leaders, had become. While the book's preface declared it a work of fiction, she later wrote to a Chilean friend that it was "the pure truth, except for the names, which are easy to decipher."[25] Through her pseudonymous character, María de la Luz, Portal wrote her most intimate and revealing self-portrait.

Portal, as María de la Luz, ruminated for pages on how others perceived her public self. Through the eyes of her compañeros in the leadership, Portal was revealed as "that fragile, weak, pale woman, with her long chestnut hair and her eyes of extraordinary brilliance, full of strength, inspiring opposing feelings. Everyone knows that she has won her position in the party, her prominent standing, because of her authentic struggle, of effective battles won against the enemy. But also won against these same 'comrades.' A type of jealousy makes them feel that this woman, who has come to occupy a position of honor as high as that of the highest leaders, is a little too bold. As if women had the right to be the equal of men." Portal flatteringly wrote about herself: "She is considered intelligent, capable, active, a hard worker and loyal in her dedication. . . . But she is too intolerant, too bitter, too proud. She is not malleable, she does not mold to circumstances. She has the prejudices of the intellectuals. The wives of the leaders don't like her, because she looks down on them. The leaders don't like her, because the presence of a woman among so many men clashes. And, she is always judging."[26]

In the evocatively titled chapter "The Siege," she explained that she always seemed to be judging others because she felt besieged, not just by APRA's political or ideological enemies, but by her own compañeros. She struggled with the repeated "propositions by men who wanted to satisfy a passing appetite." For example, "One time Manuel looked her over from head to toes, taking her in completely. Later, when the others were not paying attention—and his wife was farther away—he approached her and launched the insult: 'You're ripe for the picking. Why deny yourself?' [*Estás a punto. ¿Por qué te niegas?*] She wanted to slap him, but was horrified at the scandal that would have produced, especially in the party. She limited herself to replying: 'If you continue, I will tell your wife.' "

This was not an isolated incident. Many of her "old compañeros" had also made passes at her, even though they all had wives who were putatively Portal's friends. Another time, she described how one of her closest comrades in the party, a married man, surprised her with a clumsy attempt at seduction. In rebuffing him, her principal emotional register was hurt as least as much as anger: "She feels wounded in the depths of her dignity. . . . Disgusting!" Her rebuff, she insisted, was not based on objections to adultery per se, or any "puritan scruples." She "has no prejudices" because "she believes in free love." Hence her anger: "And to think that she had assumed they were all above any such suspicions. But none of them has told her 'I love you.' She has not seen sincerity in any of them."[27] Her principal objection was their lack of sincerity, which makes their duplicitous advances an insult to her, as opposed to an insult to their wives. She hated not their immorality, but their utilitarianism—they tried seducing her because she was attractive, ready, "a punto," a phrase used to specify how one wants their meat cooked, because she was there and presumably available, not because they loved her. Portal objected to being subsumed into the collective abstraction of woman. Here, her colleagues were transforming her from Magda, an individual, into Woman, not Magda.

The feeling of impotence at being hemmed in fueled her anger to a white hot fury. In these anecdotes, her only recourse is to threaten to tell the wives, the damas Apristas who already don't like her and may well not believe her or even blame her for their husbands' wandering eyes. "Was she supposed to be the easy prey for these guys, who were seen as models of proper behavior, of morality, of discipline? A deaf rage gnawed at her breast. She wanted to spit on them." This, then, was at the root of her "reputation as sullen, bitter, proud," defining the "uncomfortable atmosphere" with which she struggled. "It's that she must always be on alert, ready to defend herself. And her smile can never be wide enough as she might like so that it isn't interpreted as an invitation. Sometimes she feels as if she moves among beasts ready to pounce."

In the novel, Portal says she initially joined APRA because it offered "the answer to her concerns about society. . . . Passionate and vehement, she had taken the ideals of the party as a new religion and had given herself to the cause totally and completely." Later, as APRA's demands shriveled in comparison to its initial aspirations, she made political adjustments like other leaders such as Seoane. "No, the party was not perfect," she conceded, and APRA "was not as radical as she had believed at the start. But its social proclamations were realistic for an unprepared nation and [its] path—petit-bourgeois demo-liberalism—would allow them to take firm steps toward the definitive conquest of all social rights. At least, that is what [her] romantic imagination supposed."

Yet *La trampa* had its lyrical moments, as when Portal describes her public speaking voice. The transcendence she found in her public role as a revolutionary was based on a subtle distinction between her voice and her words. Describing her oratory before a crowd, her narrator says that upon hearing her, "one forgets that she is speaking, if not for the revolutionary content of her words" because "when she speaks, she appears to sing."[28] Her revolutionary words were the vehicle for her speech acts, the reason she was on stage as a public woman, but she achieved transcendence through the act of speaking, through her own voice. In fact, the revolutionary words brought listeners crashing back down to reality, tethering them to the now, with all its problems and limitations. But her "warm, full, vibrant voice" with its "harmonious, deep, musical" notes, for which she "almost does not need a microphone," was the instrument of power allowing her and her audience to transcend all that, if only for fleeting moments. Thirty years earlier, in her 1921 poem "Prayer," Portal had begged God to tame, to crush her "crazy, boundless heart" and "make it not cry, make it not sing." The prayer was never answered, and while her heart and her will had made her cry, it has also led her to stand before her Aprista brethren, where women and men looked up to her, followed her, and heard her soar on this transcendent voice.

For Portal, such glimpses of transcendence offered an escape from Peru's exploitative social and economic conditions and the repressive expectations of gender conformity. It was a glimpse of the feeling she had found as a young woman in the bohemian camaraderie of 1920s Lima and as a founding comrade in APRA's top leadership. She always insisted that she genuinely believed her revolutionary ideas, "I have been a leftist since the day I was born," but in the final analysis, she discovered an equally transcendent power not in ideology but instead in what she had personally been able to do to advance its cause.[29]

In this self-portrait, Portal's relationship with Haya continues to be central. In Mexico, Haya had been the brightest star in a constellation of brothers. Now he was much more of a traditional patriarchal figure, inspiring respect for the father at least as much as the love of brothers bonding and conspiring together. Looming as the overarching figure in *La trampa*, Haya commands Portal's fearful respect; he was "the 'Jefe' who unquestionably knows more than everyone, he was above all the leaders. . . . Him she does fear." The changes in her description of their relationship thus measure the distance APRA has traveled from a student entourage to a populist cult of personality. Portal tallies Haya's messianic tendencies, his egotistical certainty that he was the party, and cataloged the deteriorating physical appearance that accompanied his aging. Presented as averse to revolutionary violence as a fault of character, Haya was softening; he was so "tired of the cheap meals, of those he had to suffer during his student years and later in persecution," that he now gorged on delicious feasts, growing fat.[30]

In such unflattering details, we see one of the implicit themes of *La trampa*: Portal's struggle to assert herself vis-à-vis Haya, to the point, almost, of seeing herself as the anti-Haya. Portal, she insists, is an original, foundational, irreplaceable leader: "Among the women there is no other leader," no one else with her "prestige and the charisma of leadership." She was "a cofounder of [Aprismo], since she affiliated at the first moments of its birth. She occupies a lifelong place in the high command." When she reviews her troops in the female rank and file with a cold, unfeeling eye, it's what generals, what leaders do, what Haya does. Like Haya, Portal was irreplaceable because women followed her. The leadership calculated shrewdly that the "damas Apristas" were not enough and that "the party needs a woman leader to attract women, so that no one can say that women don't matter, that they are only used to fill vacancies and inferior functions, like selling bonds, organizing charity balls, visiting prisoners, etc."[31]

La trampa was not an ideological polemic like *¿Quiénes traicionaron al pueblo?*, where she had outlined her ideological and strategic complaints about the leadership. There are very few ideas in these pages but many breathing, flesh-and-blood people. This was a personal attack, and not only against the highest leaders. Her sketches of the "damas Apristas," the wives, girlfriends, and, in Haya's case, relatives, closest to the male leaders were also highly unflattering. Attacking wives, daughters, mothers? The leadership moved quickly to suffocate these personal, intimate attacks. The original 1956 edition of *La trampa* never circulated, Portal claimed, "because some people who felt the text alluded to them kidnapped it."[32]

Having suffered as a prison widow herself, Portal no doubt felt deeply about the injustice befalling Carlos Steer, the triggerman still rotting in prison while those who had manipulated him into the crime walked free. In the final analysis, however, her personal attacks were the point of *La trampa*. As the painful anecdotes about her compañeros' constant propositions reveal, she felt a "deaf rage" at their assaults, impotent to defend herself or respond in kind. She had no equivalent weapon with which to return what she experienced as the wounding attacks on her self and her dignity. *La trampa* was the closest she could come to hurting them in a measure approaching that which she felt she had suffered, after being besieged for years.

In the end, Portal's self-portrait in *La trampa* is one of desolate loneliness narrated as a series of collapsed refuges, with the fading of all that had once consoled and offered the strength to persevere. Portal cataloged her emotional state with unrelenting honesty, showing the same attention to the female subjective and emotional experience that had transfixed Mariátegui about her poetry nearly twenty years earlier. Affiliation through comradeship was gone, with political and more personal consequences for her sense of self. Politically, the most visible consequence of her compañeros' discomfort with her was her systematic exclusion from "the meetings of high politics."[33] When she appears "at the high command, they deal only with formalities. And when she disagrees, the majority rebut her. She is left alone. . . . That is why, whenever possible, they push her aside, diminish her," she diagnoses, the word "diminish" suggesting the second, perhaps more debilitating psychological costs of this painful exclusion. "Many times she leaves the room in protest, and everybody breathes easier," she reports.[34] Perpetually on guard against her closest comrades and excluded from key deliberations, she felt her alienation among the high command was rooted in both the impossibility of being "one of the boys" and of ever allowing herself authentic self-expression among them.

Another missing refuge was the idea of the companionate marriage, a union she had come closest to in her relationship with Serafín, which she suspects she will never experience again. While she publicly claims not to need love, "It is not true," she confesses in an aside. She "passes long hours of the night awake, and many times it is not because of the party, nor because of her own economic problems. A desolate emptiness, a solitude that nothing fulfills, makes her toss and turn sharply in bed."[35] Another refuge is notable by its total absence: her daughter, Gloria. There is no trace of her daughter, Gloria, in *La trampa*, which in every other regard holds true to Portal's promise that it was "the pure truth," suggesting just how unresolved this wound still was for her.

Finally, her loneliness was further compounded by the distance she felt from other women. In her honesty, Portal explored the steep price she paid to draw closer to her male friends—an alienation from women so profound she perceived it as an unbridgeable distance. "In reality," she confessed, she "does not know women. . . . Her relations with them have always been very superficial. In general, she has had male friends and felt much more comfortable with them, since these had been comrades [*camaradas*] in her life as a student or social justice militant."[36] Narrating an anecdote that tellingly demotes her birthday to a footnote to a party of camaraderie [*camaradería*], she remembers a toast at that "happy night of beautiful remembrance." Magda Portal, "'may women curse you . . . !' What a strange impression that left in her, while the rest of the friends celebrated the occasion and continued toasting. It is true, women do not love her," she reflected. "Is it that her character awakens resistance? Is it that in reality she is so different from other women that she cannot find kindred spirits among her own sex?" Were they jealous because she was "usurping a place that does not belong to her?" She was different. "Maybe too introverted, she is ignorant of the frivolous manners that is the climate best suited for women."

In *La trampa*, Portal took stock of APRA's female membership with equally bruising honesty. The largest group, the female rank and file, was "entirely passive," their role "that of sponge or hungry mouth, who receive with no cup or measure the spiritual sustenance of the words of faith poured by the leaders." The next strata were the middle-class students, labor leaders, and wives of middle and subaltern leaders, who "believe that their best interest is served by serving and flattering her." These women "are useful workers, active, but filled with tremendous personal ambitions and petty jealousies among them," controlled only by Portal's "undeniable authority."

Portal assessed this group with a cold and unfeeling eye as if she weighed the strengths and weaknesses of her troops, but that emotional distance disappeared when she turned her attention to the final, smallest group of women at the top of the party: the wives, relatives, and friends of the leaders. Her discomfort with this group, the "counterweight" to her own troops, was palpable. While many of them were not even formally affiliated with the party, they "nonetheless occupy a preponderant place within it." The rank and file considered this small group of damas Apristas "the aristocracy of the party," who distributed toys and organized charity balls, "imitating the gran bourgeoisie. . . . They require another kind of approach, more frivolous, more in accordance with their position," Portal revealed. These Aprista ladies were more "worried about when their husbands' political conferences finish, rather than what is discussed at them," and while she might "use the friendly '*tú*' with all of them, she does not feel that they are really her friends."[37] Among women, among Apristas, and among Aprista women, Magda Portal stood alone.

The Ultimate Compañeros Apristas

A generation earlier, the Limeñan matriarch Lastenia Larriva de Llona advised her granddaughters that their best, and perhaps only, weapon to maneuver through their constricted lives was judiciously and circumspectly managing the emotions of the men around them. This was the only way women could exert their agency, turning patriarchs into doting fathers and potentially violent men into caring husbands. Of course, the men to be so managed dismissed and derided such feminine emotional manipulation, the waterworks of manufactured tears and the pitiful pleas of these "weapons of the weak."

In her masculinist posture, Portal shared this rejection of what were perceived to be feminine traits. While she documented the way other

Apristas used gender to dismiss and attack her, Portal nonetheless had internalized the essentialized notions of the men around her. Throughout her book, she observed that the men of the party, at every rank, often complained about "whining" and "meddling" women playing at revolution. But even when she assessed her own public speaking voice positively, she wrote that "it is not the whiny voice that generally comes from women when they present harangues or speeches." One of the most important of these internalized gender assumptions was that the expression of emotion was womanly and thus a sign of weakness and a lack of dignity, even unrevolutionary. In prison, her alter ego, she wrote, "would cry if not for the fact that it was undignified for a revolutionary woman to be seen as weak."[38] Searching for how to best wound the revolutionary credentials of the Aprista leadership in her 1950 denunciation *¿Quiénes traicionaron al pueblo?*, Portal landed on an evocative historical example in its rousing conclusion. As Aprista leaders "continue singing their chorus of laments before the tired attention of Peru and America," she declared, they provoked this increasingly exasperated audience "to apply the caustic phrase of the mother of the last Moorish king before the walls of the lost Granada: 'You cry like a woman for what you could not defend like a man.'"[39]

These assumptions, of course, also constrained male leaders. In *La trampa*, a leader needles Haya to approve a Machiavellian plan to assassinate Seoane to whip up the rank and file. As Haya demurs, the leader "jokes": "'Could it be a little sentimentalism, Jefe?'"[40] Haya's "hypersentimentalism" had long been the butt of charged "jokes" since his student days in the twenties, but perhaps those years, when many if not most of these young men primarily identified with poetry and bohemianism, were more forgiving of masculine emotional displays. Such ready access to emotion had long since melted under the duress of clandestine politics, and the implications of sentimentalism were much graver: weakness, an inability to consider the big picture, even self-indulgence.

Expressed emotions were dangerous waters in this world. Part of Haya's political genius, however, was his ability to navigate adroitly around the hidden dangers while finding an additional reservoir of political power in such performances of sentimentality. Back in 1949, when Seoane threatened to leave and splinter APRA, Haya sent him a "moving letter." "Speaking of letters, the one you wrote to Manolo touched my soul," a party confidant reported back to Haya. "The way I see it, it disarmed him. And he is a gentleman who always reacts with elegance. He was kind enough to let me read it. How beautiful! It also touched me," he confessed. "Manuel melted, and the letter had the effect that you and everyone wanted."[41]

Haya's performance of emotion bridged ideological divides, as it did in Seoane's case, by collapsing discussions back from the realm of abstract ideology to the intimate, personal, sentimental level. It recognized and valorized the individual in exactly the way that Portal yearned to be seen and recognized by Haya and the other leaders—as an individual and not a type. Haya's affection for him also can't help but touch Seoane in part because it is so unexpected of a masculine persona and therefore proves Haya's sincerity. Such a performance of emotional vulnerability, so unexpected of a patriarchal chief, could only be expected in the most dire of conditions, thus proving Seoane's worth, value, and importance. Portal never received any such "moving letter" from Haya during those sixteen months she seethed underground after October 1948, or in the three years before APRA was outlawed when her distance from the leadership was unmistakably growing.

Portal's retrospective dissection of the late-1940s period tended to be dispassionate. She alluded, but did not directly appeal to, the emotions involved: hurt, shame, and blame. "Of course it hurts anyone to break with a group for which one fought for so many years. But when one has not changed, one must not feel the blame."[42] Direct appeals to sentiment or emotion, she had learned all too well in her long history in the Aprista fraternity, would be unthinkingly dismissed out of hand as hysteria or "feminine sentimentalism." Such charges suggested that an emotional appeal would only serve to prove her failure to understand hard political realities, even as Haya's emotional appeals signaled his depth of conviction.

Ultimately, comparing Portal's with Seoane's political choices in this difficult period helps us unpack what Peruvians meant when they used "personalist" to dismiss and discount their political opponents. Branding as "personalist" her choice to publicly criticize the leadership, Aprista leaders signaled that her charges lacked an ideological basis and were merely the product of her own self-serving interests. This was at the heart of the most damaging and painful charge: that she had sold out to Odría, probably for a lot of money. This denied her the status of a principled opponent, when in her view, her deal with Odría allowed her the liberty to publicly denounce APRA as counterrevolutionary.

Yet these charges of "personalism" never stuck to Seoane, even as his political ambitions rose to presidential heights, or while gossip held that he may have informed the government about the 1948 Callao mutiny and enjoyed material comfort from his relationship with the Bustamante government, including a security detail. At heart, such "personalist" labels aimed to strip Portal of what she valued most: her principles, while attributing her actions to her suspiciously strong personality, her own force of will that dragged others in its wake. Left unsaid was the gendered assumption that such forceful women were nefarious, whereas similarly forceful, persuasive men were called "charismatic."

The gendered layers of meaning that attached to her as a woman undermined her attempts to represent herself as APRA's truth bearer, its most faithful soldier loyal to their founding principles. Female Aprista loyalists often called her *la traidora* (the traitor), which in Spanish carries an inescapable suggestion of adultery and sexual infidelity.[43] One popular line of attack against her, Portal remembered, was allegations that she was enmeshed in torrid affairs with the other male leaders, and she reported that an altered photograph circulated when she was imprisoned, which portrayed her with many faces, each one kissing a different Aprista leader.[44]

Other Aprista women remembered Portal as a woman who reacted jealously when Haya's attention strayed to more beautiful militants. Recounting her recruitment into the party, a young Aprista confessed it had nothing to do with ideas. Instead, by chance, she had been spotted at party headquarters and selected to "grace the stage with Haya because of her beauty." On the way to a meeting, she and Haya traveled alone in the first car, followed by Seoane and Portal in a second car. Portal "asked who was that young girl who accompanied the Jefe, since Haya's arm corresponded to her, since she was one of the most important women in APRA. 'I thought she felt displaced,'" the young woman concluded.[45]

The party had failed to create a "new Aprista woman" of the type Portal had argued for in the 1930s. The other templates available for people to understand Portal as a public woman remained that of a (failed) "dama Aprista," or, barring that, a mistress jealous of Haya's attention. These are the familiar and intimate roles that others—and perhaps even Portal—reflexively fell back on to understand interpersonal relations and, more importantly, political and interpersonal conflict within the party. While Portal, Haya, and Seoane could step away and intellectually recognize the actual ideological and political dimensions of their conflicts, they explained and emotionally reacted to this conflict as if it was part of an intimate family drama. These frameworks were built from experiences available to all and included a far richer repertoire of roles and tropes for males to navigate conflict, allowing Haya and Seoane to present, and perhaps understand, serious ideological and personal discrepancies as a spat between brothers.

The repertoire proved anemic, however, when dealing with conflict between men and women, relegating conflict between them to either a romantic liaison or a maternal dynamic, such as the one that years before had permeated the relationship between the younger Haya and his foreign patron, Anna Melissa Graves. Since their student days, women like Portal had always suffered from a paucity of female models—that was the crux of the predicament captured in the "orphanhood of lettered women." While young men could look to older, unrelated "Maestros de Juventud" as patrons and champions, young lettered women had only maternal models, such as their own mothers or matriarchal figures like Lastenia Larriva de Llona, who were deeply invested in defending gendered authority. At that time, there was no legible frame for a righteous sister among brothers, whose emotional force stemmed from personal conviction and political commitments. Existing frameworks more easily accommodated a woman's public vehemence as an expression of the sexual insatiability of la traidora (the traitor or adulterer) or of a woman driven by uncontrollable emotions like frustration, jealousy, and rage.

For more than twenty years, Portal's visibility as a poet and a partisan had made her a beacon for vicious sexist attacks. The situation of a public woman in Peru at that time, especially a woman who positioned herself against the Church and for revolution, was necessarily going to be a target, and Portal understood this distasteful truth. As a committed revolutionary, her partner Serafín was perhaps mentally equipped to deal with the ugly gendered attacks against Portal. But what about a young girl? Gloria was being romanced by an older man in the party, and while Portal knew how to see through and rebuff exploitative advances from men, Gloria's suicide suggested that her daughter was taken in and perhaps victimized. Portal's sister also reported that in the months before Gloria shot herself in the heart, a woman who detested Portal was sending Gloria very hurtful letters, writing terrible things to the young woman about her mother.[46] Who would do this? The vitriol and rage that would cause someone to send such terrible letters to the young daughter of a public figure could be dismissed as the acts of a vicious and deranged mind. But it is also the logical consequence of a public life that channels feelings and emotions about women in politics, women with power, professionally violent women, into these two fraught frames where conflict and emotion can only be understood as intimate family dramas. For Portal, the final dilemma was that as a committed revolutionary, she had to guard against seeming too vulnerable or excessively emotional for fear such displays would be read as weakness. Portal could not therefore publicly mourn her daughter without potentially undermining her authority.

Emotional humiliation was both a potent weapon against individual women like Portal and chillingly effective in disciplining women collectively. It helped ensure that women's public, and especially political, agendas were forever on the defensive. A generation later, women office holders in Peru in the early 1970s "expressed over and over" their "almost pathological fear of being laughed at by men," and their tentative organizing efforts were "ridiculed to death in the male-dominated press."[47] One of Portal's greatest sources of disillusionment was that her political comrades did not abandon their sexist assumptions in their broader dealings with women. Psychological research in "moral self-licensing" suggests this is not that surprising.[48] When people in power allow an exceptional individual into their club, we expect it would make it easier for others to follow; the door has been opened, the ceiling shattered. However, allowing in a "token" individual often lets people in power double down on previous social prejudice, since they have now proven to themselves and others that they do not discriminate. Any woman's sexual "honor" remained an effective target for such humiliating attacks by her own Aprista colleagues, especially on their enemies. "I found that distasteful and I would tell them, 'Why do we have to attack the honor of women?' Whether it's true or a lie, it is a very low category of propaganda. 'The public likes that, they like to hear those things, it is what captivates them the most,' they told me. That means that what they said against Aprista women also captivated them more, especially [what they said] of me."[49]

Portal claims that she "never gave the gossip and rumors any importance," because otherwise she "would have gone crazy," which would have "diminished her capacity to struggle." Yet her repeated claims that these hurtful slanders "meant nothing to her" are too forced in their carefully studied indifference. Her political work, the need to be an effective comrade, and the overriding goal of changing society had always been more important to her than her personal concerns as an individual. This allowed her, even forced her, to dismiss sexist attacks if they threatened to get in the way of her political mission. Her honor as a woman, like her poetry, was another "personal interest," another "sacrifice" she was prepared to make when she pledged herself to her revolution in Mexico in 1928. It was a relatively effective psychological strategy that allowed her to violate social conventions, face down the consequent shame, and survive the punishing social and personal consequences of her transgression, yet in the end, it was only a partial defense. She could bear the pain and forge ahead, but she would always feel the hurt, shame, and blame.

While she hated how her Aprista compañeros targeted women's sexual honor in political attacks, she was not above doing the same in her own internecine battles. In *La trampa*, when she assessed her voice, Portal contrasted it to APRA's most famous and important voice: Haya's. A key instrument of his charisma as an orator, his voice was "lightly high-pitched, with a slightly feminine variation," she suggested. "But that gives him a caressing tone when speaking publicly," although in private it could "break into falsetto." If Haya's private speaking voice suggested a dangerous, out-of-place femininity, his public speaking voice was effective because his "caressing tone" seduced the public. Her own masculine affect also made her irreplaceable to Haya, she suggested, since "the majority of the high-ranking [Aprista] women are too 'womanish.' And that bothers the 'Jefe.'"[50]

All these implicit asides about Haya's masculinity deepened into an explicit discussion of his sexuality. Haya "does not like women. They have a nefarious influence on men. . . . Like in the beautiful Greek times of Socrates and Plato, women need to be excluded from the meetings of men. . . . A world only of men! Only the problem of reproduction complicated everything." In her novel, she even imagined Haya at night, tossing and turning in bed, kept awake by his restless thoughts while mulling over the baths and massages he receives from Jorge, his valet.[51] In this time and place, this was a shocking homophobic sexual attack on Haya. *La trampa* was "the book for which [APRA] wanted to kill me," Portal confided at the end of life with no small measure of pride.[52]

Haya's homosexuality had to be a secret, because it was a shameful sin of the highest order in this patriarchal Catholic nation. One might imagine that just the rumor would have disqualified Haya as a viable political leader. It might even be thought to threaten his charismatic leadership and undermine his claims to be the ultimate patriarch of his party and the nation. Indeed, Communists had long derided him privately as a "faggot," but the issue was more complicated because Haya's sexuality was an open secret, both in Peru and abroad.[53] Books were written—and not just by enemies—trying to investigate the truth about his intimate life.[54] Indeed, his English-language biographer, Fredrick Pike, observed that "one of the most remarkable facets" of Haya's life was that he enjoyed such success in Peru's *machista* culture, "with its glorification of the male heterosexual erotic athlete," despite the fact that few doubted his homosexuality.[55] For instance, in 1969, the director of the Congress for Cultural Freedom in Peru, Jorge Luis Recavarren, told Robert Alexander that while he was "not one to get excited about homosexuality," he thought "that it has been nefarious in this case. Haya de la Torre is a 'prisoner' of a mulatto chauffeur and private secretary."[56]

From the very beginning, Haya also benefited from Portal's presence among the male leadership. Portal had already boldly transgressed on traditional gender expectations for women, which in some way made his own unorthodox sexuality less exceptional and allowed him to keep the focus on the "larger" political issues at hand. She was also important to him as an object of scandal that deflected, or absorbed, some of the prurient attention that might otherwise have settled on him and his personal life. Indeed, her compañeros were not above using Portal's hard-won visibility, even notoriety, as a lightning rod in the center of the APRA leadership. "Risk and danger always surrounded me, because the so-called leaders—or candidates to a higher political role—carefully guarded themselves from exhibition when it was not convenient," she wrote in her unpublished memoirs, "while my presence was like a sign that effectively attracted so much attention in a social environment like the Peruvian one, where only rarely had a woman taken on such a task."[57]

It may even be that the North Atlantic concept of "closet" fails to capture the nuances of Haya's "open secret." Roger Lancaster has argued that Latin America's regional public culture of sexuality was more akin to a "walk-in closet . . . a space big enough to hold you and your whole family."[58] Instead of a blanket prohibition against homosexuality, Latin American men before the Sexual Revolution lived in a landscape of spatially defined "tolerant intolerance" in which homosexual behaviors were tacitly accepted in some locales and situations while vocally and vehemently decried in other, more respectable "decent" spaces. The "open secret" was not about not knowing Haya's preference so much as it was about not saying out loud what everyone knew to be true.[59] In 2014, an old "Búfalo," a member of Haya's personal guard in the early 1960s, remembered how some taunted Haya by calling him "Lucy," a pseudonym from his youth, but he assured his interviewer that he and other guards would have eagerly jumped up to "break the face" of anyone they heard so openly insulting him.[60]

Haya's "open secret" was not entirely negative, however. Paradoxically, there were also reservoirs of political power in Haya's unorthodox sexuality. Pike even speculated that Haya's charisma benefited from trading "on the symbolism of the hermaphrodite, the being who had become whole and complete, and thereby charismatic or godlike."[61] It also reinforced a sense of community among Apristas, mapping the borders of those who "knew," and were thus implicitly tasked with protecting Haya, whose only "beard" was his party. Even the most token of marriages would have provided the necessary cover, but as Haya implausibly explained: he had no woman in his life because "an unfortunate love affair at eighteen . . . killed off his interest."[62] "Our Jefe Máximo is not a queer," an Aprista said in defending him in 1957: "He doesn't need a woman, because his woman is APRA, and to her he had dedicated everything."[63]

Haya was thus the man married to his party and his nation. In *La trampa*, Portal's alter ego had also tossed and turned night after night, tormented by thoughts of failures in love. "Yes, three sentimental failures. . . . And why does it matter? She is young, why should she feel that it's over? She will recuperate soon."[64] Portal had at least three great loves of her life, the Bolaños brothers and likely Esteban Pavletich, all in her twenties. After these "sentimental failures," men still pursued her, and she herself seemed to long for another connection. What kept her from pursuing

other loves? Perhaps if Haya was married to the nation, Portal was as devoted to the dream of revolution.

One might hypothesize that Haya and Portal, standing at the summit
of their party's leadership, were compañeros in a type of Aprista marriage,
with each trying to leverage what they could from the space that the
other's gender deviance created. Each was charismatic and able to coalesce
people around them and persuade them of their visions, if to varying
degrees. Both had what others considered "extreme personalities," although
Haya was able to use a richer spectrum of emotions, including an affec-
tionate, beseeching, even tender and loving register that strengthened the
revolutionary fraternity he led. And when the marriage fell apart, her attack on Haya's sexuality was an attempt to hurt him as effectively as other
male leaders had betrayed her. When she published *¿Quiénes traicionaron
al pueblo?* in 1950, she claimed that "they say Haya cried, that my position
wounded him deeply. Truth or lie, I don't know, but it must have hurt him
because I had been there from Apra's first moments."[65] In her recollections,
Portal wants to establish her importance to her listeners and to herself. She
was an intimate of Haya who was powerful and close enough to bring
APRA's patriarch to tears.

A Feminist Politics of Personality

After breaking with APRA and losing her drafts on her ill-fated flight to
Buenos Aires in mid-1951, Portal returned to Lima a few months later to
take care of her ailing mother, her younger sister, and her niece. Her public
profile, however, had evaporated "in the drizzle of oblivion."[66] In 1965, she
published a poetic anthology, *Constancia del ser* (Constancy of being),
which introduced her work to a new generation. Looking back on her
sixty-five years of life, during which her political fortunes waxed and
waned, many elements of her being had, in fact, remained constant. Her
first reviewer had predicted in 1923 that the painful, sorrowful "future that
Magda Portal glimpses is not happy" and made her "uneasy."[67] Life had
proven him right. But Portal also remained constant in her unflinching,
radical honesty and in the masculinist orientation with which she approached the world.

She became the Peruvian representative of the prestigious Mexican pub-
lisher Fondo de Cultura Económica, but when the Peruvian currency lost

nearly half its value in 1967, the Mexican home office, trying to recoup their losses, took Portal to court. She left the post in July 1970. Portal's reemergence on new terms was really catalyzed, however, by her work with the 1970s feminist generation who came to see her as an important foremother. In 1979, two young founders of Action for the Liberation of Peruvian Women published the book *Ser mujer en el Perú* (Being a woman in Peru), which prominently featured an interview, "I am Magda Portal," that cemented Portal's canonical position among Peruvian feminists.

This feminist second life, however, could also be a difficult fit, since Portal had long politically defined herself in opposition to feminism, which she viewed as separatist and overly focused on women's biological difference.[68] As early as 1931, her short list of Peru's most pressing problems included economics and education but not women's issues.[69] Fifteen years later, at the height of her power in the party in 1946, she reminded the National Convention of Aprista Women that she had not begun her "social and political action as a follower of the flag of the feminist cause." She had "always believed that the two sexes should in no way be separated or differentiated, creating distances that would forcibly drive us to acknowledge women as another social group," constituting "another problem."[70] She continued to deflect a feminist label until the very end of her life. Praised for being "without a doubt the true initiator of militant feminism" in Peru, Portal countered: "In reality, at the beginning, I was not a feminist but instead a fighter for social justice."[71]

Evading a label was one thing, but second-wave feminists found her history on the litmus-test issue of women's suffrage more troubling. In the early 1930s, Apristas had argued for a limited female vote as a tactical political position, not a first principle. Luis Alberto Sánchez explained that Apristas abandoned their demands for universal women's suffrage because "fanatical ultraconservatism tried to use it to its benefit"; the party downgraded their demands to a limited suffrage for only "married women, mothers of families, and working women."[72] Nothing came of these debates, however, and it would fall to the despised Odría government to usher in female suffrage in 1955.

In 1979, Portal distanced herself from this earlier Aprista position regarding a qualified female vote and retrospectively separated herself from other male leaders who "considered that it was 'premature'" and who "said women were not 'prepared'" and that they needed to be educated first.[73]

Portal, however, had in fact embraced her party's position on suffrage in the 1930s. In 1933, she insisted only women who worked or studied should wield the "weapon that is the vote"; Apristas believed that women in the "productive" classes would support them against the country's "parasitic classes."[74] Like her Aprista brethren, Portal considered as class enemies these aristocratic women who constituted "the little group of Peruvian Feminism," women willing to court any regime in power to claim political favors for themselves or for the men to whom they were attached. Their bourgeois feminist interests, including women's suffrage, were said to be directly opposed to those of working and middle-sector Aprista women.[75] APRA's Manichaean logic cast "feminism" on the side of the old generation, their political opponents, and the Catholic Church, all firm proponents of patriarchal privilege. Reflexively, APRA saw these three as of a piece and inherently, irrevocably opposed to their secular and rational party.

Everyone on the political spectrum assumed women were a conservative electoral force because they all believed the Catholic Church was the principal influence in women's lives. After the ill-fated Trujillo Revolution of 1932, Apristas rumored darkly that priests targeted "naïve devoted women" in the confessional's solitude to extract information about their party.[76] In contrast to the actions of such Catholic women, Aprista propaganda glorified the young female snipers carrying arms for their cause or the aristocratic Aprista sympathizers who, trading on stereotypes of demure women, were able to provide succor to prisoners or serve as messengers for the cause.

But it was difficult to parse whether Apristas distrusted women because they were Catholic, or distrusted the community of Catholic believers because its women wielded an uncontrollable influence over men, a form of Catholic power. One might recall how furiously Haya accused Luis Alberto Sánchez's "Señora wife" of waging a campaign for years to separate Sánchez from the party. Similarly, a few years later in 1948, Haya spoke with U.S. embassy analysts as his party's political situation spiraled from dire to disastrous; he described President Bustamante as "weak, indecisive, retiring, and easily swayed, especially by his wife, whose social climbing and ultraconservative Catholicism are 'bad influences.'"[77]

In spite of Portal's history on women's suffrage, her young feminist interlocutors in the 1970s recognized that in the 1930s Portal had in fact developed a feminist orientation. In its demand for the equal participation of women in public life, her worldview and the Aprista conception of women's rights she formulated were far broader than those she dismissed as "the feminism in fashion."[78] Portal's feminist orientation rejected any trace of separatism and assumed a compañerismo ideal, even as she recognized the complicity of male compañeros in perpetuating women's subjugation.

Portal did, however, modify her position on women's suffrage and supported it in a 1941 essay, at least for Chile. But she did not demand universal female suffrage in principle, arguing instead that Chilean women deserved the vote because they had fully developed their characters through their economic struggles and now possessed "that certainty and dominion over [themselves] that is the best symptom of personality."[79] And, in fact, the concept of personality and women's complicity in their own subjugation was a lifelong focus for Portal.[80] Portal believed that a woman, sharing men's depreciative view of herself, thus "lives her inferiority complex. She *believes* herself inferior to her male compañero. Her brain is atrophied by the lack of exercise, her will annulled by the eternal dependency, without consciousness of responsibility, everything in her begins, it is in potency. She is like a child who only recently perceives life and is preparing to understand it, to explain it, to conquer it."[81]

What did Portal mean by "personality"? Personality was self-certainty, self-dependence, and dominion over oneself, both self-control and self-sovereignty. In a letter she wrote from prison in 1935, she sketched out her position after an obligatory warning that "this is not feminism. The woman continues being an appendix of the man, the classic Biblical rib, without personality," she wrote, because "women lack faith in themselves and the courage to face the responsibility of being themselves."[82]

In her 1933 *Hacia la mujer nueva*, Portal had outlined the psychological nature of this "deeper and more total" struggle. While both men and women strove for social justice, women's ultimate goal was "the conquest of the right to reveal her own personality, marginalized by prejudice and by incomprehension, and to beat back the dependence and timidity that the patriarchal foundations of the Spanish colonial system had inculcated in women for nearly four hundred years."[83] The logical consequence of personality, this form of self-dominion was a will to action that would propel women from domestic cloister into public life. Courage comes up again and again; the courage women would need to be themselves, not demure or self-abnegating, and the need to face the inevitable responsibility for their actions. Portal's radical honesty also acknowledged that an unavoidable price had to be paid for this courage, anticipating existentialism avant la lettre. Women, she observed, would continue struggling with ambivalent emotions about the actions that even their fully formed personalities would take.

Above all else, Portal stressed that "women needed to matter in a manner other than in the home. But women had little to give because they were simply not allowed [to contribute]. In contrast, I came in through the front [*entré de frente*], and they had to accept me anyway; it was not that I asked for it but that I compelled it to happen . . . because I entered and was the first woman who was in a party that was very important."[84] This unapologetic will to action reflected a fully developed female personality. Portal used her stubborn will, understood as masculine, to barrel through life's challenges—political, artistic, and affective. Throughout her life, Portal critically appraised the bohemian poetry salon, the underground political cell, and the emotional landscape of intimate affective relationships in a society that taught a woman to submit her desires to the men around her. In all of these, Portal's will to action allowed her to reject a society that expected her to be demure, like a decent woman. Instead, Portal forced doors open and barged in, *entrando de frente*. Her actions and choices were aggressive psychological acts projecting her self against society's hegemonic discourses. It offered proof of her self-actualizing feminist personality and showed that the Aprista New Woman was possible. Women could break out of the jail built and guarded by a patriarchy that was part and parcel of Spanish colonialism. The Aprista New Woman was thus critical to Peru's decolonization. This was what she meant by "personality."

How and why did Portal develop such a will to action? How did it become the central, foundational feature of what she considered her "personality"? Even as a young girl, Portal's greatest wish was to "learn everything," to become self-sufficient and self-worthy (*valerme por mí misma*). In early-twentieth-century Latin America, female ambition to *valerse por sí misma* encompassed more than ambitions for paid employment and economic independence; for traditionalists, "it was not work but self-sufficiency" that competed with the ideal of women as the force holding together both families and the nation.[85] If women were not dependent, if they could fend for themselves, economically, socially, and psychologically, what would keep them home, taking care of others? "In truth, women, half plus one of humanity, have not had much significance in the great human drama," Portal wrote in a 1935 letter. "Their role has been not just subaltern, but dependent."[86]

Female self-sufficiency carried powerful psychological connotations because it assumed the creation of an active and autonomous female individual and agency. Scholars have shown how a robust sense of self was inculcated in bourgeois men, teaching them that "only certain people had the intellectual gifts necessary to actualize" the self that "everyone possessed potentially." The consequent hierarchy, explicitly built on class and gender with bourgeois men on top, was then institutionally replicated and reinforced, psychologically justifying their superiority.[87] Portal, in contrast, did not enjoy an educational system designed to encourage her to cultivate a self-actualizing personality. On the contrary, women in Peru at the start of the twentieth century were ruthlessly socialized to inculcate a surveyed self, a self constantly being judged and on guard to ensure it did not trespass the presumptive norms of behavior for decent women. Traditional Lima's female *I*, their internal judge, served the inverse purpose of the robust male bourgeois self, because it strove to ensure that women policed themselves and provided an incessant, internal justification for their social subordination.

The positive attributes of the autonomous individual in elite males were therefore negative attributes in women. Women who rejected society's script had to reject society's image of them. For Portal, exercising her personality, asserting her *I*, meant rejecting Lima's poetry of the home, which still held the allegiance of feminists of her time and place. They warned against women who wanted nothing to do with child-rearing or taking care of the home, much less those who terrorized their defeated lovers with a "despotic will." In such a world turned upside down, male weakness turned men into "servile vassals" and women into tyrants: a "frightful chaos."[88] A robust female sense of self and agency, a woman's "despotic will," placed her needs above others and refused to negate her self as dictated by the archetype of female self-abnegation.

Many saw Portal's transgressions as selfish, despotic, and frightfully chaotic, but she saw them as the difficult choices that allowed the full development of her personality, which was, she insisted, something very different from the willful pursuit of pleasure. "Liberty is the fundamental climate for the development of personality," she wrote in 1936. "And note

I did not say libertinage or individualism."[89] More than forty years later, while attending an international literary conference, Portal and her biographer Daniel Reedy heard the Nicaraguan poet Daisy Zamora read poems explicitly detailing oral sex in the Sandinista trenches. Portal whispered to Reedy: "If another one of these women stands [up] to talk to me about her vagina, I'm marching out. I also had an intimate life, but I don't understand why these women have to describe theirs in such detail."[90] Reedy considered her reaction against open mention of sexual intimacies a fault line between early and second-wave feminists. But this was not a reactionary modesty developed in old age. Portal was not against young women's open sexuality as much as she was against celebrating it as an ultimate good in itself; in her thinking, such an open sexual sensibility was a consequence of the full development of female personalities, but not its goal. When a young second-wave feminist historian asked her to discuss her erotic experiences, she laughed.[91]

Portal's robust sense of self and agency was for her a necessary tool for her revolutionary commitment. At first, she needed a mission for a greater good to justify breaking with such entrenched social norms. The revolution incarnated in APRA became the "great and noble cause" that allowed her to realize the full strength of her "never understood human personality." But she also accepted responsibility for the "frightful chaos" her political activity caused, disrupting the normative middle-class home, as another necessary sacrifice. "Like they say colloquially, I tore myself apart [*me rompí*]; I dedicated myself entirely to the struggle and I went through some very difficult situations. The struggle of my time in the Aprista Party was a struggle from head to toes."[92]

Portal's experience in her twenty years of Aprista militancy was profoundly marked by patriarchal assumptions and gender discrimination. However, at the time and as a matter of principle, Portal repeatedly and vehemently denied a focus on gender as the primary lens for understanding her experience. As Portal aged, however, the scholars and activists who rescued her as a pivotal Peruvian figure in politics and letters were all, to some degree, feminists. The feminist context for her reemergence into prominence shaped her later life narratives, where gender discrimination became even more central than it had been in *La trampa*. What she might have explained before as a function of economic, social, or political disadvantage she now clearly labeled as sexual discrimination, no matter how important or petty the issue might at first appear: "In Peru," she complained, "there was never money for me to travel," the first of many discriminations because "there was always money" for male leaders.[93] Yet this framework had been present even in 1950, as she broke publicly with APRA, her "great and noble cause." At her court-martial, she explained that her alienation from the party occurred in part because her status in APRA was that of a "simple sympathizer," the status accorded to all women by their party statutes.[94] Nonetheless, after her release, her writings for the 1950 Revisionist Congress focused not on women but instead on youth and labor complaints.[95]

This shift is reflected in Portal's description of her disaffection at the 1948 congress, where she struck a blow on behalf of the goal of female participation and citizenship in APRA. Thirty years after the events, the party's changes in economic ideology dropped away from the story she told, as she focused on the changes in APRA's philosophy concerning women's political rights in the party. At the closing plenary meeting, Portal recalled, she was incensed when a motion was put forward declaring, she paraphrased, that "women are not active members of the party, they are only compañeras, because they do not have the quality of citizenship." When she challenged the motion, she was told it was a declaration not open to discussion. Furious, she dramatically left the plenary session in protest. "I said, 'Ah, this I don't accept. This is Fascism.'"[96] In another interview a few months later, a few details had changed. Portal was seated in the first row of the audience. Haya, in the concluding remarks, said, "'We have considered that the women of the party, as they do not yet have the vote, cannot be considered authentic members of the party. They cannot be anything but sympathizers.' I stood up and said, 'I demand the floor.' Haya said, 'There is nothing under discussion.' I insisted, 'I demand the floor!' 'There is nothing under discussion!' And he violently shut the minute book. He looked every bit a dictator."[97]

The 1931 First National Party Congress, she explained, had established that its female militants were eligible to become official party members and called for women's suffrage. Now, Portal fumed, one of the "many doctrinal aberrations" in the new Aprista statutes denied a woman the right to be an official party member "while she did not have political rights." Further, when women were granted suffrage in the future, the new APRA position was to make women eligible to vote when they turned twenty-five, while men would be eligible when they turned eighteen.[98] After twenty years of revolutionary militancy and untold energy spent recruiting and organizing women, the elderly Portal described this as not just a political but a personal betrayal, "the greatest disloyalty with the Aprista woman," and it became a pivot in Portal's later life narrative explaining her break with APRA focusing the injury on gender.

Yet the putatively retrograde gender politics of the Second National Congress cannot fully explain Portal's reactions. The party's position on making unmarried women eligible for citizenship at twenty-five while men were eligible for citizenship at eighteen had actually been official Aprista doctrine for four years. The APRA Ideology, Program, and Statutes approved unanimously by plenary session in 1948 had already been approved four years earlier in a clandestine 1944 party meeting and made official in 1945 when the party was registered as the Partido del Pueblo. This was therefore not an "aberration" but a settled question, although the party statutes did assert the "constitutionality of the political rights of women and of their legal capacity to execute any political, municipal, or judicial office."[99] A previous plenary session in that same 1948 congress had just approved a motion proposing a constitutional reform that recognized a woman's right to citizenship when she turned eighteen, to "satisfy the longing of the feminine element and of the masculine element who supports her."[100]

The official published minutes are thus at odds with Portal's retrospective accounts. It is certainly possible that heated words thrown during discussion reflected the general tenor of the massive plenary meeting that Portal believed signaled a conservative turn on women's participation; we don't have a full transcript. Yet there is reason to doubt such a retreat on principle, given a regional political context where their reformist counterpart parties were supporting women's right to vote: Guatemala in 1944, Venezuela in 1945, Argentina in 1947, and Chile in 1949. Rejecting female membership would also have been at odds with the party's formal institutional architecture, which included an entire secretary-level office, the Woman's Unit (Comando Femenino), solely dedicated to bringing women into Aprista politics.[101] Ultimately, APRA's 1948 position on women's rights is best understood as oscillating between Portal's categorical extreme (women should have identical political rights and not be treated in any way differently from men) and a more measured accommodation, though still radical for Peru's conservative political culture. This had been true since the First National Party Congress walked back the most radical demands of the Lima Department Congress in 1931. The clash in 1948 most likely reflected Portal's intraparty scuffles after she was awarded only an honorific subsecretary general position, which she considered weaker than leading the Women's Unit that they "took" from her, a position she had built into "a force to be reckoned with."[102]

A Force, and a Woman, to be Reckoned With

Being a force to be reckoned with was critical to Portal's feminist politics of personality. Another "curious" story Portal told about herself made this clear or, perhaps more precisely, made clear how vital it was for her to be recognized as a force to be reckoned with. Arrested in Chile, she found herself on a ship, being transferred to face prison in Peru. "When they changed the guard, I was carrying a small suitcase, waiting to disembark, . . . when an *oficialito* came up to me and asked me: 'What do you [*Ud.*] need, señorita? Has someone attended to you?' I was looking at him, [and] it seemed that he was making fun of me. I committed an error there, maybe because I was tired, because I answered him immediately: 'You don't know who I am?' 'No,' he told me. 'I am Magda Portal.' 'Ay . . .' and he took me by the arm . . . locking me in a room. . . . He thought I was one of the many [women] who had gone to see a prisoner." Elsewhere, she expanded on his "very flustered" reply. "'You, you are Magda Portal?' 'Yes, I am, who did you think I was?' And once again, the absurd supposition that I did not appear to be a revolutionary, appearing to be instead a young woman without any other complications. Yes, I replied to him, you thought I should be a manly woman, [*mujerona*] with a revolver in my pocket . . . and you found instead something completely different: and we laughed as if we were friends."[103]

When approached with the courtesy offered women of her presumed class, Portal feels humiliated because the "oficialito" has failed to recognize her. Portal's dress and physical appearance meant she was not immediately legible as a revolutionary agent; this should have been a tactical advantage, as it was for the young elite women in Trujillo who no one suspected as Aprista insurgents. Yet, in Chile, Portal chose instead to immediately reveal her political and revolutionary identity. Asserting her self is a psychological necessity for her, but it is also a personal emotional response that costs her the chance to escape; in other words, revealing her identity is a sudden loss of revolutionary discipline she can only explain later as "the error she committed" because of understandable physical limitations, "maybe she was tired." It occurred in a split second. When she had to make an immediate decision, instead of seizing an opportunity to escape, she chose to prove she was much more than just a "señorita": she was Magda Portal, a woman her captor knew was a force to be reckoned with.

Portal diffused the emotional pain of this systemic misreading of her appearance, this "absurd supposition," with a shared laugh, "as if we were friends," which momentarily bridged the political divide ripping Peru apart. But this was no laughing matter to Portal, as attested by the fact that this interaction—being mistaken by others as not revolutionary because she was a beautiful woman, only to be corrected by Portal, who then also diffuses the uncomfortable confusion with humor—appears again and again in her memoirs. Touring the Caribbean in 1929, she recalled "I was thin then, I wore vaporous suits. In Santo Domingo, leaving the ship they confused me with one of the dancers who were coming to perform there. The journalists came up to me. Then, I told them I was Magda Portal. 'Ah . . . Magda Portal . . .' They thought I was coming with two bombs in hand. They could not imagine that I could be like any normal girl."[104]

Portal needed to be seen as both a political agent but also as a normative woman: two of her central personas that her time and place assumed were incompatible. Portal could revel in the masculine ways other political players read her public life, which proved other players in the game considered her a worthy, even dangerous adversary. "Of course machismo is a fact. This is a machista country. But they are machistas without pants." A high military officer and Aprista sympathizer, she remembered, "always told me: 'You are more [of a] man than all those in the party,' and yet he added: 'But you are one hundred percent woman.'"[105] His final flirtatious remark is the anecdote's real punch and signals that he admired her not just for her masculine politics, her effectiveness, but also as a feminine, sexually attractive woman.

That Portal chose to repeat his compliment reveals her need to highlight that *she* still considered herself a normative woman. But by introducing the compliment with "and yet," she suggests that her femininity, inherent in being "one hundred percent woman," was a surprise; Portal remained deeply ambivalent about her feminine-masculine persona. To be a successful political figure, Portal needed to adopt a militant masculine approach that transformed her in the eyes of others, and perhaps her own, into something other than a normal girl. Portal's precarious balancing act involved seeing herself simultaneously as an active masculine agent able to fight for the causes she held dear and to handle her personal affairs as she saw fit, while remaining feminine enough to be socially normative. Others would look at Portal and resolve the ambiguities into one camp or another, either overly masculine or too feminine; this was the unforgiving logic of a politics of respectability. In some of these anecdotes, the most jarring detail clashing with the presumed identity of normative womanhood was that she was symbolically armed—either carrying bombs or a revolver—as symbols of her political commitment and her identity as professionally violent.

This was the enduring tension confronting Latin American women with aspirations to public—and especially political—life. Latin Americans generally regarded feminism "as divesting" women of feminine qualities; it masculinized them by stripping meanings away instead of adding or layering additional meanings onto femininity. The tension between struggling for rights while preserving femininity and respectability was a "constant" issue for lettered men and women, both feminists and antifeminists.[106] Reconstructing Portal's historical context and her actions lets us map the distance between society's understanding of an "acceptable" or an "excessive" female agency and Portal's own political, creative, and personal behavior. But she herself remained deeply ambivalent about this painful distance; she struggled throughout her life with defining and patrolling this limit, simultaneously claiming an aggressive masculine privilege while staunchly defending not a feminine decency, which she rejected as sterile and bourgeois, but a feminine persona rooted in her sense of herself as sexually attractive to men. Portal painfully negotiated among qualities her time and place considered mutually exclusive: political efficacy, poetic relevance, self-defense against physical and emotional male exploitation, and her own desire to be an attractive woman.

If she could not escape the emotional price of being a gender rebel, neither could she revel in her accomplishments as a gender pioneer. The tightrope Portal walked lay in recognizing men's refusal to surrender patriarchal privilege while not discounting her own achievements by viewing them as a "gift" granted to her for being a token woman. "Men, in

general, do not like to feel equal to women. But neither is it about searching for or asking for privileges," she explained. "Because when they give
us privileges, they are belittling us. That was precisely what I did not want,
that they considered me weak, a poor little thing, conceited, no, not that."[107]
But to assert the importance of what she had achieved, and to avoid feeling humiliated for being considered "weak, a poor little thing, conceited,"
by those who looked at her and saw "just" a woman, she could not define
her own importance and her achievements based on her gender.

This deep ambivalence about her gendered persona also characterized
her personal life. "Somebody told me once," she confessed, "that I had not
been born to be married, being very feminine. And that is the truth. I can
bear neither the *tutoría* [tutelage, guidance, or guardianship] of a man, nor
the tutoría of a home."[108] Portal articulated femininity with matrimony. Is
this meant to convince us that she could have easily married because others
considered her feminine and attractive, but that something else, some inner
destiny, prevented her? Being married inevitably meant being subjected
to the will of another—her husband—and perhaps more dangerously,
subjected to the will of a strict domestic ideology, Lima's poetry of the
home. As a young woman, Portal had tried to create a different kind of
marriage, one defined as a voluntary affective union between two companions, who joined to create a home and a life project dedicated to art and
political militancy. The failure of that project, however, confirmed what the
elderly Portal now asserted as fact: in a world where the institution of marriage refused to evolve, she was unsuited for marriage, and perhaps, she at
times suspected, not fully a woman.

Portal was not alone in confronting this tension, but she was exceptional
because, unable to mold matrimony into what she needed, she discarded
marriage and the social privileges it conferred. "Even though I have sometimes felt the need for protection, I never felt myself less for not having a
man. And in general, I did not miss the protection of a man. I lived for
years and years without feeling that presence."[109] In stark contrast to her
earliest romantic illusions about marriage as a partnership with emotional
rewards of love and intimacy, these end-of-life reflections reduce the benefits of marriage to masculine protection. But the key is her aside, "I never
felt myself less for not having a man." The traditional mentality Portal
spent a lifetime fighting valued women only in relation to the men who
called them theirs—first fathers, then husbands, finally sons. Portal

claimed worth for her independent self and its actions in the world and did not assume it her failure that she could not "keep" a husband. But the fact that she raises the issue underlines her continued ambivalence and struggle with the emotional weight of these inescapable social expectations. This was the ultimate reality at the heart of Portal's feminist politics of personality: the New Woman, even the self-actualizing, self-sufficient, self-dependent woman sovereign over herself and her life, was never truly free from the emotional hold of these deeply entrenched patriarchal understandings.

With her expanded public profile in the early eighties, Portal reissued a slightly revised version of *La trampa* in 1982, and with the support of six other feminist intellectuals, in 1983 rewrote an earlier essay into a small book on the famed French-Peruvian nineteenth-century Socialist Flora Tristán.[110] The book looked to the latest generation of Peruvian feminists to address the list of concerns she had presented to their mothers and grandmothers, eliminating "the old scheme of the woman as domestic" and carving out a space for women in public life. There were other continuities. Fifty years after writing *Hacia la mujer nueva*, Portal still emphasized collaborating with men. Tristán, she wrote, was "a true torch" illuminating the consciousness of those around her, "without antimasculine confrontations" or "hating men, never ceasing to be an authentic woman." Portal's heteronormative orientation remained as she continued to define her ultimate goal, even after all these years, as the struggle for "the most complete equilibrium of the human couple." The main change in her thinking was her new sympathy for the early-twentieth-century suffragists she had once attacked as class enemies who, she now argued, had "waged real battles to gain the vote, a necessary step, according to them, to reach equality with men, [and who] were taunted, humiliated, their claims derided," who she now raised as "exalting examples of women's character."[111]

Portal's biography strikingly echoed Tristán's a hundred years later. Tristán (1803–1844) was the daughter of a wealthy Peruvian living in France and a European mother. When her father died when Flora was five years old, it cast the young family from the comfortable lap of wealth to a miserable penury. Her mother pressured a seventeen-year-old Flora to marry her older and established employer.[112] Tristán bore him two children, but she was increasingly estranged from an unhappy and abusive relationship that was further stressed by the family's deteriorating economic situation. Expecting their third child, Tristán fled from her husband, and spent years battling his legal claims over her and their children in court. After being forced to relinquish her son to her hated husband, Tristán left her daughter in the care of an acquaintance and boarded a ship to the end of the world—she sailed to Peru to plead with her paternal uncle for a part of her father's inheritance. But this "adventure of her life" ended unhappily when her father's family refused her everything but a ticket home and a small pension because her parents' marriage was illegitimate. When she returned to France, her enraged husband attacked and shot her.

Free at last from her despised, and now imprisoned, husband, Tristán devoted herself to organizing the Socialist Workers Union, embarking on a series of exhausting tours throughout France that Portal called "proselytizing tours," the same name she gave her own travels to build APRA throughout Peru a century later.[113] Tristán unflinchingly documented the unhappiness and violence that characterized most proletarian homes and argued that the key to ending ignorance and misery was the education of women. The Workers Union demanded equality in education, professional training, and wages so women could gain economic independence from men; the right to freely elect their husbands; the right to divorce; the rights of single mothers before the law; and the right of illegitimate children to their paternal inheritance.

Both women, a century apart, were attacked for personalities that were too extreme and unbending; Tristán was "dogmatic, a woman's principal defect." And both women had to resolve a devastating crisis of faith. Tristán's journey to Peru had by all rights ended in failure: she was rejected by her father's family and refused any part of the inheritance that she so desperately needed in her long-shot legal battle to divorce her hated husband. Portal tells us Tristán fell into "a tremendous depression" and bordered on suicide. "But she repents and thinks about how she is still young and has to defeat her sufferings and return to the struggle." Tristán resolved to reorient her struggle to fight for all the disenfranchised. "From now on, all Humanity is my fatherland! The Woman Messiah (Mujer Mesías) has been born."[114]

Portal used this phrase, "Mujer Mesías," with its many rich, inescapable connotations, to describe the last phase of Tristán's life, when she threw herself completely into building the Workers Union. Of course, this evocative phrase just as neatly captures what Portal may have thought of her own efforts a hundred years later. A messiah is first a leader: in this case, a leader of women who, once gone, was never really replaced in Peru's public life. At the end of her life, Portal was asked what role she had played in the women's liberation movements. "Before women had not been promoted, and I had to come for that to happen; to give women importance, work with them, so that they would not be pushed into oblivion. . . . Once I left politics," she continued, women have been neglected. "They have always been left behind." Women came to APRA "because I was there," she explained. "If I had not been there, they would not have come. That's how the party became filled with women."[115]

Yet a messiah is also a deliverer, a redeemer like Tristán, whose outsized personality compensates for other women's weakness and aims to create a political community where they can be educated about their interests and fully develop their personalities. "In a country like ours, a little behind, it was difficult for women to have public activities, and my proselytizing action was directed at letting them have it," Portal explained. "I remember well that one time we were in a little village and a *negrita* came up to me and nobody believed that the negrita would be able to say something, and she told me: 'I want to speak, compañera.' 'Go, *hijita*, go ahead and speak!' And she began to speak about her conditions of poverty, and it happened that she knew as much as I did. I was left amazed to see that a woman of her very popular class could express herself as well as I could."[116]

In a country as Catholic as Peru, of course, a messiah was always finally a savior. As the female Aprista torchbearer, Portal was a savior whose instrument of salvation was her irrepressible will to action. At times, Portal's high opinion of herself seems megalomaniacal. "Now," she explains, "women have in a certain form unlinked themselves from me, and I consider it magnificent. . . . Sometimes young people have asked me: 'Why is it that before you were [active in politics] women did not exist?' And I have always answered: they did not exist . . . because they did not have the action [*la acción*]."[117]

Conclusion

> Wide smiles illuminate the weathered, miserable faces. Breasts expand in a relieved breath. Now we really are on top of an erupting volcano. Soon we will be the masters of Peru. . . . And the reactionaries, the old exploiting caste, the great landowners and bankers, will feed on dust. There will be well-paid work, there will be free schools, there will be cheap homes. . . . The earth will belong to the campesinos who labor on it. . . . No more hunger, no more persecution, no more misery. Ah, how beautiful it is to fight for all of this! What does that which has been suffered matter? . . . Finally, we have arrived and the long years of suffering were well worth it!
>
> Portal, *La trampa*, 107

THIS WAS HOW MAGDA PORTAL depicted the emotional impact of a massive APRA rally in her novelistic memoir *La trampa*. This communal euphoria was shaped by the revolutionary dream of a Peru freed from the structures of exploitation and inequality rooted in hundreds of years of colonial and neocolonial rule. Apristas were possessed by a sense of heroic agency that flooded over them, certain they were called forth to make this dream a political reality. The leaders on stage faced the challenge of harnessing an erupting volcano. How must they have felt as they conducted this performance of APRA's "collective madness"?

After her 1950 break with APRA, Portal rejected the party to the very end of her life. When APRA finally reached the presidency in 1985, Portal flatly refused even a symbolic rapprochement when the wives of APRA leaders, a new generation of damas Apristas, approached her about reaffiliating with the party at its moment of triumph. "I advance and advance; I don't retreat."[1] APRA was no longer a dream that had been worth all her suffering; instead, it was a bitter reminder of aborted potential.

Yet when interviewed in 1978 she answered a whimsical question with conviction. "If reincarnation existed? I would have liked to have been reborn as a revolutionary leader. It can be a woman, too, to not speak only of a masculine model. As for me, in this regard, I have failed by being a woman; if I had been a man, I would have triumphed. They never gave me the opportunity to go beyond what I was in the party." "And you know," she mused, "maybe I would have liked to have been born a man. I see how men can go from this to that place, free, without censures, and can go out at night without problems. In contrast, they regulate us. Because of that I would have liked to have been a man."[2]

This was about much more than politics; Portal dreamed of a more complete escape as she imagined that, as a man, she would have been freed from the condemnation society heaped on her for her unregulated personal as well as public life. This book has teased out the many layers of meaning in Portal's fantasies of self and revolution. To her last day, she was proud of her political achievements and of a lifelong ideological fidelity that she contrasted with those of her former political comrades like Haya who had strayed from the ideals of social revolution they had shared in their twenties. Back then, she had found transcendence in affiliating with a group of young bohemians who would as mature men attack her for her ferocious political commitment, her "outsized" sense of agency, and the strength of her stubborn will. They now condemned her as an "extremist" personality oriented, they claimed, toward her own selfish and personalist ends. In her old age, Portal still raged at a society that frustrated her interventions in public life, whether in politics or art; a society set on trampling her independence and challenging her right to make her own choices in politics, love, and life.

In another end-of-life reflection, however, Portal was equally emphatic that she and APRA's leaders had been "compañeros, absolutely." Her peers treated her equally, she insisted. "No one discriminated against me."[3] Back in 1935, writing privately to Anna Melissa Graves, she was more forthright. "We women who struggle have a double enemy: against the common enemy, social injustice, and against the prejudices of our environment, whose seeds are found even in our own compañeros!"[4] Would women gain rights and reach equality because of their exemplary actions, or did equality necessarily mean men had to surrender patriarchal privileges? Portal's writings suggested the first, implying women could gain equality without men necessarily losing status and privilege. Her lived experience, however, taught her the second; equality and justice for women would require both. In some ways, it was analogous, but in reverse, to APRA's shifting position on economic justice, from arguing in the late twenties for taking and redistributing the wealth of the ruling class to a position, twenty years later in 1945, that promised to create more wealth to distribute to all without demanding that the rich give up theirs.

After World War I and the Russian Revolution, this generation's American hour began as a moment of incandescent possibility full of potential for radical change, which formed their personalities and channeled the will to power of the young like Haya, Mariátegui, and Portal. But as that historical window closed, a more limited pragmatism necessarily emerged during the Popular Front, with its existential global fight against Fascism, followed by the Cold War chess game. Under these shifting conditions, Portal could not revise, much less shed, her maximalist political imagination. The heroic agency underlying her revolutionary romanticism remained at the core of her political thinking and her creative relevance as a poet, as well as being the foundation of her own feminist personality. Her transformative dreams had emerged simultaneously, interwoven from the first, beginning with her Promethean effort to become a poet, a revolutionary, and, above all, a free woman.

When the political and historical circumstances changed and new opportunities for power arose, many of her male peers were able to change with them. They could catch and soar on new political winds, "regaining their reason," as Portal wryly noted when recalling her first defeat in the party in 1931 when Haya vetoed their Minimum Program as too radical. For her to do so would mean shedding the heroic self she had constructed as Portal the poet, Portal the activist, and Portal the authentic and fully realized human woman. Portal's version of a shared revolutionary self-delusion, the "collective madness" tying them together, was more inflexible and thus more brittle because it was tightly woven with her gendered identity as a free woman. It limited how accurately she could see, assess, and react to people and situations as they evolved.

Looking back over her life in her later years, Portal may have wondered whether her two dreams—a commitment to revolution and to an uncompromising will to action as a free woman—had not been, somehow, enough. Even after her public break with APRA, friends and allies like Rómulo Betancourt continued to court her, convinced that her revolutionary mission remained morally imperative. In 1950, he had written Portal a letter in which he had questioned her public renunciation of APRA. Two years later, in 1952, Betancourt and his Acción Democrática Party were still living under a dictatorship that in Venezuela in 1948, as in Peru, had brought down a progressive reformist postwar government. He wrote Portal a letter addressing her as "My dear Magdita" and acknowledged his error in having sent her that earlier rushed letter, when he could not "see her clearly." But I have never doubted "your honesty as a fighter," he insisted, and continue to "trust you, born of a fraternal friendship that is about to celebrate its silver anniversary."[5]

Yet Betancourt, as unquestioned a leader of AD as Haya was of APRA, did not shy away from their political differences. Her "attitude of public belligerence" toward APRA, he insisted, was illogical even if she "had already reached that intimate state of feeling 'disgust' for politics." Appealing to her as a politician, he suggested that if she was "already in the trance of a complete disenchantment," she should have retreated quietly back to her intellectual life, which would keep the revolutionary faith of the masses alive. "And don't forget," he reminded her, "your attitude took me by surprise, because you were never completely frank with me regarding your profound divergence" from the leadership. Portal, he suggested, had guarded her growing doubt from even her closest, most trusted friends. "How many times did we talk in Caracas, but you never wanted, with a modesty that I respected, to get to the bottom of the question."[6]

Aware of the devastating loss of her papers en route to Argentina, Betancourt pleaded with her to keep working for the revolution rather than going down the path of "defeatism." I understand "perfectly that you want to step aside from the political struggle," which, he admitted, could be "nauseous." Yet you still have "a message, as an intellectual, as a writer, and . . . must continue offering it. Write, and if you lost the originals, or they stole them from you, rewrite them" and continue. In a testament to what may have been her deepest friendship among her political compañeros, Betancourt recalled that "you were more developed as a revolutionary when we met, in Santo Domingo in '29," and "you helped me a lot, in my training, with your mystical adhesion to the social struggle. . . . Now I return that lesson," he continued, to say "with rude sincerity that . . . you are not a pure poet, nor a sharpshooter who can do what they want with their life. You have a past that obligates you, a commitment to your people and with the peoples of America" that she should not "throw overboard, in an individualist gesture. I know how much you suffer and have suffered; I understand that if any life has been dramatic, it is yours. But . . . you have a mission, a destiny, and you cannot be disloyal to them."[7]

This searching letter shows the measure of Betancourt's friendship in 1952. Meant to bolster her spirits, it recognized Portal's value to him as a political mentor and as a close friend, as suggested by his use of the matrimonial milestone "silver anniversary" to describe their long journey together. It also showed that, at least in 1952, they still shared a common language of dedication to revolution. Seven years later, in 1959, Betancourt returned to power in Venezuela, just as the region was shaken by the eruption of a new political volcano: a revolution in Cuba led by a new generation of radical students. Rather than join Fidel Castro in a common anti-imperialist struggle, President Betancourt—at one time an avowed Communist—set out to crush the Venezuelan revolutionary groups inspired by Cuba, who opposed him.[8]

The Cuban Revolution changed everything. It rekindled Portal's maximalist political imagination even as leaders like Haya and Betancourt turned sharply toward the Right in their bid to prove to the United States that their non-Communist reformist parties were its best allies in a Latin America battered by revolutionary storms. Just a year later, Portal wrote to a Chilean friend in 1960 that "with Rómulo," she had "suffered one of the most painful disappointments. . . . I believed him a brother," but "when I realized his attitude—and his flirtations with yanqui imperialism—I wrote him a letter where I broke with the fraternal affection that always united us and I told him some very energetic things."[9]

The Cuban Revolution cast Portal's life story in a new light. Fidel's Caribbean revolution, and the insurgencies it inspired over the next twenty years, proved she had been correct in breaking from APRA and denouncing its leadership by making clear just how little APRA or Betancourt's Democratic Action had achieved in exchange for betraying the region's hopes for revolutionary change. Using the political language of Marxism, Portal would explain that Betancourt destroyed their long friendship because of his "adhesion to social democratic doctrines, married to the extreme reactionary right wing," a political assessment shared by the Cuban and Latin American Left.[10] The abrupt end of one of her closest friendships proved that, for Portal, politics mattered more than friendship.

The Cuban Revolution vindicated her as a revolutionary in the 1960s, but it also inevitably called into question her decision forty years earlier to choose Haya over Mariátegui, the founder of the Peruvian Communist Party. Although the Communists never became a mass party like APRA, the two defined the continuum of the Peruvian Left and remained combative rivals. Portal had been a national leader in the anti-Communist APRA for over twenty years, but her Aprista period was more than a decade behind her in the 1960s. In 1960, she became part of a newly constituted Peruvian Soviet Institute and seven years later she formally joined the Peruvian Communist Party.[11] When she affiliated with APRA's principal leftist rival, she declared that she had no regrets about her Aprista past; it was "part of my own human situation, part of my personal burden and my fate. I don't believe in guilt." Even with what she now deemed "all its faults and heresies," APRA "had readied the ground, it had raised consciousness, it had created conditions for a leap ahead."[12]

In the 1970s, she returned to organizational leadership working with the leftist Peruvian National Association of Writers and Artists (Asociación Nacional de Escritores y Artistas; ANEA), serving as its president from 1981 to 1986. This work allowed her to travel the world attending political and literary conferences in the Soviet Union, Czechoslovakia, Bulgaria, Cuba, Mexico, France, and even the United States. She served as president of the Peru-Cuba Friendship Association, defended the 1979 Soviet invasion of Afghanistan, and organized solidarity campaigns for the embattled Sandinistas in the 1980s.[13] At the age of seventy-eight, she even ran for office on the Socialist Revolutionary Action Party ticket for the 1978 constitutional assembly tasked with writing a new constitution for Peru's 1980 democratic elections.[14]

Scholars have long asked what, in the end, had APRA, even with "all its faults and heresies," achieved? Leftist scholars would argue it had never been a revolutionary party and it was a "mistake" to take APRA's insurrectionary eruptions seriously, since they never meant to really take power, but used violence only to "dramatize" their politics and strengthen Aprista solidarity.[15] For those who tried and failed to spur the party to more radical measures, the failed Callao insurrection loomed as the last great lost opportunity to realize APRA's revolutionary potential. In 1954, Major Villanueva published a book about that failed revolt he titled *La tragedia de un pueblo y de un partido* (The tragedy of a people and of a party). Echoing Portal's 1950 denunciations, the prologue claimed that the Aprista leadership's relationship to revolution was only one of romantic identification. The faithful Aprista rank and file "did not know, had no way of knowing, that some of the highest leaders in the party had only an abstract concept of revolution, or better said, a lyrical, agreeable understanding, like the taste of a ripe peach."[16]

Villanueva's indictment of the APRA leadership did not include Portal, who remained, in her words, "rabidly leftist." She believed, as she explained in this 1960 letter, that there could be no real solutions to the people's problems through elections, but only with "the triumph of the total rights of the people." Looking back in the late seventies, Portal maintained that "the APRA of 1930 proposed anti-imperialism as a weapon of struggle. It was the moment to carry out the revolution. . . . In the letters I received from Haya . . . he told me: 'through the pink paths we will go to the red ones.' . . . But I was also defrauded in all my revolutionary expectations, because as the years passed, they went from pink to light blue, to white or to black, I don't know. But to red, like he claimed, never."[17] Portal's own map for social change, her own map of Red Paths, had started with tyrannicide; and while it had evolved from such a provocation, it brooked few compromises. Any new Peru, she was certain, was never going to be achieved through votes and negotiation, a certainty that seemed to be confirmed with revolutionary victories in Cuba and Nicaragua.

The logic of her judgment, ironically enough, had been echoed by the U.S. charge d'affaires in 1948. After reviewing Peruvian history, he torturously conceded that "it may be that only by some form of revolution can the vested interests of the ruling class be so reduced as to give the Indian what might be considered his place in a democratic society." Revolution, in other words, was perhaps necessary. "Apra's failure may therefore, in the last analysis, be due to a failure to equate its means with its ends. Apra is the social revolution, and the elite is fully aware of that fact. It may be puerile to believe, as Apra has, that in a country which in the middle of the twentieth century is still completely lacking in a liberal, democratic tradition a social revolution can be carried through by democratic means."[18]

North American analysts also wrestled with how to understand Haya and his party. "In his role as philosopher and prophet," the U.S. Charge d'Affaires suspected, Haya's ambitions probably "go higher than the presidency." He "often takes a very long-range point of view of the Peruvian scene and may place his hopes on a future far more distant." The U.S. diplomat suggested that "while he might accept it as a stepping stone to greater fame, he might prefer to spend the remainder of his life as the 'prophet of Indo-America' than to have to face . . . the mundane problems of governmental leadership and administration as President of the Republic."[19]

More than a decade after the U.S. embassy ruminated over Haya's ambition to be the region's leftist prophet, it became clear that the role would go to Fidel Castro and Che Guevara, not Haya or Betancourt. As a young student radical, Castro had watched and learned from the trajectories of Haya and Betancourt, as well as from Jacobo Árbenz's government in Guatemala, whose relatively modest reforms were nonetheless deemed enough of a threat to be overthrown in a CIA-orchestrated coup. This new generation of radicalized students arrived at Portal's position on the central questions facing this generation of Latin American leftists as they journeyed through the twentieth century. Was revolutionary violence and the overthrow of the state necessary? Could the social and economic suffering of millions be substantively addressed by a political system designed to serve the needs of the wealthy European-descended few that emerged from over four hundred years of the region's colonial and neocolonial history? Was Latin America inevitably fated by both history and geography to be subject to the political and economic desires of the United States? In leading a successful armed Socialist revolution just ninety miles from Florida, Castro and his band of brothers definitely displaced Haya and his cohort as leaders of the Latin American Left and conductors of its revolutionary hopes. In 1960, Portal gleefully recounted how Haya was upstaged before a massive rally by the future Chilean president Salvador Allende with a "tremendous" speech in favor of Fidel Castro and against U.S. imperialism.[20]

This generational changing of the guard sharply contrasted the aging Haya as the violence-averse philosopher with Castro, a virile martial figure branded in the global imagination as the eternal guerrilla commander ever ready in his military fatigues, while successfully administering a country besieged by its enemies. Haya's homosexuality was another ready contrast with the vocally homophobic Cuban revolutionary leaders. In his widely read 1967 testimony about life as a twentieth-century Communist, the Salvadorean Miguel Mármol casually referred to Haya as "that old faggot."[21] Recent work on the gendered contours of revolutionary fraternity in the Cuban Revolution, however, offers suggestive hints about the power of a strand of revolutionary androgyny in Che Guevara's Socialist "New

Man" and in the dynamics of Castro's charismatic leadership. Similar processes may well have been in play in the Aprista adulation for the young Haya, with the collective fervor of their mass rallies, the devotional literature and individual manifestations such as the poems Delmar and others wrote to him, and the intense, homosocial bonding that characterized their Aprista faith.

Che Guevara's "New Man" layered onto the paradigmatic masculine martial traits of bravery, courage, and patriotism the feminine traits of "nineteenth-century domestic heroism: endurance, tenderness, discipline, love, sacrifice, surrender, suffering."[22] From these, Ileana Rodríguez focuses on *tendresse,* the tender love that defined bourgeois romanticism, which these revolutionaries believed the old male needed to become the New Man.[23] Expressing this tender love for their fellow guerrillas, and especially for (and receiving it from) their ultimate leader, Castro, became a patriotic duty. The guerrillas' "homosociality," created by expressing this tender love among themselves, "remapped desire" and transformed their quasi-erotic commitment to Castro into an index for measuring their devotion to Cuba. In short, such *tendresse* allowed Che Guevara and the New Man he theorized to embody a somewhat more feminized masculinity that made possible a wider range of homosocial bonding, strengthening their revolutionary fraternity and, ultimately, their insurgent military project. And, in the Socialist tomorrow, this androgynous New Man would become the "model for the new social subject."[24]

A generation earlier, in her own masculinist orientation, Portal had embodied a similar revolutionary androgyny. In her 1933 *Hacia la mujer nueva,* she had explicitly argued that a similarly androgynous subjectivity would be the necessary transitional bridge between the colonial mentality still burdening women and the fully realized Aprista New Woman of the future. "Partly masculine and partly feminine in spirit," this transitional woman "is the pure type of the social revolutionary, courageous, energetic, but not sharply delineated in her sexual identity." Since "the feminine is still synonymous with *dulzura,*" with sweetness, gentleness, tenderness, and docility, the woman transitioning toward the New Woman "had no choice but to fight 'like a man' and forget she is a woman." Guided by APRA's revolutionary vision, however, Portal distinguished this from other modern, gender-confused women like the "ambiguous" and "asexual" woman, the "Yankee flapper," or the French "*garçonne*" because APRA had led her "to realize her true place in society," which was to create a future world where she would "attain authentic stature" as a woman.[25]

But at heart, the power of revolutionary androgyny was not available to Portal in the same measure as it was for aspiring New Men of the 1960s in Latin America. The feminized masculine subject was not the same as the masculinized feminine one she discussed in theory and created in her attempt to live as a free woman. The first made men more human and gave tender love to soldiers, the legitimate, "authorized" agents of revolution. It allowed brothers in arms to "love" each other more fiercely, and through that love, reinforced their collective love for their revolutionary vision for their country and beyond. The second layered the threat of violence on what should have been an uncomplicated canvas of dulzura, of sweet, tender love, either romantic or maternal. It did not legitimate or authorize women as revolutionary subjects even as it transformed them into not-quite-women. Instead of producing more loving brothers-in-arms, the masculinized feminine was the anxious terror of the woman with a gun.

That anxiety and fear still resonate in how Peruvians remember Portal. She remained a heroic, almost messianic figure for many of the women she worked with in APRA and for the feminists a generation later who saw her as a pioneer. Thirteen years after Portal's death, María Julia Luna de Ciudad, who had participated in the 1946 National Convention of Aprista Women, eulogized her: "Magda, with her arms open in a cross, raised symbol of the struggle for liberation, extends, rises, nails herself so that many women, with love, follow a similar path, with no truces, with more strength but less pain."[26] But the other side of the aisle, the latest generation of Aprista women, who, had everything worked out differently, should have been the Aprista New Women Portal had hoped for, saw something entirely different; something abnormal and nefarious.

At the dawn of a new century, when a young female Aprista, a journalist like the younger Portal, tried to track down information about her, she found that among the older Apristas she interviewed, "not everyone remembers" her. "Nobody gave me a reason, only some loose facts, sometimes vague and contradictory," she reported. "Magda Portal gathered a group of *La Tribuna* workers and formed a revisionist commando,'" an elderly female Aprista told her. "I wanted to know more, because, according to her, this revisionist commando was organized to assassinate various high-order leaders of APRA, among them Haya de la Torre, because

Portal judged that they were not 'fighting for the people.'" The young journalist concluded that "nobody wants to remember her" because "the difference between defiance and rebellion [*rebeldía y rebelión*] is the same as that which exists between waving a fist and killing someone. Magda Portal was much more than rebellious and much more than passionate. . . . The silence that today exists about her does not permit us to learn what drives a woman who fights to be, at best, a devastating woman [*una mujer devastadora*]. And I think about this, nonetheless, now that night has fallen and the sun has set, and I can't find the light to see what are the paths that take one toward that darkness that at one time was a constructive passion for freedom."[27] Portal would be proud to see how her spirit lived on in this political condemnation, which echoes the rumors about her as a violent, chaotic destroyer, someone willing to kill, who literally walked in darkness.

Portal's masculinist agency, which she had argued offered an androgyny full of revolutionary potential, did not legitimize her as someone with a "constructive passion for freedom" for this later generation of Apristas. Instead, it stripped or erased whatever dulzura Portal may have had, leaving, "at best, a devastating woman." Whether being cast as messiah or as the "devastating woman" who haunted APRA, Portal had established herself as Peru's principal female revolutionary and as a woman of revolutionary importance in its history. Portal had long ago decided that inspiring anger and rage in her opponents was preferable to being "dismissed" as a "human tragedy," a pity case that, in her view, was necessarily condescending, humiliating, and psychologically demeaning. It was better to pick a fight; to become hated but feared and, at best, warily respected.

Portal did walk through darkness but not because of her "excessive" passion, agency, or will to action; instead her darkness was lodged in the emotional pain and scars of all she had lost and sacrificed along the way, including her daughter. That was her victory: becoming herself by building APRA, which she used as a vehicle to develop her freedom and, when she felt it politically necessary, as in 1950, choosing her ideals over the party. Ironically enough, the battles that characterized Portal's own fraught marriage with APRA were fought on a terrain that was curiously similar to the field of battle that defined the traditional Limeñan marriage Portal had rejected. A century earlier, the conservative matriarch Lastenia Larriva de

Llona, the closest woman Portal and Lima's other orphaned lettered women had to a Maestra de Juventud, had counseled them that their marriages would be measured only "in the quotidian small battles of existence" on fields of "unknown heroisms . . . in tight quarters, surrounded by four walls . . . which Fame does not make known," producing "no medals or crosses of honor."[28] The emotional dynamics of marriage in Lima's "poetry of the home" would inevitably be cramped, hidden, and conflictive. Portal discovered a similar battle, as rife with emotional undercurrents, that played out within a similar gendered logic in her most enduring relationship: her political marriage with her party that made her one of their band of Aprista brothers.

In publishing *La trampa*, Portal publicly exposed the seamy underside of what her increasingly oppressive political relationship to APRA had become. Critics point to *¿Quiénes traicionaron al pueblo?* as her moment of courage in accusing the Aprista leadership of betraying the rank and file's revolutionary aspirations. But in *La trampa*, Portal once again showed a different kind of boldness, the courage to expose to the world, with an almost immolating honesty, her emotional landscape with its peaks of high emotion and its valleys of desolation. Mariátegui had praised Portal's poetry in 1928 for her courage in exploring the landscape of female sexuality and desire, which he declared tore Peruvian literature from its Spanish colonial moorings. In politics, as much as Portal's revolutionary significance rested on her political and doctrinal ideas, it also rested on how she unabashedly revealed and explored her own subjectivity in a life full of unflinching self-portraits.

Her portraits allowed Portal to reveal her inner workings rather than remaining modestly demure. It gives us the opportunity to witness Portal's trials as she valiantly attempted to live as a free woman, "a true revolutionary," in the words of Seoane, "a new woman in this Latin America full of antiquated defects."[29] The documentation she left behind showed an exhausting but nonetheless exhilarating effort to develop a heroic will to action that allowed her to force herself out on public stages. It was also, however, the ambivalence of living with the knowledge that, in choosing that public life, she lost her dulzura and necessarily became something other than a "normal girl," and recognizing how that affected her family, her lovers, and her child. It meant finding a way to grimly live through and endure gendered trauma within what should have been her beloved community, a fraternity of brothers in arms where homosocial emotion was the "cement" binding them together as they hurtled toward the new Peru.

She offered, in short, the full, searching, fearless, almost shameless exploration of her gendered plunge into politics as lived experience. She recognized the power of shame in disciplining individuals, making them feel guilty for behaviors they should have known were wrong. Portal experienced these feelings of guilt and regret in her effort to become the New Woman, but she accepted the need to make difficult choices and to live with the consequences. Yet, in revealing her emotional landscape, especially those tortured, conflicted emotions, she boldly insisted that the blame lay in the "antiquated defects" and the structural conditions of her society. This is the revelatory, emancipatory power of Magda Portal: why should she feel ashamed about choosing to be free? *She* was the dream worth all the sacrifices, not APRA.

As she aged, Portal saw Seoane die in 1963, while her old friend Salvador Allende stepped onto center stage as the president of the Western

Magda Portal in 1981. Courtesy of Kathleen Weaver, photographer.

Hemisphere's first elected Socialist government in Chile. When Augusto Pinochet's troops attacked the Presidential Palace in 1973, Allende gave his life defending his dream of revolution with a machine gun given to him by Castro. Haya died in 1979, right after overseeing Peru's Constitutional Convention as the nation's eldest statesman; Betancourt followed two years later in 1981, lionized as the "father of Venezuelan democracy," his party rightly considered Venezuela's most important but destined within the decade to be totally discredited by the rise of another revolutionary leader, Hugo Chávez. APRA finally reached power in 1985 when Alan García Pérez was elected to the presidency at only thirty-six years old. Portal's health and mind began deteriorating in 1987, and she suffered a stroke in December 1988, losing the ability to speak. She died seven months later, on July 11, 1989.[30] Luis Alberto Sánchez was the only one of the original band of brothers to serve in an APRA government, and he died in 1994.

By the time APRA held the reins of power, Peruvians who had spent fifty years fearing Aprista revolutionary violence no longer considered APRA an existential threat, but a stable part of their political firmament. The politics of Latin America's neoliberal age discredited revolutionary vanguardism and the armed struggle against the state. APRA had executed its rightward shift long before, thus "regaining its reason," and had evolved from a movement qua insurgency into a mass electoral party. Conflict over society and the economy would continue in Peru, of course, but now within a political system where the interests, needs, and votes of the masses were accommodated and elections were the uncontested legitimizing principle. At the turn of the twenty-first century, the question of revolutionary violence was seen in the light of a new, much more terrifying political project that had exploded on the scene with the rise of a faction of avowed Maoist revolutionaries fiercely devoted to using violence to achieve their ends. On fire with the incandescent revolutionary certainty that they were Peru's luminous Red Path, this new messianic group flayed the country bare, exposing the potential dangers that now inhered, or perhaps still inhered, in an uncompromising, masculinized maximalism: Sendero Luminoso.

Notes

Abbreviations

AMGP   Anna Melissa Graves Papers; Archives of Labor History
                and Urban Affairs, Wayne State University, Detroit,
                Michigan.
Benson   Magda Portal Papers, Nettie Lee Benson Library Special
                Collections, University of Texas at Austin. Austin, Texas.
CENDOC-Mujer   Centro de Documentación sobre la Mujer, Lima, Peru.
CGRAELP   Classified General Records, American Embassy, Lima,
                Peru.
DPAELP   Diplomatic Posts, American Embassy, Lima, Peru.
GRAELP   General Records, American Embassy, Lima, Peru.
Portal Estate Papers   Portal Estate Papers, Lima, Peru. In care of Rocío
                Revolledo Pareja, now deposited at the Biblioteca
                Nacional del Perú (BNP) and available electronically at
                http://www.lib.utexas.edu/taro/utlac/00221/lac-00221
                .html#series4 as 2011 Additions to the Benson Special
                Collections at the University of Texas at Austin.
RG 84   Record Group 84, Records of the Foreign Service Posts of
                the Department of State, National Archives deposited at
                College Park, Maryland.

Introduction

1. Manuel González Prada, Peruvian anarchist and Maestro de Juventud, from a lecture he gave in Lima in 1888. All translations are my own unless otherwise indicated.

2. Werlich, *Peru*, 175.

3. López Lenci, "La poesía," 20.

4. Arrington, "Magda Portal"; Monguió, *La poesía*, 134.

5. Mariátegui, *Peruanicemos al Perú*, 22; Mariátegui, *Siete ensayos*, 322.

6. Hollinger, "From Identity to Solidarity," 24–25.

7. Vaughan, *Portrait*, 3.

8. Portal Estate Papers, "La vida que yo viví," undated manuscript, Benson, Box 2, Folder 7, 1.

9. Rivero-Ayllón, *Haya*; Klarén, *Modernization*, 84–106.

10. Villanueva del Campo, "Haya y Vallejo," 120, 123.

11. Walker, "Lima," 71–88; Stansell, *American Moderns.*

12. Jrade, *Modernismo*, 5, 12.

13. Portal, "Una revista de cuatro nombres," 102.

14. Portal, "Un llamado a la juventud revolucionaria de América Latina," reprinted in Del Mazo, *La Reforma Universitaria*, 1:1.

15. Rama, *La ciudad letrada.*

16. Garrison, *"Empire of Ideals,"* 41, 197.

17. Lavrin, "Some Final Considerations," 310.

18. French, "Social History."

19. Vaughan, *Portrait*, 3.

20. Nasaw, " 'Introduction' to AHR Roundtable," 574.

21. Cited in Kessler-Harris, "Why Biography?," 626.

22. Spiegel, "Comment on A Crooked Line," 411–12; French, "Social History."

23. Banner, "Biography as History," 583.

24. Biographies of Portal include Reedy, *Magda Portal*; Weaver and Portal, *Peruvian Rebel*; García-Bryce, "Transnational Activist."

25. Miller, *Latin American Women*, 101–2.

26. Stein, "Paths to Populism," 104–5.

27. Lavrin, "Some Final Considerations," 303, 316–17; Chaney, "Old and New Feminisms," 334.

28. Kuhnheim, "Verbal Society," 206.

29. William K. Wimsatt, cited in Wood, "We Do It All the Time," 8.

30. William Empson, cited in Wood, "We Do It All the Time," 8.

31. Izenberg, "Psychohistory," 139–55.

Chapter 1

1. Stein, *Populism*, 142–44.

2. Ibid., 137.

3. Ibid., 134.

4. Werlich, *Peru*, 176.

5. Seoane, *Páginas escogidas*, 21.

6. Stein, *Populism*, 139–40.

7. Ibid., 143–44.

8. Sánchez, *Leguía*, 102.

9. Walker, "Lima," 77.

10. Garret, *Oncenio*, 23.

11. Castañeda Vielakamen, *El vanguardismo*, 15; Sánchez, *Testimonio*, 1:282.

12. Walker, "Lima," 74, 80.

13. Herrera, "Magda Portal," 9; Sánchez, *Testimonio*, 1:288.

14. "Los Juegos Florales," *Mundial*, August 31, 1923.

15. Apollinaire, *Alcools*, 73–74.

16. Walker, "Lima," 79; Lauer, *La polémica*, xxxiii.

17. Lauer, *Antología*, xxx.

18. Monguió, *La poesía*, 58.

19. Reedy, *Magda Portal*, 63.

20. Walker, "Lima," 79.

21. Sánchez, *Testimonio*, 1:148.

22. "Juegos Florales de 1923: Acta-fallo del jurado," *El Tiempo* (Lima), August 22, 1923, cited in Reedy, *Magda Portal*, 59.

23. Sánchez, *Testimonio*, 1:148; Cossío del Pomar, *Víctor Raúl*, 131; Alberto Guillén, "Haya Delatorre ha dicho la verdad," *Repertorio Americano* (Costa Rica) 7, no. 10, September 18, 1928, 151.

24. Sánchez, *Testimonio*, 1:314.

25. Iwasaki Cauti, "Maldito y canalla," 162, 165.

26. Herrera, "Magda Portal," 9–10.

27. "La hermosa velada de anoche en el Teatro Forero," *La Crónica* (Lima), August 26, 1923, 9, 18.

28. Herrera, "Magda Portal," 9–10.

29. Seoane, "Escorzo," 13.

30. Reedy, *Magda Portal*, 63–64.

31. *Claridad*, Edición en facsímile, 85.

32. Seoane, *Páginas escogidas*, 22–23.

33. Sánchez, *Testimonio*, 1:193–94.

34. Andradi and Portugal, "Magda Portal," 212–13.

35. Ibid., 211; Reedy, *Magda Portal*, 30–31; Weaver, "Interview," 55.

36. Parker, *Middle Class*, 6–7, 17, 20, 24–28, 52.

37. Portal Estate Papers, "La vida que yo viví," Benson, Box 2, Folder 7, 8; Weaver, "Interview," 54–55.

38. Mannarelli, *Limpias*, 156; Reedy, *Magda Portal*, 34.

39. Portal Estate Papers, "La vida que yo viví," Benson, Box 2, Folder 7, 8, 10.

40. J. Croniquer, "Por esas calles," *La Prensa* (Lima), August 7, 1912, cited in López Lenci, *El laboratorio*, 66; Basadre, *Historia*, 9:4127–34; Basadre, "La aristocracia y las clases medias," 464–65.

41. González de Fanning, *Educación femenina*, 39, cited in Mannarelli, *Limpias*, 138.

42. Parker, *Middle Class*, 19.

43. Matto de Turner's *Herencia*, cited in Mannarelli, *Limpias*, 36–37.

44. Mannarelli, *Limpias*, 34.

45. Gálvez, *Una Lima*, 173–74.

46. Larriva de Llona, *Cartas a mi hijo*, 258–60.

47. Ibid., 258–59.

48. Parker, *Middle Class*, 38, 60; Basadre, *Historia*, 9:4184.

49. Reedy, *Magda Portal*, 12; Portal Estate Papers, "La vida que yo viví," Benson, Box 2, Folder 7, 10.

50. Parker, *Middle Class*, 28, 31.

51. Mannarelli, *Limpias*, 156.

52. Portal, "Trazos cortados [drafts]," Benson, Box 4, Folder 10, 15; Basadre, "La aristocracia," 466–67.

53. Portal Estate Papers, "La vida que yo viví," Benson, Box 2, Folder 7, 11; Andradi and Portugal, "Magda Portal," 211.

54. Reedy, *Magda Portal*, 35; Mannarelli, *Limpias*, 48–51. Population figures from *Extracto Estadístico del Perú de 1926*, 135.

55. Sánchez, *Testimonio*, 1:234.

56. Portal Estate Papers, "La vida que yo viví," Benson, Box 2, Folder 7, 9.

57. Sánchez, *Testimonio*, 1:297.

58. Portal, "Response to '¿Con quién coquetearía Ud.?,'" *Mundial*, January 1, 1923, 74.

59. Portal Estate Papers, "La vida que yo viví," Benson, Box 2, Folder 7, 13.

60. Roberts, *Disruptive Acts*, 88–89.

61. Reedy, *Magda Portal*, 349–50.

62. Weaver, "Interview," 60.

63. "La hermosa velada de anoche en el Teatro Forero," 9, 18; *El Tiempo* (Lima), August 22, 1923, cited in Reedy, *Magda Portal*, 59.

64. Ladislao Meza, "Magda Portal, Laureada," *Mundial*, July 27, 1923.

65. Mariátegui, *Peruanicemos al Perú*, 22; Mariátegui, *Siete ensayos*, 322.

66. Andradi and Portugal, "Magda Portal," 214; Weaver, "Interview," 58.

67. Roberts, *Disruptive Acts*, 96.

68. "Quien será Reina del Carnaval?," *Mundial*, February 2, 1923, 16.

69. Reedy, *Magda Portal*, 63.

70. Ladislao Meza, "Magda Portal, Laureada," *Mundial*, July 27, 1923.

71. *El Tiempo*, August 22, 1923, cited in Reedy, *Magda Portal*, 59.

Chapter 2

1. Larriva de Llona, *Cartas a mi hijo*, 86.

2. Mannarelli, *Limpias*, 276, 137–39.

3. Portal, "Trazos cortados [drafts]," Benson, Box 4, Folder 10, 2, 16.

4. Portal, "Plegaria," *Mundial*, September 30, 1921. Myrna L. Wallace aided with the translation.

5. Basadre, *Historia*, 9:4127, 4133.

6. Sánchez, *Testimonio*, 1:160–62, 164–68; Guardia, *Mujeres peruanas*, 80.

7. Portal Estate Papers, "La vida que yo viví," Benson, Box 2, Folder 7, 14; Guardia, *Mujeres peruanas*, 81.

8. Franco, *César Vallejo*, 7.

9. Weaver, "Interview," 59–61; "Magda Portal: Primera militante Aprista," *Mujer y Sociedad* (July 1986), CENDOC-Mujer 5671, 42; Portal, "Trazos cortados [drafts]," Benson, Box 4, Folder 10, 13.

10. Portal, "China-Town," *Mundial*, June 10, 1921.

11. Weaver, "Interview," 56–60.

12. Portal, "Trazos cortados [drafts]," Benson, Box 4, Folder 10, 18.

13. Sánchez, *Testimonio*, 1:163–64.

14. Drinot, *Allure of Labor.*

15. Stansell, *American Moderns*, 82.

16. Portal, "Trazos cortados [drafts]," Benson, Box 4, Folder 10, 18. Women in the city's intellectual, artistic, and bohemian circles included Dora Mayer de Zulen, Carmen Saco, Julia Codesido, María Wiesse, Blanca del Prado, Ángela Ramos, Alicia del Prado, and Blanca Luz Brum. Guardia, *Mujeres peruanas*, 74.

17. Weaver, "Interview," 59–60.

18. Berger, *Ways of Seeing*, 47.

19. Portal, "Trazos cortados [drafts]," Benson, Box 4, Folder 10, 18.

20. Weaver, "Interview," 59–60.

21. Reedy, *Magda Portal*, 35, 66.

22. Weaver, "Interview," 58.

23. Reedy, *Magda Portal*, 70, 73.

24. Larriva de Llona, *Cartas a mi hijo*, 251; Olcott, *Revolutionary Women*, 15–17.

25. Andradi and Portugal, "Magda Portal," 229.

26. Weaver, "Interview," 55.

27. Stansell, *American Moderns*, 246–47.

28. Portal, "Oración conmovida," handwritten note, Portal Estate Papers.

29. Portal, "18 cantos emocionados de vidrios de amor," *Repertorio Americano* 19, no. 24, December 21, 1929, 379–80.

30. Theweleit, *Male Fantasies*, 1:244, 252, 288.

31. Ibid., 284.

32. Portal, "18 cantos emocionados de vidrios de amor," 379.

33. Portal, "Mi homenaje al Día de la Madre," undated manuscript, Portal Estate Papers.

34. Garrison, *"Empire of Ideals,"* 35, 37.

35. Hubbs, *Queer Composition*, 9.

36. Unruh, *Performing Women*, 8; Stansell, *American Moderns*, 232.

37. Ladislao Meza, "Magda Portal, Laureada," *Mundial*, July 27, 1923, 5.

38. Unruh, *Performing Women*, 15.

39. Portal, "Alfonsina Storni," reprinted in Castañeda Vielakamen, *El vanguardismo*, 131.

40. Unruh, *Performing Women*, 176.
41. Portal, "Trazos cortados [drafts]," Benson, Box 4, Folder 10, 16.
42. Andradi and Portugal, "Magda Portal," 229–31.

Chapter 3

1. Larriva de Llona, *Cartas a mi hijo*, 227, 256.
2. Reedy, *Magda Portal*, 87–89; López Lenci, *El laboratorio.*
3. Mannarelli, *Limpias*, 211, 221, 229.
4. Stansell, *American Moderns*, 250–51.
5. Miller, "La mujer obrera," 19; Mannarelli, *Limpias*, 209.
6. Chang-Rodríguez, *Una vida agónica*, 161–64.
7. Castañeda Vielakamen, *El vanguardismo*, 30, 95–98.
8. Reedy, *Magda Portal*, 91.
9. Castañeda Vielakamen, *El vanguardismo*, 44, 31.
10. Mannarelli, *Limpias*, 130–34.
11. Mariátegui, *Temas de educación*, 171.
12. Wiesse, *Etapas de su vida*, 37.
13. Guardia, *El amor*, 14, 22.
14. Ibid., 18.
15. Portal, "Response to '¿Con quién coquetearía Ud.?'"
16. Larriva de Llona, *Cartas a mi hijo*, 153.
17. Ibid., 153.
18. Ibid., 153, 157.
19. Mannarelli, *Limpias*, 217–20.
20. Larriva de Llona, *Cartas a mi hijo*, 207.
21. Ibid., 227.
22. Andradi and Portugal, "Magda Portal," 228–29.
23. Ibid., 229.
24. Ibid., 228–29.
25. Reedy, *Magda Portal*, 88.
26. Castañeda Vielakamen, *El vanguardismo*, 118.
27. Portal, "Vidas de milagro," *Mercurio Peruano* (Lima) 15, no. 81–82 (March 1925), 133.
28. Jrade, *Modernismo*, 134–35; Unruh, *Performing Women.*
29. Reedy, *Magda Portal*, 97.
30. Andradi and Portugal, "Magda Portal," 228–29.
31. Larriva de Llona, *Cartas a mi hijo*, 93.
32. Barquero, *Serafín Delmar.*
33. Delmar, *Los campesinos*, 55. See especially "*Noche de lluvia*" and "*Dos policías.*"
34. Weaver and Portal, *Peruvian Rebel*, 28; Andradi and Portugal, "Magda Portal," 229.

35. Larriva de Llona, *Cartas a mi hijo*, 241.

36. Andradi and Portugal, "Magda Portal," 229.

37. Larriva de Llona, *Cartas a mi hijo*, 252.

38. Reedy, *Magda Portal*, 96, 98, 137.

39. Ibid., 98.

Chapter 4

1. Delmar and Portal, *El derecho*, n.p.

2. Reedy, *Magda Portal*, 351; López Lenci, *El laboratorio*, 73.

3. Fasey, "'Shock of Recognition,'" 92, 97–98.

4. Delmar and Portal, *El derecho*, n.p.

5. Reedy, *Magda Portal*, 111.

6. Portal, "La rara," *Mundial*, March 16, 1923.

7. Delmar and Portal, *El derecho*, n.p.

8. Reedy, *Magda Portal*, 100, 104–5.

9. Andradi and Portugal, "Magda Portal," 213; Reedy, *Magda Portal*, 105.

10. *Rascacielos*, November 1926, reprinted in Portal, "Una revista de cuatro nombres," 101–4.

11. Weaver, "Interview," 58–59.

12. Delmar and Portal, *El derecho*, n.p.

13. Reedy, *Magda Portal*, 105.

14. Guardia, *Mujeres peruanas*, 82.

15. Klarén, *Peru*, 214.

16. Guardia, *Mujeres peruanas*, 81.

17. Ibid., 78.

18. "Magda Portal: Primera militante Aprista," CENDOC-Mujer 5671, 42.

19. Guardia, *Mujeres peruanas*, 78, 80.

20. Reedy, *Magda Portal*, 111–12.

21. Urquieta, "Izquierdismo," 68, 76, 78–79.

22. Portal, "Réplica," 80–81." Portal's formulation positing that the future lies at the heart of the present is strikingly similar to Sartre's. See Sartre, *Search for a Method*.

23. Guardia, *Mujeres peruanas*, 81–82; Andradi and Portugal, "Magda Portal," 231; Portal, "37 poema," *Boletín de las Universidades Populares González Prada* (Lima), January 1927, 5, reprinted in *Claridad*, Edición en facsímile.

24. Andradi and Portugal, "Magda Portal," 213.

25. Ibid., 213.

26. Guardia, *Mujeres peruanas*, 82–83; Weaver, "Interview," 65–66.

27. Portal Estate Papers, "La vida que yo viví," Benson, Box 2, Folder 7, 34–35; Andradi and Portugal, "Magda Portal," 213.

28. Guardia, *Mujeres peruanas*, 82–83.

29. Weaver and Portal, *Peruvian Rebel*, 52.

30. Eudocio Ravines, quoted in Werlich, *Peru*, 179.

31. Haya to Graves, January 2, 1923, AMGP, Box 1, Folder 1.

32. Haya to Graves, December 26, 1923, AMGP, Box 1, Folder 1.

33. Haya to Graves, February 29, 1924, AMGP, Box 1, Folder 2.

34. Haya to Graves, postmarked May 1924, AMGP, Box 1, Folder 3.

35. Haya to Graves, August 9, 1924, AMGP, Box 1, Folder 3.

36. Zoila de la Torre to Graves, July 31, 1924, AMGP, Box 6, Folder 9.

37. Haya to Graves, September 8, 1925, AMGP, Box 1, Folder 14.

38. Weaver, "Interview," 65–66; Andradi and Portugal, "Magda Portal," 213.

39. Werlich, *Peru*, 183.

40. Klarén, *Peru*, 261.

41. Sánchez, *Apuntes*, 1:76–80.

42. "Magda Portal: Primera militante Aprista," CENDOC-Mujer 5671, 42.

43. Reedy, *Magda Portal*, 78–79; Guardia, *Mujeres peruanas*, 82.

44. Andradi and Portugal, "Magda Portal," 213.

45. Mathews Carmelino, "Magda Portal: Entre la palabra y el silencio," Thesis, CENDOC-Mujer 19552, 67, 69, 70, 76–77.

46. Ibid., 66.

47. "Magda Portal: Primera militante Aprista," CENDOC-Mujer 5671, 42.

48. Andradi and Portugal, "Magda Portal," 213; Portal Estate Papers, "La vida que yo viví," Benson, Box 2, Folder 7, 32–33.

49. Weaver, "Interview," 65–66.

50. Ibid.

51. Portal Estate Papers, "La vida que yo viví," Benson, Box 2, Folder 7, 34.

52. Saldaña-Portillo, *Revolutionary Imagination*, 9, 66.

53. Reedy, *Magda Portal*, 78–79.

54. Haya letter, February 4, 1929, AMGP, Box 3, Folder 4.

55. Portal Estate Papers, "La vida que yo viví," Benson, Box 2, Folder 7, 36.

56. Haya to Ravines, March 22, 1929, in Pedro Planas, *Los orígenes del APRA*, cited in Reedy, *Magda Portal*, 159.

57. Scrapbook: Portal's Antilles Tour, Benson, Box 10, Folder 11.

58. José Abad Ramos, cited in García-Bryce, "Transnational Activist," 678.

59. Suárez Figueroa, "El joven Betancourt," 91; *Archivo de Rómulo Betancourt*, 4:285–86.

60. Gómez, *Rómulo Betancourt*, 29.

61. *Archivo de Rómulo Betancourt*, 4:95.

62. *Archivo de Rómulo Betancourt*, 3:90–91.

63. Portal, "Dos poemas proletarios para los compañeros de Vitarte," *Amauta* (Lima), July 1929, 18–20.

64. Werlich, *Peru*, 185.

65. Portal Estate Papers, "La vida que yo viví," Benson, Box 2, Folder 7, 34, 42–44.

Chapter 5

1. Weaver, "1981 Portal Interview," unpublished manuscript, Portal Estate Papers, 12.

2. Portal, "Trazos cortados [drafts]," Benson, Box 4, Folder 10, 22.

3. Andradi and Portugal, "Magda Portal," 227–28; Weaver, "1981 Portal Interview," 16.

4. Weaver, "1981 Portal Interview," 16.

5. Andradi and Portugal, "Magda Portal," 228.

6. Weaver, "1981 Portal Interview," 15.

7. "Nuestros líderes en gira por el país," *APRA* (Lima), 5, no. 4, December 7, 1933, 5.

8. Portal, *Hacia la mujer nueva*, 49.

9. Drake, *Money Doctor*, 212–16, 244.

10. Klarén, *Modernization*, 120.

11. Sánchez, *Apuntes*, 1:193.

12. Werlich, *Peru*, 188–89.

13. Stein, *Populism*, 84, 102; Werlich, *Peru*, 187.

14. Sánchez, *Testimonio*, 1:326.

15. Sánchez, *Apuntes*, 1:195–98.

16. Pike, *Politics*, 150.

17. Seoane, "Escorzo," 14.

18. Sánchez, *Apuntes*, 2:23.

19. Sánchez, *Apuntes*, 1:222.

20. Heilman, "We Will No Longer Be Servile," 509.

21. Sánchez, *Apuntes*, 1:200; Announcement of Provisional Executive Committee, *APRA* (Lima) 1, no. 2, October 20, 1930, 3.

22. Sánchez, *Apuntes*, 1:199, 203, 205.

23. Delmar to Betancourt, December 9, 1930, *Archivo de Rómulo Betancourt*, 2:447.

24. Portal, "La hora del Perú," *Repertorio Americano* 22, no. 4, January 24, 1931, 58–59.

25. Petrovick, "Informe de la Secretaría de Organización del Comité Ejecutivo Nacional del P.A.P," *APRA* (Lima) 3, no. 5, August 22, 1931, 8.

26. Sánchez, *Apuntes*, 1:213.

27. Weaver, "1981 Portal Interview," 11–12.

28. Stein, *Populism*, 95.

29. Sánchez, *Testimonio*, 1:369, 347, 349.

30. "El Aprismo es una fuerza nueva y constructiva, así dijo ayer Magda Portal," *La Tribuna* (Lima), June 22, 1931, 3.

31. Chang-Rodríguez, *Una vida agónica*, 101.

32. Delmar to Betancourt, June 5, 1931, *Archivo de Rómulo Betancourt*, 3:91.

33. Weaver, "1981 Portal Interview," 13–14.

34. Haya to Sánchez, January 31, 1931, Haya and Sánchez, *Correspondencia*, 33; Sánchez, *Testimonio*, 1:347.

35. Sánchez, *Víctor Raúl Haya de la Torre*, 195; "Exhibición de Fuerzas Políticas," *APRA* (Lima) 4, no. 5, September 30, 1931, 5.

36. Sánchez, *Testimonio*, 1:347.

37. Delmar to Betancourt, June 5, 1930, *Archivo de Rómulo Betancourt*, 3:90.

38. Portal, "La hora del Perú," 65.

39. Weaver, "1981 Portal Interview," 5.

40. "Continuó sus labores el Congreso Departamental Aprista de Lima," *La Tribuna*, June 30, 1931, 3; Klarén, *Modernization*, 122.

41. "Balance del Congreso Departamental Aprista de Lima," *APRA* (Lima) 3, no. 2, July 8, 1931, 2.

42. Portal, "La hora del Perú," 66.

43. "Ponencias presentadas por la Sección Femenina y aprobadas por el CAD del L," *APRA* (Lima) 3, no. 2, July 8, 1931, 15.

44. Portal, "Definición de la mujer aprista," *APRA* (Lima) 2, no. 3, March 18, 1931, 5; Portal, "Rol de la mujer revolucionaria: El voto femenino," *APRA* (Lima) 2, no. 7, April 2, 1931, 10; Portal, "Llamamiento a las mujeres del Perú," *APRA* (Lima) 4, no. 7, October 22, 1931, 4; Portal, "Las mujeres peruanas ante el proceso electoral," *APRA* (Lima) 4, no. 9, November 6, 1931, 11; Portal, "El voto femenino debe ser calificado," *APRA* (Lima) 5, no. 15, December 31, 1931, 7.

45. Divorce decree, May 19, 1931, Portal Estate Papers.

46. Sánchez, *Víctor Raúl Haya de la Torre*, 188, 193.

47. Masterson, *Militarism*, 47; Klarén, *Modernization*, 131.

48. Stein, *Populism*, 210.

49. Werlich, *Peru*, 190.

50. Portal, "Trazos cortados [drafts]," Benson, Box 4, Folder 10, 21.

51. Stein, *Populism*, 107.

52. Sánchez, *Haya de la Torre y el Apra*, 182, 191, 195.

53. Sánchez, *Testimonio*, 1:352, 369, 347, 349.

54. Pike, *Politics*, 152–53.

55. Sánchez, *Testimonio*, 1:360.

56. Werlich, *Peru*, 94.

57. Klarén, *Modernization*, 132.

58. Sánchez, *Víctor Raúl Haya de la Torre*, 192.

59. Stein, *Populism*, 163–64.

60. Portal, "La hora histórica del Perú." *Repertorio Americano* 23, no. 5, August 1, 1931, 1.

61. "Las mujeres y el APRA," *APRA* (Lima) 3, no. 4, August 8, 1931, 11.

62. Petrovick, "Informe de la Secretaría de Organización del Comité Ejecutivo Nacional del P.A.P.," 13.

63. Portal, "La hora histórica del Perú," 1.

64. Delmar to Betancourt, December 20, 1930, *Archivo de Rómulo Betancourt*, 2:455.

65. Weaver, "1981 Portal Interview," 12.

66. Haya, "Haya a la nación," *Repertorio Americano* 24, no. 14, April 23, 1932, 218.

67. Portal, "Una nueva época," *APRA* (Lima) 3, no. 4, August 8, 1931, 4; Portal, "22 de agosto," *APRA* (Lima) 3, no. 5, August 22, 1931, 14–15.

68. "El homenaje de las mujeres a Víctor Raúl Haya de la Torre," *APRA* (Lima) 3, no. 5, August 22, 1931, 5.

69. Portal, "Panorama de América," *APRA* (Lima) 4, no. 2, September 8, 1931, 6; Portal, "Panorama de América," *APRA* (Lima) 4, no. 3, September 15, 1931, 7.

70. "Los libros del momento," *APRA* (Lima) 4, no. 2, September 8, 1931, 7.

71. "Reportaje a nuestros líderes: Magda Portal," *APRA* (Lima) 4, no. 4, September 23, 1931, 10.

72. "Los libros del momento," *APRA* (Lima) 4, no. 4, September 23, 1931, 14.

73. "Magda Portal El Comité Femenino de la Victoria recepcionó en forma magnífica a la c," *La Tribuna*, September 18, 1931, 6.

74. "Conferencia de Haya Delatorre en la Plaza de Acho," *APRA* (Lima) 4, no. 1, September 1, 1931, 8–9.

75. Werlich, *Peru*, 192.

76. Drinot, "Creole Anti-Communism," 721.

77. Pike, *Politics*, 155.

78. "Conferencia de Haya Delatorre en la Plaza de Acho."

79. Stein, *Populism*, 189.

80. Murillo Garaycochea, *Historia*, 120.

81. Stein, *Populism*, 189, 192.

82. Klarén, *Modernization*, 136.

83. Pike, *Politics*, 198–99; Chang-Rodríguez, *Una vida agónica*, 44, 104. The most detailed accounting of the 1931 election remains Stein, *Populism*, 188–202.

84. Werlich, *Peru*, 195.

85. Ciccarelli, *Militarism*, 20.

86. Sánchez, *Testimonio*, 1:362–63.

87. Portal, "Refutación al General Arévalo Cedeño," *Repertorio Americano* 24, no. 24, June 20, 1932, 371.

88. Sánchez, *Testimonio*, 1:355.

89. Masterson, *Militarism*, 47–48.

90. Klarén, *Modernization*, 137; Masterson, *Militarism*, 47–48; Stein, *Populism*, 199.

91. Sánchez, *Apuntes*, 2:16–19.

92. Pike, *Politics*, 161.

93. Sánchez, *Apuntes*, 2:16.

94. Haya, "Haya a la nación (III)," *Repertorio Americano* 24, no. 16, May 7, 1932, 246.

95. Masterson, "Soldiers, Sailors, and Apristas," 25.

96. Masterson, *Militarism*, 43, 48.

97. Portal, "Refutación al General Arévalo Cedeño," 371; Haya and Cox, *Cartas*, 20.

98. Dearing, Cable 1381: January 6, 1932, DPAELP, Correspondence, 800 1932, Volume 12, RG 84.

99. "El Comité Ejecutivo Nacional del Partido ha quedado reorganizado totalmente," *APRA* (Lima) 4, no. 16, January 7, 1932, 3.

100. Murillo Garaycochea, *Historia*, 153–54.

101. Dearing, Cable 1497: February 4, 1932, DPAELP, Correspondence, 800 1932, Volume 12, RG 84.

102. Sánchez, *Apuntes*, 2:52, 56.

103. "El director de APRA se dirije al C.E.N. del P.A.P," *APRA* (Lima) 4, no. 18, January 21, 1932, 3.

104. Pike, *Politics*, 165.

105. Murillo Garaycochea, *Historia*, 160.

106. Reedy, *Magda Portal*, 179–80.

107. Seoane, "Sobre una sentencia de muerte," *Repertorio Americano* 24, no. 19, May 28, 1932, 299–300.

108. Haya, "Haya a la nación," 217.

109. Portal, "Refutación al General Arévalo Cedeño," 371.

110. Reedy, *Magda Portal*, 179; "Notas bibliográficas: El 'Año trágico' de Serafín Delmar," *APRA* (Lima) 5, no. 9, February 1, 1934, 8.

111. "Entrevista con Magda Portal," *El Observador* (Lima), April 5, 1982.

112. Carmen Lyra, "Gloria, la hijita de Magda Portal," *Repertorio Americano* 24, no. 11, April 2, 1932, 175.

113. Murillo Garaycochea, *Historia*, 99.

114. Juan Seoane, *Hombres y rejas*, 20, 35, 73–75, 142, 263; Andradi and Portugal, "Magda Portal," 225.

115. Seoane, "Escorzo," 14.

116. Andradi and Portugal, "Magda Portal," 221–22; Seoane, "Escorzo," 15.

117. Seoane, "Escorzo," 15.

118. Andradi and Portugal, "Magda Portal," 212.

119. Juan Seoane, *Hombres y rejas*, 263.

120. Sánchez to Betancourt, March 20, 1932, *Archivo de Rómulo Betancourt*, 4:94–95.

121. Seoane, "Escorzo," 14; Portal, "La mujer en el Partido del Pueblo," Portal Estate Papers, 13.

122. Portal, "Refutación al General Arévalo Cedeño"; Portal, "Los Apristas peruanos informan y dan las gracias," *Repertorio Americano* 25, no. 12, September 24, 1932, 190.

123. Betancourt to Hermanitos, September 17, 1931, *Archivo de Rómulo Betancourt*, 3:241–49.

124. Betancourt to Mariano Picón-Salas, October 12, 1932, *Archivo de Rómulo Betancourt*, 4:328–29.

125. Betancourt to Portal, March 11, 1932, ibid., 85–86.

126. Ibid., 167.

127. Ibid., 195–97.

128. Unsigned letter, probably from Miguel Otero Silva, to "Nelly and Peter," likely Pedro and Josefina Juliac, January 1935, *Archivo de Rómulo Betancourt*, 5:216.

129. Juan Seoane, *Hombres y rejas*, 42.

130. Delmar, "Haya de la Torre," *Repertorio Americano* 26, no. 17, May 6, 1933, 270.

131. Portal, "Poemas de la prisión," *Repertorio Americano* 25, no. 22, December 10, 1932, 349–50.

132. Manuel Seoane, "Sobre una sentencia de muerte," 299; "Un gesto heroico," *Repertorio Americano* 24, no. 19, May 28, 1932, 297, 300.

Chapter 6

1. Thorndike, *El año*, 229–30, 237, 284.

2. William Burdett, "Aviation in Trujillo Revolution," DPAELP, Correspondence, 800 1932, Volume 12, RG 84.

3. Thorndike, *El año*, 237, 288, 293.

4. Díaz Paredes, *Las mujeres*, 135–36.

5. Berrocal Neciosup, "Trujillo."

6. Thorndike, *El año*, 308–9.

7. *Diario El Norte* (Trujillo), July 7, 1934, cited in Berrocal Neciosup, "Trujillo."

8. Liga de Escritores Revolucionarios del Perú, *Cantos de la Revolución*, 49–50.

9. Thorndike, *El año*, 173–74.

10. Werlich, *Peru*, 197–98.

11. Masterson, *Militarism*, 44; Masterson, "Soldiers, Sailors, and Apristas," 26.

12. Klarén, *Modernization*, 139.

13. Thorndike, *El año*, 194.

14. Fred Morris Dearing, "Man-NY#3469: Revolution, July 20, 1932," DPAELP, Correspondence, 800 1932, Volume 12, RG 84, 5.

15. Thorndike, *El año*, 227; Masterson, *Militarism*, 49–50; Werlich, *Peru*, 197–98.

16. Fred Morris Dearing, "Man-NY#3469: Revolution July 20, 1932," 5.

17. Thorndike, *El año*, 254, 246, 273, 336.

18. Werlich, *Peru*, 198.

19. William Burdett, "Cable No. 1953: Developments in the Peruvian Revolution," DPAELP, Correspondence, 800 1932, Volume 12, RG 84, 5.

20. Thorndike, *El año*, 284, 342, 351.

21. William Burdett, "Aviation in Trujillo Revolution"; William Burdett, "Cable No. 1953," 5.

22. Burdett, "Cable No. 1953," 6–7.

23. Masterson, *Militarism*, 50–51.

24. Werlich, *Peru*, 205; Klaiber, *Religion*, 148.

25. Werlich, *Peru*, 198–99.

26. Murillo Garaycochea, *Historia*, 286, 294.

27. Portal, *Hacia la mujer nueva*, 31.

28. Juan Seoane, *Hombres y rejas*, 351.

29. Werlich, *Peru*, 203–5.

30. Sánchez, *Apuntes*, 2:163.

31. Ciccarelli, "Fascism and Politics," 411.

32. Pike, *Politics*, 169; Werlich, *Peru*, 206.

33. Haya, "Discurso de VRHT a los Apristas," *APRA* (Lima) 5, no. 2, November 2, 1933, 6–7.

34. Werlich, *Peru*, 204–5.

35. "Comité Ejecutivo Nacional Partido Aprista Peruano 1933," *APRA* (Lima) 5, no. 1, November 12, 1933, unpaginated supplementary insert.

36. While Stein argued that APRA's middle-class leadership never altered its views of working-class inferiority, the 1933 CEN suggests that after the "sixteen tragic months," the leadership's efforts to include workers was more than rhetorical. Stein, *Populism*, 154–55.

37. Front matter to Portal, *Hacia la mujer nueva*.

38. Sánchez, *Apuntes*, 2:162–63.

39. Seoane, "Escorzo," 15.

40. "Reportaje a nuestros líderes: Serafín Delmar," *APRA* (Lima) 4, no. 14, December 22, 1931, 12.

41. "Reportaje a nuestros líderes: Magda Portal," *APRA* (Lima) 4, no. 4, September 23, 1931, 10.

42. "Reportaje a nuestros líderes: Julián Petrovick," *APRA* (Lima) 4, no. 10, November 13, 1931, 11.

43. "Reportaje a nuestros líderes: Luis E. Heysen," *APRA* (Lima) 4, no. 5, September 30, 1931, 4.

44. Chang-Rodríguez, *Una vida agónica*, 91, 100, 103; "Reportaje a nuestros líderes: Luis E. Heysen," *APRA* (Lima) 4, no. 5, September 30, 1931, 4; Portal, *Hacia la mujer nueva*, 16; Thorndike, *El año*, 381.

45. Heysen, *El ABC*, 20–21; emphasis in original was in all caps.

46. Portal, *Hacia la mujer nueva*, 16.

47. Heysen, "La rebelión de la mujer," *APRA* (Lima) 4, no. 13, December 4, 1931, 8–11; emphasis in original was bolded.

48. As John D. French and Mary Lynn Pedersen Cluff's work on postwar São Paulo has shown, intense political struggle from below leads to bending the boundaries of those eligible to be "mobilized" and targets women to increase their numbers. French and Cluff, "Women and Working-Class Mobilization."

49. Portal, "Las mujeres peruanas ante el proceso electoral."

50. Portal, "Definición de la mujer Aprista," *APRA* (Lima) 2, no. 3, March 18, 1931, 5.

51. Ibid.

52. Portal, "Rol de la mujer revolucionaria: El voto femenino," *APRA* (Lima) 2, no. 7, April 2, 1931, 10.

53. Portal, *Hacia la mujer nueva*, 33; emphasis in original.

54. Ibid., 51.

55. Ibid., 52–53.

56. Ibid., 42.

57. Ibid., 41, 44, 47, 53.

58. Ibid., 52.

59. Ibid., 56.

60. Ibid., 42.

61. Ibid., 43, 53.

62. Ibid., 58.

63. Ibid., 48.

64. Chambers, *From Subjects to Citizens*.

65. Portal, *Hacia la mujer nueva*, 24–25.

66. Seoane, "Escorzo," 13.

67. Haya to Portal, April 10, 1934, Benson, Box 1, Folder 1. Haya got his wish, and sent Portal a note on April 22 after their visit. "Magdita: It's good. I was very happy with your visit. I think we should always see each other because then we give each other strength." The visit touched on more than ideas, however. "I know that you have to struggle, but isn't that our life? Will we ever have the right to rest, those of us who have voiced the urgency of a permanent insurgency against everything that today overwhelms the people?" Haya to Portal, April 22, 1934, Benson, Box 1, Folder 13.

68. Portal, *Hacia la mujer nueva*, 56–57.

69. "Reportaje a nuestros líderes: Julián Petrovick," *APRA* (Lima) 4, no. 10, November 13, 1931, 11.

70. Sánchez, *Testimonio*, 1:351.

71. Ibid., 394.

72. Sánchez, *Apuntes*, 2:162–63; Sánchez, *Testimonio*, 1:351. The phrase "APRA's court historian" is Werlich's.

73. Portal, *Hacia la mujer nueva*, 48, 53–54.

74. Liga de Escritores Revolucionarios del Perú, *Cantos de la revolución*, 54–57.

75. "El Despertar del Sur"; "Nuestros líderes en gira por el país," *APRA* (Lima) 5, no. 4, December 7, 1933, 5.

76. Portal, *La trampa*, 96.

77. Díaz Paredes, *Las mujeres*, 138–39.

78. Berrocal Neciosup, "Trujillo."

79. Sánchez, *Apuntes*, 2:178.

80. Federación Aprista Juvenil, *Código de Acción FAJ*, 5–7; emphasis in original in all caps.

81. Sánchez, *Apuntes*, 2:178.

82. "Reportaje a nuestros líderes: Manuel Seoane," *APRA* (Lima) 4, no. 3, September 15, 1931, 13.
83. See "Conclusion" in Wallace Fuentes, "Becoming Magda Portal"; Wohl, *Generation of 1914*, 220.
84. Wohl, *Generation of 1914*, 220.
85. "Reportaje a nuestros líderes: Magda Portal," *APRA* (Lima) 4, no. 4, September 23, 1931, 10.
86. Betancourt, "Magda Portal y el voto femenino," *Repertorio Americano* 22, no. 21, June 6, 1931, 332.
87. "Cable 517: Ideario del PAP," *La Tribuna*, June 16, 1948, GRAELP, 350.1–360.2, Box 356, Folder: 800 APRA, RG 84.
88. Portal, *"La mujer en el Partido del Pueblo,"* xx.
89. Ibid., 10–11, 14–15; Portal, *Hacia la mujer nueva*, 26.
90. Portal, *"La mujer en el Partido del Pueblo,"* 10–12, 16.
91. Portal, *Hacia la mujer nueva*, 30–31.
92. Seoane, "Escorzo," 15.
93. Federación Aprista Juvenil, *Código de Acción FAJ*, 5; caps in original.
94. Ibid., 5.
95. Seoane, "Escorzo," 15.
96. Werlich, *Peru*, 204–5, 220.
97. Masterson, *Militarism*, 53–54.
98. Reedy, *Magda Portal*, 193–94.
99. Pike, *Politics*, 175.
100. Reedy, *Magda Portal*, 203.
101. Seoane, "Escorzo," 15.
102. Reedy, *Magda Portal*, 201.
103. Seoane to Sánchez, June 1935, #1683, Luis Alberto Sánchez Papers (1764), Historical Collections and Labor Archives, Special Collections Library, Pennsylvania State University, State College, Pennsylvania.
104. Frontispiece in *Magda Portal: Su vida y su obra.*
105. Portal, "Dawn in Jail," *Costa sur*, 117–20.
106. Portal to Graves, October 10, 1935, Benson, Box 1, Folder 1.
107. Portal, *Costa sur*, 121–23.
108. Wohl, *Generation of 1914*, 220.
109. Portal, *Costa sur*, 121–23.
110. Seoane, "Escorzo," 15.

Chapter 7

1. Haya to Sánchez, March 8, 1934, Haya and Sánchez, *Correspondencia*, 214.
2. Haya to Sánchez, March 1, 1936, Henderson, Pérez, and Sánchez, *Literature*, 200; Portal to PAP in Chile, May 1, 1936, Benson, Box 1, Folder 2.

3. Klarén, *Peru*, 280.

4. Sánchez to Godoy Alcayaga, June 12, 1939, Henderson, Pérez, and Sánchez, *Literature*, 114; Reedy, *Magda Portal*, 202, 206.

5. Sánchez to Haya, December 22, 1939, Haya and Sánchez, *Correspondencia*, 393.

6. Drake, "International Crises," 110–11, 113, 117–18.

7. Davies and Villanueva, *300 documentos*, 423.

8. "Magda Portal, líder Aprista, sufrió prisiones, es antiimperialista y no cree en el Tío Sam," *Ercilla* (Santiago de Chile), November 29, 1939, Portal Estate Papers, 8; Graves to Portal, September 30, 1939, Benson, Box 1, Folder 3.

9. Sosa Abascal, *Rómulo Betancourt*, 437, 440.

10. Drake, "International Crises," 122.

11. Certificate of Participation, Primer Congreso de Partidos Democráticos y Populares de América Latina, Santiago, October 3–8, 1940, Portal Estate Papers.

12. Drake, "International Crises," 122, 124.

13. Ibid., 119, 121–22, 127–28.

14. Sánchez to Haya, January 9, 1943, Haya and Sánchez, *Correspondencia*, 409.

15. Sánchez to Haya, December 22, 1939, ibid., 389–92.

16. Sánchez to Haya, January 9, 1943, ibid., 408, 412.

17. Sánchez to Haya, March 9, 1943, ibid., 419–20.

18. Ibid., 419–20.

19. Portal to Haya, June 20, 1941, Portal Estate Papers, 1–3.

20. Ibid., 4.

21. Haya to Portal, July 7, 1940, Portal Estate Papers.

22. Portal to Haya, June 20, 1941, Portal Estate Papers, 4.

23. Schneider, *Comparative*, 260.

24. Haya to Sánchez, March 29, 1943, Haya and Sánchez, *Correspondencia*, 421, 422, 430, 431, 434, 435.

25. Haya to Sánchez, March 29, 1943, ibid., 435.

26. Ibid., 422–23.

27. Betancourt to Portal, March 19, 1945, Benson, Box 1, Folder 7.

28. Del Mazo to Portal, March 23, 1945, Benson, Box 1, Folder 7.

29. Betancourt to Portal, March 19, 1945, Benson, Box 1, Folder 7.

30. Alfonso Tealdo, "Historia del APRA: Entrevista con Magda Portal," *¡DDT!* (Lima), May 17, 1950, Portal Estate Papers.

31. Reedy, *Magda Portal*, 177.

32. Vásquez Díaz to Delmar, March 2, 1942, Benson, Box 1, Folder 14.

33. Portal, *La trampa*, 96–97.

34. Vásquez Díaz to Portal, December 29, 1944, Benson, Box 1, Folder 7.

35. Weaver and Portal, *Peruvian Rebel*, 141.

36. Villanueva, *La gran persecución*, 201; Barquero, "Serafín Delmar"; Weaver and Portal, *Peruvian Rebel*, 141.

37. Weaver and Portal, *Peruvian Rebel*, 141.

38. [Illegible] to Portal, November 4, 1945, Benson, Box 1, Folder 7.

39. Andradi and Portugal, "Magda Portal," 228–29; Reedy, *Magda Portal*, 87–89, 95.

40. Schneider, *Comparative*, 258; Pike, *Politics*, 225.

41. Bertram, "Peru," 426, 404.

42. Pierrot, "Confidential Cable No. 700: A Study of Apra: 1945–1948," August 31, 1948, CGRAELP, 1936–1963, Box 53: 1948, 800–810.8, Folder: 1948 800, RG 84, 15–16.

43. Drake, "International Crises," 127.

44. Pierrot, "Confidential Cable No. 700: A Study of Apra," 7, 15, 17.

45. Schneider, *Comparative*, 273.

46. Drake, "International Crises," 128.

47. Reedy, *Magda Portal*, 235.

48. Andradi and Portugal, "Magda Portal," 215; [Illegible] to Portal, November 4, 1945.

49. Portal to Haya, July 16, 1946, Portal Estate Papers.

50. Haya to Portal, July 31, 1946, Portal Estate Papers.

51. Chang-Rodríguez, *Pensamiento y acción*, 300–301; Villanueva, *La gran persecución*, 280–83.

52. Klarén, *Modernization*, 259–60, 273.

53. Parker, *Idea of the Middle Class*.

54. Drinot, "Creole Anti-Communism."

55. Heilman, "We Will No Longer Be Servile"; Nugent, *Modernity*.

56. Pike, *Politics*, 225.

57. Chanduví Torres, *APRA por dentro*, 342.

58. Andradi and Portugal, "Magda Portal," 216.

59. Pierrot, "Confidential Cable No. 700: A Study of Apra," 11.

60. Klarén, *Peru*, 297.

61. Chanduví Torres, *APRA por dentro*, 344.

62. Pierrot, "Confidential Cable No. 700: A Study of Apra," 18.

63. Weaver, "1981 Portal Interview," 21.

64. Weaver and Portal, *Peruvian Rebel*, 145–46.

65. Portal, *"La mujer en el Partido del Pueblo,"* 45.

66. "Hoy se clausura la Convención femenina Aprista," *La Tribuna*, November 24, 1946, 3; Reedy, *Magda Portal*, 241.

67. "En Asamblea Plenaria se denominó 'Zoila Victoria de la Torre de Haya,'" *La Tribuna*, November 20, 1946, 13.

68. "El hogar y el estado," *La Tribuna*, November 25, 1946, 6.

69. Weaver, "1981 Portal Interview," 21.

70. "Magda Portal fue nombrada por unanimidad Presidenta," *La Tribuna*, November 16, 1946, 10.

71. Portal's sister, cited in Weaver and Portal, *Peruvian Rebel*, 150–51.

72. Ibid., 150–51.

73. Reedy, *Magda Portal*, 245; Weaver and Portal, *Peruvian Rebel*, 153–54.

74. Portal, *Constancia del ser*, 130.

75. Forgues, *Palabra viva*, 54.

76. Garrison, *"Empire of Ideals,"* 40.

77. Werlich, *Peru*, 239.

78. Prialé, "Pone a órdenes de la policía su archivo el PdP," *La Tribuna*, January 14, 1947, 1.

79. Pierrot, "Confidential Cable No. 700: A Study of Apra," 1, 17.

80. Andradi and Portugal, "Magda Portal," 229–31.

81. Schneider, *Comparative*, 273.

82. Undated clippings from *La Tribuna* and *El País* (Venezuela) collected in clippings album 1929–1948, Benson, Box 10, Folder 10.

83. Pierrot, "Confidential Cable No. 700: A Study of Apra," 17–18.

84. Luna Vega, *Contribución*, 87.

85. Pierrot, "Confidential Cable No. 700: A Study of Apra," 18, 20.

86. Werlich, *Peru*, 235.

87. Pierrot, "Confidential Cable No. 700: A Study of Apra," 20–21.

88. Klarén, *Peru*, 298.

89. Chanduví Torres, *APRA por dentro*, 370–71.

90. Werlich, *Peru*, 241–42.

91. Klarén, *Peru*, 296.

92. Pierrot, "Cable No. 517: Conclusions of the Second National Congress of Apra (Party of the People)," June 28, 1948, GRAELP, 350.1–360.2, Box 356, Folder: 800 APRA, RG 84, 6.

93. "'La mujer como todo militante Aprista será elegida delegada al Congreso,'" *La Tribuna*, May 15, 1948, 7; "El aprismo reivindica en la mujer su derecho de ciudadanía integral," *La Tribuna*, May 28, 1948, 8.

94. Pierrot, "Cable No. 517," 6.

95. Pierrot, "Cable No. 517," 2, 6.

96. Chanduví Torres, *APRA por dentro*, 387–88.

97. Ibid., 387.

98. Sánchez, *Apuntes*, 3:240; Pike, *Politics*, 221.

99. Chanduví Torres, *APRA por dentro*, 387–88.

100. "Informative Bulletin," June 1948, Pierrot, "Cable No. 517."

101. Pareja Pflücker, *Arturo Sabroso*, 88.

102. "Expresión de fraternidad Aprista en el homenaje del sábado a Magda Portal," *La Tribuna*, June 11, 1948, 6.

103. Werlich, *Peru*, 241–42.

104. Masterson, "Soldiers, Sailors, and Apristas," 30–32. See also Pike, *Politics*, 231–32.

Chapter 8

1. "Naval Attaché Report, October 7, 1948," CGRAELP, 1936–1963, Box 53: 1958, 800–810.8, Folder 1948 800, RG 84, 2–3; Werlich, *Peru*, 244.

2. "Naval Attaché Report, October 7, 1948," 4–5.

3. Harold Tittman, "Confidential Airgram to Secretary of State, October 11, 1948," CGRAELP, 1936–1963, Box 53: 1958, 800–810.8, Folder 1948 800, RG 84.

4. "SECRET Memorandum, October 27, 1948," CGRAELP, 1936–1963, Box 53: 1958, 800–810.8, Folder 1948 800, RG 84.

5. Werlich, *Peru*, 244–45.

6. "Naval Attaché Report, October 7, 1948," 3.

7. Andradi and Portugal, "Magda Portal," 220.

8. Weaver, "1981 Portal Interview," 22.

9. Schneider, *Comparative*, 273.

10. Drake, "International Crises," 134.

11. Bertram, "Peru," 430.

12. Quoted in Luna Vega, *Contribución*, 86.

13. Villanueva, *La tragedia*, 138, 145–46.

14. Ibid., 161; Luna Vega, *Contribución*, 86.

15. Tittman, "Despatch No. 805," CGRAELP, 1936–1963, Box 53: 1948, 800–810.8, Folder: 1948 800, RG 84.

16. "SECRET Memorandum, October 27, 1948."

17. Tittman, "Confidential Telegram, October 6, 1948, 5 pm," CGRAELP, 1936–1963, Box 53: 1948, 800–810.8, Folder: 1948 800, RG 84.

18. Tittman, "Confidential Despatch 922," CGRAELP, 1936–1963, Box 53: 1948, 800–810.8, Folder: 1948 800, RG 84.

19. Bertram, "Peru," 430, 404.

20. Sánchez, *Apuntes*, 3:242–43.

21. Villanueva, *La gran persecución*.

22. Ibid., 319.

23. Reedy, *Magda Portal*, 264.

24. Masterson, "Soldiers, Sailors, and Apristas," 35–36; Bertram, "Peru," 432.

25. "Naval Attaché Report, October 7, 1948," 4.

26. Tittman, "Cable No. 424," CGRAELP, 322.1–350, Box 380, Folder: 350 Revolutions 1950, RG 84.

27. Portal Estate Papers, "La vida que yo viví: Segunda parte," Benson, Box 2, Folder 8, 2.

28. Nugent, "States, Secrecy, Subversives," 681, 686, 692–93.

29. Ibid., 688–89, 694, 698.

30. Ibid., 694–95.

31. Portal to President of the Military Governing Junta, December 16, 1949, Benson, Box 10, Folder 8.

32. Portal Estate Papers, "La vida que yo viví: Segunda parte," Benson, Box 2, Folder 8, 2.

33. Villanueva, *La gran persecución*, 392, 410.

34. "Magda Portal: No quiere hablar," *Cocodrilo* (Lima) 1, no. 2, April 4, 1950, Portal Estate Papers.

35. Reedy, *Magda Portal*, 260.

36. "Magda Portal, líder Aprista, acusa al APRA," *Semanario Peruano* (Lima) 4, no. 7, February 13, 1950, Benson, Box 11, Folder 3, 5.

37. Nugent, "States, Secrecy, Subversives," 690, 695–96.

38. Ibid.

39. "Magda Portal, líder Aprista, acusa al APRA," 6.

40. Tittman, "Cable No. 424."

41. Portal, "Trazos cortados, Segunda parte [drafts]," Benson, 2.

42. Portal, *¿Quiénes traicionaron al pueblo?*, 25.

43. Ibid.

44. Ibid., 8–10.

45 Andradi and Portugal, "Magda Portal," 217, 220, 226.

46. Ibid., 226, 217.

47. Weaver, "1981 Portal Interview," 19.

48. Portal, *¿Quiénes traicionaron al pueblo?*, 9.

49. Ibid., 22; Reedy, *Magda Portal*, 256.

50. *La Crónica*, February 11, 1950, Benson, Box 11, Folder 3, 8.

51. Portal, *¿Quiénes traicionaron al pueblo?*, 19–20; Tealdo, "Historia del APRA: Entrevista con Magda Portal."

52. Pierrot, "Cable No. 517," 5.

53. Portal, *¿Quiénes traicionaron al pueblo?*, 21.

54. Chanduví Torres, *APRA por dentro*, 387–88.

55. Carlos Hall, "Cable No. 83 from Santiago Desk," GRAELP, 350.1–360.2, Box 381, Folder 350.1, 1952, RG 84.

56. Portal, *La trampa*, 122.

57. *La Crónica*, February 11, 1950, Benson, Box 11, Folder 3, 8.

58. Andradi and Portugal, "Magda Portal," 218.

59. Weaver, "1981 Portal Interview," 23; Portal, *¿Quiénes traicionaron al pueblo?*, 23.

60. Reedy, *Magda Portal*, 265.

61. Tittman, "Cable No. 424."

62. Reedy, *Magda Portal*, 245.

63. Pierrot, "Confidential Cable No. 700: A Study of Apra," 25.

64. Reedy, *Magda Portal*, 266–67.

65. Portal, *¿Quiénes traicionaron al pueblo?*, 10.

66. Haya to Sánchez, March 29, 1943, Haya and Sánchez, *Correspondencia*, 433.

67. Portal, *¿Quiénes traicionaron al pueblo?*, 29.

68. Weaver, "1981 Portal Interview," 23.

69. Portal, *¿Quiénes traicionaron al pueblo?*, 29.

70. *La Crónica*, February 11, 1950, Benson, Box 11, Folder 3, 8.

71. Tealdo, "Historia del APRA: Entrevista con Magda Portal."

72. Magda Portal, "Discurso de Clausura," *Tiempos* (Lima) 1, no. 1, September 15, 1950, 14.

73. "Conclusiones del III Congreso Revisionista," *Tiempos* (Lima) 1, no. 1, September 15, 1950, 14–15, 21, 27.

74. "El Aprismo está liquidado," *Tiempos* (Lima) 1, no. 1, September 15, 1950, 16.

75. Pierrot, "Confidential Cable No. 700: A Study of Apra," 24.

76. Sánchez, *Testimonio*, 3:1011–12.

77. Major Villanueva to Portal, June 6, 1950, Benson, Box 1, Folder 11.

78. "El Aprismo está liquidado."

79. Portal, "Discurso de Clausura," 27.

80. "Movimiento de Juventud Revisionista," *Tiempos* (Lima) 1, no. 7, October 27, 1950, 16.

81. "Conclusiones del III Congreso Revisionista," 22.

82. "Revisionismo," *Tiempos* (Lima) 1, no. 2, September 22, 1950, 5; "Convención ex-Apristas," *Tiempos* (Lima) 1, no. 2, September 22, 1950, 16; "Una carta," *Tiempos* (Lima) 1, no. 6, October 20, 1950, 17.

83. "Movimiento de Juventud Revisionista," *Tiempos* (Lima) 1, no. 7, October 27, 1950, 16; "Una carta," *Tiempos* (Lima) 1, no. 6, October 20, 1950, 17.

84. "Editora 'Tiempos,'" *Tiempos* (Lima) 1, no. 7, October 27, 1950, 10.

85. Nugent, "States, Secrecy, Subversives," 695.

86. Luis Varrios Llona to Seoane, December 15, 1951, in Chanduví Torres, *APRA por dentro*, 506–7.

87. Nicanor Mujica Álvarez Calderón to Luis Barrios, January 9, 1951, in ibid., 545.

88. Weaver, "1981 Portal Interview," 23.

89. "Editora 'Tiempos.'"

90. Weaver and Portal, *Peruvian Rebel*, 163.

91. Andradi and Portugal, "Magda Portal," 219; Díaz Paredes, *Las mujeres*, 151–52.

92. Weaver and Portal, *Peruvian Rebel*, 164.

Chapter 9

1. Villanueva, *La tragedia*, 195.

2. Chanduví Torres, *APRA por dentro*, 469; Partido del Pueblo, *40 preguntas*, 9–10.

3. Haya and Sánchez, *Correspondencia*, 2:201; Chanduví Torres, *APRA por dentro*, 469.

4. Villanueva, *La tragedia*, 195.

5. Werlich, *Peru*, 248.

6. Chanduví Torres, *APRA por dentro*, 469.

7. "El Jerarca Número 2," *Tiempos* (Lima) 1, no. 8, November 3, 1950, 16; Braun, *The Assassination of Gaitán*.

8. "El Jerarca Número 2," *Tiempos* (Lima) 1, no. 8, November 3, 1950, 16.

9. Sánchez, *Testimonio*, 3:910.

10. "Breve reseña de una vida grande," *La Tribuna*, September 12, 1963, cited in Seoane, *Izquierda aprista*, 363–65.

11. Seoane to Sánchez, December 11, 1949, annotated in Henderson, Pérez, and Sánchez, *Literature*, 405.

12. Carlos Hall, "Cable No. 83 from Santiago Desk," 1. Seoane to Sánchez, February 20, 1950, in Henderson, Pérez, and Sánchez, *Literature*, 409.

13. Seoane, *Carta de 1952*, 8.

14. Luna Vega, *Contribución*, 95; Seoane, *Carta de 1952*.

15. Pike, *Politics*, 221.

16. Carlos Hall, "Cable No. 83 from Santiago Desk," 2.

17. Seoane, *Carta de 1952*, 61.

18. "Seudo Congreso Aprista," *Tiempos* (Lima) 1, no. 8, November 3, 1950, 17; Chanduví Torres, *APRA por dentro*, 480.

19. Pike, *Politics*, 221.

20. Pierrot, "Confidential Cable No. 700, A Study of Apra."

21. Seoane, *Carta de 1952*, 4, 61.

22. Sánchez, *Apuntes*, 3:240.

23. "Movimiento de Juventud Revisionista," *Tiempos* (Lima) 1, no. 7, October 27, 1950, 16.

24. Chanduví Torres, *APRA por dentro*, 491.

25. Portal to Olga, May 13, 1960, Benson, Box 1, Folder 12, 2.

26. Portal, *La trampa*, 102, 122.

27. Ibid., 84–86.

28. Ibid., 103–4.

29. Forgues, *Palabra viva*, 55.

30. Portal, *La trampa*, 76, 104–5, 113–15.

31. Ibid., 102, 122.

32. *El Observador* (Lima), April 5, 1982, cited in Luna Vega, *Contribución*, 117.

33. Portal, *La trampa*, 122. She repeats this complaint in later interviews. León de Vivero's faction "had it in for me," she remembers, and male leaders "always" met when she was absent. Andradi and Portugal, "Magda Portal," 221.

34. Portal, *La trampa*, 102, 122.

35. Ibid., 84.

36. Ibid., 90–91.

37. Ibid., 87–92.

38. Ibid., 104, 40.

39. Portal, *¿Quiénes traicionaron al pueblo?*, 27–28.

40. Ibid., 62.

41. Luis Barrios to Haya, July 27, 1949, reprinted in Chanduví Torres, *APRA por dentro*, 477.

42. *El Observador*, April 5, 1982, cited in Luna Vega, *Contribución*, 117.

43. Weaver, "1981 Portal Interview," 23.

44. Andradi and Portugal, "Magda Portal," 221.

45. Díaz Paredes, *Las mujeres*, 143–45.

46. Weaver and Portal, *Peruvian Rebel*, 150–51.

47. Chaney, "Old and New Feminisms," 341.

48. Merritt, Effron, and Monin, "Moral Self-Licensing."

49. Andradi and Portugal, "Magda Portal," 221.

50. Portal, *La trampa*, 76, 104–5, 113–15.

51. Ibid., 116, 124–27.

52. Andradi and Portugal, "Magda Portal," 219.

53. Mármol and Dalton, *Miguel Mármol*, 205.

54. Macedo, *La vida íntima*.

55. Pike, *Politics*, 101.

56. Interview, December 29, 1969, archived in *Robert Jackson Alexander Papers: The Interview Collection*, Microfilm (Leiden: IDC Publishers), 2002.

57. Portal Estate Papers, "La vida que yo viví," Benson, Box 2, Folder 7, Proemio, 4.

58. Lancaster, "Tolerance," 262–64.

59. French, "Rethinking Police Violence," 170; Taussig, *Defacement*, 51.

60. "Los enemigos de Haya lo llamaban 'Lucy,'" *Velaverde* (Lima), February 24, 2014.

61. Pike, *Politics*, 164.

62. Ray Josephs, "Uncle Sam's Latin Salesman," *Collier's*, October 16, 1948, cited in ibid., xiii.

63. Eduardo Sierralta Lorca, *El Apra y la sombra*, cited in Pike, *Politics*, 117.

64. Portal, *La trampa*, 84.

65. Andradi and Portugal, "Magda Portal," 226–27.

66. Portal to Portugal, November 7, 1957, Benson, Box 1, Folder 12; Reedy, *Magda Portal*, 282.

67. Ladislao Meza, "Magda Portal, Laureada," *Mundial*, July 27, 1923.

68. Forgues, *Palabra viva*, 54.

69. "Reportaje a nuestros líderes: Magda Portal," *APRA* (Lima) 4, no. 4, September 23, 1931, 10.

70. Portal, "Mi experiencia en la lucha por la emancipación de la mujer," undated manuscript, Portal Estate Papers, 1.

71. Forgues, *Palabra viva*, 53, 60. Portal twice deflected the "militant feminist" label. Forgues asks Portal if Micaela Bastidas, the wife of the colonial rebel Túpac Amaru, was "also . . . a symbol, before its time, of militant feminism?" Portal replies: "Not actually, but instead [a symbol] of a woman who is capable of giving herself, of surrendering herself. She was a leader" (60).

72. Sánchez, *Testimonio*, 1:380.

73. Andradi and Portugal, "Magda Portal," 215.

74. Portal, *Hacia la mujer nueva*, 16–17; Portal, "El voto femenino debe ser calificado," *APRA* (Lima) 5, no. 15, December 31, 1931, 7.

75. Portal, "Rol de la mujer revolucionaria: El voto femenino," *APRA* (Lima) 2, no. 7, April 2, 1931, 10.

76. Chang-Rodríguez, *Pensamiento y acción*, 342.

77. R. M. de Lambert, "Cable 520," CGRAELP, 1936–1963, Box 53: 1948, 800–810.8, Folder 800, Confidential 800, RG 84.

78. Portal, "Definición de la mujer Aprista," *APRA* (Lima) 2, no. 3, March 18, 1931, 5.

79. Portal, "Voto político para la mujer chilena," January 1941, Benson, Box 4, Folder 1.

80. Portal, "Rumbo femenino," *Repertorio Americano* 32, no. 9, September 5, 1936, 143; Reedy, *Magda Portal*, 203.

81. Portal, "Rumbo femenino"; emphasis in original.

82. Portal to Graves, October 10, 1935, Benson, Box 1, Folder 1.

83. Portal, *Hacia la mujer nueva*, 49, 53–54.

84. Forgues, *Palabra viva*, 53, 60.

85. Mead, "Beneficent Maternalism," 137.

86. Portal to Graves, October 10, 1935, Benson, Box 1, Folder 1.

87. Goldstein, *The Post-Revolutionary Self*, 11.

88. María Jesús Alvarado, "La educación moral en el hogar," *El Hogar y la Escuela* 1, no. 11, June 1, 1909, 320, cited in Mannarelli, *Limpias*, 120.

89. Portal, "Rumbo femenino."

90. Reedy, *Magda Portal*, 293–94.

91. Weaver and Portal, *Peruvian Rebel*, 179.

92. Forgues, *Palabra viva*, 54.

93. Weaver, "1981 Portal Interview," 14.

94. *La Crónica*, February 11, 1950, Benson, Box 11, Folder 3, 8.

95. "Conclusiones del III Congreso Revisionista," 15.

96. Andradi and Portugal, "Magda Portal," 218.

97. Weaver, "1981 Portal Interview," 21.

98. Portal, *¿Quiénes traicionaron al pueblo?*, 22.

99. "Emitieron sus dictámenes las Comisiones de Ideario, Programa Político y Estatutos," *La Tribuna*, May 31, 1948, 5; "Importantes Acuerdos Adoptó el Congreso del Partido en su Tercera Sesión Plenaria," *La Tribuna*, June 1, 1948, 6.

100. "Importantes dictámenes sobre problemas de interés nacional fueron aprobados en el Plenario del lunes," *La Tribuna*, June 2, 1948, 7.

101. Comando Nacional de Capacitación Femenina del Partido del Pueblo, "40 preguntas y 40 respuestas sobre el Comando de Capacitación Femenina Primera de la Organización," Benson, Box 10, Folder 5, 3–5.

102. Andradi and Portugal, "Magda Portal," 218.

103. Ibid., 223–24; Portal Estate Papers, "La vida que yo viví," Benson, Box 2, Folder 7, 75–76.
104. Andradi and Portugal, "Magda Portal," 229.
105. Ibid., 229, 221.
106. Lavrin, "Some Final Considerations," 315.
107. Andradi and Portugal, "Magda Portal," 229.
108. Ibid.
109. Ibid.
110. Reedy, *Magda Portal*, 296–98.
111. Portal, *Flora Tristán*, 12, 14–15.
112. Ibid., 36–38, 40.
113. Ibid., 97, 101.
114. Ibid., 102, 48–49.
115. Forgues, *Palabra viva*, 54–55.
116. Ibid., 57.
117. Ibid., 54.

Conclusion

1. Reedy, *Magda Portal*, 282–83, 279, 288, 294–96.
2. Andradi and Portugal, "Magda Portal," 221.
3. Forgues, *Palabra viva*, 55.
4. Portal to Graves, October 10, 1935, Benson, Box 1, Folder 1.
5. Betancourt to Portal, July 27, 1952, Benson, Box 1, Folder 11.
6. Ibid.
7. Ibid.
8. See Velasco, *Barrio Rising*.
9. Portal to Olga, May 13, 1960, Benson, Box 1, Folder 12, 2.
10. Portal, "Trazos cortados [drafts]," 41.
11. Portal to Olga, May 13, 1960, Benson, Box 1, Folder 12, 2.
12. Weaver and Portal, *Peruvian Rebel*, 177.
13. Ibid., 178, 183.
14. Reedy, *Magda Portal*, 282–83, 279, 288, 294–96.
15. Bertram, "Peru," 403, 405.
16. Villanueva, *La tragedia*, 9.
17. Andradi and Portugal, "Magda Portal," 226–27.
18. Pierrot, "Confidential Cable No. 700: A Study of Apra," 24–25.
19. Ibid.
20. Portal to Olga, May 13, 1960, Benson, Box 1, Folder 12, 2.
21. Mármol, *Miguel Mármol*, 205.
22. Saldaña-Portillo, *Revolutionary Imagination*, 78–79.
23. Butler, *Deconstructing an Icon*, 64, 76; Rodríguez, *Women, Guerrillas, and Love*, 33–34.

24. Saldaña-Portillo, *Revolutionary Imagination*, 78–79.

25. Portal, *Hacia la mujer nueva*, 51–52.

26. María Julia Luna de Ciudad, "Magda Portal: Jardinera Política," *Somos Mujeres* (Peru), 7, no. 43, 2001, CENDOC-Mujer, No. 36627.

27. Díaz Paredes, *Las mujeres*, 151–53.

28. Larriva de Llona, *Cartas a mi hijo*, 227.

29. Seoane, "Escorzo," 15.

30. Weaver and Portal, *Peruvian Rebel*, 184–85; Reedy, *Magda Portal*, 325–26.

Bibliography

Archives

Centro de Documentación sobre la Mujer (CENDOC-Mujer), Lima, Peru.

Classified General Records. American Embassy, Lima, Peru.

Diplomatic Posts. American Embassy, Lima, Peru.

General Records. American Embassy, Lima, Peru.

Graves, Anna Melissa. Papers. Archives of Labor History and Urban Affairs, Wayne State University, Detroit, Michigan.

Portal Estate Papers, Lima, Peru. In care of Rocío Revolledo Pareja, now deposited at the Biblioteca Nacional del Perú (BNP) and available electronically at http://www.lib.utexas.edu/taro/utlac/00221/lac-00221.html#series4 as 2011 Additions to the Nettie Lee Benson Library Special Collections, University of Texas at Austin, Austin, Texas.

Portal, Magda. Papers. Nettie Lee Benson Library Special Collections, University of Texas at Austin, Austin, Texas.

Record Group 84: Records of the Foreign Service Posts of the Department of State. National Archives deposited at College Park, Maryland.

Sánchez, Luis Alberto. Papers (1764). Historical Collections and Labor Archives, The Eberly Family Special Collections Library, Pennsylvania State University, State College, Pennsylvania.

Newspapers and Periodicals

Amauta (Lima, Peru)

APRA (Lima, Peru)

Boletín de las Universidades Populares González Prada (Lima, Peru)

Claridad (Buenos Aires, Argentina)

La Crónica (Lima, Peru)

La Tribuna: Diario Informativo de la Mañana (Lima, Peru)

Mundial (Lima, Peru)
Repertorio Americano (San José, Costa Rica)
Tiempos: Revista de Historia y Cultura (Lima, Peru)

Books and Articles

Alexander, Robert J., and John D. French. *Robert Jackson Alexander Papers, 1890 (1945)–1999: The Interview Collection.* Leiden: IDC Publishers, 2002.

Andradi, Esther, and Ana María Portugal. "Magda Portal, escritora y política: 'Yo soy Magda Portal.'" In *Ser mujer en el Perú*, 209–32. Lima: Tokapu Editores, 1979.

Apollinaire, Guillaume. *Alcools.* Edited by Anthony Edward Pilkington. Oxford: Blackwell, 1970.

Archivo de Rómulo Betancourt, Tomo 2: 1930. Caracas: Editorial Fundación Rómulo Betancourt, 1990.

Archivo de Rómulo Betancourt, Tomo 3: 1931. Caracas: Editorial Fundación Rómulo Betancourt, 1991.

Archivo de Rómulo Betancourt, Tomo 4: 1932. Caracas: Editorial Fundación Rómulo Betancourt, 1994.

Archivo de Rómulo Betancourt, Tomo 5: 1933–1935. Caracas: Editorial Fundación Rómulo Betancourt en coedición con el Congreso de la República, 1996.

Arrington Jr., Melvin S. "Magda Portal, Vanguard Critic." In *Reinterpreting the Spanish American Essay: Women Writers of the 19th and 20th Centuries,* edited by Doris Meyer, 148–56. Austin: University of Texas Press, 1995.

Banner, Lois W. "Biography as History." *The American Historical Review* 114, no. 3 (2009): 579–86.

Barquero, J. "Serafín Delmar, precursor de la literatura social del Perú." http://www.pueblocontinente.com/serafin_del_mar_pc.pdf (accessed July 8, 2009).

Basadre, Jorge. *Historia de la República del Perú.* 10 vols. Lima: Ediciones "Historia," 1964.

———. "La aristocracia y las clases medias civiles en el Perú republicano." *Mercurio Peruano* 437–440 (1963): 461–71.

Berger, John. *Ways of Seeing.* London: BBC and Penguin, 1972.

Berrocal Neciosup, Leonel. "Trujillo: La revolución de 1932." http://www.voltairenet.org/article160918.html (accessed October 14, 2009).

Bertram, Geoffrey. "Peru, 1930–1960." In *The Cambridge History of Latin America.* Vol. 8, *Latin America Since 1930: Spanish South America,* edited by Leslie Bethell, 385–449. Cambridge: Cambridge University Press, 1991.

Braun, Herbert. *The Assassination of Gaitán: Public Life and Urban Violence in Colombia.* Madison: University of Wisconsin Press, 2003.

Butler, Krissie. "Deconstructing an Icon: Fidel Castro and Revolutionary Masculinity." PhD diss., University of Kentucky, 2012.

Castañeda Vielakamen, Esther. *El vanguardismo literario en el Perú: Estudio y selección de la revista Flechas (1924)*. La Victoria, Peru: Amaru Editores, 1989.

Chambers, Sarah C. *From Subjects to Citizens: Honor, Gender, and Politics in Arequipa, Peru, 1780–1854*. University Park: Pennsylvania State University Press, 1999.

Chanduví Torres, Luis. *El APRA por dentro: Lo que hice, lo que vi, y lo que sé, 1931–1957*. Lima: N.p., 1988.

Chaney, Elsa M. "Old and New Feminisms in Latin America: The Case of Peru and Chile." *Journal of Marriage and the Family* 35, no. 2 (1973): 331–43.

Chang-Rodríguez, Eugenio. *Pensamiento y acción en González Prada, Mariátegui y Haya de la Torre*. Lima: Fondo Editorial, Pontificia Universidad Católica del Perú, 2012.

———. *Una vida agónica: Víctor Raúl Haya de la Torre, Testimonio de parte*. Lima: Fondo Editorial del Congreso del Perú, 2007.

Ciccarelli, Orazio Andrea. "Fascism and Politics in Peru during the Benavides Regime, 1933–39: The Italian Perspective." *Hispanic American Historical Review* 70, no. 3 (1990): 405–32.

———. *Militarism, Aprismo, and Violence in Peru: The Presidential Election of 1931*. Buffalo, N.Y.: Council on International Studies, State University of New York at Buffalo, 1973.

Claridad: Órgano de la Federación Obrera Local de Lima y de la Juventud Libre del Perú. Edición en facsímile. Lima: Editora Amauta, 1994.

Cossío del Pomar, Felipe. *Víctor Raúl: Biografía de Haya de la Torre*. Mexico City: Editorial Cultura, 1961.

Davies, Thomas M. Jr., and Víctor Villanueva. *300 documentos para la historia del APRA: Conspiraciones apristas de 1935 a 1939*. Lima: Editorial Horizonte, 1978.

Delmar, Serafín. *Los campesinos y otros condenados*. Santiago de Chile: Editorial Orbe, 1943.

Delmar, Serafín, and Magda Portal. *El derecho de matar*. La Paz: Impresa Continental, 1926.

Del Mazo, Gabriel. *La Reforma Universitaria*. Vol. 1, *El movimiento argentino*. Lima: Universidad Nacional Mayor de San Marcos, 1967.

Díaz Paredes, María Luz. *Las mujeres de Haya: Ocho historias de pasión y rebeldía*. Lima: Editorial Planeta, 2007.

Drake, Paul W. "International Crises and Popular Movements in Latin America: Chile and Peru from the Great Depression to the Cold War." In *Latin America in the 1940s: War and Postwar Transitions*, edited by David Rock, 109–40. Berkeley: University of California Press, 1994.

———. *The Money Doctor in the Andes: The Kemmerer Missions, 1923–1933*. Durham, N.C.: Duke University Press, 1989.

Drinot, Paulo. *The Allure of Labor: Workers, Race, and the Making of the Peruvian State.* Durham, N.C.: Duke University Press, 2011.

———. "Creole Anti-Communism: Labor, the Peruvian Communist Party, and APRA, 1930–1934." *Hispanic American Historical Review* 92, no. 4 (2012): 703–36, doi:10.1215/00182168-1727981.

Fasey, Rosemary. "The 'Shock of Recognition': Alberti's Indebtedness to Russian Writing." *Revista Canadiense de Estudios Hispánicos* 24, no. 1 (1999): 87–104, doi:10.2307/27763596.

Federación Aprista Juvenil. *Código de Acción FAJ.* Lima: Editorial Cooperativa Aprista Atahualpa, 1934.

Forgues, Roland. *Palabra viva: Las poetas se desnudan.* Lima: Editorial El Quijote, 1991.

Franco, Jean. *César Vallejo: The Dialectics of Poetry and Silence.* Cambridge: Cambridge University Press, 1976.

French, Jan Hoffman. "Rethinking Police Violence in Brazil: Unmasking the Public Secret of Race." *Latin American Politics and Society* 55, no. 4 (2013): 161–81.

French, John D. "Social History and the Study of 'Great Men'? The *Hispanic American Historical Review,* William Spence Robertson (1872–1956), and the Disciplinary Debate about Biography." *Anuario Colombiano de Historia Social y de la Cultura* 40, Supplement 1 (2013): 99–138.

French, John D., and Mary Lynn Pedersen Cluff. "Women and Working-Class Mobilization in Postwar São Paulo, 1945–1948." In *The Gendered Worlds of Latin American Women Workers: From Household and Factory to the Union Hall and Ballot Box,* edited by John D. French and Daniel James, 176–207. Durham, N.C.: Duke University Press, 1997.

Gálvez, José. *Una Lima que se va.* Lima: Editorial P. T. C. M., 1947.

García-Bryce, Iñigo. "Transnational Activist: Magda Portal and the American Popular Revolutionary Alliance (APRA), 1926–1950." *The Americas* 70, no. 4 (2014): 677–706.

Garret, Gary Richard. "The Oncenio of Augusto B. Leguía: Middle Sector Government and Leadership in Peru, 1919–1930." Albuquerque: University of New Mexico, 1973.

Garrison, Justin D. *"An Empire of Ideals": The Chimeric Imagination of Ronald Reagan.* New York: Routledge, 2013.

Goldstein, Jan. *The Post-Revolutionary Self: Politics and Psyche in France, 1750–1850.* Cambridge, Mass.: Harvard University Press, 2005.

Gómez, Alejandro. *Rómulo Betancourt y el Partido Comunista de Costa Rica, 1931–1935.* Caracas: Fondo Editorial de Humanidades y Educación, Universidad Central de Venezuela, 1985.

González de Fanning, Teresa. *Educación femenina. Colección de artículos pedagógicos, morales y sociológicos.* Lima: Tipografía El Lucero, 1905.

Guardia, Sara Beatriz. *El amor como acto cotidiano.* Lima: Librería Editorial Minerva, 1994.

———. *Mujeres peruanas: El otro lado de la historia.* Lima: Tempus Editores, 1986.

Haya de la Torre, Víctor Raúl, and Carlos Manuel Cox. *Cartas de Haya de la Torre a los prisioneros apristas.* Lima: Editorial Nuevo Día, 1946.

Haya de la Torre, Víctor Raúl, and Luis Alberto Sánchez. *Correspondencia 1924–1951: Víctor Raúl Haya de la Torre; Luis Alberto Sánchez.* Vol. 1. Lima: Mosca Azul Editores, 1982.

———. *Correspondencia 1952–1976: Víctor Raúl Haya de la Torre; Luis Alberto Sánchez.* Vol. 2. Lima: Mosca Azul Editores, 1982.

Heilman, Jaymie Patricia. "We Will No Longer Be Servile: *Aprismo* in 1930s Ayacucho." *Journal of Latin American Studies* 38, no. 3 (2006): 491–518, doi:10.1017/S0022216X06001143.

Henderson, Donald C., Grace R. Pérez, and Luis Alberto Sánchez. *Literature and Politics in Latin America: An Annotated Calendar of the Luis Alberto Sánchez Correspondence, 1919–1980.* University Park: Pennsylvania State University Libraries, 1982.

Herrera, Óscar. "Magda Portal." *Claridad* 14, no. 294 (1935): 9–10.

Heysen, Luis E. *El ABC de la peruanización.* Lima: Editorial APRA, 1931.

Hollinger, David. "From Identity to Solidarity." *Daedalus* 135, no. 4 (2006): 23–31, doi:10.2307/20028069.

Hubbs, Nadine. *The Queer Composition of America's Sound: Gay Modernists, American Music, and National Identity.* Berkeley and Los Angeles: University of California Press, 2004.

Iwasaki Cauti, Fernando. "Maldito y canalla: La linterna de Alberto Guillén." *Hueso Húmero* 39 (2001): 161–67.

Izenberg, Gerald. "Psychohistory and Intellectual History." *History and Theory* 14, no. 2 (1975): 139–55, doi:10.2307/2504610. http://www.jstor.org/stable/2504610.

Jrade, Cathy L. Modernismo, *Modernity, and the Development of Spanish American Literature.* Austin: University of Texas Press, 1998.

Kessler-Harris, Alice. "Why Biography?" *The American Historical Review* 114, no. 3 (2009): 625–30.

Klaiber, Jeffrey L. *Religion and Revolution in Peru, 1824–1976.* Notre Dame, Ind.: University of Notre Dame Press, 1977.

Klarén, Peter F. *Modernization, Dislocation, and Aprismo: Origins of the Peruvian Aprista Party, 1870–1932.* Austin: Published for the Institute of Latin American Studies by the University of Texas Press, 1973.

———. *Peru: Society and Nationhood in the Andes.* Latin American Histories. New York: Oxford University Press, 2000.

Kuhnheim, Jill S. "Verbal Society: Poetry and Poets at the End of the Twentieth

Century." Review Essay. *Latin American Research Review* 38, no. 3 (2003): 200–209.

Lancaster, Roger N. "Tolerance and Intolerance in Sexual Cultures in Latin America." In *Passing Lines: Sexuality and Immigration*, edited by Bradley S. Epps, Keja Valens, and Bill Johnson González, 255–74. Cambridge, Mass.: Harvard University Press, 2005.

Larriva de Llona, Lastenia. *Cartas a mi hijo: Psicología de la mujer.* Lima: Estado Mayor General del Ejército, 1919.

Lavrin, Asunción. "Some Final Considerations on Trends and Issues in Latin American Women's History." In *Latin American Women: Historical Perspectives*, edited by Asunción Lavrin, 302–32. Westport, Conn.: Greenwood Press, 1978.

Liga de Escritores Revolucionarios del Perú. *Cantos de la revolución.* Lima: Editorial Aprista Atahualpa, 1934.

López Lenci, Yazmín. *El laboratorio de la vanguardia literaria en el Perú: Trayectoria de una génesis a través de las revistas culturales de los años veinte.* Lima: Editorial Horizonte, 1999.

———. "La poesía de Magda Portal: Tránsito del postmodernismo a la vanguardia." Licenciatura thesis. Lima: Pontificia Universidad Católica del Perú, 1991.

"Los enemigos de Haya lo llamaban 'Lucy.'" *Revista Velaverde* 55, February 24, 2014. http://www.revistavelaverde.pe/los-enemigos-de-haya-lo-llamaban -lucy/ (accessed August 15, 2016).

Luna Vega, Ricardo. *Contribución a la verdadera historia del APRA, 1923–1988.* Historia. Lima: Editorial Horizonte, 1990.

Macedo, Alberto. *La vida íntima de Haya de la Torre.* Lima: Organización Gráfica Victoria, 1963.

Magda Portal: Su vida y su obra. Special Issue. *Claridad*, no. 294 (1935).

Mannarelli, María Emma. *Limpias y modernas: Género, higiene y cultura en la Lima del novecientos.* Lima: Ediciones Flora Tristán, 1999.

Mariátegui, José Carlos. *Peruanicemos al Perú.* Ediciones Populares de las Obras Completas de José Carlos Mariátegui. Lima: Editora Amauta, 1988.

———. *Siete ensayos de interpretación de la realidad peruana.* Ediciones Populares de las Obras Completas de José Carlos Mariátegui. Lima: Editora Amauta, 1996.

———. *Temas de educación.* Ediciones Populares de las Obras Completas de José Carlos Mariátegui. Lima: Editora Amauta, 1998.

Masterson, Daniel M. *Militarism and Politics in Latin America: Peru from Sánchez Cerro to Sendero Luminoso.* Contributions in Military Studies. New York: Greenwood Press, 1991.

———. "Soldiers, Sailors, and Apristas: Conspiracy and Power Politics in Peru, 1932–1948." In *The Underside of Latin American History*, edited by John J. Bratzel and Daniel M. Masterson, 24–42. Michigan State Latin American

Studies Center Monograph Series 16. East Lansing: Latin American Studies Center, Michigan State University, 1977.

Mármol, Miguel, and Roque Dalton. *Miguel Mármol*. Willimantic, Conn.; New York, N.Y.: Curbstone Press; distributed by Tallman Co., 1987.

Mead, Karen. "Beneficent Maternalism: Argentine Motherhood in Comparative Perspective, 1880–1920." *Journal of Women's History* 12, no. 3 (2000): 120–45.

Merritt, Anna C., Daniel A. Effron, and Benoit Monin. "Moral Self-Licensing: When Being Good Frees Us to Be Bad." *Social and Personality Psychology Compass* 4, no. 5 (2010): 344–57.

Miller, Francesca. *Latin American Women and the Search for Social Justice*. Hanover, N. H.: University Press of New England, 1991.

Miller, Laura. "La mujer obrera en Lima, 1900–1930." In *Lima Obrera, 1900–1930*, edited by Steve Stein and Laura Miller, 2:11–152. Lima: Ediciones El Virrey, 1986.

Mirko, Lauer. *La polémica del vanguardismo, 1916–1928*. Lima: Fondo Editorial de la Universidad Nacional Mayor de San Marcos, 2001.

Monguió, Luis. *La poesía postmodernista peruana*. Mexico City and Buenos Aires: Fondo de Cultura Económica, 1954.

Murillo Garaycochea, Percy. *Historia del APRA, 1919–1945*. Lima: Editora Atlántida, 1976.

Nasaw, David. "'Introduction' to AHR Roundtable: Historians and Biography." *American Historical Review* 114 (2009): 573–78.

Nugent, David. *Modernity at the Edge of Empire: State, Individual, and Nation in the Northern Peruvian Andes, 1885–1935*. Stanford, Calif.: Stanford University Press, 1997.

———. "States, Secrecy, Subversives: APRA and Political Fantasy in Mid-20th-Century Peru." *American Ethnologist* 37, no. 4 (2010): 681–702, doi:10.1111/j.1548–1425.2010.01278.x.

Olcott, Jocelyn. *Revolutionary Women in Postrevolutionary Mexico*. Next Wave: New Directions in Women's Studies. Durham, N.C.: Duke University Press, 2005.

Pareja Pflücker, Piedad. *Arturo Sabroso Montoya: Entre el sindicalismo autónomo y la militancia política*. Lima: Asociación Demokracia, 2002.

Parker, David S. *The Idea of the Middle Class: White-Collar Workers and Peruvian Society, 1900–1950*. University Park: Pennsylvania State University Press, 1998.

Partido del Pueblo. *40 preguntas y 40 respuestas sobre el Partido Aprista Peruano*, Incahuasi, Peru: Editorial Indoamericana, 1941.

Pike, Fredrick B. *The Politics of the Miraculous in Peru: Haya de la Torre and the Spiritualist Tradition*. Lincoln: University of Nebraska Press, 1986.

Portal, Magda. "Andamios de vida." In *La polémica del vanguardismo, 1916–1928*, edited by Mirko Lauer, 64–67. Lima: Fondo Editorial de la Universidad Nacional Mayor de San Marcos, 2001.

———. *Constancia del ser.* Lima: Talleres Gráficos P. L. Villanueva, 1965.

———. *Costa sur.* Santiago de Chile: Imprenta Nueva, 1945.

———. "18 cantos emocionados de vidrios de amor." *Repertorio Americano* 19, no. 24 (December 21, 1929): 379–80.

———. "Dos poemas proletarios para los compañeros de Vitarte." *Amauta*, no. 25 (1929): 18–20.

———. *Flora Tristán, precursora.* Lima: Editorial La Equidad, 1983.

———. *Hacia la mujer nueva: El aprismo y la mujer.* Lima: Editorial Cooperativa Aprista "Atahualpa," 1933.

———. *La trampa.* Lima: Ediciones Raíz, 1956.

———. *¿Quiénes traicionaron al pueblo?* Lima: Salas e Hijos, 1950.

———. "Réplica." In *La polémica del vanguardismo, 1916–1928*, edited by Mirko Lauer, 80–81. Lima: Fondo Editorial de la Universidad Nacional Mayor de San Marcos, 2001.

———. "Una revista de cuatro nombres." *Hueso Húmero* 7 (1980): 101–4.

Rama, Ángel. *La ciudad letrada.* Hanover, N.H: Ediciones del Norte, 1984.

Reedy, Daniel R. *Magda Portal, la pasionaria peruana: Biografía intelectual.* Lima: Ediciones Flora Tristán, 2000.

Rivero-Ayllón, Teodoro. *Haya de la Torre y el Grupo Norte.* Trujillo, Peru: Trilce Editores, 2005.

Roberts, Mary Louise. *Disruptive Acts: The New Woman in Fin-de-Siècle France.* Chicago: University of Chicago Press, 2002.

Rodríguez, Ileana. *Women, Guerrillas, and Love: Understanding War in Central America.* Minneapolis: University of Minnesota Press, 1996.

Saldaña-Portillo, María Josefina. *The Revolutionary Imagination in the Americas and the Age of Development.* Latin America Otherwise. Durham, N.C.: Duke University Press, 2003.

Sánchez, Luis Alberto. *Apuntes para una biografía del APRA.* Vol. 1, *Los primeros pasos, 1923–1931.* Lima: Mosca Azul Editores, 1978.

———. *Apuntes para una biografía del APRA.* Vol. 2, *Una larga guerra civil, 1931–1934.* Lima: Mosca Azul Editores, 1979.

———. *Apuntes para una biografía del APRA.* Vol. 3, *La violencia, 1935–1948.* Lima: Mosca Azul Editores, 1981.

———. *Haya de la Torre y el APRA; Crónica de un hombre y un partido.* Santiago de Chile: Editorial del Pacífico, 1955.

———. *Leguía: El dictador.* Lima: Pachacútec, 1993.

———. *Testimonio personal: Memorias de un peruano del Siglo 20.* Vol. 1. Lima: Ediciones Villasán, 1969.

———. *Testimonio personal: Memorias de un peruano del Siglo 20.* Vol. 3. Lima: Ediciones Villasán, 1969.

———. *Víctor Raúl Haya de la Torre o el político: Crónica de una vida sin tregua.* Lima: Editora Atlántida, 1979.

Sartre, Jean Paul. *Search for a Method.* New York: Knopf, 1963.

Schneider, Ronald M. *Comparative Latin American Politics*. Boulder, Colo.: Westview Press, 2010.

Seoane, Juan. *Hombres y rejas*. Santiago de Chile: Ediciones Ercilla, 1937.

Seoane, Manuel. *Carta de 1952. Proposiciones para el 20 Congreso Postal de Desterrados Apristas (C.P.D.) y algunas conclusiones del 1.er C.P.D.* Santiago de Chile, 1952.

———. "Escorzo de Magda Portal." *Claridad* 14, no. 294 (1935).

———. *Izquierda aprista: El verbo vigoroso de Manuel Seoane marca con fuego una posición política*. Lima: OKURA, 1984.

———. *Manuel Seoane: Páginas escogidas*. Edited by Eugenio Chang-Rodríguez. Lima: Fondo Editorial del Congreso del Perú, 2002.

Sosa Abascal, Arturo. *Rómulo Betancourt y el Partido del Pueblo, 1937–1941*. Caracas: Editorial Fundación Rómulo Betancourt, 1995.

Spiegel, Gabrielle M. "Comment on *A Crooked Line*." *The American Historical Review* 113, no. 2 (2008): 406–16.

Stansell, Christine. *American Moderns: Bohemian New York and the Creation of a New Century*. New York: Metropolitan Books, Henry Holt and Company, 2000.

Stein, Steve. "The Paths to Populism in Peru." In *Populism in Latin America*, edited by Michael L. Conniff, 110–31. Tuscaloosa: University of Alabama Press, 1999.

———. *Populism in Peru: The Emergence of the Masses and the Politics of Social Control*. Madison: University of Wisconsin Press, 1980.

Suárez Figueroa, Naudy. "El joven Betancourt: La socialdemocracia venezolana de 1928 a 1930." *Nueva Política* 14 (1974): 3–129.

Taussig, Michael T. *Defacement: Public Secrecy and the Labor of the Negative*. Stanford, Calif.: Stanford University Press, 1999.

Theweleit, Klaus. *Male Fantasies: Theory and History of Literature*. Vol. 1, *Women, Floods, Bodies, History*. Minneapolis: University of Minnesota Press, 1987.

Thorndike, Guillermo. *El año de la barbarie: Perú 1932*. Lima: Editorial Nueva América, 1969.

Unruh, Vicky. *Performing Women and Modern Literary Culture in Latin America*. Austin: University of Texas Press, 2006.

Urquieta, Miguel Ángel. "Izquierdismo y seudoizquierdismo artísticos." In *La polémica del vanguardismo, 1916–1928*, edited by Mirko Lauer, 68–79. Lima: Fondo Editorial de la Universidad Nacional Mayor de San Marcos, 2001.

Vaughan, Mary K. *Portrait of a Young Painter: Pepe Zúñiga and Mexico City's Rebel Generation*. Durham, N.C.: Duke University Press, 2014.

Velasco, Alejandro. *Barrio Rising: Urban Popular Politics and the Making of Modern Venezuela*. Oakland: University of California Press, 2015.

Villanueva del Campo, Armando. "Haya y Vallejo: Evocaciones." *Hueso Húmero* 41 (2002): 110–24.

Villanueva del Campo, Armando, and Guillermo Thorndike. *La gran persecución, 1932–1956.* Lima: Empresa Periodística Nacional, 2004.

Villanueva, Víctor. *La tragedia de un pueblo y de un partido: Páginas para la historia del Apra.* Santiago de Chile: Alfa y Roa, 1954.

Walker, Charles. "Lima de Mariátegui: Los intelectuales y la capital durante el oncenio." *Socialismo y Participación* 35 (1986): 71–88.

Wallace Fuentes, Myrna Ivonne. "Becoming Magda Portal: Poetry, Gender, and Revolutionary Politics in Lima, Peru, 1920–1930." PhD diss., Duke University, Durham, North Carolina, December 2006.

Weaver, Kathleen. "An Interview with Magda Portal: The Early Years." In *Contemporary Women Writing in the Other Americas.* Vol. 1, *Contemporary Women Writing in Latin America,* edited by Georgiana M. M. Colvile, 51–70. Lewiston, N.Y.: Edwin Mellen Press, 1996.

Weaver, Kathleen, and Magda Portal. *Peruvian Rebel: The World of Magda Portal, with a Selection of Her Poems.* University Park: Pennsylvania State University Press, 2009.

Werlich, David P. *Peru: A Short History.* Carbondale: Southern Illinois University Press, 1978.

Wiesse, Maria. *José Carlos Mariátegui: Etapas de su vida.* Obras Completas de José Carlos Mariátegui. Lima: Editora Amauta, 1985.

Wohl, Robert. *The Generation of 1914.* Cambridge, Mass.: Harvard University Press, 1979.

Wood, Michael. "We Do It All the Time." *London Review of Books* 38, no. 3–4 (2016): 7–9.

Index

Page numbers in *italics* refer to illustrations.